Karl Krolow and the Poetics of Amnesia

Karl Krolow (1915–1999) was one of the most prominent German poets of the second half of the twentieth century. His work has a representative stature for the period, and his production as one of Germany's leading critics of poetry is almost as impressive. Yet his poetry has surprisingly not received sustained critical attention. This study locates for the first time the hidden thread that runs through Krolow's work: his uneasy relationship to the recent German past. During the entire postwar period, he engaged his technical virtuosity as a poet in a stunning avoidance of historical content, both Germany's and his own. He never addressed publicly his own activities in the Third Reich and during the war: this study examines for the first time, with new historical research and documentation, Krolow's activities during the Nazi period and his literary production before 1945. With this new foundation, Neil H. Donahue presents Krolow's career from a wholly new perspective, presenting in sum, but overturning, decades of Krolow criticism that, begun on a false footing, missed the real historical depth in Krolow's poems: the depth of avoidance.

Neil H. Donahue is Professor of German and Comparative Literature at Hofstra University in Hempstead, New York.

Studies in German Literature, Linguistics, and Culture

Edited by James Hardin
(*South Carolina*)

Karl Krolow

and the Poetics of Amnesia in Postwar Germany

Neil H. Donahue

CAMDEN HOUSE

First published 2002
by Camden House

Camden House is an imprint of Boydell & Brewer Inc.
PO Box 41026, Rochester, NY 14604–4126 USA
and of Boydell & Brewer Limited
PO Box 9, Woodbridge, Suffolk IP12 3DF, UK

ISBN: 1–57113–251–1

Library of Congress Cataloging-in-Publication Data

Donahue, Neil H.
Karl Krolow and the poetics of amnesia in postwar Germany / Neil H.
Donahue.
    p. cm. — (Studies in German literature, linguistics, and culture)
Includes bibliographical references and index.
ISBN 1–57113–251–1 (alk. paper)
    1. Krolow, Karl—Criticism and interpretation.   I. Title.   II. Studies in
German literature, linguistics, and culture (Unnumbered)

PT2621 .R695 .D66 2002
831'.914—dc21

                                                        2002019362

A catalogue record for this title is available from the British Library.

This publication is printed on acid-free paper.
Printed in the United States of America.

To

John O. McCormick
Scholar and Teacher
for his advice and example

Contents

Acknowledgments

THE IMPETUS FOR THIS STUDY developed from several reviews I wrote for *World Literature Today* in the 1990s of Karl Krolow's most recent volumes. After having completed a study of Gerhard Falkner's work in the immediate context of contemporary German poetry, those reviews gave me the opportunity to ponder the trajectory of a very different poet's career in the context of postwar German literature in general. I would like to thank the editor of *World Literature Today*, Bill Riggan, for his consistently friendly and supportive professionalism over the years. For their help in getting my project off the ground, I also thank: Andreas Huyssen, Frederick Lubich, Joachim Sartorius and especially Jerry Glenn, who also later provided advice and practical help at critical junctures in my research, especially relating to Krolow's contact with Paul Celan. In the United States, I was able to begin the basic research for this project, but both the broad research into Krolow's scattered publications and the in-depth archival research had to be done in Germany — to an extent that I had not even anticipated when I began. That research in Germany, which changed the nature of my study fundamentally, could not have been done without the support of a grant from the Alexander von Humboldt Foundation that allowed me to live and work in Munich for one year. It would be difficult to understate the importance of the practical support for research in Germany that the Humboldt Foundation provides, and I wish to register my deepest gratitude for their many acts of assistance and generosity, large and small.

Once in Munich, Gerhard Neumann provided essential dialogue about my topic, thoughtful practical advice for my research, and invaluable assistance as a reader of early drafts as well as crucial logistical support at all stages: this study owes a great deal to his support and collegiality. Also in Munich, Volker Dahm, at the Institut für Zeitgeschichte, was generous with his time and patience in helping me understand the bureaucratic intricacies of life as a writer during the Third Reich. Hans-Peter Söder, the Director of the Wayne State Junior Year in Munich Program, also helped with practical and critical advice by lending a hand and an ear and, on one occasion, by providing emergency assistance in deciphering crucial handwritten documents. In the

Deutsches Literaturarchiv in Marbach, where my research quickly led me, I was fortunate to find in Reinhard Tgahrt and Jochen Meyer two extraordinary partners in dialogue, whose extensive knowledge of Krolow's work and its particular literary contexts both helped and inspired my research. Reinhard Tgahrt also granted permission to include my chapter on Karl Krolow and Oskar Loerke from the proceedings of the 1997 Marbacher Loerke Kolloquium. In 1996 Karl Krolow kindly granted me permission to consult the papers he had already deposited in the Marbach archive. Because of his illness in the last years of his life, I was unable to meet him in person before his death in June 1999, but I have always appreciated his willingness to meet if circumstances had allowed. His wife, Luzie Krolow, has given generous permission for me to quote materials from my research in German archives and has extended a cordial offer of future assistance. For that, I wish to thank her most warmly. Likewise, the Suhrkamp Verlag has shown great support of scholarship and generosity in granting permission for me to quote abundantly from Krolow's poems. The Schiller Museum/Deutsches Literaturarchiv in Marbach am Neckar granted permission to quote Krolow's letter to Dolf Sternberger. Also in Marbach I was able to consult the correspondence between Paul Celan and Karl Krolow, and I wish to thank Eric Celan for kindly granting me permission to do so; the section on Karl Krolow and Paul Celan first appeared in the electronic journal *Glossen* No. 11 (2000) and I thank its editor, Wolfgang Müller of Dickinson College in Pennsylvania, for his assistance. In Regensburg, Hans-Dieter Schäfer animated my labors by sharing his vast and detailed knowledge of the period along with his lively spirit of critical inquiry; his own trenchant writings on the nonfascist literature in the 1930s and 1940s in Germany served as a model for my own engagement with the topic. In Berlin, Christoph Meckel was generous with his time and gracious in his hospitality in agreeing to meet me for a lengthy discussion of my topic and related matters. In this study I have benefited, as always, from hours and hours of discussion with Gerhard Falkner on poetry and its changing historical situation in Germany and in general. Dr. Leonard Smolka, director of the university archives in Wroclaw (formerly Breslau), kindly responded to my inquiries about their records on Krolow. Rolf Paulus helped me to clarify some vexing bibliographical issues. I thank him for that assistance and, of course, for his prior studies and bibliography of Krolow.

Numerous institutions provided support for my research. In addition to the Humboldt Foundation, Hofstra University granted me leave from teaching duties during my year (1996–97) in Munich as a Humboldt Fellow and made important other arrangements to allow my research abroad for a year. Provost Herman Berliner and Dean Bernard J. Firestone of the College of Arts and Sciences have always shown their support in word and deed. In subsequent years, Hofstra has consistently provided funding, through its Faculty Research and Development grants and Presidential Research awards, for further research trips to Germany, which were essential for the completion of this project. In Munich, the Ludwig Maximilians Universität hosted me for the year and allowed me full use of its library, as did the Bavarian State Library, where they retrieved Krolow's pornographic *Bürgerliche Gedichte* out of the *Giftschrank* for my inspection, the Institut für Zeitgeschichte, and the Monacensia Literature Archive. The latter archive generously granted me permission to cite a letter from Karl Krolow to Oda Schaefer, and I would like to thank the director, Frau Ursula Hummel, for her assistance. Surrounded by these excellent facilities in Munich, I had the perfect location for my research. Elsewhere, outside of Munich, the Deutsches Rundfunkarchiv kindly provided me with a list of Krolow's radio interviews and readings; at Norddeutscher Rundfunk in Hannover, I would like to thank Dr. Beyer and the literary editor, Wend Kässens, for providing me with specific materials (Karl Krolow — öffentl. Lesung, 13.03.85; Sendung: 19.03.85/NDR 3). The Bundesarchiv Berlin and the Universitätsarchiv Göttingen allowed me valuable access to their files, as did the Niedersächsisches Staatsarchiv in Hannover, where my thanks go to Herr Leerhof in particular for his cordial assistance. All of these institutions were crucial for the development of my thesis, which in turn changed as I discovered new materials or foreclosed lines of further inquiry.

For sustaining me in this project with their informed conversation and wise counsel, I would like to thank Peter Burgard and Sylvia Schmitz-Burgard, Alexandar Mihailovic and Helga Druxes, Jeffrey and Dietlinde Hamburger, Kalyan Basu, Stephen Brockmann, Doris Kirchner, Hans-Peter Söder, Gerhard Falkner, Erk Grimm, Franz Josef Czernin, Frank Trommler, Jerry Glenn, Colin Riordan, Fred Lubich, Todd Kontje, Glenn Cuomo, James K. Lyon, Michael Sharp, George Greaney, Barbara Lekatsas, and Russell Harrison, who deserves special thanks also for having given my whole manuscript a careful reading, which was an act of invaluable assistance. The editors at Camden House, Jim Hardin and Jim Walker, have provided speedy responses and steady advice on all editorial matters, large and small, and I have greatly appreciated their reliable assistance, as well as the hard work and professionalism of the very competent copyeditor. My family shared a wonderful year in Munich as I went about my research for this book, which is thus imbued with innumerable fond memories of that place and time, including the birth of our son. My wife, Christine Rota-Donahue, has given continuous support and encouragement, and our children, Alice and Julian, have always provided many forms of happy distraction in order to ensure that my scholarship would not interfere with what is really important.

N. H. D.

April 2002

Introduction:
Karl Krolow's Relation to the Past —
The Poetics of Amnesia

KARL KROLOW'S LONG CAREER as a poet and critic of poetry
stretches over six decades from the years of National Socialism in
Germany, through the war and postwar division of Germany, to re-
unification. His career spans the history of the Federal Republic of
Germany, and like the Federal Republic, had its roots in the experience of National Socialism and war. In the years since German reunifi-
cation, historians and literary historians have begun, particularly since
the fiftieth anniversary of Allied victory and the birth of the Federal
Republic, to look back at the immediate prewar and war years, and the
immediate postwar period.[1] At times, those revisions have led to dramatic reappraisals and new understanding of an individual's actions or
of a historical phenomenon. Historical research on such different figures in German literature as Günter Eich, Stephan Hermlin, Peter
Huchel, or Walter Koeppen, and others, or the Germanist Hans
Schwerte (a.k.a. Hans Ernst Schneider), not to mention such figures
as François Mitterand in France, has provided a more detailed understanding of an epoch. The specific circumstances and actions (or inac-
tions) of individuals revealed through such research often only raises
further questions. With his death in June 1999, Krolow's career can
now also be examined in its full historical dimensions, but an understanding of its phases depends first on an understanding of its beginnings. Over six decades Krolow has produced what Kurt Drawert aptly
calls "ein heute kaum mehr zu überblickendes Werk" (349), which
includes not only his many volumes of poetry and literary prose, but
also collections of essays in literary history and criticism, as well as an
enormous output of uncollected literary journalism, from innumerable
book reviews to occasional reflections on topics ranging from the birth-
day or death of an author to impressions of a landscape. In retrospect,
Krolow maintained a second career as a journalist in literary affairs.

During that time, however, and in that broad range of topics,
Krolow has rarely broached the topic and never reflected publicly in
any concrete detail on his experiences during the Nazi period from his
years in Gymnasium and at the university, to his beginnings as a writer

under National Socialism, his experiences during the war years, and then again after the war. In his speech when awarded the prestigious Büchner Prize in 1956, Krolow speaks of his attempts after the war "mich von den Bedrückungen zu befreien, von jenem Cauchemar zu lösen" (*Ein Gedicht entsteht,* 196) and remarks, in summary, upon his development as a poet: "Ich wollte mich aus der Umklammerung der Erinnerung befreien, die ich an die Zeit zwischen meinem zwanzigsten und dreißigsten Lebensjahre hatte, zwischen 1935 und 1945" (*Ein Gedicht entsteht,* 197). Here he makes a rare specific reference to that period, but he has never described for public consumption the circumstances of his life during that time nor those specific "oppressions" that indirectly or even directly molded his work. Krolow has also never reflected publicly on the events of the war and the Holocaust in general as Klaus Jeziorkowski has noted.[2] In the considerable number of accounts of his life and work, the same few dates and events repeat without detail or further inquiry or elaboration, yet a historical understanding of his work first requires biographical detail to establish his experience at the beginning of his career and then its relation to his later work.

Yet the scholarship and literary criticism on Krolow has been reluctant, at risk of indiscretion, to pose questions about his early work and his life at the time. In fact, scholars and critics have too often followed Krolow's directions as critic of his own work. For example, in the introduction to Krolow by Gerhard Kolter and Rolf Paulus, *Der Lyriker Karl Krolow* (1983),[3] the authors note the lack of available information about Krolow's biography and, after citing Gabriele Wohmann's character portrait of him, they simply adopt Krolow's views on the matter as critical principle:

> Wollte man nach dieser Momentaufnahme einen ausführlichen biographischen Abriß mit dem Anspruch, Leben und Werk ständig aufeinander zu beziehen, schreiben, hätte man zu wenig Material. Auch hält Krolow selbst dies nicht für sinnvoll, er betont im Gespräch, daß er ein relativ unauffälliges Leben geführt habe, ohne Sensationen und ohne Katastrophen. Die Bedeutungen und die Zufälle des literarischen Lebens seien von größerer Bedeutung als private Hintergründe.[4]

This passage pre-emptively blocks inquiry into Krolow's life. To examine the relation between a writer's life and work is not at all the same as "To relate the life and the work constantly to one another." To inquire into relevant biographical background does not turn the poetic work into mere autobiographical document or gossip, but allows critical discrimination and contextualization. In fact, some pertinent details about the life are necessary in order to separate life and work. A basic principle of criticism dictates that the author, however respected and consulted, does not have the last word. Krolow has written anecdotal and incidental accounts of his early biography and the formation of his sensibility in the landscapes of his youth that, in their exclusion of facts and broader context, reinforce a self-fashioned image of timeless reverie and devotion to poetry outside of historical context. This study aims to restore the historical context to Krolow's life as a poet and then to the poems themselves. In terms of general literary history, Krolow himself rightly remarks that the Stunde Null did not exist and that lines of continuity apply to the period and to his own work; yet his understanding of literature seems curiously and insistently removed and set apart from nonliterary, historical experience and from that period in particular, or elsewhere strictly confined to the historical present or to literary experience only. The many phases of his development, his work as a whole is determined by what is left unsaid or unaddressed, and by the calculated blind spot in his reflections, in his poetics, in his poems, and in his literary criticism. In effect, a notion of literariness within which Krolow develops variously as a poet over fifty years becomes a refuge from the past, from his life between the ages of twenty-five and thirty-five.

Krolow's 1975 essay on memory, "Sich erinnern können," seems at first to address the issue of inquiry into the recent past, but in fact portrays, in exemplary and almost systematic fashion, Krolow's manner of dealing with this issue as in the first paragraph, which requires quotation in full, as much for what he says as for what he does not say:

> Wir leben in einer Zeit, die Gedächtnis, Erinnerungsvermögen oder gar den Wunsch, sich zu erinnern, eher verdrängt als fördert. Viele wollen vieles, was ihnen geschah, nicht wahrhaben, weil es ihnen unbequem ist. Nichts scheint einfacher als das Lästige nicht zuzulassen und so zu tun, als hätte es Unannehmlichkeiten nicht gegeben. Aber mit ihnen wird oft auch das Angenehme abgetan. Das 'Speichern' überläßt man den Computern, die bei rechter Fütterung sogar etwas ausscheiden, das manche voreilig als Gedichte proklamiert haben. Sich erinnern können, ist — so hieß es früher — meist eine Sache der Erfahrung. Ältere Menschen verstanden sich (und verstehen sich hoffentlich auch heute noch) zuweilen auf die Kunst der Erinnerung, die nicht nur auf Kindheit und junge Jahre begrenzt ist. Das sensible Arsenal Gedächtnis bleibt freilich bei den meisten ungenutzt. Gedächtnis sei, sagt ein französischer Schriftsteller unserer

Tage, die Mutter der Musen. Er hatte freilich mit diesem Anspruch ein besonderes Gedächtnis, das poetische, im Sinne.

The opening indirectly reflects the cultural climate of anamnesis in post-1968 Germany and in its tone anticipates a serious effort at *Vergangenheitsbewältigung*. As a literary journalist, Krolow responded in his way to the themes of the day, if not to specific events. Though the logic of transitions in this paragraph is not always clear, this first paragraph nonetheless delineates the direction of the essay as a whole in textbook fashion. The first three sentences strike a note of critical provocation and invoke the need to recognize denial and repression, to confront the past and overcome amnesia, however disagreeable and discomfiting the task might be, but the fourth sentence shifts surprisingly to regret merely that such amnesia also blocks pleasant memories. The subsequent associations abandon the initial line of argumentation, surround the topic with disconnected reflections that drain the essay and its initial argument of urgency, and narrow its scope from historical memory and *Vergangenheitsbewältigung* to computer memory and computer poetry, to the "art of recollection" among the elderly and finally to poetic memory. Though one might object that such a journalistic essay does not deserve such close attention, the journalistic medium allows Krolow a margin of imprecision that nevertheless contains a precise logic that also seems to comment upon itself. Krolow's essay on memory exemplifies what it at first seems to confront: the mechanism of ignoring what is unpleasant in the past, and it thereby enacts the poetics of amnesia.

After having broached a topic with a given framework in postwar Germany and shifting the terms of discussion from history to poetry, the second paragraph reduces the task, the project of postwar remembering, to routine and harmless reflections upon the passing of a calendar year. The implicit, but specific and serious historical context, has dwindled to the common, human foible of taking stock of one's failures or successes during the year, though he notes aptly: "Wortreich wird ja bekanntlich bei uns der Verdrängungsprozeß ausgestattet. Im Schwall der Worte geht unter, was nicht ins Konzept paßte, . . ." (!). The third paragraph also seems without logical transition by suddenly introducing "eine Art Unschuld des Erinnerns von Augenblicken," but in fact, it represents a logical step in the further reduction of memory now from epochs and decades to years, and then to single moments in which tightly circumscribed memory can now coincide with innocence. The explicit moral condemnation of forgetting at the outset has reversed into praise of memory of single, isolated impressions outside of any historical continuum or context ("Ein Mosaik von Kleinigkeiten, von Belanglosigkeiten") that constitute therefore a form of innocence ("momentanes Staunen, Entzücken und Sprachlosigkeit, ein Schweigen vor einem schönen Bild, einem schönen Gesicht, einer schönen, noch unverdorbenen Landschaft"). Memory becomes entirely aesthetic and timeless, a series of discrete epiphanies of beauty without depth or coherence. In the third and fourth paragraphs, Krolow advances, instead of memory, a sort of eidetic impressionism without cognitive function that does not give emotional depth or intellectual understanding to experience, but rather, distracts and entertains "wie ein kleiner persönlicher Film" and ultimately comforts: "so sehr ist man seiner Erinnerung verpflichtet, die einem hilft, in der Kunst, sich wohlzufühlen, Fortschritte zu machen." Krolow presents memory as a balm for the soul, as a means of forgetting (!), rather than as a means of recuperating and reflecting upon the past; memory becomes an art of selection and isolation of aesthetic impressions: "Die inzwischen verstrichene Zeit wirkte als Filter. Wirklichkeit wurde zur Erscheinung. Das Wiedererscheinen eines Jahres oder eines ganzen Lebens kommt auf diese Weise zustande." The dissimulation of memory allows the artful self-fashioning of an epoch, or a life, into an aesthetic construction, an "appearance."[5]

Most interviews with Krolow over the years have politely avoided the matter of his experiences during the Nazi period and the war or touched upon it only tangentially. Krolow's responses tend to deflect the question into vague existential generalities. In his interview with Rolf Paulus and Gerhard Kolter in 1982, the two interviewers, cued by their discussion of the general difficulties of establishing one's literary identity, asked directly about his literary beginnings, "wie das in Ihren Anfängen war" (*Text + Kritik*, 51), to which Krolow replied:

> Wissen Sie, meine Situation ist die — jetzt: Ich gehe weg, ich gehe davon, ich verschwinde. Gut — wie lange das dauert, weiß ich nicht, noch lebe ich, aber es hat nicht gleich etwas mit Leben und Sterben zu tun: man stirbt sowieso als Autor, als Verfasser von diesem und jenem mehrmals vor sich hin und wird dann wieder aus irgendeiner Ecke hervorgezerrt und ist eine Weile am Leben und so schleudert man durch die Gegend.
>
> Also die Anfänge — ja . . . Man weiß glücklicherweise nicht, was man tut, wenn man also auch über das noch nachdächte — wer sich vornimmt, Schriftsteller zu werden, das ist ein Thema für ein beschädigtes Gedicht. Verstehen Sie? Ich bin da hineingeraten durch die Umstände, durch die Zeitumstände, durch Begabung, freilich.
> (*Text + Kritik*, 41)

His response begins with the existential platitude that one moves on and passes on, but his words, "Ich gehe weg," characterize the movement of his response, his flight from the issue, and his evasion of the question, which addressed concrete matters of historical record. The interviewers then return to inquire more pointedly into the specifics of his historical situation: "Für uns ist interessant die Situation, die wir ja selbst nicht kennen, die Nachkriegszeit; wie ist das literarische Leben gewesen?" (51). Krolow's response, though a full page in length, amounts to: "Aber einiges setzte sich fort, einiges fiel weg, das ist alles" (51), with allusions to the general historical climate and his general literary activities. The interviewers indeed do try to insist, delicately enough, on a discussion of the period: "Sie sagten, einerseits war alles sehr reduziert, sehr einfach, wenig verfügbar, mußte erarbeitet werden, war nicht parat; andererseits wäre für uns schon interessant zu wissen, was es dann an Veröffentlichungsmöglichkeiten gab" (52). Krolow again answers in broad historical generalities: "Es gab sehr viele Chancen, wer sie nutzte." Krolow simply does not allow a discussion of the historical particularities of his experience in the Third Reich and during the Second World War or immediately afterward.

In 1985, in an unscripted radio broadcast of a reading and open discussion,[6] an unidentified man from the audience went furthest in probing Krolow's activities in this period; the man posed his question bluntly and directly: "Ich möchte gern was aus Ihrer Biographie fragen [. . .] Sie haben in Göttingen und Breslau studiert; das war zur Zeit des Dritten Reiches. Sind Sie zu der Zeit in die Innere Emigration gegangen? Oder wie haben Sie sich verhalten?" After some hesitation, Krolow responded, "Das sind so Fragen." To which the man in the audience, anticipating an evasion, exclaimed, "Hab ich mir gedacht!" Thus put under pressure in public, Krolow launched into a prolonged answer, which I have transcribed and quote in full:

> Mein Herr, ich hatte nicht mehr als Wörter im Kopf, . . . die waren mir geblieben. Sonst sah ich und hörte ich ziemlich viel um mich herum, das war ziemlich laut. Ich bemühte mich, was heißt bemühen? Ich war in Breslau eine Art Robinson, in Göttingen war es etwas anders . . . Uhhh . . . Ich stand da, und es sah wie Studium aus, ein Studium, das nicht zu Ende gehen durfte, weil kein Examen gemacht werden durfte. Ich vertrieb mir auf meiner Weise die Zeit mit meiner Begabung, d. h. umgangs mit Wörtern, die ich, wie ich glaubte, zu Worte kommen ließ, ganz anders als heute, aber immerhin auch schon auf einer, na, sagen wir, literarischer Weise. Ich war, jedenfalls, nicht mehr allein mit dieser Zeit, die mich nicht allein lassen wollte. Ich wollte mir aber schon diese meine Individualität und

Umgang mit dem, was ich wollte, und das war Literatur bestimmter Art und die Wiedergabe, Literatur, von Literatur bestimmter Art auf meiner Weise erhalten wissen, dies tat ich, bis heute, es hat sich zwischen den Jahren 1940 und 1980, so gesehen, überhaupt nichts geändert, für mich als Vorgang beim Schreiben, beim Tun, meine Sache, die ich nicht lassen konnte, für die ich disponiert war, und da mir damals, sozusagen, nichts anderes übrig blieb, ich streiche das, sozusagen, es blieb mir nichts anderes übrig.

This question represents the most direct inquiry on record into Krolow's life under National Socialism. The question was never posed or pondered in critical commentary at that point for forty years and, not surprisingly, came from a member of the audience, from outside of the literary-critical community in which Krolow for decades had wielded influence and authority. The occasion also reflects Krolow's best opportunity on record to examine, at age seventy, the circumstances of his years under National Socialism and the war. Yet Krolow stonewalled instead of providing any descriptive detail of his life, activities, studies, early publications, and dealings with editors (as recorded, for example, in his correspondence with Paul Alverdes, the editor of *Das Innere Reich*), or describing the various pressures upon the writer or on the individual in general at that time, in those places, or on just what exactly he observed during those ten years. In a tone of defensive condescension ("Mein Herr, . . ."), Krolow's first response ("Ich hatte nicht mehr als Wörter im Kopf . . .") seems a rather pathetic and unsatisfactory dodge that indeed meets with immediate, scoffing skepticism; his follow-up is convoluted and dissolves the issue in garbled verbiage that nonetheless advances the position of *inner emigration* that his initial prevarications seem to rebuff. Yet he did not respond directly that he went into *inner emigration,* as asked.[7]

Krolow's inability to reflect upon the third decade of his life and his beginnings as a writer, or about the phenomenon of the war and Holocaust, becomes, in retrospect, the framework for reconsidering his work and its reception in the decades after the war more than half a century later. What Krolow said in his interview with Gerhard Kolter and Rolf Paulus of his literary practice in the early 1980s seems to apply to his beginnings as a writer as well: "dennoch benehme ich mich so, als könne man sehr viel vergessen, nämlich das ganze 20. Jahrhundert, als gäbe es den Expressionismus nicht, als gäbe es Liliencron nicht, als gäbe es nicht die Celanisierte Lyrik oder was Sie wollen. . . . Dies ist unter anderem für mich interessant, das Rückspringen und Überspringen — wie weit das möglich ist, etwas, was man überhaupt nicht tun darf und kann; wenn man anfängt, dann ist man verloren" (*Text + Kritik*, 47). Krolow grants himself the license to ignore certain literary periods, but he specifically cites and wishes out of existence poetry in the vein of Celan, whose work centers on the historical experience and memory of the Holocaust. In the numerous prior representations of his career, the very early period is left unquestioned, if discussed at all. A closer look at available documentation of Krolow's life and work in that period, and the gap in his reflections on that period, provides here a basis for re-examining the subsequent developments of his work, and the particular nature of his poetics as articulated in his critical essays, reviews, interviews, and ultimately, in his poetry.

Until the 1980s, most of the discussions of Krolow's work were by friends such as Friedrich Rasche and Sabais, and friendly poets, whose work Krolow also in turn reviewed such as Hans-Egon Holthusen, Hans-Jürgen Heise, Walter Helmut Fritz, and Harald Hartung. Gerhard Kolter has systematically studied the reception of Krolow's poetry in postwar West Germany and comes to two conclusions. First, Krolow's reception initially remained bound to outdated, even atavistic concepts of poetic *Erlebnis* and genius theory that provided no basis for textual criticism: "Solche Haltungen sind vor allem erstaunlich, weil man Neuorientierung nach dem Faschismus erwarten konnte. . . . Natürlich scheinen solche Gedanken nach dem Kriege in gemäßigter Form, aber die magische Komponente, die Emotionsbasis, die Verachtung der Ratio sind Grundkonstante, die sich nahezu unverändert in die Nachkriegszeit hinüberretten konnten" (80). And second, Krolow's reception remained captivated by formulaic verbiage that was obfuscatory rather than critical: "Ähnlich verhält es sich mit solchen Kategorien wie 'Sensibilität,' 'Virtuosität,' 'Klarheit' u.v.m. Sie können über Leerformen nur dann hinauskommen, wenn sie durch Beispiele illustriert und in ihrer spezifischen Ausformung gegenüber anderen Autoren sichtbar gemacht werden; das geschieht jedoch in den seltensten Fällen" (82). The intrinsic examination of his poetics and poetry, based on close readings of his poems in their historical context, requires a complementary examination of prior discussions of Krolow's work in order to gain the benefit from previous insights as well as to locate previous blind spots in the criticism.

Since there has been very little exploration by Krolow's commentators into his activities and experiences in the period of National Socialism and in the immediate postwar period, there is in that regard little to go on. The years of university education and early career establish, or at least bear a relation to, a writer's later style and sensibility. Though the myth of a Stunde Null or Zero Hour has been reconsidered and refuted repeatedly, it seems to perdure in the consideration of individual biographies, though in the last decade new research and debate on figures such as Günter Eich, Walter Koeppen, and others has changed substantially our understanding of the prior activities of subsequently well-known postwar writers. Indeed, despite the fact that a forty-one-year-old Krolow was the youngest recipient ever of the Büchner Prize in 1956 and was enshrined by Hugo Friedrich in his epoch-making study *Die Struktur der modernen Lyrik*, virtually no sustained study of Krolow's work appeared until the 1980s! In her 1975 dissertation, Renate Beyer rightly wonders why one of the most well-known and established poets of the postwar period, prominently included in all literary histories of the period, had not yet been the object of serious study. This study seeks an answer to that question in the function that Krolow assigns to the poem in its relation to experience in general and to memory in particular, to the past, and to his past.

Therefore, this study combines historical, archival research on Krolow's past with detailed close readings of his poems, including those early poems that he published in the Nazi period and chose not to include in his *Gesammelte Gedichte*. This study requires extensive explication of individual poems in order to trace a narrative of his development from his own willful Stunde Null, the blind spot about his past, through his various phases into the mid-1970s. That blind spot about German history in the Third Reich figures in his own postwar reflections on his career and in his poetics and poetry, as I demonstrate. Krolow's particular and peculiar blindness and ahistoricism emerges as the defining characteristic of his oeuvre, which is at first in alignment, but then increasingly at odds with postwar German sensibility about the past as I make clear in my discussion of Krolow's relation to poets of very different historical sensibility, Oskar Loerke and Paul Celan. The archival research and close readings along with these comparisons restore the historical dimension to his work in all genres and, by so doing, highlight the scope of Krolow's poetics of amnesia.

Notes

[1] See the two recent historical studies by Jeffrey Herf and Norbert Frei, and the collection of essays edited by Stephen Brockmann and Frank Trommler on the notion of *Zero Hour.*

[2] In his 1973 essay, Jeziorkowski raises an important question: "Krolow tat also genau das, was Brecht in den Svendborger Gedichten im Ton der Klage über finstere Zeiten 'fast ein Verbrechen' genannt hatte und was Adorno später noch pauschaler als Möglichkeit negierte: er sprach nach dem Massaker 'über Bäume,' ja über besondere Baum-, Stauden- und Gräserspezies in Linneschem Artenreichtum. Das war gerade kein Kahlschlag. Er sprach dafür — zunächst — so gut wie gar nicht über den vorausgegangenen Massenmord und dessen Folgen. Vielleicht weil das übergroße Entsetzen ihm nicht so bald artikulierbar erschien? War dieses 'Schweigen über so viele Untaten' in dieser Weise beredt?" (396). Jeziorkowski raises the question but provides no answer, though his speculations lead the reader toward certain conclusions: that his silence was due to trauma and that therefore the silence was eloquent. Jeziorkowski's interpolation of "at first" also suggests that Krolow did later address the "mass murder and its consequences," but to my knowledge that is not the case.

[3] *Der Lyriker Karl Krolow* (1983) by Kolter and Paulus should not be confused with the separate studies of Krolow by each author.

[4] To be fair, Paulus and Kolter did try to pose such questions in a prior interview and were rebuffed; I discuss this below. Yet here they accede to Krolow's management of the inquiry.

[5] An earlier short essay on memory titled "Wege, die man ging" (*Stuttgarter Nachrichten,* July 20, 1952, 165) also reduced the scope and gravity of memory to "minor matters" or "Kleinigkeiten" and, instead of addressing serious issues of one's remembered life, shifts from the general topic quickly to "Wege der Kindheit zum Beispiel" in the second paragraph, enumerates sentimental recollections, and concludes with "der unausrottbaren Lust am Dasein, dem Hang, zu triumphieren und alle Kreuzwege in einem Glück enden zu lassen, das die Märchen kennen," outside of history in autobiographical fairy tale.

[6] "Autoren lesen im Funkhaus Hannover: Karl Krolow; Einführung Gisela Lindemann" (taped March 13, 1985; broadcast March 19, 1985). Norddeutscher Rundfunk. HW 207 394/1–2.

[7] I choose to italicize this term throughout the text in order to highlight the ambiguous or dubious nature of this term and concept.

1: The Early Career (1940–1943): The Writer and the Regime

KARL KROLOW (B. 1915) IS A FIGURE OF continuity in German letters over the last sixty years or more, even beyond the dates of his own publications. His earliest work links tendencies from the late years of the Weimar Republic and extends through the Nazi period to the early years of the Federal Republic of Germany and the post-reunification 1990s. Krolow's continuity lies not at all in a single style, since his style changed dramatically from decade to decade, but rather in his dedication to the genre of poetry through the writing of his own poetry as well as in his attention to the work of others. Numerous critics and other poets have cited Krolow as an exemplary figure in postwar German poetry.[1]

Krolow belongs to a generation that reached maturity during the Nazi period and began to write and publish during that time, if not before; this generation of writers later shaped German literature in the postwar period, either as part of the Gruppe 47, or not. In contrast to the many writers, artists, critics, and others who left Germany by choice or necessity, Krolow stayed and therefore belongs to the writers grouped under the rubric of *inner emigration,* though that term is notoriously imprecise and inadequate.[2] In order to understand Krolow's early development, one must keep in mind the context of literary production in the Nazi period in general and the particular development (or dilemmas) of other writers and artists. Still, Krolow does not fit readily into any of the usual generational and ideological paradigms. The particular problems of his career as a writer from its beginning have to be addressed in its own concrete details and particulars.

Unlike so many others of his generation in the 1930s, Krolow was able to avoid military conscription, at first because of his frail constitution and later, presumably, because of his status as a student. In his "Rede auf Karl Krolow," Peter Rühmkorf remarks, "Wie unzählige andere junge Menschen seiner Generation [. . .], wurde Krolow im Jahre 1943 gemustert, vermessen, gewogen — und: für zu leicht befunden (88 Pfund wog der spindelige Kerl bei einer Körpergröße von

1 Meter 77), Grund genug für einen glücklichen Verschonten, seiner Fortuna noch viele Preislieder auf die Leichtgewichtigkeit zu singen" (144). Though not acceptable weight for military service, one cannot help wonder whether before the war or especially during the war, a recruit would so easily be released from military service. Rühmkorf does not cite a source, but such a detail presumably comes from Krolow himself; in his "Nachruf zu Lebzeiten" (1970) Krolow mentions about himself "Er war glücklicherweise von zarter Konstitution" (140) and "Mit dreiundsechzig Kilo blieb er zu lange zu leicht für ein ernsthaftes Dasein" (142). I have found no other more specific explanation than "frail health" for why Krolow did not do military service. Rühmkorf slyly brings together the biographical and poetological; the notion of Krolow's poems as "Preislieder auf die Leichtgewichtigkeit" is witty since it links Krolow's poetics of *Leichtigkeit* to the questions of poetic substance and biography. Rühmkorf precedes that comment with the remark: "Von den Schüssen der frühen Jahre hallen unheimlich noch die spätesten Gedichte und Erzählprosa wider. Das bedrohliche Blitzen von Messern, Dolchen und Bajonetten pflanzt sich als leitmotivischer Angstreflex bis in die astralen Höhen seines Metaphernhimmels fort" (144). He does not explain his use of the word *unheimlich* but indirectly invites one to wonder what direct experience of violence so deeply affected Krolow as to remain pervasive in his work. Rühmkorf's casual-seeming but careful remarks make the connection that other scholarship on Krolow has never made between his biography and his aesthetics, and between his metaphors and his experience. One need not be surprised by the subtle critical edge to Rühmkorf's address. After Krolow had won the Büchner Prize in 1956, Rühmkorf, under the pseudonym Leslie Meier, published a blistering commentary on Krolow as the representative figure of German poetry in the 1950s. In his regular column, "Leslie Meiers Lyrik-Schlachthof," in the journal *Studenten-Kurier,* Rühmkorf wrote: "Die zeitgenössische Lyrik ist gekennzeichnet durch einen ganz entschiedenen Zug zur Verharmlosung und Verniedlichung. Da ist das meiste auf freundlich frisiert, gepflegte Metaphern, adrette Formeln, geschmackvolle Kunstgewerblichkeit, kein gewagter Griff, kein schiefer Ton, kurz und gut: die geschniegelte Mediokrität" (5). With direct citations from Krolow's poems, Rühmkorf tilts against "miniaturism with existentialist posturing" and identifies the poet ("der Oberparfumeur") at the end of his vituperations as Krolow. Nonetheless, Rühmkorf is virtually alone in having isolated, however fleetingly, this dimension in Krolow's work: Krolow's poetry is otherwise generally

perceived in the main as far from violent, but rather as a sort of verbal filigree, intelligent and sensitive, bold at times and even incisive, but ultimately ahistorical and ornamental.

According to most accounts of Krolow's life in this period, he pursued his studies at the university, first in Göttingen, then in Breslau, and then again in Göttingen in the field of Romance languages, even though he was never registered as a student of Romance languages at Göttingen.[3] In his digest of folksy anecdotes and local history, *Deutschland, deine Niedersachsen* (1972), Krolow includes autobiographical passages about his family and the landscape, but in the long section on Göttingen, under the heading *Individuelle Zeiten*, he passes over his own years there with the characterization: "Man beließ einem Individualität, im Rahmen des Studienganges. Man konnte unauffällig verbummeln oder vorankommen, und Göttingen blieb Göttingen, unveränderbar" (163). This statement defies credibility for the period during the Third Reich as well as Krolow's own later response to the man in the audience about the period, about the "Zeit, die mich nicht allein lassen wollte." Krolow then abstracts the town out of any specific historical context into the banal timelessness of stereotypes about student life. Rolf Paulus indicates that Krolow was *Studienrat* in the Philosophical Seminar in Göttingen, but could not advance to the position of *Assistent* (assistant professor) without belonging to the National Socialist Party (NSDAP; hereafter, the Party) or affiliated organizations.[4] However, according to documents he filled out at the time, Krolow was indeed a member of the Hitler-Jugend (HJ) and of NSDAP. In the *Lebenslauf* that accompanied his membership application of January 16, 1941 in the Reichsschrifttumskammer (RSK), Krolow indicates, "Mitglied der NSDAP bin ich seit dem 1. April 1937." Documents in the Bundesarchiv in Berlin indicate that Krolow applied for membership to the Göttingen local branch (*Ortsgruppe*) of the Party on May 1, 1937 with a Party membership number (*Parteianwärterkarte Nr. 500 30*) and officially became a member on January 3, 1938 in the Ortsgruppe Göttingen (*Mitgliedsnummer 4819613*). This information is also given in five different matriculation certificates (*Anmeldeschein der Studentenführung*), where a rank of service is given, though illegible (*Mitglied des Be*[fehls]*stabs*). He also indicates that he has performed some sort of compensatory, non-military service "Ausgleichdienst abgeleistet: Ja von 17. 5. 1935 bis 12. 10. 1935." This would have been between his completion of Tellkampf Oberschule, the Gymnasium in Hannover, and the beginning of his studies at the university. His temporary membership card, which had to be returned when the regular membership card was issued, is among the materials in the Bundesarchiv Berlin. Likewise, in his file for the university, Krolow indicates that he had belonged to the Hitler Youth since April 10, 1934 and to the Nazi Party since May 1, 1937.[5]

In an official Party questionnaire of 1939, Krolow also checks both columns next to HJ, indicating *Mitglied* and *darin führend tätig.* Krolow seems to have participated actively in the organizations of the Hitler Youth and the Nazi Party, neither of which was automatically open to one and all, and both of which were designed to train elites. On the second page of that same questionnaire, Krolow indicates in section D, *Tätigkeit als Polit. Leiter — Nur auszufüllen von zur Zeit tätigen Politischen Leitern,* on line three, *Dienststellung,* that he held the office of *Blockleiter.* Line four asks, *Wie wird die vorgenannte Tätigkeit ausgeübt?* He indicates *ehrenamtlich,* that is, without salary. He further indicates that the service is performed in his locality. An understanding of that position requires reference to the Nazi Party guidelines for background.

The *Organisationsbuch der NSDAP* (7th ed., 1943) defines the position of the block leader in the Nazi Party hierarchy as the lowest level of decorated political leader or *Hoheitsträger,* all of whom are responsible at their different levels for a geographical area and for their subordinates: "Die Hoheitsträger üben die allgemeine Dienstaufsicht über alle ihnen nachgeordneten Parteidienststellen aus und sind für die Aufrechterhaltung der Disziplin in ihrem Bereich verantwortlich" (98a). As the lowest level of political leader, the block leader connected both the self-styled elite of Party leadership with the regular Party members and the *Volk* in general, that is, the tip with the base of the pyramid, and therefore needed to stay in "dauernder lebendiger Fühlungnahme mit den Politischen Leitern und der Bevölkerung ihres Bereiches" (98a), in part through regular office hours. The block consisted of forty to sixty households and "*Der Blockleiter ist für die gesamten Vorgänge in seinem Bereich,* welche die Bewegung betreffen, *zuständig* und dem Zellenleiter *voll verantwortlich*" (emphasis in original, 100). Given the crucial position as liaison between Party leadership and the general population, the block leader had to meet certain requirements: "Der Blockleiter muß Parteigenosse sein. Er soll zu den besten Parteigenossen innerhalb der Ortsgruppe zählen" (100), but he could not apply or volunteer for such position; the candidate had to be proposed by the group leader of the town or locality and then named by the regional leader: "Nach erfolgter Bewährung und Beibringung der vorgeschriebenen Personalunterlagen (Nachweis arischer Abstammung bis 1800) wird er 3 bis 4 Monate nach kommissarischer Einsetzung offiziell vom zuständigen Kreisleiter ernannt" (100). The block leader had the duty to "enlighten" the population "im Sinne der Bewegung" (101) and to report rumors detrimental to the Party: "Der Blockleiter muß nicht nur der Prediger und Verfechter der national-sozialistischen Weltanschauung gegenüber den seiner politischen Betreuung anvertrauten Volks- und Parteigenossen sein, sondern er muß auch dahin wirken, daß seinem Blockbereich angehörende *Parteigenossen praktische Mitarbeit leisten*. . . . Der Blockleiter soll die Parteigenossen immer wieder auf ihre besonderen Pflichten gegenüber Volk und Staat aufmerksam machen" (emphasis in original, 101–2). The block leader is required to maintain records on the activities of Party members and to record their dues payments as well as the configuration of individual households, which are not necessarily families but all individuals under one roof.

As the most immediately visible and accessible local representative of the Party, the block leader "hat sich beim Tragen des Dienstanzuges besonders korrekter Haltung, Sauberkeit und strikter Einhaltung der Uniform-Vorschriften zu befleißigen" (103) and to demonstrate an exemplary attitude in public and private life as a model to the public, "kurz und gut, der Blockleiter ist ein unablässig sich mühender Aktivist und Propagandist der Bewegung" (103). Of course, such a description might not always coincide with actual practice, but nonetheless indicates that Krolow, as block leader, would have had a position of responsibility and an active role in local Party affairs. The organizational handbook emphasized the positive social function of National Socialism and the beneficial engagement of the block leader in helping individuals and families become integrated into the Party, which remained somewhat exclusive, or into related support organizations for the masses including the NS-Frauenschaft and the DAF. As the monitor of local activities and the link to higher Party echelons, the block leader would have also been feared by those individuals not in the Party, or those individuals of a faith, racial minority, or political conviction not acceptable to the Party.

Without additional knowledge of Krolow's actual experience, it is impossible to determine how his individual performance in that office might have varied from the general description and prescription of the function of a block leader. My later research indicates that he claimed afterward to have only substituted unofficially and short term for the person in that position, who had to be away, but in this official survey he makes no mention of any such qualifications. Krolow's 1939 Party questionnaire does not indicate the length of his service as block leader, but as indicated in the handbook, that position was given to individuals of proven Party credentials, as in Krolow's long term membership in the Hitler Youth with a leadership role. Presumably, his activities as block leader came to an end with his move to Breslau in 1940.[6] Little is known of his experience in Breslau, at the university or otherwise. He exmatriculated on September 12, 1942.[7]

Gerhard Kolter's biographical sketch indicates, contrary to Paulus, that Krolow was an *Assistent* for a short period without his degree, but that claim is undocumented.[8] In his questionnaire for the RSK dated January 25, 1941, Krolow indicates that he also did editorial work for the scholarly journal *Junge Wissenschaft/Göttinger Semesterhefte,* where his first known publication also appeared: an essay on Rilke's poem "Ausgesetzt auf den Bergen des Herzens" in 1939.[9] In this essay, Krolow distinguished Rilke from Paul Valéry, leaning on longstanding stereotypes of cultural difference between German *Kultur* and French *Zivilisation,* according to the fullness of intellectual and emotional experience that enters into the language of the poem: "Aber — und das ist der deutliche Unterschied zu ähnlich Erlebenden romanischer Herkunft und französischen Sprachbereichs wie etwa Paul Valéry — der errungene Innenraum bleibt nicht Raum der ratio, kein intellektueller Filtrat, — kein purer Geist-Raum, darauf noch intim Sinnenhaftes, noch das Pretiöse eines beliebigen Intérieurs Bezug hat, sondern weitet sich zum Raum aus Geist und Herz des deutschen Dichters" (123). He adopts that widespread distinction, which aligns him with conservative thinking over the prior 30 or more years, but neither links him nor too greatly distances him from more fervent or rabid Nazi discourse, yet he adds a footnote (no. 4) about the particular intellectuality of Valéry, calling it positively "ein zartes Geheimnis des Geistes." The term *zart* will emerge in his poetics much more frequently later on and suggests here perhaps, in retrospect, a discreet or secret identification on his part with Valéry or French culture.[10] In the choice of topic and content, Krolow evinces an early identification with Rilke and the situation of existential dis-ease or painful exposure to circumstances that nonetheless and necessarily broaden the sensibility, which in turn elevates those circumstances, or dissolves and clarifies that pain in the beauty of formed language.[11] In a sort of dialectic of evasive self-affirmation as an aesthete, Krolow discretely manages, while appearing to make necessary concessions to nationalism, to speak not only of Valéry, but also to speak positively of him and to delineate a path, seemingly incongruous with the time and place, toward refinement of the spirit in poetic language. This essay marks perhaps the first steps in print in his aesthetic progress toward the relative (or compromised) independence of *inner emigration* and outward conformity, a sort of calculated hypocrisy for the sake of survival and artistic self-fulfillment, which is neither admirable nor heroic, but also not an egregious instance of art in the service of the state.[12] Marie Luise Kaschnitz, as quoted in Kirchner, describes the situation with candor as follows:

> Worin soll sie denn bestanden haben, unsere sogenannte innere Emigration? [. . .] nicht heimlich im Keller Flugblätter gedruckt, nicht nachts verteilt, nicht widerständlerischen Bünden angehört, von denen man nicht wußte, daß es sie gab, es so genau aber gar nicht wissen wollte. Lieber überleben [. . .] Wir sind keine Politiker, wir sind keine Helden, wir taten was anderes. Das andere hielt uns aufrecht [. . .] Und an der Wichtigkeit unserer Arbeit zweifelten wir keinen Augenblick, eine wissenschaftliche Erkenntnis, eine gelungene Verszeile, auch eine nie gedruckte, konnten nach meiner damaligen Auffassung die Welt verändern, verbessern, das war unsere Art von Widerstand. (63)

Of course, the term *inner emigration*, already inadequate in Krolow's case, is especially so in this light since he worked hard to emerge fully into the public sphere of Nazi Germany at this time with numerous publications. He thereby actively served the Party in the 1930s and 1940s. Between 1940 and 1945, Krolow published in the following newspapers, magazines, and journals: *Schlesische Tageszeitung, Deutsche Allgemeine Zeitung, Hannoverscher Kurier, Münchner Neueste Nachrichten, Berliner Börsen Zeitung, Brüsseler Zeitung, Ostdeutsche Morgenpost, Das Reich, Hamburger Tageblatt, Kölnische Zeitung, Das Innere Reich*, and probably also *Krakauer Zeitung*.[13] *Inner emigration* suggests a retreat from public life that in Krolow's case simply does not seem to have taken place. Instead, his early career shows a gradual, hard-earned breadth of exposure in print, about which he is evidently proud. The notion of emigration, even reversed, does not capture the specific contours of his early career. Whether as a true believer in Nazi ideology and a willing servant of the regime or not, his position at the time, despite the activities he indicates, seems to have been one of imagined aesthetic insularity, which allowed him to pursue, without reservation or compunction, opportunities to publish poems, lyrical prose, and reviews or critical essays on a broad basis during the war years of most severe censorship. Indeed, after his student essay, Krolow's first known publication was a poem in the *Schlesische Tageszeitung,* which can be further identified as the "Amtliches Blatt der NSDAP und sämtlicher Behörden. Breslau: NS-Gauverlag Niederschlesien," which indicates, at least, his willingness to publish wherever possible.[14] Yet these earliest publications in various newspapers are not propagandistic; his poems and short passages of lyrical prose describe the seasons and do not resemble Nazi discourse, but rather seem, out of context, simple exercises, often cloying, in capturing nuances of perception. Nonetheless, the context, for example in the *Deutsche Allgemeine Zeitung,* reminds one of the dialectical complicity of such pabulum, perhaps even a paradoxical consistency between conventional and insipid nature poetry and Party membership. One cannot ignore that these poems also served the Party by preserving the threadbare illusion of apolitical space. In these organs, such poetry had Party approval, not just tolerance; accordingly, Krolow lists them in seeking admission as full member of the RSK.

For the period after his semesters at the university, Krolow appears in the standard brief chronologies after 1942 as a *freier Schriftsteller,* which is misleading terminology. Despite the longstanding acceptance of this information in Krolow criticism, no such position existed in German society at the time. In order to publish, one had to belong to the RSK or rather one published under the administrative authority of the RSK. In his "Periodisierung" essay of 1977, Hans Dieter Schäfer lists Krolow (105) among authors who shaped postwar German literature, but who were also registered in the Directory of Authors of the RSK; in a footnote, Schäfer explains his use of an asterisk in a list of those authors who were "von der Mitgliedschaft befreit" and quotes the passage from the RSK regulations that makes the distinction between authors who supported themselves fully by their writing and those who did not, only publishing "in geringfügigem Umfange." It deserves emphasis that this was not a matter of self-definition. Whether as vocation or avocation, the criterion was one's income. Those writers who were released from full membership were simply less financially successful and not required to pay full dues or to have their income taxed at the same rate as full members, and could get a blanket permission to publish up to twelve small items at a time, thus reducing the bureaucratic burden for both parties of separate requests for permission to publish.

The distinction between full and released members (*befreit*) sounds substantial and morally significant, but both groups were registered in the RSK and subject to the exact same requirements such as:

proof of Aryan lineage, a personal questionnaire, Party review, Gestapo review, and so forth, as well as the same surveillance and censorship. The distinction is, in fact, only internal and resembles more accurately the difference between categories in the dues schedule of any organization. Despite what the word *befreit* leads one to assume or believe outside of the specific historical context of the Reichsschrifttumskammer, the term does not carry moral weight or implications. In financial terms, a release was simply a dues waiver and therefore something of an advantage for younger, less established, or less productive writers, though surely designed to reduce paperwork. The distinction was not an evaluation of the work along either literary or Party lines. One way or another, one had to belong to the RSK in order to publish, that is, under their authority; if one published during that period in Germany on any regular basis, one was equally a member of the RSK, regardless of this internal bureaucratic distinction. This distinction is defined on the reverse side of the *Befreiungsschein* as well as in the bylaws.[15]

A writer who was released of the obligation of full membership simply did not earn enough to gain that status and was accordingly not subjected to the same taxation and dues requirements. On that basis, Krolow was routinely granted his release or waiver, but he applied anyway for "Aufnahme als Mitglied der Reichsschrifttumskammer, Gruppe Schriftsteller" on January 25, 1941. This status was apparently not granted, since Krolow petitioned to have his status upgraded to that of full member and wrote two postcards from Hannover to inquire further, to protest, and to request a repeated and expedited review of the matter. His two cards were followed by an insistent letter sent from Kattowitz on March 8, 1942, and stamped on arrival March 10, 1942:

Ich bitte um Aufnahme in die Reichsschrifttumskammer.
Im vergangenen Jahre veröffentlichte ich laufend in einer grossen Anzahl deutscher Zeitungen ca. 75 Beiträge (Ausschliesslich Lyrik). Mit dem Ausbau meiner Mitarbeit an deutschen Grosszeitungen ist zu rechnen. Zudem bin ich mit einem Verlag in Verhandlungen über Buchveröffentlichung [*sic*] getreten.
    Ich halte daher meine Anmeldung mit der Bitte um Aufnahme für unumgänglich. Januar 41, zu Beginn meiner Veröffentlichungen, setzte ich Sie bereits schon einmal in Kenntnis. Damals vereinbarten wir vorläufige Befreiung. Meine Papiere betr. arischen Nachweis lagen seinerzeit vor und wurden von Ihnen überprüft.

Ich bitte um möglichst baldige Antwort.
Heil Hitler!
Karl Krolow
Referent (K) beim Reichsführer SS
Reichskommissar f. d. F. d. V.

The possible reasons for his impatience and persistence in this matter are obscure, aside from the added degree of official recognition and validation within that state as a writer.[16] One can only assume that Krolow was willing to pay higher fees and higher taxes for that institutional recognition as a fully established, self-supporting writer. Whatever his reasons, the letter has a note of desperate supplication, which is hard to fathom since concrete, material advantages to such a change in bureaucratic status were not likely, although the financial disadvantages were certain. Perhaps he could have then expected higher honoraria for small publications and better terms for the book publication, which he seems at that point to have expected.[17] The fact that the Reichsschrifttumskammer did not respond to his several petitions for full membership, based on income, raises the question of how Krolow supported himself and his family. At the end of his letter, apparently to impress the RSK, Krolow adds a title that connects him ominously to the SS as a *Referent* for the "Reichskommissar für die Festigung des deutschen Volkstums" — an organization that determined who was and who was not of German ancestry in the East, particularly in Poland, a decision which had dire consequences for those individuals.[18]

Krolow's use of this title and position as *Referent* in that notorious commission — in an attempt at persuading the RSK to upgrade his status — is the only indication of any such activity on his part. His status there will receive some clarification here, though without independent corroboration. Nonetheless, at the time, such a title could have been checked easily. A *Referent* is normally a salaried position of some authority in a bureaucracy with responsibility for an area; the indication (K) presumably refers to *Kultur* or *Kulturabteilung,* the cultural section. At this point, it is only necessary to note that, despite his efforts with the RSK, Krolow's status was not changed. This indicates that he simply did not earn enough income as a writer, despite his growing number of publications; his newspaper publications were, for the poems at least, brief in word count and probably also small in remuneration.[19] If he had a salary from his bureaucratic position as *Referent* in that organization, he may have wanted the status as full member to suggest that he earned his full living from his writing.

Without drawing conclusions beyond the evidence, this episode shows Krolow's willingness to advance his career for whatever reasons under the Nazi state.

Krolow's most substantial publications of this period were review essays of recent poetry that appeared in *Das Innere Reich*. More than his own artistic efforts in that period, which seem rather more like exercises than accomplishments, his essays show a mature, critical intelligence and have to alter the impression that arises from the meager biography provided in previous criticism that Krolow was a fledgling author, who published quantitatively little and qualitatively little more than juvenilia during the Nazi period. He had, to the contrary, completed his studies and established himself as a professional writer of some modest early success with very good prospects, according to his own account. Rolf Paulus alludes to extensive work with radio, which may have been an additional source of income, though he gives no dates or listings. Krolow's criticism, even under the restrictions of the day, is marked by a mature, well-informed, and discerning intelligence. When the war ended, Krolow was thirty years old, and had been publishing regularly for five to six years. He occupies a place between the older authors with whom he is often linked such as Horst Lange, Günter Eich, Oskar Loerke, Wilhelm Lehmann, Oda Schaefer, Georg Britting, and many more, and the generation that emerged into prominence with the Gruppe 47 (Paul Celan, Ingeborg Bachmann, Günter Grass, and others). In these review essays, probably written at age twenty-seven or twenty-eight, Krolow shows a broad view of the genre in Germany, limited as it was by political circumstances, and also demonstrates his knowledge and appreciation of poetry outside Germany. In his reviews, Krolow limits himself to matters of genre, although marked with some inflections of ideological conformity, and in his prose, to matters of perception. During this period, Krolow seems to have successfully tried to cultivate the development of his own sensibility, technical facility, and critical acumen with respect to the genre of poetry within the restrictions imposed by the state. Thus a highly developed sense of genre effectively becomes the cocoon of his *inner emigration* or aesthetic insularity tempered by a critical awareness of his compromises, which also emerges in the intriguing dissonances of his first volume of poetry in 1943.

Notes

[1] In his editorial note to his collection of criticism *Über Karl Krolow* (1972), Walter Helmut Fritz cites his "exemplarische Bedeutung" (7). Also in that year, Ludwig Büttner remarks in summation: "So zeigt sich Krolows Gedichtwerk wandlungsfähig und mehrschichtig; es läßt sich an ihm gleichsam die Verschiedenheit der Nachkriegslyrik ablesen" (88). Harald Hartung, in 1985, disputes any suggestion that Krolow simply conforms poetically to the tastes of the day and suggests in contrast: "Wichtige Entwicklungsschübe der Nachkriegslyrik sind in seinem Werk modellhaft repräsentiert" (164). Even his harshest critic, Hans Dieter Schäfer, in 1981, still considers him a negative representative of the period: "An Krolows Arbeiten läßt sich eindrucksvoll das literarische Klima der fünfziger Jahre erfahrbar machen" ("Zusammenhänge der deutschen Gegenwartslyrik," 168).

[2] In 1962, an American Germanist, Charles W. Hoffmann, focused attention on a third branch of German literature during the 1930s and 1940s by individuals who were neither targeted by the regime nor supporters of it, who neither went into exile nor joined or supported the Nazi Party, and whose work did not belong to either the literature of exile or an openly programmatic Nazi literature. Hoffmann drew attention to what he called "opposition poetry," which he equates with "resistance poetry" or "anti-Nazi" poetry. Under these conflated rubrics, he offers valuable but limited deliberations on four poets (Werner Bergengruen [b. 1892], Reinhold Schneider [b. 1903], Albrecht Haushofer [b. 1903] and Rudolf Hagelstange [b. 1912]), whose works affirm humane values through the stylistic traditionalism of the sonnet and religious confession. Though popular, their work did not, however, release any new impulses for the postwar period. They may indeed have constituted a "heimliche Gegenöffentlichkeit" (Bormann, 202) during the Nazi period, but neither Hoffmann's terminology nor his choice of authors adequately addressed the third branch of literary production in the Nazi period, though Hoffmann provided an initial impetus to this inquiry. Later studies by Ralf Schnell, Hans Dieter Schäfer and Karl Heinz Schoeps increasingly opened the range of inquiry into the particular circumstances and works of individual authors. Schäfer's term "nichtfaschistische Literatur" provided the necessary conceptual handle or tool for inquiry into this gray area and thereby allowed for an increasingly differentiated understanding of the real conditions and choices of individuals. See also the forthcoming collection of essays *Flight of Fantasy: New Perspectives on Inner Emigration in German Literature, 1933–1945,* edited by Neil H. Donahue and Doris Kirchner (New York and London: Berghahn Books, 2003).

[3] Krolow entered the university in Göttingen in the Wintersemester 1935/36 after completing the *Ausgleichdienst* referred to in his *Anmeldeschein der Studentenführung;* the university records of his matriculation read as follows, with semester, discipline and address:

Student #2212 Krolow, Karl

Wintersemester 1935/36	*Theol.*	*Kirchweg 44*
Sommersemester 1936	*phil.*	*Kirchweg 44*

Wintersemester 1936/37	*phil.*	*Münchhausenstr. 23*
[no matriculation records for summer semester 1937]		
Wintersemester 1937/38	*germ.*	*Friedl. Weg 34*
Sommersemester 1938	*germ.*	*Friedl. Weg 34*
Sommersemester 1939	*phil.*	*Friedl. Weg 34*
Herbsttrimester 1939	*phil.*	*Friedl. Weg. 34 beurlaubt*
I. Trimester 1940	*phil.*	*Hannover Bandelstr. 23*
II. Trimester 1940	*[no listing]*	
III. Trimester 1940	*[no listing]*	
I. Trimester 1941	*[no listing]*	
II. Trimester 1941	*[no listing]*	
Winter 1941–42	*[no listing]*	
Sommer 1942	*[no listing]*	

[at the university in Breslau from the third trimester 1940 to spring/summer 1941, according to Nazi Party personnel file]

Student #11285

Wintersemester 1942–43	*phil.*	*Feuerschanzengraben 15*
Sommer 1943	*phil.*	*Langemarckstr. 58 II*
Winter 1943–44	*phil.*	*Langemarckstr. 58 II*
Sommer 1944	*German.*	*11 Semester [noted in records]*

[4] See fn. 14 in this chapter.

[5] For historical context from a personal perspective, see Bernt Engelmann's accounts. In a discussion of the pressures to belong to the Hitler Youth, he notes, "Es war wirklich nicht allzu schwierig gewesen, sich von der HJ fernzuhalten" (*Im Gleichschritt*, 76), though he adds, "Tatsächlich war erst von 1937 an der Druck stärker geworden, und im März 1939, als man uns schon zum Reichsarbeitsdienst und etwas später zur Wehrmacht eingezogen hatte, war ein Gesetz erlassen worden, nach dem alle Jugendlichen für den Dienst in der Hitlerjugend in ähnlicher Weise wie für den Wehrdienst erfaßt werden sollten" (78). Krolow, however, was already in the Hitler Youth in 1934 and became a Nazi Party member in 1937. Engelmann's partner in dialogue remarks: "Wir jedenfalls mußten nicht zur HJ [. . .] und wer dem Verein beitrat, der war entweder wirklich dafür oder tat so, als ob er es wäre aus dem einen oder anderen Grund . . ." (78). Without additional information, we cannot draw further conclusions about Krolow's participation in the HJ or the Nazi Party.

[6] For comparison, see Günter Eich's comment in his correspondence of September 20, 1939, with Adolf Artur Kuhnert on the advantages of being away from Berlin: "daß es reichlich Butter gibt und daß zur Verpflegung Zigaretten gehören. Von anderen Dingen ganz zu schweigen. (Blockwart kann man hier nicht werden)" [cited in Karst, 53]. This suggests that he was happy to avoid the pressures to serve the Party in that manner on the home front. Eich did, however, serve in other ways through his radio plays.

[7] According to a letter dated April 7, 1997, from Dr. Leonard Smolka, Director of the University Archives in Wroclaw, the archive contains no other information

than a listing for Krolow as a student of Kulturwissenschaft in the years 1935–45 without the specific dates of his attendance.

[8] In *Der Lyriker Karl Krolow* by R. Paulus and G. Kolter, the authors state first: "Mit dem Studium der Germanistik, Romanistik, Kunstgeschichte und Philosophie in Göttingen, Breslau und wieder Göttingen hätte Krolow Studienrat für Deutsch und Französisch werden können. Er mußte aber auf einen Abschluß verzichten, weil er nicht den entsprechenden Organisationen angehören wollte" (10), then, in apparent contradiction, they write: "Eine Anstellung als Assistent des Philosophischen Seminars schützt ihn vor Wehrdienst und anderem" (10). The university archive in Göttingen has no record of Krolow as an "Assistent des Philosophischen Seminars." The only professor of philosophy at the time (Heyse) had few "Assistenten," whose documents such as letters of contract, pay records, recommendations, and so on are present in the archive, including the "Treue-Gelöbnis" of allegiance to the National-Socialist Party as required at the time. If Krolow did have such a position, such an oath would have also been required.

[9] Karl Krolow, "Bemerkungen zu einem späten Gedicht Rilkes: 'Ausgetzt auf den Bergen des Herzens.'" *Junge Wissenschaft/Göttinger Semesterhefte* 2 (1938/39): 122–26.

[10] One might compare this moment from his earliest publication to his comments on French culture in conversation with Vera B. Profit some fifty-five years later (*Menschlich*, 67).

[11] Rolf Paulus remarks about the different phases of Krolow's poetics: "Immer handelt es sich um ein Ausgesetztsein, das aber eine beträchtliche Variationsbreite hat" (*Lyrik und Poetik Karl Krolows*, 30).

[12] Here one has to think of the whole spectrum of writers and artists who served the state as propagandists, like Leni Riefenstahl, despite her assertions to the contrary, or as a functionary, issuing public statements on behalf of *Gleichschaltung*, like at first Gottfried Benn, or celebrated Nazi writers like Hanns Johst, or even writers who worked for the more closely watched and remunerative medium of radio, like Günter Eich (see Glenn Cuomo's study).

[13] *Krakauer Zeitung* is not included in Paulus; see Orlowski.

[14] In his "Antrag zur Bearbeitung der Aufnahme als Mitglied der Reichsschrifttumskammer, Gruppe Schriftsteller" of January 25, 1941, Krolow lists his publications as follows:

Mitarbeit seit dem 15. Dezember 1933 an Zeitungen:

Deutsche Allgemeine Zeitung	*Okt.-Dez. 1940*	*fünf*
Berliner Börsenzeitung	*Dez. 1940*	*einer*
Schlesische Tageszeitung	*Okt.-Dez. 1940*	*drei*
Hannoverscher Kurier	*Nov.-Dez. 1940*	*drei*
Münchner Neueste Nachrichten	*Nov.-Dez. 1940*	*zwei*

It is possible that Krolow lists here some poems accepted for publication in 1940 that did not appear until the next year. Even if one takes into account publications from 1941, his list of fourteen still adds at least several poems to the eight listed for 1940 in the Paulus bibliography: an additional two poems published by his own account in the *Schlesische Tageszeitung* and two more also in the *Hannoverscher Kurier*.

[15] See "Amtliche Bekanntmachung Nr. 88" in *Handbuch der Reichsschrifttums-kammer,* ed. Wilhelm Ihde, which is quoted by Schäfer, though not fully enough. Also, in a letter to Karl Krolow, Volker Dahm, an authority on the Reichsschrifttumskammer (Institut für Zeitgeschichte, Munich) clarified this terminological distinction as merely one of nomenclature, but not substance. I thank Dr. Dahm for valuable discussions on the intricacies of RSK bureaucracy.

[16] Jan-Pieter Barbian, the most knowledgeable chronicler of the RSK, cites a passage from this letter in his essay in English translation (though not in his book in German), but offers no further commentary there to a situation that is not at all self-evident or self-explanatory.

[17] At the time, Krolow was circulating a manuscript of his poetry. In a letter from August 10, 1943 (in Marbach), Paul Alverdes, the editor of *Das Innere Reich,* finally responds to the manuscript from his much appreciated reviewer with much descriptive praise. He cites more and different poems than *Hochgelobtes, gutes Leben* contains. Krolow was probably trying at this time to place a second manuscript. In fact, under wartime restrictions on paper, Krolow's first book of the following year, *Hochgelobtes, gutes Leben,* was a tandem publication and contained only six poems by each of its two authors, printed as an unbound brochure on poor paper. Krolow cannot have expected to advance financially from that publication. The RSK did not respond to his prospects.

[18] See the studies by Koehl, especially in his *The Structure and Power Struggles of the Nazi SS,* 186–93, on "The RKFDV System"; see also Martin Broszat, especially 62–65), and Vladis O. Lumans.

[19] In his application for membership to the RSK in 1941, Krolow indicates that he had received in the last months of the previous year "etwa 150 RM in den letzten 8 Wochen des Jahres 1940" for the fourteen poems he had published, thus earning roughly 10 RM per poem. In 1941, he published 18 poems; in 1942, nineteen poems; in 1943, seventeen poems (six of which were in his first volume, not in newspapers); in 1944, twelve poems; and in 1945 none, though in all cases, the bibliography is probably not complete. Nonetheless his earnings per year from poetry probably did not exceed several hundred RM. His prose vignettes might have been paid somewhat better, since longer, though they also were short (in their later book publication, from one to five pages each, though with illustrations): in 1943, he published seven vignettes, in 1944, ten, and in 1945, only one, though again the bibliography is probably incomplete. For his several long review essays, he also would have had additional earnings. Nonetheless, it is hard to imagine that he would have gained more than, estimating generously, 1000 RM per year from his writings. The older and more established Georg Britting's account of his income gives a basis for comparison (see Britting, 254–55); also David Basker's description of Wolfgang Koeppen's "comfortable financial position" (Pre-1945, 682–83) of RM 12,000. for 1941 and 1942. Basker additionally cites Timothy Mason's study *Sozialpolitik im Dritten Reich* (1978) to the effect that in 1936 RM 128 per month (!) was a subsistence wage. Thus, Krolow's sporadic earnings hardly constitute a living wage, even for himself alone, much less with family.

2: Blüte und Boden: *Inner Emigration* in the Uncollected Poems (1940–1945)

KARL KROLOW'S LONG CAREER began almost sixty years ago with the publication of his first poems in 1940. Since then he has regularly published a volume of poetry at least every few years. Aside from the longevity of his career and his extraordinary productivity, many critics have considered Krolow particularly representative of postwar German poetry because of his ability to absorb new impulses, to transform himself, and to reflect in his own work the dominant phases of the genre in each decade up to the present. His origins in the tradition of German *Naturlyrik* linked him closely to an older generation of poets such as Oskar Loerke, Wilhelm Lehmann, Elisabeth Langgässer, Marie Luise Kaschnitz, and Günter Eich, all born between 1884 and 1907, but his numerous translations of French and Spanish poets after the war distanced him from that tradition. Krolow's early work never figured as part of the literature of *inner emigration* in Nazi Germany;[1] rather he appeared in the public eye as a new talent in the 1950s, like Ingeborg Bachmann and Paul Celan, whose poetry also exhibited acute linguistic consciousness, surrealistic metaphors, and an allusive, cosmopolitan flair. Between these two literary generations, Krolow helped open postwar German poetry to new impulses as poet, translator, and critic.

In 1952 Krolow presented his poems at the same epoch-making Group 47 meeting in Niendorf that introduced Paul Celan and Ingeborg Bachmann; that same year his volume *Die Zeichen der Welt* was published with the Deutsche Verlags-Anstalt in Stuttgart as was Celan's *Mohn und Gedächtnis*. Along with Bachmann and Celan, Eich, and Huchel, Krolow gained a place at once among the most important poets of the period. He received the Büchner Prize in 1956 and was at the time the youngest recipient ever. In that same year his poems were included, with very few other German poets, in Hugo Friedrich's landmark study *Die Struktur der modernen Lyrik*. Friedrich subsequently wrote an afterword to a selection of Krolow's poetry in 1963, and in 1965, Suhrkamp began to publish Krolow's *Gesammelte Gedichte* in ten-year intervals: the fourth volume appeared in 1997.

Early on, Krolow belonged to the canon of postwar German poetry. In 1973 Klaus Jeziorkowski touted Krolow as the "Repräsentativge-stalt der deutschen Nachkriegslyrik überhaupt. . . . Seine Entwicklung ist in singulärer Weise repräsentativ, muster- und modellhaft [. . .] für die [. . .] Entwicklung der deutschen Lyrik nach dem Zweiten Welt-krieg. Heute ist er der Doyen der deutschen Gegenwartslyrik" (409).

Beyond his poetry, Krolow also secured his position in German letters with regular volumes of literary prose and occasional essays on sundry topics. He also produced innumerable reviews of poetry for newspapers such as the *Frankfurter Allgemeine Zeitung,* essays in liter-ary criticism that have been collected in several books, and a literary history of postwar German poetry. Krolow regularly arranged for the multiple publication of his poems, reviews, and essays in various news-papers and journals, either verbatim or with slight alterations under different titles, before they appeared in book form. As of 1980 Krolow had the largest bibliography of any postwar German writer. Further-more, Krolow did extensive work for radio and increasingly sat on ju-ries for literary awards, a fact not recorded in bibliographical accounts. He gained an uncommon influence in the world of German poetry from these experiences; his work was not only part of the literary canon, but as critic he had also become an institution in the business of German literature.

As a result of his critical and institutional influence, Krolow shaped the reception of postwar German poetry and of his own work, which enjoyed a broad, generally uncritical, and friendly reception, as a study by Gerhard Kolter has documented. Little attention was paid to his early work, which was not available anyway. His *Gesammelte Gedichte* of 1965 did not include the poems from his early volumes between 1943 and 1949, which were first reprinted by Suhrkamp in 1989. In Krolow's 186-page entry in *Kindlers Literaturgeschichte der Gegenwart* titled "Die Lyrik in der Bundesrepublik seit 1945," he in-troduces his own work next to Eich's with the comment "Wie Günter Eich ist Karl Krolow (*1915) bald nach 1945 mit Gedichten hervor-getreten" (416), but makes the distinction: "Während Eichs Anwe-senheit in der deutschen Lyrik, wie die Huchels, in den dreißiger Jahren in Umrissen erkennbar ist, tritt Krolow später auf den Plan" (417). In the appendix to that volume, Krolow's name appears neither on the list of authors who emigrated nor among those who "der 'In-neren Emigration' zugerechnet sind," though, for example, Luise Rinser (b. 1912), only three years older than Krolow, fell into this latter category. As a critic, Krolow stylized the historical dimension of his early career as a poet and critic, which, if not in need of wholesale revision, does require closer scrutiny. In fact, Krolow began his busy career as poet, prose writer, and critic in the Third Reich with approximately 105 publications of poetry and lyrical prose from 1940 to 1945 in various newspapers and with substantial discussions of poetry in the journal *Das Innere Reich.*

Instead of mere juvenilia, this earliest phase of Krolow's literary career, between the ages of twenty-five and thirty, represents the serious production of a mature intellectual, who has decided to advance his literary career under the given circumstances. His first poem, "Ende des Sommers," appeared in the *Schlesische Tageszeitung* in October 1940 in Breslau, where Krolow had gone as a student for two years from 1940 to 1942; that newspaper bore the caption "Amtliches Blatt der NSDAP und sämtlicher Behörden" and was published by the NS-Gauverlag in Breslau, though Walter Tausk, in his *Breslauer Tagebuch, 1933–1940,* calls another newspaper, the *Schlesische Tagespost,* the leading "Naziblatt von Breslau" (67). Both that caption and Tausk's diary recall the historical context of invasion, persecution, and resettlement in the Breslau of Krolow's first published poem, which begins: "Laß es genug sein. Komm und ruhe aus. / Schau auf das Land und spür das große Licht."[2] In quietly compromised innocence, Krolow's earliest poetry describes, predictably, the changes of the seasons from month to month or the changing times of day; the final lines of the poem "November," also from 1940, offer what amounts to a poetics of *inner emigration:* "Groß war das Jahr. Schließe die Augen nur / Und horch auf Regenguß und Krähenlaut."[3] Some of the poems strike a tone of folksy simplicity as in the prayer-like poem "An einen Herbst," which invokes the lingering warmth of summer in the air: "Die Heimweh macht nach einem Frauenkinn, [. . .] und Haaren, blond wie Flachs." It pleads: "Gib den Geruch von milden Arzenein, / Von Lorbeerblatt und trocknem Thymian. / Gib den Geschmack von frischem Apfelwein / Und schütz das Korn vor Brand und Mäusezahn." Such poems provide a touch of uncomplicated, sentimental, and atmospheric *Innerlichkeit* to the official ideology of racial purity and rural rootedness ("blond wie Flachs"). They comfort the newspaper reader with familiar emotions linked to the eternal rhythm of the seasons beyond daily political news and propaganda that otherwise filled the same pages and frame the events of the day in the illusion of a benign and natural order. This sort of idyllic *Blüte-und-Boden* literature was not as trite and innocuous as it sounded but served a precise ideological function.[4]

In that context, other poems allow a certain allegorical reading in terms of *inner emigration*, which absorbs, naturalizes, and defuses anxiety, again providing comfort and blunting potential criticism. The poem "Nebelweg," published in the *Berliner Börsen Zeitung* on December 28, 1940, demonstrates Krolow's allegory:

> Du gehst verstummt durch blindes Land,
> Die Stirn voll Trug und Traum.
> Du greifst den Nebel mit der Hand
> Und ahnst den Schlehenbaum.
>
> Und weißt: hier schlangen Blatt und Dorn,
> hier trieben Kraut und Halm,
> hier atmete das Sommerkorn,
> hier hing der träge Qualm
>
> Des Reisigfeuers in der Luft. —
> Es schwand das Gartenhaus,
> Der Kiesweg schwand, der Beerenduft.
> Du kennst dich nicht mehr aus.
>
> Du suchst und irrst und hörst dein Herz
> Und bist mit ihm allein.
> Und schwindest selbst, gehst ohne Schmerz
> In Gottes Dunkel ein.

In the first lines, the poem seems to describe, within this natural scenario, an oppressed individual ("verstummt") wandering in a landscape of uncritical conformity ("durch blindes Land"), trapped in anguish between ideological deception and dreams of transcendence ("Die Stirn voll Trug und Traum"). The direct address creates a personal bond of understanding and sympathy for that individual's predicament and tribulations. The situation of existential confusion and desperate *Ausweglosigkeit* leads to utter isolation and communion with one's self that leads, instead of to action or analysis, to paralysis in a sort of quietist self-abnegation before the mystery of revelation.

The poems of this period range between these two poles of solidarity in the benign order of nature or in shared anxieties. The poem "Geist des Abends," which appeared in the *Düsseldorfer Nachrichten* on July 24, 1941, combines the two modes:

Guter Geist des Abends, komm und schweb
Wie ein Falter her und atme Mohn.
Bring den Duft der späten Blume, leb
Leicht in Vasen und im Weinglas. Wohn

Unter uns. Die Dämmerung ist lang.
Gib, daß wir den dunklen Baum versteh'n.
Wehr den Wind, der weht. Er macht uns bang.
Laß uns tief in nahe Augen seh'n.

Sei im Druck der warmen Menschenhand,
Wie sie zärtlich in der andern ruht.
Nimm von uns die letzte, dünne Wand,
Die uns heimlich trennt und wehe tut.

In this poem the enjambment between the first two strophes almost shocks as stylistic radicalism in its partial departure from strict convention since it breaks the utterance in order to maintain the rhyme scheme, whereas thought and rhyme usually converge with seeming inevitability. Such rare moments highlight the transparency, if not invisibility, of poetic style in these poems, where the external consistency of rhyme matches the internal uniformity of content to create a soothing, almost sedative affect, stripped of dissonances. The parts seem almost interchangeable. As a rule, therefore, the poems avoid any direct mention of historical events or even traces of modern urban society. They only relate dialectically through that evacuation of historical content or in terms of what might be called allegorical mood, where certain phrases might suggest a ponderous relation to events in the world. Only one poem, the elegiac "Einem Toten des Krieges," published in the *Brüsseler Zeitung* on March 4, 1943, refers directly to the war and transports the fallen soldier into eternity: "Wie ein Sternbild, das uns jäh entrückte, / Bist du in das Ew'ge ausgesetzt. / Und der Totenkranz, der knapp dich schmückte, / Wuchs zum stillen Lorbeer dir zuletzt." This poem also reveals the ideological function of the others to translate and abstract historical experience into ahistorical terms through the mythology of nature. It gives events, whether named or unnamed, a patina of transcendence, a nimbus of eternity, as defined in Krolow's 1943 essay, "Glanz des Ewigen im Gedicht."

That short essay appeared in the *Deutsche Allgemeine Zeitung* (April 17, 1943) in an issue mainly devoted to commentary on the mass murder in Katyn, Poland, along with more routine articles on new tanks and other developments in the war. The page preceding the single page of feuilleton carries, for example, an article captioned "Durch Genickschuß erledigt: Weitere Einzelheiten zur jüdisch-bolschewistischen Mordtat in Katyn." The "Glanz des Ewigen im Gedicht" stands in relation to such events in the same pages, whether as individual flight from that reality or instrumental diversion from the same, or both. The essay defines the contents of a poem as: "Im wahren Gedicht sind, nicht anders als in einer zarten Streichermusik oder einer gewaltigen Doppelfuge, wie im echten Werk bildender Kunst, dem strengen Profil einer Novelle und im großen Hingang des Dramas alle guten Geister eines Volkes gesammelt" (3). All art serves the same function of distilling the good spirits "eines Volkes" from the various soothing experiences he enumerates in the subsequent paragraphs, from the "sanfte Traurigkeit der kleinen Städte" to the "starken Bauernschädel des Pflügers." The bad or evil spirits "eines Volkes," are implied here, but do not, cannot, enter into the poem. The poem must function as an anodyne, an aesthetic anaesthesia that removes historical experience from an analytical context or even from an interrogatory openness, and uplifts the reader to an eternal realm of sublimely uncritical reflection; the last paragraph of the essay evokes that realm:

> Die Luft, die solche Gedichte umweht, verbraucht sich nicht. In ihr geht der Atem der Unsterblichen um, der nicht schwindet. — Seltsam, zu sagen: Blume, Baum, Haus, Stern, Tier und dies alles ins Gedicht zu nehmen, in dem es dauern darf, in den behutsamen und geduldigen Gang eines kurzen Verses oder es in wilder Bewegung Strophen durchstürzen zu lassen, hinreißend schön, und beides vom gleichen Aufgehobensein gezeichnet, das den Tod nicht kennt, dem wir erliegen, und dem der Mund erlag, der es zum ersten Male hinsprach und nachsprach.

The poem, like other arts, is marked "vom gleichen Aufgehobensein" and comforts the reader, in the face of dire news in those same pages, against fears of death "dem wir erliegen."

That view of the poem was also defined in the short, unattributed text that accompanied the publication of Krolow's poem "Herbstsonett" in Goebbels's propaganda organ *Das Reich* (December 17, 1944), where the affirmative function of the poem is defined as follows: "Im Gedichte liegt das Bekenntnis zur 'guten Welt.' Das gebundene Wort ist ein Teil der ewigen Ordnung. Es ist der Glaube an Sinn, Klarheit und Bezogenheit des Lebens, der den Reim aufklingen und Widerhall finden läßt" (4). Of course, as the war dragged on and turned against the German forces, especially after the battle of Stalingrad and the surrender by German forces there on February 2, 1943, the need for such *Trostdichtung* became more urgent; in 1944 Krolow began to publish in *Das Reich,* where the eternal order of nature evoked in the poems appears to complement the detailed and rabid propagandistic reports on the war that were introduced in each weekly issue by Goebbels's own lead editorial. Nonetheless, even in such proximity to the center of Nazi power and propaganda, the feuilleton retained a certain limited measure of editorial latitude, though that latitude was of course also purposeful.[5] Krolow published three poems and two columns of lyrical prose in *Das Reich.* In one of those two prose texts, "Die Tulpen," the description of flowers takes on a different coloration in the context of its time and place of publication; the narrator reminisces about the tulips that his mother would bring home for the table, and how he used to watch their slow movements:

> Das Erregende war für mich jedesmal, zu sehen, wie die sterbenden Blumen von wilder Bewegung gepackt wurden, die eine nach der anderen ergriff. Einzelne krochen über den Krugrand und wollten zu Boden, begaben sich in tiefste Demut. Welche warfen sich nach hinten, bäumten sich, stemmten sich gegen das Unsichtbare, das ihnen Gewalt antat. Etwas Verzweifeltes war an diesen Blumen. Sie wehrten sich und mußten doch unterliegen. Welche schienen in der Schräge zu drehen und brachen auseinander. Ein Tulpenglas konnte über Nacht zu einem Schlachtfeld werden. Verwüstung war mit der Finsternis eingebrochen, vor der es keine Rettung gab. Und man mußte es geschehen lassen und vielleicht noch einen halben Tag zusehen oder einen vollen, wie sie der Reihe nach verdarben. Für Viertelstunden war ich manchmal im Anblick dieses blumenhaften Sterbens versunken, das gar nicht unauffällig und wehrlos geschah, wie man uns gern erzählt hatte, bei dem erbittert Widerstand geleistet wurde, wenn auch schrecklich lautlos. Und es ist sicher ein großes Wort, aber man erfuhr dabei ein wenig über die schwer beschreibliche Tapferkeit der Geschöpfe. (Included in *Von nahen und fernen Dingen,* 1953: 17)

Krolow adopts the diction of the front pages and describes the wilting tulips in terms of war: the passage personifies the flowers and describes their desperate movements as they seem to succumb to violence. The flower vase becomes a scene of anguished, writhing helplessness and fatal violence, a "Schlachtfeld" or mass execution, "wie sie der Reihe nach verdarben," before which there is "keine Rettung." The observer likewise becomes helpless as passive witness, anonymously detached from the scene: "Und man mußte es geschehen lassen." The second paragraph seems to counter the first with a description, like a clandestine battle report from the front that contradicts the official account of events, of the scene of death ("dieses blumenhaften Sterbens"), whereby the victims were not "wehrlos," but rather mounted "erbittert Widerstand" and showed their bravery. In the context of the regular war reports on the preceding pages of every issue of *Das Reich*, this description takes on a troubling verism, though framed within a childhood reminiscence. The diction elaborates a complex metaphor of battle that can be reported either as physically passive but anguished submission to violence or as brave resistance to the inevitable. The elaborate metaphor completely overtakes and virtually detaches itself from its object to yield an unnerving description of a scene of mass death. Most of the prose of this volume remains in the manner of overblown and empty nature reverie, entirely confectionery, which meets the expectations of *inner emigration*, and against which the metaphoric violence of this passage stands out and shocks all the more with its political diction.[6]

This description inverts the usual relation of the literary idyll in this period to the violence of war that surrounded it: instead of the usual simple exclusion, this unusual passage includes the violence of battle and summary mass execution as metaphor applied, grotesquely, to the slow, usually graceful undulations of wilting tulips. Through its elaborate metaphor, this passage links the recollected scenario from the narrator's childhood past to the present reality of total war reported each week by the periodical. The conscious grotesqueness of the violent images of flowers stands in equal but inverted relation to the arbitrary stylization, the artifice, of all propagandistic reporting, which exalts in order to obscure the actual brutality of events. Through its metaphors, this passage reveals what the landscape idylls in this period, in prose or poetry, labor in their artifice to conceal: here the dialectical relation between the sanitized idyll that bans any visible relation to external historical reality has been incorporated into the text itself as the gulf between the described reality of tulips and the reality of the description of mass death in war. This self-conscious passage casts light on Krolow's other prose and poetry, and on *inner emigration* in the Nazi period in general, as a sort of *Blüte-und-Boden* literature of prettified complicity that hides the historical complexities and concrete barbarities of the Second World War behind a screen of unreflected formulas.

In addition to his poems, scattered in newspapers throughout the Reich, and his lyrical prose vignettes, which he did not repudiate but later collected and reissued as a book titled *Von nahen und fernen*

Dingen in 1953, Krolow also published literary criticism of a sort. Krolow became a regular contributor to the journal *Das Innere Reich* in 1942 with several poems and four book reviews, two of single volumes and two long review essays. That journal, like the cultural section of *Das Reich,* tried to maintain an unpolitical, intellectual profile, which of course had its own function in the cultural strategy of the regime: to represent relative freedom of thought and expression to the outside world and to attract, or at least assuage, conservative but critical intellectuals.[7] Krolow joined the contributors to *Das Innere Reich* during its third and last phase: the first phase from 1934 to 1937 was relatively liberal and open insofar as the journal was not fully "ideological" and still accommodated a balance of nationalist-conservative authors and other Christian or humanist conservatives, who tended toward opposition to the Party, including Reinhold Schneider, Rudolf Alexander Schröder, and Konrad Weiß, or others such as Eugen Gottlob Winkler, Georg von der Vring, Walter Bauer, Wilhelm Lehmann, Günter Eich, and Peter Huchel; in the second phase from 1938 to 1941, during the period of unhindered Nazi territorial expansion, many of those figures refrained from further contributions and allowed uncritical conservatives and national-socialists to predominate, which gave the journal a tone of "radical nationalism" (Mallmann, 136); in the third phase, during the war years, the journal seemed more acutely apolitical in its avoidance of current issues and its return to bourgeois traditionalism, partly as a result of official party policy and partly as a reflection of general disillusionment and resignation (Mallmann, 137). The more apolitical the journal appeared, the more fully it fulfilled its ideological function; as Horst Denkler notes in his study of the journal: "Da Überlebenschance und Langzeiterfolg des NS-Regimes in nicht geringem Grade von solcher Seelen- und Gehirnmassage abhingen, wurde dem Dichter erhöhter Rang zugesprochen und ihm zugleich die dichterische Rolle aufgabengerecht vorgeschrieben" (389). Since the general prohibition of criticism in 1936 (Strothmann, 274f.), and especially since the brief ban on the journal from 1937 to 1938 (Mallmann, 138–51), the editors had been careful all along to screen the content and formulations of all contributions. Of that third phase, Marion Mallmann clarifies: "Von einer echten Liberalisierungstendenz kann also nicht gesprochen werden. Junge, neu hinzutretende Mitarbeiter wie Krolow blieben die Ausnahme. Ihn beispielsweise als 'oppositionell' einzustufen, ist nur möglich, wenn der Begriff so weit gefaßt wird, daß darunter der Verzicht auf jegliche aktuelle Bezugnahme zur realen Situation verstan-

den wird, was problematisch erscheint" (97). Krolow was an exception, but since he had longstanding Hitler Youth and NSDAP credentials, he did not pose a risk. He served instead to provide
unpolitical but also unchallenging intellectual product.

Such allegiance was particularly necessary for essayists and book
reviewers. His reviews in *Das Innere Reich* of 1942/43 demonstrate
his breadth of familiarity with the poetry of that period, which he is
obliged to characterize in positive terms in light of the prohibition on
criticism.[8] In the essay "Betrachtungen zu Gedichtband-Titeln"
(1943), his comments on thirty-four volumes, from Georg Britting,
Georg von der Vring, and Friedrich Jünger to Hermann Stüppack and
Hans Baumann, revolve around the distinction between sensual apprehension of nature and a more intellectual apprehension of reality:

> Konnte man bei den bisher angeführten Buchtiteln und den hinter
> ihnen stehenden Lyrikern empfinden, daß sie bei aller Verschieden-
> heit im Einzelprofil im Grunde von gleicher sinnenhaft erlebter Na-
> turnähe und Gefühlsverbundenheit waren im Gang durch Jahr und
> Landschaft, so wird man schwerlich bei einem bemerkenswerten Teil
> unseres Lyrik-Schrifttums den Zug zum Idealischen, Geistgebunde-
> nen, weitesten abendländischen Traditionen Verpflichteten verken-
> nen können.

The forms of feeling in nature need no further justification in their
proximity to National-Socialist ideology, but the German intellectual
has to be distinguished from the domination of intellectuality elsewhere: "Unsere Wirklichkeit, die von anderen Elementen getragen
wird und die wir nicht ins Bodenlose reiner Geist-Vorgänge verflüch-
tigt sehen möchten, ist eine durchaus andere" (98). Krolow cites
Mallarmé, Valéry, and late work of Rilke as examples of a "Trostlosig-
keit . . . mit der sich selbstherrlich gewordene Intelligenz in der Kunst
noch immer rächte" (101). Krolow taps into longstanding German
conservative suspicions of French or Latinate *Zivilisationskunst*, inspired by intellect rather than the collective feeling of common *Kultur*, in order to reinforce through negation the positive function of
German poetry as *Trostdichtung*. In the simple dialectic of this essay,
after the initial "*Gefühlsverbundenheit*" in nature poetry, the negative
tendency of intellectualism, even when mastered in German poetry, is
elevated by impulses that link it back to the *Volk* and its imperatives
(102–3):

> Am elementaren Ereignis des Krieges endlich hat sich auch die Lyrik
> zu bewähren. Aus der Namenlosigkeit derer, denen der Gang der
> Waffen, das Geschrei der Kämpfer und der Blick der Sterbenden den

Mund öffnete und Stimme gab, sind einzelne über das Erscheinen in Zeitschrift und Tageszeitung hinaus, seit geraumer Zeit mit Gedichtbüchern hervorgetreten. Wir könnten unsere Betrachtung nicht besser abschließen als im Hinblick auf das [. . .] Wunderbare der Erscheinung, das an diesen soldatischen Menschen deutlich wird, die im Begriffe sind, ein neues, härteres und unsentimentales Gedicht des Krieges zu schaffen. [. . .] Es ist Ausdruck für die wissende Entschlossenheit, mit der unser Volk in diesem zweiten Weltkrieg sein Leben dranzugeben gewillt ist.

The essay closes with an evocation of Hans Baumann's volume *Der Wandler Krieg* (War. The Transformer, 1943), which "faßt aufs glücklichste das nicht nur für unsere völkische Gesamtexistenz sondern auch für unser Schrifttum als dem 'geistigen Raum der Nation' Ergiebige einer Zeit zusammen, die keinem etwas schenken darf" (104). In this verbose gloss of thirty-four titles and volumes, Krolow marshals all of them to the higher purpose of self-transformation. With a closing citation from Rilke, "Geh in die Verwandlung aus und ein," which harkens back to Baumann's *Der Wandler Krieg,* the conclusion resounds with an affirmative sense of mission in war but also quivers with ambiguity.

Notes

[1] Almost all criticism of Krolow either passes over his early work or lumps it under the moniker of *Naturlyrik* or Wilhelm Lehmann's influence. Though several critics, whom I indicate, are intelligently discriminating in their views and reservations, rarely does there appear a decidedly critical tone. Therefore, Manfred Seidler surprises when he indicates that Krolow began publishing "1943 (!) [his parenthetical exclamation] als Weltmaler von biederer Blindheit für das Geschehende" (104). Without supporting detail, that sort of sweeping candor is refreshing, but only shifts to the other extreme and does not add to our analytical understanding of his early years. Chapter 3 links the background of his general literary activity in the Nazi period to a reading of his first volume of poetry. Throughout my discussion, the German term *Naturlyrik* refers to the specific body of nature poetry in Germany in the Weimar, Nazi, and postwar periods as opposed to nature poetry in general in other periods or places. This tradition is peculiar to Germany at this time.

[2] This poem was also published under the title "October" in another newspaper. Krolow does not mention this poem or any specific instance from his own experience in his short essay "Jeder hat seine kleine persönliche Sahara: Lyriker und das erste gedruckte Gedicht." *Frankfurter Allgemeine Zeitung* 217 (September 19, 1961): 20.

[3] Fausto Cercignani does not examine these poems in two important studies of Krolow's early corpus. He notes a motif in his 1986 article "aus den frühesten, zwischen 1940 und 1941 geschriebenen Gedichten" from *Hochgelobtes, gutes Leben* (1943).

[4] In the section on "NS-Lyrik" (133–56) in his study of *Literatur im Dritten Reich*, Karl-Heinz Schoeps cites a passage from an essay that appeared in the journal *SA-Mann* by SA-Oberführer Gerhard Schumann on Nazi art:

> Ein nationalsozialistischer Künstler macht nicht halt an den Schranken des im engeren Sinn Politischen; er hat in seiner Gestaltung alle Bezirke des Seins einzuschmelzen, er hat in sich zu reißen und aus sich herauszustellen das *Leben in seiner Ganzheit,* er hat die harte Größe unserer heroischen Zeit ebenso zu gestalten wie die Stille deutscher Landschaft, das Wunder deutschen Menschentums, das Suchen deutscher Seele nach Gott, das persönliche ebenso wie das Allgemeine. Denn gerade der Nationalsozialismus faßt das Kunstwerk nicht auf als das mechanische Produkt eines Kollektivs, sondern als die organisch gewachsene Frucht einer Gemeinschaft. (Schoeps, 133)

Not all literature of National Socialism had to share the appearance of its most strident variants, but could represent the same ideology less directly as "die Stille deutscher Landschaft," which, though less aggressive, was still instrumental.

[5] Goebbels himself wanted to create with *Das Reich* a journal without the obvious appearance of a propaganda organ in order to draw in conservative intellectuals, though of course his column itself made clear the propagandistic function of the journal. For the initial rationale of the journal, see Josef Wulf's documentation *Presse und Funk im Dritten Reich*, 158–61. In her study of *Das Reich*, Erika Martens notes: "Der Kulturteil beschäftigte sich mit dem in- und ausländischen Kulturleben auf den Gebieten Theater, Film, Musik und bildende Künste. Er brachte Buchbesprechungen, Erzählungen und ausgewählte Lyrik. Auch Probleme der Wissenschaft und Erziehung fanden Platz in seinen Spalten. Diese thematische Vielfalt war einzigartig in der Zeit des Dritten Reiches. Sie erlaubte es, einer großen Gruppe nicht-nationalsozialistischer Fachkräfte aus allen Bereichen des öffentlichen Lebens eine Art Refugium zu bieten. Doch auch der Kulturteil mußte Zugeständnisse an das Regime machen und überzeugte Nationalsozialisten in seinen Spalten zu Wort kommen lassen. Seine im allgemeinen jedoch hohen geistigen Anforderungen und die stilistische Brillanz seiner Beiträge machten ihn zu einer Oase feuilletonistischer Kunst inmitten der phrasenhaften Sprache und primitiven Argumentation der nationalsozialistischen Propaganda in den meisten übrigen Blättern. . . . Trotzdem haben sie — wie alle anderen Journalisten im Dritten Reich — der nationalsozialistischen Diktatur gedient und mit ihren Namen und ihrem journalistischen Können das Regime im In- und Ausland aufgewertet" (51–52).

[6] Paulus and Kolter cite this sketch, astonishingly, only as an example of Krolow's powers of observation, but drop the passage I cite above; the "Schlachtfeld" becomes evidence of "eine gewisse Dynamisierung und Verschärfung des Phänomens" (17). In contrast, Fausto Cercigniani refers to this passage only in relation to other images of tulips in the poems, without commenting on the specific, un-

settling enactment of this image. In early 1940s Germany, one might read this passage quite differently than he does.

[7] Marion Mallmann notes at the outset of her study: "Kulturelle Zeitschriften, wie 'Das Innere Reich,' hatten zwar eine ganz bestimmte Funktion innerhalb des nationalsozialistischen Kultur — und Propaganda — apparates — sonst wäre ihre Existenz a priori unterbunden worden" (18), though she also notes that such a journal's significance was not central to any such strategy and cannot represent the whole. One could argue, however, that Goebbels's own journal, *Das Reich*, was central to the same strategy that gave a certain latitude, always revocable, to *Das Innere Reich*. Later, Mallmann defines the propaganda function of that latitude in cultural commentary: "Gerade die Lyrik, die den zum Nationalsozialismus tendierenden Stapel abstieß, war in der Anfangszeit durch Autoren vertreten, die der Zeitschrift sicherlich weitere Mitarbeiter (und wohl auch Leser) zuführte, die dem Regime gegenüber kritisch, wenn auch nicht notwendigerweise wegen ihrer demokratischen oder gar sozialistischen Position, eingestellt waren" (74). This holds for later arrivals, like Krolow, though by then less recruitment was necessary or even possible.

[8] As Jörg Drews notes pointedly: "Goebbels hatte mit gutem Grund die Kunstkritik verboten und angeordnet, sie sei durch 'Kunstbetrachtung' zu ersetzen. Die Ausschaltung von Kritik als einer Haltung bedeutete, daß Paraphrase und Akklamation an die Stelle jenes Unterscheidens getreten waren, [. . .] Kritik mußte verboten werden, weil sie sich ja auch gegen die Nazi-Kunst wenden konnte. Ohne die Möglichkeit differenzierter und aggressiver Haltung gegenüber Kunstwerken als geistigen Sachverhalten war aber dem Sprechen über Kunst die Unwahrhaftigkeit an die Stirn geschrieben bzw. grundsätzlich aufgezwungen worden" (126).

3: Cornerstone of a Career: *Hochgelobtes, gutes Leben!* (1943)

KROLOW'S FIRST VOLUME OF POETRY, with poems also by Hermann Gaupp, appeared in a series at the Heinrich Ellermann Verlag called *Das Gedicht: Blätter für die Dichtung.* That publisher occupies an unusual place in German literary history: Ellermann's small press tried to maintain the integrity of poetry as a genre inside Germany during the Nazi period. Ellermann managed not only to keep his series in print from 1934 to 1944 with the help of numerous supporters in Germany and Switzerland, but also to keep Nazi Party pulp out of the volumes, as Christoph Perels notes:

> Fast vollständig ist es Ellermann gelungen — Herbert Böhme präsentiert sich hier ganz von seiner epigonalen, ja trivialen Seite, die große Zahl der berüchtigten Namen fehlt ganz. Die Reihe blieb ein Organ nichtnationalsozialistischer Lyrik, letzteres nicht selten auch durch die Texte, die Heinrich Ellermann aus dem Werk nicht mehr lebender Dichter auswählte. (7)

Perel's qualification is important beyond the single example of the Nazi author he cites since it reminds us of the obvious: what was at stake for Ellermann's press was not direct resistance, but a relative degree of freedom from National-Socialist doctrine and denunciation, which would allow a meeting of minds around the idea of the poem inside Germany but outside the party. Ellermann's series provided an external structure for the hypostatized but urgent understanding of genre by poets in Germany in this period. Ellermann printed poems by German Romantic poets like Hölderlin, Goethe, Eichendorff, Brentano, Novalis, von Arnim; by German Realist poets like C. F. Meyer, Hebbel, Droste-Hülshoff, Mörike; and by Expressionist poets such as Georg Trakl, Ernst Stadler and Georg Heym. He also published more recent but lesser known talents such as Wilhelm Lehmann, Oskar Loerke, Friedrich Georg Jünger, Georg von der Vring, Georg Britting, Elisabeth Langgässer, Johannes Thor (a.k.a. Yvan Goll), Hermann Kasack, all born between 1882 and 1899. The series was discontinued in 1944, but Ellermann was able to resume publication again after the war, and in 1949, in the same series, he also published Krolow's fourth volume, *Auf Erden:* that incidental and extrinsic framework allows the treatment of Krolow's first four volumes of poetry in the 1940s as a separate group in order to isolate his origins as a poet and his early development. These first four volumes, however, reveal intrinsic relations that justify their presentation as a coherent but not static period of his development.

The title *Hochgelobtes, gutes Leben!* is taken from Gaupp's poem "Mittag im Gebirge," the first in the volume. In this slight publication, more of a brochure than a book, there is no page to separate the two series of poems, probably due to shortages of paper, though a table of contents at the back indicates the order and authorship of the poems. Nonetheless, the change in tone from Gaupp's naive jubilation in the first half to Krolow's sense of ubiquitous menace in his first poem "Der Wald" is striking, even jarring. In retrospect, the collocation of the two provides an interesting measure of the tensions in Krolow's earliest volume and the difference in his use of the idiom when compared to the average use of the same idiom among his contemporaries. A comment from Oda Schaefer's correspondence with Krolow puts the title into historical perspective; in her letter of December 28, 1943, she writes to Krolow: "Schreiben wir also einen Lobgesang auf das Leben, ich kann mir eben nichts Schöneres denken, trotz der Hekatomben von Opfern." But she is not aware of Krolow's publication. In her next letter of January 26, 1944, she writes: "Und siehe da, ich schrieb, Sie sollten einen Lobgesang auf das Leben schreiben und Sie haben es schon getan bei Ellermann! Das ist doch sonderbar." But of course she had not yet seen the poems to realize the discrepancy between the title and Krolow's poems. Yet one gets a sense of the forced exuberance in embracing life and culture in her letters. She discusses Proust, Joyce, Faulkner, Wolfe, Hemingway, Apollinaire, surrealism, French painting, and so on and adds: "Es hat mich sehr gefreut, dass auch Sie so überaus crazy auf alle jene Dinge sind, hinter denen ich wie ein Narr her bin." Krolow's poems capture the uneasiness behind that frantic attempt to find comfort in nature or in art during the war.

In his 1986 article, Fausto Cercignani examines closely these early poems in Krolow's first volume for the first time as a group and takes issue with the passing commentary of the few previous critics of the cycle. He indicates and underscores that the poems do not participate in the mood suggested by the title, nor do they express a simple desire for dissolution into nature. The poems do contain such elements, but close reading of each poem individually and in relation to the others

complicates to the point of flat refutation such impressionistic and reductive readings. Cercignani rightly emphasizes that the poems reflect
an attempt "eine durch die tragischen Ereignisse der Zeit verschärfte
Existenzunruhe zu überwinden" (75), and correctly insists on the
need for eliciting the historical dimension of the poems, which manifests itself "in einem ungelösten Widerspruch zwischen zwei entge-
gengesetzten Aspekten des poetischen Empfindens" (75): a wish to
transcend general human and specific historical conditions or limitations, and the contrary recognition, based on skepticism toward religious or "natural" mysticism, that such a transcendence can only be
artificially stimulated, by drink for example, and therefore only simu-
lated. Cercignani's essay is particularly important for clearing away
understandable misconceptions about these poems and shifting the
terms of discussion. However, though his own individual readings in
each case maintain and reinforce the general terms he establishes, the
interpretations do not enter fully into the language and form of the
poems, and instead often only recapitulate, albeit in correct context,
the content.[1] As a result, his essay cannot go far enough to secure
Krolow's texts to the historical context and draw more far-reaching
conclusions about the type of literary and historical moment they represent. In the specific formal intricacies of these early poems lies the
first instance of what Hans Egon Holthusen called, with regard to
Krolow's work in the 1950s, a "hochempfindliche Dialektik" (104).

Krolow's first poem, "Der Wald," captures the dilemma of such
poetry of *inner emigration:*

Mag sein: der Sturm befuhr ihn orgellaut und groß
Und zog mit Fahnen Staub und stumpfem Blitz
Und ließ die schwarzen Donner auf ihn los
Und jagte Regen aus dem Wolkenschlitz.

Mag sein: der Wintermond zerbarst ihm Baum um Baum
Und Vogelschwärme fielen wie ein Stein
Und tot ans Herz ihm aus dem leeren Raum.
Im Eisgestrüpp zerstob das Tiergebein.

Mag sein: die fackelgelbe Sonne brannte aus,
Schwang ihm zu Häupten, feurignaher Bolz,
Und knisterte im trocknen Blätterhaus,
Verdarb den Eichbaum, spliß sein hartes Holz.

> Mag sein: es warb um ihn der tausendfache Tod,
> Warf Frost und Feuer in sein offnes Haar. —
> Vom Zorn des Donn'rers wolkenwild umdroht,
> Bestand er atemlos sein Wälderjahr. (9)

The four quatrains all begin with the clipped phrase "mag sein" and lack the normal impersonal subject pronoun. The repetition highlights the idiomatic uses of that phrase, which normally indicates an impersonal condition that creates certain expectations, but in the given case, leads to a response contrary to those expectations. The repeated phrase frames a scenario of contrariness or even resistance to what prevailing circumstances might otherwise seem to dictate. The anaphoric "Und" increasingly elevates the pressure to succumb. The full colon after each spondaic "mag sein" creates a caesura, an analytical detachment from the concrete details that follow, which thus invite explication: "Mag sein: der Sturm befuhr ihn orgellaut und groß / Und zog mit Fahnen Staub und stumpfen Blitz." The personal pronoun refers at first glance to the forest of the title, but nonetheless that pronoun becomes more personal, more suggestive of an individual with each repetition. The poem develops from description to allegory. The title functions as a cover of sorts, providing a screen, a blind, as a public notice of a nonpolitical topic, behind which cover another reading can develop. In other words, the personal pronouns increasingly beg, or even assert, an allegorical explication: the title separates the concrete referent from its abstract significance, the signifier from the signified, the vehicle from the tenor, in order to allow a twofold reading.

The personal pronoun is acted upon by violent forces: the words *Sturm, Fahnen,* and *Blitz* suggest military invasion, though here that conquering expansion has reversed and flung itself back "orgellaut und groß" upon the forest, upon the mystical sanctum of German identity, its mythic *Waldeinsamkeit.* In the second stanza, that terrain is devastated from above as if by Allied air raids: "Und Vogelschwärme fielen wie ein Stein / Und tot ans Herz ihm aus dem leeren Raum."[2] In the third stanza, the storm obscures the sun, which here does not symbolize enlightenment; instead, *fackelgelb* suggests the torchlight processions of Nazis and the reign of collective delusion that could no longer be sustained when the war, the storm, came back home: "die fackelgelbe Sonne brannte aus." The active, violent verbs in the poem, including *jagte, zerbarst, fielen, zerstob, schwang, knisterte, verdarb, warb, warf, spliß,* capture the frenzy of destruction.

The fourth stanza culminates the rapidly gathering atmosphere of ubiquitous menace: "es warb um ihn der tausendfache Tod," where the number might first seem meaninglessly great, then to suggest an abstractly eschatological, indeed millenary, apocalypse, but also, more concretely historical, the collapse of Hitler's vaunted 1,000-year Reich into a thousandfold death. The initial spondee *Warf Frost* and the alliterations *warb/warf, tausendfache Tod,* and *Frost und Feuer* in the first distich concentrate phonetically and reinforce a sense of violence and then release it, without alliteration, into "sein offenes Haar," raining it down upon the individual.[3] At this point, the process of personification has also culminated with the inversion of the allegory; the person to whom the hair belongs now has to represent the forest, rather than the opposite, as earlier. By the end of the poem, the allegory has, so to speak, come out of the woods.

Then a dash separates the last distich from the first fourteen lines to lend the poem's conclusion a static prominence set against the deadly storm. The third line of the stanza, the first of that distich, attributes the *Sturm* and *Blitz* to a mythic figure, a Zeus-like pagan god, who has unleashed the forces from which the individual is now, in a strikingly dramatic phrase, "wolkenwild umdroht." The repeated preposition "um" in lines one and three of that final stanza bridge the caesura marked by the dash, reinforce in sense and sound the mood of surrounding menace, and isolate the last line: "Bestand er atemlos sein Wälderjahr." In that line, for the first time, the allegorical *er* is the subject, the grammatical agent of the action, not its object. The action, however, consists of simply standing ground, to hold out and survive against hostile forces, not falling for that god, despite the storm, the show of force; though outwardly passive, the individual has withstood the storm by staying in place without succumbing to its frenzy. The personified forest is now a symbol of intractable but outwardly passive resistance to aggressive historical forces, against which the individual is breathless with suffocation by the striking force of the storm, breathless from the effort of standing ground, as if running in place, and poetically breathless, without voice, unable to publish without the awareness and possible censure, or worse, of Party officials. Thus, the poet's early years of learning his craft, his traditional *Wanderjahre* have become his *Wälderjahr,* a training in cryptically allegorical nature poetry.

With its emphasis on surviving and holding out, this 1943 poem could also appear as a sort of *Durchhaltegedicht,* a parallel in literature to the official Nazi propaganda that encouraged Germans to bear up under the strain and to believe in final victory. Or rather, the motif of the storm reflects a common attitude among nonfascist writers in Nazi Germany that the regime could not last long; as Oda Schaefer notes in her memoirs of the period:

> Unversehens waren wir in etwas hineingeraten, das wir nicht übersehen konnten. Zuerst hielten wir alles, trotz der Haussuchung, für einen Alptraum, der wohl Opfer fordern, doch rasch vorübergehen würde. . . . Max Born, der nach England emigrierte Wissenschaftler, schrieb an Einstein im Jahre 1938, er sähe alles wohl voraus, den Krieg und das Ende, "aber an diesem Geschehen kann man nichts ändern. Das läuft ab wie ein Gewitter." (249)

The illusion that the Nazi regime would run its course like a storm might signal between the lines that a community exists that outwardly cannot be recognized. Inwardly, it is at odds with the regime and does not share its doctrine, yet the image of the storm nonetheless also serves to naturalize those political circumstances. It thereby neutralizes any impulse toward active opposition and instead reinforces passivity (although other options were not necessarily available).[4] Schaefer's casual allusion to the "Alptraum, der wohl Opfer fordern, doch rasch vorübergehen würde" is unsettling in its smugness and in the ease with which real victims are included in the calculus of weathering the storm. Reinhold Grimm has also noted how the image of the storm often served to define the "Lebensform" (418) of *inner emigration:* "Dieses Bild von der windstillen Mitte des Taifuns dürfte überhaupt eine Art Urerlebnis der 'inneren Emigration' zum Ausdruck bringen" ("Im Dickicht," 419). Krolow's poem reflects that same view of the period, in which passive rootedness appears as resistance, but the poem also breaks up that smugness and makes felt the immediate menace of the storm.

The second poem of the series thematizes the imaginative life of the poet-subject, who has turned inward, away from the storm of historical reality. After emerging in profile at the end of "Der Wald," the subject is now present, active, and assertive from the outset, almost defiant in stating the primacy of self, imagination, and nature ("Ich träume grün") over the surrounding pressures to conform to Nazi doctrine, to what is not green; in fact, the color green, symbolic of nature, has become a coded denunciation of National-Socialist brown:

Ich träume grün. Wie ich die Augen schließe,
Ist noch das Dunkel meiner Lider grün.
Wenn ich den Baum jetzt in mir wachsen ließe,
Die zarte Blume dürfte weiterblühn.

Wenn hinter meinen Augen Blattgedränge,
Die grünen Ruten vom Holunderstrauch,
Vom Wind gepeitscht, noch einmal wären! Schwänge
Die grüne Sonne! Düftete der Lauch!

Und grüne Luft und Buschwerk, halb im Dämmer!
Ein Vogel pfiffe mir sein grünes Lied.
Und ferne wo des Spechtes helle Hämmer
Ein Rasenstück, das in den Morgen sieht,

Gelänge mir mit Beinwell und Ranunkel,
Voll Wegerich und Tausendguldenkraut. —
Ich wüchse selig über alles Dunkel
Und wäre Blume, Baum und Vogellaut.

Although that refusal to conform inwardly might constitute a paradoxical sort of active passivity or passive resistance, it remains at the
same time a refusal to bear witness to the adversities and crimes of the
period. Indeed, the poet closes his eyes in the first lines in order to
create that imaginative retreat into nature. The poet has adapted to
nature a Rilkean sense of *Weltinnenraum* as the *locus hortus* or *locus
amoenus* where he can cultivate that "delicate flower" of poetry. Yet
the subsequent three stanzas, extending from the use of the subjunctive in those last lines of the second distich of the first stanza, perform
a dual maneuver of protracted ambiguity that is typical of Krolow's
earliest poetry of *inner emigration.* The subsequent stanzas are dense
with nouns, a battery of names, mainly botanical, that evoke concretely and almost microscopically the enclosure of nature. At the
same time, the stanzas are also dense with active verbs in the subjunctive mood: *ließe, dürfte, wären, schwänge, duftete, pfiffe, gelänge,* and
wüchse. These verbs call to mind the unreality of that retreat. The
combination of overly exact denomination and retraction through the
use of hypothetical subjunctive creates an irony of simultaneous description and effacement. The longing for wholeness of unspoiled nature outside of historical reality reveals its own absurdity: both the
specific emblematic details and the verb conjugations begin to appear,
not as the exfoliation of the delicate flower of poetry, but as its systematic disfiguration, its elaboration into an all so tender grotesque.

Again the last distich is separated by a dash from the body of the poem in order to highlight its summary character: "Ich wüchse selig über alles Dunkel / Und wäre Blume, Baum und Vogellaut." The poet strains to express his wish to transcend the dark hour of history through a sort of joyously vegetative proliferation in poetry and to become "flower, tree and birdsong"; that wish, that subjunctive, becomes the indirect measure of the historical reality itself, of how *unselig* life is outside of nature in the culture of Nazi Germany.

The poet's hypothesized desire for transformation into song creates a transition to the next poem "Waldmusik" (11), where the poet figure appears first as the direct object, *mich,* who is disturbed while trying to hide from the heat:

Wenn mich schattend aus Akazien rief
Mund des Horns und Klage der Oboe,
Wie die Hitze ich im Holz verschlief:
Und ich fuhr aus Träumen und entlief
Und verbarg mich stumm im Weidicht wo.

Wenn der Nachmittag im Himbeerwald
Dunkelte im Tönen des Fagott:
Hornklee roch und Nebel braute bald,
Schauder überrieselte mich kalt,
Und ich sah den starken Hirtengott.

Und ich lauschte, vom Gesang berückt
Zarter Flöten, die der Baumgeist blies,
Den der braune Kranz aus Lattich schmückt. —
Wie im Spiel er schwarze Beeren pflückt,
Hängt der tiefe Abend ihm im Vlies.

The poet-subject *ich* in the third line is ensconced in his hideout in the middle of the line, wrapped around phonetically by the several alliterations ("Wie die Hitze ich im Holz verschlief"), in a cocoon of sorts, a protected bower, until the *Klage* or lament, perhaps an awareness of history, guilt, sorrow, or mourning, startles him out of that dream into a new flight in order to seek a new hideout, where he will remain "stumm im Weidicht wo." The noun *Weidicht* is an unusual noun for a variation of *Weiderich* as either a type of grass pastureland or the plant purple loosestrife (*lythrum salicaria*). The prefix *Weid* also retains an allusion to the hunt. Here those terms and senses are compressed into two syllables, *Weidicht,* to make both the word and the hideout "dicht" or thickly dense and secure. In other words, the first-person subject *ich* has taken refuge where word and place (*Wort* and *Ort*) converge in *Dichtung*. The *ich* in the thicket of *Dichtung* hides out in the density of details about nature, here in the *Wei(dicht)*. This refuge of the poet in the poetry of nature is a type of countermystification, a concealment of self in the rhythmic obscurities of mythological and mystified nature: "Dunkelte im Tönen. . . ." Yet even here in these depths of concealment, terror can strike at the sight of the powerful, deified leader: "den starken Hirtengott." The caesura marked by the period and the end of the stanza, without any enjambment, separates the two collocated actions: "Und ich sah . . . / Und ich lauschte . . ." Instead of joining the "herd" of followers, the poet-subject "heard" around, listening to nature; the subject neither follows nor flees as before, but remains still, not transfixed by the spectacle of what he saw, but rather transported by a music he is attuned to: "Vom Gesang berückt / zarter Flöten, die der Baumgeist blies." The personified spirit of the trees, with their tender melodies, provides another sort of concealment, a means of escaping inwardly into nature, instead of being drawn out into a society dominated by a "starken Hirtengott."

Accordingly, the next poem "Nußernte" (12) celebrates the transcendent principle of nature, including its sweet and bitter sides:

> Süßer Kern und bitter Kern
> Schlagt mit Stangen an die Äste!
> Mächtig trägt der Walnußbaum.
> Feiert schwelgerische Feste,
> Schmeckt das Fleisch und seid voll Traum!
> Süßer Kern und bitter Kern.
>
> Dunkle Erde, schöner Stern!
> Beizt die Haut das Unkrautfeuer,
> Brennt der Strauch der Hasel rot,
> Schlingt Clematis am Gemäuer,
> Nußkern nehmt zum Bauernbrot!
> Dunkle Erde, schöner Stern!
>
> Buben mögen Nüsse gern:
> Füllen sich die Körnersiebe,
> Liegt zum Trocknen Nuß bei Nuß,
> Lauern schon die ersten Diebe,
> Nahen sich mit bloßem Fuß . . .
> Buben mögen Nüsse gern.

> Schreit die Kranichschar von fern,
> Ist die letzte Nuß geschlagen,
> Schwebt im Dunst der Walnußbaum,
> Wollen wir uns nicht versagen
> Herben Nußschnaps. — Wie im Traum
> Schreit die Kranichschar von fern.

The poet invites others to partake (in a German variant of Mallarmé's grape) of the fullness of nature as a passage into the realm of imagination, but recognizes already in the second stanza the paradox of that position: "Dunkle Erde, schöner Stern!" The darker the hour down below on earth, the more brilliantly and beautifully shine the stars; the more somber the historical reality, the more aesthetically intense the desire to transcend, the more extravagantly lush the overlay of artistry: "Schlingt Clematis am Gemäuer." Here that artifice is made evident by the framing repetitions of lines one and six in each stanza. As if now in consequence of that dialectic, after the crisp, densely evocative second stanza, the third stanza slips back into a trite Biedermeier idyll of boys stealing walnuts, which forces the realization, that "schwelgerische Feste . . . voll Traum," outside of history, will soon become kitsch, indeed the fate of so much nature poetry. Yet the last stanza here recovers an unsentimental distance from which to observe nature without the intrusion of "Buben" and instead with detachment: "Schreit die Kranichschar von fern." That line already seems to fulfill an aesthetic impulse toward depersonalization in Krolow's work, for which he credits the influence of Oskar Loerke in allowing nature its separateness, its self-sufficiency in the poem, without the pathos of the poet. Yet here the aesthetic distance to the object-nature, the heightening of perception is gained through drink: "Wollen wir uns nicht versagen / Herben Nußschnaps." The line combines folksy kitsch again with an image of the false transcendence of nature poetry; like the first three poems, the last lines are set off by a dash, repeating the first line of the stanza with an added comparison: "— Wie im Traum / Schreit die Kranichschar von fern." The poem captures the contradiction between dream and historical experience, and the ultimate illusion of a refuge in nature in poetry.

The motif of drinking as false transcendence emerges fully in the next poem, "Der Trinkende."[5] In "Nußernte," the "Nußschnaps" at the end bridged the gap, marked by the dash, to aesthetic perception, "as in a dream," related to but not representing historical reality. The poet-subject is within a festive, though tritely folkloric community, with a discreet awareness of the illusion, the unreality of his art, "as in a dream"; now the figure of the drinker is alone and conscious of the strictures that both prevent full engagement with historical and social experience, and that make such an art of anaesthesia necessary. The poet-subject once again confronts, or rather faces and helplessly dwells upon the conditions of his existence: "Noch einmal steigt in Schein und Widerschein / Mein Leben mir aus diesem Glas, das klingt." He has surrendered priority of imagination in the face of adverse circumstances and recognizes his lack of control, his loss of political *Mündigkeit:* "Wie er selig singt // In meinen Adern! Wie ein Kind, voll Traum, / fühle ich die Dämmerung und bin ihr gut." It is not the poet who sings but the wine. The poet-subject is reduced to a childlike dreamer in a subdued state of *Dämmerung,* both crepuscular and alcoholic: "Wie wohl das tut." Paradoxically, by portraying the existential anguish of the isolated thinker turned drinker, the poem attains a measure of visceral historical veracity in the lines: "Die Nacht schaut mich aus tiefen Augen an. / Ich trinke Schatten aus dem Schattenglas." The personified Night has witnessed much and looks at the poet ("mich") accusatively "aus tiefen Augen." The depths of the eyes of night open onto the nightmare of history in those years, though without specific detail; the poet regains his *Mündigkeit* as a subject, as an individual, in the simple and moving line, recalling distantly Odysseus in the Underworld and anticipating Celan: "Ich trinke Schatten aus dem Schattenglas." Drinking becomes an inconspicuous act of mourning and of numbing the pain of losses. Like the poet in the "Vorrede" to Goethe's *Faust I,* the poet here also encounters those who are now lost: "Noch einmal sind mir alle Menschen nah, / Die mich verließen und die ich verließ / Und winken mir." The end of the poem imagines a religious transcendence, an apotheosis, that brings into harmonious balance the joys and sorrows: "Das Leid, das mir geschah, / Und alles Glück gehn ein ins Paradies. // Der Engel Gottes nimmt mich bei der Hand / Und führt mich sicher übern Sternensteg / Ins große Licht und lächelt unverwandt / Und bleibt zurück und segnet meinen Weg." After recognizing the deception of aesthetic escape and depicting the anguish of helpless, paralyzed awareness, the simplistic and conventional image of apotheosis regains as well some affective force as a drunken vision born of sorrow.[6]

The final poem in the series seems at first simply objectionable, in light of the historical moment, from its opening line: "So nah am Tode ist das Leben süß." The fin-de-siècle cliché only aggravates the historical blindness that such a sentiment evinces. Here, after foreshadowing the falsity of a transcendence into nature in the previous poems, the poet projects himself entirely into that sidereal realm: "Und Stern und Wolke waren Paradies" before descending back to earth to glorify Nature's superabundance:

> Der Tonkrug schwang. Der Brotlaib lud zu Tisch.
> Zertretne Traube und geschlitzter Fisch,
> Vergoßner Wein: O Überfluß, du färbst
> Die Seele dunkler mir und machtest satt.

Oddly, in the last line, that excess only makes him more somber, more obscurely melancholy, even "satt," which can mean both satisfied and fed up. The Petrarchan form of the sonnet, with the caesura between the octet and sestet, highlights the tension between the unreal excess and the dark soul of the poet, who envisions nature ("Ich schau dich, Birnbaum!") and discovers himself there:

> Und weiß: ich bin mit Baum und Tier vertauscht,
> Bin Vogelwolke, die am Abend rauscht
> Und meine Spuren in die Sterne trägt.

What had been longing for escape in the last lines of the second poem "Traum von einem Wald": "Ich wüchse selig über alles Dunkel / Und wäre Blume, Baum und Vogellaut," now seems to have been realized: "Ich bin mit Baum und Tier vertauscht, / Bin Vogelwolke," and the poet is taken up into idealized Nature. No dash separates the lines from the body of the poem as before. Yet the full colon in the last tercet allows a more subtle irony of disjunction. After "Und weiß," the voice of the poem seems merely to acknowledge an unquestionable given, while that fact of consciousness at the same time gives the lie to the assertion. Consciousness separates the visionary from the vision and reveals it as fabrication. While appearing to mark the final stage of transcendence into nature, the last lines also reflect the bad consciousness that accompanies such an escape, the bad conscience at having to avoid history and take to the stars. The poem is an elaborately trite conceit, whereby the excess of cliché reveals the poem as a self-conscious, ironic construct that bores into the dilemma of the inner emigrant hiding behind a façade of nature: "O Überfluß, du färbst / Die Seele dunkler mir und machtest satt." The poem closes the initial cycle of Krolow's poetic career where each poem operates on two levels: at first glance, as competent but unexciting, if not excruciating, poetic handiwork in the manner of conventional nature poetry. It contains, at second glance, a series of disjunctive moments of self-consciousness that signal the friction of conflicted conformity, the chafing of the poet working under restraints within imposed limits, trying subtly to indict the idiom of nature poetry to which he, literally — *sub rosa* so to speak — subscribes himself. That latter dimension frames the existential quandary, the muted suffering of an unhappy inner emigrant.

Notes

[1] Horst Daemmrich notes briefly that "Die Natur wird zur Zauberformel, die einen Weg aus der menschlichen Begrenzung und Erniedrigung der Jahre bietet. Sie gewährt Zuflucht zum organischen Lebensrhythmus, der in der Welt zerstört ist, und ermöglicht eine verhüllte Kritik an den gesellschaftlichen und politischen Zuständen" (6). Daemmrich rightly indicates that dimension of critique, but does not demonstrate how it functions in the poems: that critique seems, for Daemmrich, to result simply from the choice of nature as topic.

[2] For historical context from a personal perspective and for pertinent descriptions of the conditions during the 1943 Allied air raids in Berlin, see Oda Schaefer, 303 f. Also, see Ernst Loewy's study of Nazi literature for a discussion of the use of the storm metaphor in works of open doctrinal conformity.

[3] Cf. Georg Britting's poem "Da hat der Wind die Bäume in den Haaren" (39).

[4] Krolow echoes that attitude in using the same word *hineingeraten*, which is an important concept to describe this generation of would-be apolitical writers. It is comparable as a slogan to Brecht's *Nachgeborene* after the war, or to Uwe Kolbe's *Hineingeborene* in the GDR, and also emphasizes the danger of simply waiting for the storm to pass. Both Schaefer's use of the term and Krolow's refer to external circumstances; Max Picard adds an internal, psychological dimension to that term by commenting on the confused inner life of individuals, exposed in the early twentieth century to new forms of media inundation that defuse or numb critical consciousness, and he concludes: "Auch Adolf Hitler: er ist dann auch im Innern des Menschen, ohne daß man es merkt, wie er hineingeraten ist" (*Hitler*, 13–14).

[5] This poem was first published in the *Deutsche Allgemeine Zeitung* (November 3, 1940). Rümmler cites the external resemblances in title and topic of several poems by Krolow to others by Rilke, including Rilke's "Das Lied des Trinkers," but rightly adds: "Doch werden dieselben Motive bei beiden sehr verschieden realisiert" (118). Krolow's very first publication in the previous year, a short essay on one poem by Rilke, documents his familiarity with Rilke at this very early, formative phase of his career.

[6] Jong Ho Pee cites (59) this poem in order to establish his reading of Krolow's fundamental irony, between "Schein und Widerschein" in line one, without any mention of the historical context or commentary on the third and fourth stanzas. In introducing this poem from Krolow's first volume *Hochgelobtes, gutes Leben*,

Pee attributes the same irony to the volume's title, which in fact was not chosen by Krolow and derived from one of Hermann Gaupp's poems in that shared volume, and is consistent in its utter lack of irony with Gaupp's poems. Pee had to know this from Fausto Cercigiani's article, but this moment indicates the degree to which Pee's reading of irony in Krolow is forced onto the material. Krolow's work in this volume certainly has much greater complexity than Gaupp's, as indicated in the present discussion, but complexity need not always equal irony and thereby remain entirely textual. Precisely in the literature of *inner emigration,* the ambiguity or simple doubleness of the texts requires its external framework. Pee then focuses on the motif of the "Glas." Krolow's irony does emerge in the last strophe of the poem and I agree with Pee that that strophe "als allegorische Einübung der Selbstkritik fungiert" (60).

4: The Postwar Period: Trials and Tribulations

WHATEVER THE FURTHER DETAILS of Krolow's activities for the Nazi Party as Hitler Youth leader, block leader or *Referent* for the *Reichskommissar für die Festigung des deutschen Volkstums,* the American authorities after the war had enough material to initiate a denazification hearing (*Entnazifizierungsverfahren*) in 1946. No mention or record of this process appears in any commentary on Krolow to date; no mention of it appears, as far as I could determine, in the materials he has deposited in the Deutsches Literaturarchiv in Marbach. However, also in Marbach, in the estate of Dolf Sternberger, the social historian and editor of the journal *Die Wandlung,* two letters by Krolow refer to his hearing and inform the editor of his work prohibition, which made it impossible for him to publish right away after the war; the first letter to Dolf Sternberger reads as follows:

> Göttingen, 19. XI. 46
>
> An die Redaktion der "Wandlung"
>
> Die amerikanische Militär-Regierung hat auf Grund einer schwer- wiegenden politischen Unterstellung über mich ein Arbeitsverbot verhängt. Ich nehme an, daß Sie hierüber inzwischen in Kenntnis ge- setzt wurden, beeile mich aber trotzdem, Ihnen von dieser Maß- nahme (die ich selber aus zweiter Hand habe) zu schreiben, damit es keinerlei Unannehmlichkeiten für Sie setzt. Die beiden von Ihnen seinerzeit erworbenen Gedichte "Furie" und "Fische" betrachte ich bis zur Klärung meines Falles als zurückgezogen.
>
> Ich werde so energisch wie möglich meine Rechtfertigung betreiben (was sich freilich kompliziert, da ich nicht US-Zonen-Angehöriger bin) und hoffe mich solcherart aus der absurden Situation befreien zu können, in die ich durch Irrtum, Denunziation oder andere Um- stände geraten bin.

Krolow acknowledges that the grounds for the work prohibition are "serious," though he suggests that his predicament derives from "er- ror, denunciation or other circumstances" that suggest his innocence, but leaves open the question of his activities during the Third Reich. Krolow never addressed or reflected further in public upon this "error" or imputation, or his actual activities that might have given rise to such suspicions.

In a letter to Oda Schaefer on January 28, 1947, he expresses his concern over the upcoming denazification proceeding and gives some of the immediate background:

Göttingen, 28. I. 47

Liebe Oda Schaefer,

Haben Sie vielen Dank für Ihre herzliche Anteilnahme an meinem bösen Mißgeschick. — Inzwischen hat sich noch nichts Neues getan. Ich warte auf die Aufförderung eines englischen Militärgerichts, die hoffentlich schnell sich einfindet. Ich will mich gerne und ohne Furcht verantworten, wenn mir und meinem Anwalt das Wort gelassen wird. Freilich will es mir manchmal bange werden, wenn ich sehe, wie sich die Gerechtigkeit oft und oft verstossen findet und — sie nach einem finsteren Gesetz — sich verschoben sieht. — Nein, in meinem Fall braucht das alles ja nicht passieren. Ich werde den Beistand von Göttingen und von allen Hannoverschen Freunden haben. Vor allem der gute [name deleted] wird nichts unversucht lassen, um mir zu helfen. Und er ist in Hannover ein Mann von einigen Beziehungen und entsprechendem Einfluß. Ich kann mich ganz auf ihn verlassen.

Natürlich hatten die Briten nichts gegen mich. Die Sache kam hier auf amerikanischen Einspruch von Berlin aus Information Control Division in Gang. Nun haben die englischen Stellen Unterlagen angefördert, nach denen dann gegen mich vorgegangen sein soll. Bei der Koordinierung der Information Control lag dann als erstes das Publikationsverbot auch in unserer Zone auf der Hand. Nun ist mir publizistisch eben nur das Zipfelchen Südwesten [the French occupation zone] geblieben im Augenblick.

Ich selber neige — die Anwalt und meine Angehörigen — immer noch dazu, eine Denunziation anzunehmen. — [. . .] ist's schließlich gleich. So oder so muß ich durchs finstre Tal hindurch und wünsche mir, daß ich die "Wendung" [?] würdig bestehe, sei bei meiner ja auch ganz hübsch verrückten Nerven immerhin nicht von vornherein als sicher gelten kann. — Mit [. . .] war's vielleicht doch noch ganz anders als bei mir. — Es ist wirklich schade, daß ich Ihnen nicht *erzählen* kann. Mündlich löst sich alles leichter, zwangsloser auf. Und ich bin schon so weit, daß ich einfach keine Lust spüre, trotz meine Affäre brieflich durchzukauen und so genau zu erörtern, wie's richtig wäre um nicht mißverstanden zu werden. — Wie gesagt, den Kopf habe ich nicht verloren, weil ich weiß, daß ich weder Nazi noch den Nazis gedient habe. [one word] von dieser Feststellung abgesehen, ist der *Gewissenszwang,* der derzeitig auf Menschen ausgeübt wird, für meine Begriffe so absurd und inhuman, daß ich's nicht in Worte fassen kann. — Hier kann man nun wohl keinen beschuldigen, es ist eines der zahlreichen Verhängnisse, eine der stillen, zähen Verzweiflungen, denen unsere Modernität immer nachhaltiger ausgesetzt wird.

Für die "Zeit," in der ich mich eben mit einem kleinen Aufsatz über Paul Appel verabschiedete, sollte ich über Ihre Gedichte schreiben, die ich überhaupt in letzter Zeit sehr häufig von [. . .] gebracht wurde. Schade! — Nun: halten Sie mir heftig die Daumen, wenn Sie gerade an mich denken sollten: Geht's schnell und für mich günstig aus, hoffe ich, in absehbarer Zeit nachholen zu können, was mir nun verwehrt ist. — Ist das nicht grotesk, daß man seiner friedlichen Bemühungen nicht froh werden soll!? Daß alles derart unheilvoll miteinander verquickt sind!! — Nun, ich will mich gar nicht erst mit Jammern anfangen, mir vielmehr das Maul verbinden und für — [ellipsis with hyphen in text] arbeiten versuchen.

Denken Sie an, ich habe mich unter dem Eindruck der letzten Zeit seit Jahresbeginn in ein ganz blödsinniges Arbeiten gestürzt: ich übersetzte — um alle Befürchtungen, alle [. . .] alle Enttäuschungen zu neutralisieren — die alberne französische Lyrik des 19. Jahrhunderts. Das tat ich ab und zu nun freilich auch früher schon. Aber in den letzten Wochen habe ich — Tag und Nacht — bei gespendeten Kaffeeextrakt und Tee 30 Gedichte von Gautier, Baudelaire, Banville, Madame Desbordes, Valueve, Nerval, Verlaine, Jammes, Rimbaud, u.a. übertragen: so in einem richtigen Arbeitssturz, in herrlichen Euphorien! Ich war selten so — intellektuell — auf Touren! Und vielleicht ist das eine oder andere Poem mir halbwegs gelungen. [letter continues with another page of description of activities]

Krolow does not explain here what might have led to an inquiry by the American and British authorities. He only states his inclination to attribute their inquiry to a denunciation, which is ambiguous. He does state clearly that he was not a Nazi and never served them, but his records clearly indicate the contrary. Astonishingly, he seems to resent most the *Gewissenszwang* [coerced conscience] that the occupying authorities "practice" upon the German population after the war, which he finds unspeakably "inhumane" (!). Interestingly, this letter suggests that his intense activity as a translator at this point was directly connected to: (1) his anxieties about the denazification hearing, and (2) the fact that he was only allowed to publish in the southwest of Germany, that is, the French occupation sector, not in the American and British zones. The prohibition on publishing in the

British and American sectors seems to have propelled, even compelled, Krolow toward the translation of French poetry.

The prohibition on Krolow's working or publishing (he makes reference to both a *Publikationsverbot* and an *Arbeitsverbot*) was lifted over one year later, as he indicates in a subsequent letter to Dolf Sternberger that concerned the delayed but now permissible publication of two poems, "Fische" and "Furie," in *Die Wandlung*.[1] The information from the Bundesarchiv about those years, along with the references in these letters to a denazification hearing and ban on publishing, is sufficient to beg the question of Krolow's involvement in the Nazi Party and his later reluctance to address the issue. The documents cited above, filled out or written and signed by Krolow himself, define a specific absence of information, reflection, and candor in Krolow's self-presentation and critical reception during his long career. That gap affects our understanding of his work as a poet and critic. This study is not primarily concerned with Krolow's biography, but with the relation of that gap in Krolow's biography to his poetics, poetry, and criticism since the 1940s. The files for Karl Krolow's denazification hearing are in the Niedersächsisches Hauptstaatsarchiv in Hannover (Archivsignatur Nds. 171 Hannover Nr. 19096). After Krolow's death on June 21, 1999, I was granted access to the file on Karl Krolow's denazification proceeding; as of August 1999, I was the first and the only person to have ever consulted these files since the hearings took place.

The details of the hearing provide an essential but incomplete view of Krolow's activities during the Nazi period. Below, I summarize the proceeding according to the documents held in that file. By plotting the steps of the proceeding as evidenced by the sequence and exchange of documents, I wish to reveal the texture of Krolow's historical experience at that moment, as well as to provide the facts of his life as he portrays them. The file only partially fills the gap in the long-standing postwar understanding of Krolow's past during the Third Reich and the immediate postwar period, which he never chose to address. For that reason, I also quote at considerable length the several formal biographical accounts that Krolow submitted in response to queries by the denazification panel about his activities during that time.

The exact circumstances of Krolow's denazification proceeding, as indicated by his dossier, are as follows: The file begins with letters on behalf of Krolow as character references; I have omitted the names of those letter writers. Initiating the proceeding is the actual questionnaire for the Military Government of Germany, the *Fragebogen*. With knowledge of the NSDAP documents, that is, the survey questionnaire he filled out seven years earlier, some discrepancies emerge; the occupation authorities, unbeknownst to Krolow, had that document in their possession: under "Record of Employment and Military Service," Krolow writes, "Seit 1942 im freien Beruf als Schriftsteller." This is Krolow's simple and direct version of his activities during the period, which he maintains throughout his career: later in the questionnaire, he indicates a rising income from a level of 1500 RM in 1941 from a part-time job during college), to levels of 2000 RM in 1942, 3000 RM in 1943, 4000 RM in 1944, and then only 400 RM in 1945, all from publication in newspaper and magazines. On line 41 concerning membership in the NSDAP, Krolow responds "Nein (seit 1. Mai 1937 Anwärter)"; in section 6.46 concerning "HJ einschließlich BdM," Krolow responds, "Nein, nicht betreffend." On line 6.71, concerning "Reichsschrifttumskammer," Krolow responds, "Nein (Befreiungsschein vom 27. Januar 1944)," and in section 6.74 Krolow responds, "Nein" to the question: "Sind Ihnen von einer der oben angeführten Organisationen irgendwelche Titel, Orden, Zeugnisse, Dienstgrade verliehen oder andere Ehren erwiesen worden?" In section 29, Krolow responds first with an erasure and then "Ja" to the question: "Haben Sie jemals, und falls ja, in welcher Rolle in der Zivilverwaltung in einem von Deutschland eingegliederten oder besetzen Gebiet gedient oder gearbeitet? Falls ja, geben Sie Einzelheiten an über Ihr Amt, Ihren Pflichtenkreis sowie Ort und Zeitdauer des Dienstes." Krolow answers: "Angestellter beim Oberpräsident in Kattowitz, Archivarbeiten (Presse und Kultur) als Nebenverdienst während des Studiums." In response to the question "Sind Sie jemals auf Anordnung einer der Alliierten Regierungen oder der Militärbehörde irgendeines Postens enthoben oder an einer Berufsausübung oder Beschäftigung verhindert oder ausgeschlossen worden?" Krolow writes: "Ja Seit November 1946 werden meine Arbeiten in der amerikanischen Zone bis zur politischen Entlastung auf Grund einer Anordnung der dortigen Militär-Regierung nicht mehr gedruckt." In an attachment to that questionnaire, Krolow lists the journals and newspapers in which he had published and comments "Es handelt sich um Gedichte der Landschaft und der Jahreszeiten in den Jahren 1942–1945 in folgenden Tageszeitungen und Zeitschriften"; he lists the *Deutsche Arbeiter Zeitung* and *Das Innere Reich*, but he does not list *Das Reich*, the newspaper edited by Goebbels with his own editorials. A comparison of his responses to similar questions on the Nazi questionnaire of 1939 and the Allied questionnaire of 1946 reveals troubling discrepancies that caught the attention of the military intelligence authorities.

The next step in the process was to assign the individual to a category, which constituted basically a classification of guilt according to actions or documented allegiance to the Party. There were five categories, given in both English and German:

(1) No objection / Keine Einwände

(2) Nominal Nazi supporter — Retain / Nazianhänger nur dem Namen nach — im Amt belassen

(3) Ardent Nazi Supporter — Remove Immediately / Eifriger Nazianhänger — sofort zu entlassen

(3b) Remove within one month / Innerhalb eines Monats entlassen

(4) Special Case (reasons to be given) / Besonderer Fall (Angabe der Gründe)

(5) No opinion of KP / Keine Beurteilung durch den Kreis-Ausschluß.

Instead of "No opinion," category five should bear the translation no verdict or no penalty since it also implied a formal exoneration after the objections were removed that kept the case out of category one to begin with. Initially, the German Denazification Panel[2] placed Krolow in category two with the reason given in German and English: "Nominal Nazi supporter — Retain. Since 1937 K. was in the Party. He did not belong to another organization. It cannot be proved that he held a rank or was active — therefore Group 2 (two)." The criterion was not just Party membership since membership was not required and was in fact selective. It was also based on documented rank or activity, which would testify to ideological convictions in support of the Party.

The Military Government of Germany, according to the Action Sheet of February 25, 1947, accepted that determination. It was however subsequently revoked, in the bottom section of the same Action Sheet, by the Intelligence Section on April 25, 1947 with the notification: "Suspended. Handed over to Public Prosecutor (falsification of FB)." When Krolow completed the American questionnaire, he could not have known what documentation the intelligence branch of the Military Government had on him. The intelligence unit in fact had in its possession the materials discussed in chapter 1 and noticed the discrepancies between the 1939 Nazi questionnaire and the 1946 American-Allied questionnaire.[3] In an internal communication of the same date, the same major in the Intelligence Section summarizes the case:

K. hat, wie sich aus den beiliegenden Fragebogen ergibt, die Partei-Mitgliedschaft verschwiegen, aber sich als "Anwärter" bezeichnet.

Aus seinen Original-Eingaben an die Reichsschrifttumskammer ergibt sich, dass er sich stets als Parteimitglied ausgegeben hat. In einem Antrag vom 8.3.1942 unterschreibt er als "Referent (K) beim Reichsführer SS, Reichskommissar f.d.F.d.V. (für die Festigung deutschen Volkstums)."

Es ist beabsichtigt, ihn wegen Fragebogenfälschung zu verfolgen.

Auf Grund der neuen Tatsachen wird um nochmalige Überprüfung der Göttingen Entscheidung gebeten.

In response to that turn of events, the reopening of his case for further review with specific attention to his Party activities, Krolow submitted the following biographical account as sworn testimony:

Eidesstattliche Erklärung

Ich, der Schriftsteller Karl Krolow, wohnhaft Göttingen, jetzt Beethovenstr. 58, erkläre eidesstattlich folgendes:

Unterm 1. Mai 1937 trat ich in die NSDAP ein. Der Eintritt erfolgte lediglich auf Drängen meines Vaters, von dem ich als 23 Jähriger Student wirtschaftlich abhing. Mein Vater, der selber niemals Nationalsozialist war, glaubte dadurch seinen einzigen Sohn im späteren Berufe gesicherter zu sehen. Er handelte wider seine politische Überzeugung. (— Auch später habe ich mich anläßlich meines kurzgefaßten Lebenslaufes zum philologischen Staatsexamen oder bei der Bewerbung um Mitgliedschaft in der Reichsschrifttumskammer als Mitglied bezeichnet (Anmerkung: ich glaubte der Reichsschrifttumskammer angehören zu müssen, weil ich zu veröffentlichen begann. Jedenfalls wurde es mir damals so gesagt, und ich hatte ja natürlich hier nicht die geringste Erfahrung. Übrigens wurde ich von der Mitgliedschaft befreit).

Während der folgenden Jahre bis zum Zusammenbruch habe ich im guten Glauben gelebt, Mitglied zu sein, obwohl ich von der Partei lediglich bei den monatlichen Beitragszahlungen hörte. Nach dem Zusammenbruch wurde im alliierten Fragebogen die Unterscheidung zwischen Pg. und Anwärter gemacht. Mir war bei meiner Desinteressiertheit bis dahin diese Unterscheidung nie recht zum Bewußtsein gekommen. Noch im Mai 1945, wenige Tage nach der Besetzung Göttingens durch die Amerikaner, habe ich mich in der im Rathaus damals ausliegenden Liste ausdrücklich als Pg. bezeichnet.

Nun aber glaubte ich korrekter und genauer zu handeln, wenn ich künftig mich als Anwärter bezeichnete. Ich tat dies im vollen Bewußtsein, mich bestimmter ausgedrückt zu haben. Gründe: ich besaß nie das rote Parteibuch, lediglich die rosa vorläufige Mitgliedskarte, die als vorläufiger Ausweis bezeichnet wurde. Ferner wurde ich nie vereidigt!

Ich meine auch heute noch auf Grund dieses Sachverhaltes mich als Anwärter bezeichnen zu müssen. Als was ich in den Akten der NSDAP geführt wurde, entzieht sich meiner Kenntnis. Den vorläufigen Mitgliedsausweis zerriß ich in den Tagen des Zusammenbruchs.

Studiert habe ich u.a. an der Universität Breslau, und zwar, laut Matrikel-Eintragung des Rektorats, vom 13.9.40–12.9.42. — Während dieses Studiums (und ohne mich exmatrikulieren zu lassen. Siehe Studienbuch, Seite 5) habe ich von Ende 1941 — Sommer 1942, ein gutes halbe Jahre also, den Nötigungen nachgebend, denen ich als Student, der nicht wehrdienstfähig war und bisher nicht einen einzigen Einsatz abgeleistet hatte, mich für befristete Zeit als Reichsangestellter beim Gauleiter und Oberpräsidenten von Oberschlesien, in seiner Eigenschaft als Kommissar für die Festigung deutschen Volkstums verpflichtet. Ich betone, daß diese Dienststelle dem Gauleiter und Oberpräsidenten unterstellt war, er war es, der inspizierte, ernannte, usw. Ich führte die [margin ripped] Bezeichnung Kulturreferent. Ich hatte als einzige Beschäftigung die deutsche Presse, die jeden Tag einlief, nach Artikeln über den sog. "kulturellen Aufbau" in Oberschlesien durchzusuchen, die fraglichen Aufsätze auszuschneiden, auf Pappe zu ziehen und einzuordnen, dh. eine Kartei anzulegen. Ich trug nie Uniform, war nie Mitglied, Anwärter oder fördender Mitglied der SS oder SA. Die Tätigkeit verlief vor dem Hintergrund meines Studiums, das ich nach Beendigung dieser Art von Ferieneinsatzes aufnahm (Siehe Studienbuch, Seite 5).

Meine Publikationen sind ohne die geringste Anleihe beim Nationalsozialismus konzipiert. Im Gegenteil habe ich — wie ich nachweisen kann — während der Tschechenkrise, September 1938, einen Gedichtzyklus gegen den Krieg "Tu ne tueras point" (Du sollst nicht töten) geschrieben. Im Januar 1944 wurde meine Lyrik vom Braunen Haus, München angegriffen (dekadent, untergangssüchtig, zersetzend). Auch dies kann ich belegen. [name deleted], z.Z. Redaktion "Die Welt," Hamburg kann dies bestätigen.

Meine Gedichte sollten in die Anthologie Deschs der sog. Inneren Emigration aufgenommen werden. — Der Ulenspiegel, Berlin, bezeichnete mich im Novemberheft 1946 als künstlerischen "Aktivisten" (Beleg vorhanden. Zur gleichen Zeit bekam ich Publikations-verbot in der US-Zone) — Auf der Gründungsveranstaltung der KulturLiga, München, wurden im Mai 1946 neben Gedichten Bechers und Langes auch meine Verse gesprochen. — Wolfgang Weyrauch hatte mich zur Mitarbeit an der von ihm ins Leben zu rufenden großen Anthologie zeitgenössischer Widerstandsdichtung im Aufbau-Verlag, Berlin, aufgefördert.

Durch die Verbote der Information Control Division (US Army) im November 1946 und der PRISC Regional Staff, Hannover, am 13. 1. 1947, ist mir aber jegliche publizistische Tätigkeit untersagt.

Göttingen, am 27. August 1947

Karl Krolow

(Karl Krolow)

Of course, much of Krolow's account of his activities could not then and cannot now be verified: the pressures from his father; his belief that he needed to be in the RSK in order to publish; or his belief that he was not exactly a member of the Party, even though he indicates that he was paying regular monthly dues as a member. His dramatic account of ripping up his temporary membership card at the end of the war would, however, have raised eyebrows. His temporary Party membership card was in the file with his picture on it, along with the instructions that the temporary card is to be returned when the permanent membership card is issued. A more likely and plausible scenario is that he ripped up his regular NSDAP membership card. Hence, the military intelligence authorities might have had reason to exercise skepticism about the mere cutting and pasting duties of a *Kulturreferent*. Krolow indicates that the position with the *Reichskommissar für die Festigung deutschen Volkstums* was subordinate to the [district leader] *Gauleiter*. Accordingly, Krolow is aware of the district leader's specific duties, including inspections and appointments. Presumably, the district leader appointed him directly as well. It is unlikely that such a titled position, however short term, would go to someone, even a Party member, not in good standing. Krolow worked in the offices of a notorious organization and would have had to be aware of their activities, hence the sensitivity to how those activities relating to the *kulturellen Aufbau* in the Eastern territories, such as the resettlement of Jews, would appear in the press.

Krolow's explanation seems to have satisfied the local authorities, since they reached the following conclusion on September 18, 1947:

Beschluß

In der politischen Ueberprüfung des Schriftstellers K. Krolow in eingehender Ueberprüfung und Beratung kommt der Ausschuß zur Einstufung nach Gruppe 2 (zwei). Wenn sich K. in einer anderen Form als Anwärter der Partei und früher als Parteimitglied bezeichnet hat, so ist das nach unserem Eindruck nicht geschehen um frühere ideologische Bindungen an die Partei zu verschweigen. K. war und ist in seinen Dichtungen ein bewußter Vertreter für Menschenrechte.

Der Vorsitzende

However, on September 9, 1948, the official decision or administrative verdict on Krolow places him in category four with the following penalties:

1. Krolow hat den Nationalsozialismus unterstützt.
(Kategorie IV) (4)
Massnahmen: Die Wählbarkeit wird auf 5 Jahre abgesprochen.

2. Die Kosten des Verfahrens werden auf DM 50. festgesetzt.

Gründe: Jugendliche, NSDAP ab 1937. "Referent (K) beim Reichsführer SS, Reichskommissar f.d.F.D.V." (für die Festigung Deutschen Volkstums). Nach Mitteilung der Zeugen ist K. jedoch nicht als wesentlichen Förderer oder Nutzniesser anzusehen.

Beweis: (1) Fragebogen
(2) Eigene Angaben
(3) Zeugenniederschriften
(4) Beschluss Göttingen v. 18. 9. 1947
(5) Interne Mitteilung v. 25. 4. 47

That decision went into effect on January 10, 1949. In a letter from January 21, 1949, Krolow applies for a waiver of the outstanding payment of costs for the proceedings: he paid 20 DM and wishes to have the remaining 30 DM of the total of 50 DM waived because it constituted "für mich eine ungeheure wirtschaftliche Belastung. . . . Ich bitte Sie daher sehr, mir angesichts dieser wirtschaftlichen Not diesen Restbetrag zu erlassen."

Subsequently, the public prosecutor initiated a review of the deliberations to that date and forwarded the case to the public prosecutor for special professions. In a memo of February 1, 1949, he states:

In der genannten Sache werden die Vorgänge zurueckgereicht.

Gegen die Entscheidung bestehen Bedenken: Der Betroffene gehört gemaess Paragr. 3 Abs. 2) der Verordnung vom 3. 7. 1948 nicht zu dem zu überprüfenden Personenkreis, da die Voraussetzung des Paragr. 3 Abs. 1 nicht vorliegen.

Die Einstufung in die Kategorie IV ist ferner offenbar deswegen erfolgt, weil die Intelligence Section (vergl. Das vorletzte Bl. d. Handakte) angegeben hat, Krolow habe sich im Jahre 1942 einmal in einem Antrag als Referent (K) beim Reichsführer SS Reichskommissar für die Festigung des deutschen Volkstums bezeichnet. Diese Stellung ist dann in der Begruendung der Entscheidung übernommen worden, ohne den Betroffenen, der nur angegeben hat, ca. ½ Jahr als Reichsangestellter beim Gauleiter und Oberpräsidenten von Oberschlesien taetig gewesen zu sein, Gelegenheit zu geben, sich hierzu zu aeussern. Aufgrund des Gesamtbildes der Akten besteht der Eindruck, dass der Betroffene durch die Einstufung in die Kategorie IV benachteiligt ist. Der Vorgang ist daher dem Oeffentl. Klaeger Entscheidung und insbesondere dazu zu hoeren, ob und warum er sich durch diese Entscheidung fuer benachteiligt haelt.

Thus, upon Krolow's letter of complaint and distress at the costs for him of that decision, he is given the opportunity to address the commission in order to explain more fully his activities in that office. The commission neither ignores the fact of that reference nor jumps to undue conclusions, but reverses the review and adjudication process in order to accommodate the defendant who has now become the plaintiff.

On March 4, 1949 Krolow appeared in person to state his case as described in the record of the proceedings:

Auf Vorladung erscheint Herr Karl Krolow, geb. Am 11. 3. 1915 in Hannover, wohnhaft in Göttingen, Beethovenstr. 58 und sagt zur Wahrheit ermahnt folgendes aus:

Unter Bezugnahme auf die mir im Januar 1949 zugestellte Entnazifizierungsentscheidung im schriftlichen Verfahren, A.Z.: R/H, VE/364/Kult. vom 16.12.1948 erkläre ich, daß ich mich durch diese Entscheidung benachteiligt fühle und zwar mit folgender Begründung:

Ich habe mich Ende 1937 auf Drängen meines Vaters bei der NSDAP angemeldet und ich erhielt etwa 1938 die rosa Anwärterkarte. Als Eintrittsdatum war darin der 1. 5. 1937 angegeben. Ein Mitgliedsbuch habe ich später niemals erhalten und bin auch nicht vereidigt worden. Aus diesem Grunde habe ich auch in meinem Fragebogen angegeben, daß ich nur "Anwärter" der NSDAP gewesen sei.

Über die Tätigkeit als "Referent" (K) beim Reichsführer SS, Reichskommissar f.d.F.d.V. (für die Festigung deutschen Volkstums) habe ich folgendes zu sagen:

Ich habe 1940 mein Studium an der Universität Breslau wieder aufgenommen. Die Möglichkeit dazu war mir gegeben, da ich infolge
Wehrdienstunfähigkeit nicht eingezogen wurde. Ende 1941 meldete
ich mich auf Grund eines Ausschreibens am schwarzen Brett der
Universität Breslau zum Ferieneinsatz beim Gauleiter und Oberpräsidenten von Oberschlesien. In der Ausschreibung war angegeben,
daß für archivarische Tätigkeit ein Philologe gesucht wurde. Etwa
Mitte der Ferien erhielt ich meine Einberufung nach Kattowitz und
wurde dort mit dem Ordnen von Pressemeldungen über den kulturellen Aufbau in Oberschlesien beschäftigt. Ich hatte die Aufgabe,
sämtliche eingehenden Zeitungen auf entsprechende Pressenotizen
durchzusehen, diese auszuschneiden, aufzukleben und zu ordnen.
Diese Tätigkeit übte ich da ich sie infolge verspätete Einberufung
nicht gleich zu Anfang der Ferien hatte beginnen können, etwas län-
ger aus und zwar bis Sommer 1942. Der Grund für meine Meldung
war einmal der Druck, der auf die Studentenschaft der Universität
ausgeübt wurde und dahin ging, die Studenten, die nicht zum
Wehrdienst einberufen wurden, irgendwie in den Ferien zu beschäf-
tigen, zum anderen sah ich in dieser Tätigkeit für mich die Möglichkeit, mir die finanziellen Mittel für die Beendigung meines Studiums
zu verschaffen.

Während dieser Tätigkeit führte ich die oben genannte Dienstbe-
zeichnung, ich möchte aber ausdrücklich bemerken, daß ich mich
niemals um irgendeinen Eintritt in die SS beworben habe und auch
nicht von irgendwelcher Seite dazu aufgefordert wurde.

Nach Abschluß meiner Tätigkeit im Sommer 1942 — ich konnte die
Stellung nur sehr schwer wieder verlassen und nur unter Hinweis auf
meine Krankheit gelang mir die Aufgabe meiner Tätigkeit — ging
ich noch kurze Zeit an die Universität Breslau zurück und setzte an-
schließend mit dem Winter-Semester 1942/1943 mein Studium in
Göttingen fort.

Dem NS-Studentenbund oder anderen Parteigliederungen oder an-
geschlossenen Organisationen (ausser der Studentenschaft, in der ich
automatisch während meines Studiums angeschlossen war), gehörte
ich nicht an. Gleichfalls gehörte ich nicht der Reichsschrifttums-
Kammer an. Ich hatte mich zwar um die Aufnahme bemüht, da ich
annahm, dass jeder, der schriftstellerisch tätig sein wollte, dieser Institution angehören müsse, erhielt aber das erste Mal im Jan. 1944
einen Befreiungsschein von der Zwangsmitgliedschaft in der Reichsschrifttumskammer. Irgendwelche andere sonstige Tätigkeit im Sinne der nazistischen Ideen habe ich niemals ausgeübt.

Unter Hinweis auf die zu den Akten eingereichten Zeugnisse und unter Berücksichtigung der oben gemachten Angaben bitte ich, meine Kategorisierung nochmals zu überprüfen und mich nach V (entlastet) einzustufen.

v. g. u.
Karl Krolow

Krolow was then invited back to speak again in order to explain a matter that he had left out of his previous declarations on the original questionnaire and in his first appearance in person before the board of inquiry. In his NSDAP questionnaire of 1937, he had indicated that he had served as a block leader about which the commission seeks clarification:

Göttingen, am 16. März 1949

Auf Vorladung erscheint Herr Karl Krolow, geb. Am 11. 3. 1915, Göttingen, Beethovenstr. 58, zur nochmaligen Vernehmung und sagt, zur Wahrheit ermahnt, folgendes aus:

Auf Vorhalt:
Zu meiner Vernehmung vom 4. 3. 1949 habe ich, nachdem mir der Fragebogen über die parteistatistische Erhebung 1939, von mir unterschrieben am 30. 6. 1939 vorgelegt war, noch folgendes zu sagen:

(1.) Ich habe in den Jahren 1938/1939 den Blockleiter nur vorübergehend vertreten, m.E. etwa auf die Dauer eines Monats. Irgendeine Funktion habe ich meines Erinners [sic] nicht ausgeübt. Ich habe auf dem oben erwähnten Fragebogen angegeben, daß ich Blockleiter sei, und zwar deswegen, weil die Stimmung unter meinen Kollegen, ich war damals Student an der Universität Göttingen, sehr gegen mich gerichtet war, da ich nicht im geringsten das war, was man mit "einsatzfreudig" bezeichnen konnte. Ich möchte aber nochmals bemerken, dass ich mich weder als Blockleiter gefühlt habe — ich habe ja auch nie irgendeine Bestätigung erhalten oder die dafür erförderlichen Papiere wie Ahnennachweis usw. eingereicht — noch dass ich die Tätigkeit eines solchen praktisch überhaupt ausgeführt habe. Die ganze Angelegenheit war eine Abrede zwischen dem für mich zuständigen Blockleiter und mir, da der zuerst Genannte in dieser Zeit anderweitige Verpflichtungen hatte.

(2.) Zu meinen Angaben in dem Fragebogen über meine Mitgliedschaft zur und meine Tätigkeit in der HJ habe ich folgendes zu bemerken: Ich war während meiner Schulzeit und zwar im letzten Jahr Angehöriger einer Schüler-Spielschar. Diese Gruppe wurde etwa 1934/35 geschlossen in die HJ überführt und zwar wurde sie, so-

weit mir erinnerlich, eine Art Gebietspielschar oder ähnliches. Solan-
ge ich noch auf der Schule war — bis Ostern 1935 — war die Ue-
berführung, soviel ich mich erinnern kann, noch nicht endgültig,
d.h. wir erhielten weder eine Mitgliedskarte, noch wurde Uniform
getragen, noch wurden Beiträge bezahlt. Wie ich von jüngeren Angehörigen der Spielschar später hörte, ist die Gruppe dann aber im
Jahre 1935 endgültig in die HJ übernommen worden und die Angehörigen der Spielschar wurden nach kurzer Zeit irgendwie als
Spielscharanwärter eingesetzt und erhielten einen entsprechenden
Rang.

In dem oben erwähnten Fragebogen habe ich m. E. aus denselben
Gründen, aus denen ich mich als Blockleiter bezeichnet habe, eine
Zugehörigkeit zur HJ und eine Führertätigkeit darin angegeben. Ich
war aber niemals Mitglied der HJ und bin selbstverständlich auch nie
darin irgendwie führend tätig gewesen.

In später von mir ausgefüllten Fragebogen habe ich auch nie wieder,
soweit mir erinnerlich ist, angegeben, daß ich Blockleiter und Führer
in der HJ gewesen sei, da ich dann jenen in meiner ersten Vernehmung erläuterten dekorativen Titel eines Referenten (K) beim
Reichsführer SS, Reichskommissar f.d.F.d.F. (für die Festigung deutschen Volkstums) zum Beweis meiner politischen Einstellung und
meines Einsatzes angeben konnte.

Weitere Angaben kann ich nicht machen.

v. g. u.

Karl Krolow

Further correspondence in the file simply confirms that Krolow was
heard on March 4, 1949, concerning the discrepancies between his
responses on the questionnaire and his responses for the NSDAP's
statistical survey of 1939.[4] The Public Prosecutor for Cultural Affairs
responded on April 4, 1949, to request a face-to-face discussion of the
case, an administrative hearing: "Auf Veranlassung des Hauptklägers
wird Einspruch gegen den Entnaz. — Entscheid im schriftlichen Verfahren vom 16. 12. 1948 erhoben und mündliche Verhandlung beantragt." Krolow then agreed to a hearing and asked for it to be
scheduled "as soon as possible." The hearing took place on May 2,
1949, with a full record of the proceeding, which is here given in full:

Protokoll

Oeffentliche Verhandlung des Spruchausschusses für Kultur-
schaffende im Sitzungssaal des Verwaltungsgerichtes, Am
Aegidientorplatz 4,

am 2. Mai 1949

in dem Entnazifizierungsverfahren: Karl Krolow

Vorsitzender:	[names deleted]
Beisitzer die Herren:	[ ]
	[ ]
	[ ]
	[ ]
Oeff. Kläger:	[ ]
Protokollführerin:	[ ]

Der Vorsitzende eröffnet die Verhandlung und trägt den Sachverhalt
vor.

Der Betroffene ist im schriftlichen Verfahren vom 9. 12. 1948 in die
Kat. IV eingestuft mit der Massnahme, dass ihm die Wählbarkeit abgesprochen wird. Er hat hiergegen frist- und formgerecht Einspruch
erhoben und mündliche Verhandlung beantragt.

Der Betroffene sagt aus (1) zur Person: Karl Krolow

Schriftsteller
geb. 11. 3. 1915
Göttingen, Langemarckstr.58

(2) zur Sache: Er sei am 1. 5. 1937 auf Veranlassung seines
Vaters in die NSDAP eingetreten. Sein Vater sei Parteigegner
gewesen, der ihm aber im Hinblick auf sein berufliches Fort-
kommen zum Parteieintritt zugeredet habe. Er habe das Parteibuch nie erhalten, sondern nur die rosa vorläufige
Mitgliedskarte und sich deshalb im Fragebogen nur als "Anwärter" bezeichnet. 1940 habe er sein Studium wieder aufgenommen bis 1942. Ab 1942 sei er als schriftstellerischer
Mitarbeiter an Zeitungen und Zeitschriften tätig gewesen.

Der öffentliche Kläger stellt fest, dass der Betroffene das Amt des
Blockleiters im Fragebogen verschwiegen hat.

Der Betroffene erklärt dazu, dass er 1938 oder 1939 den Blockleiter
für kurze Zeit vertreten hat. Das sei eine private Vereinbarung zwi-

schen ihm und dem Blockleiter gewesen. Offiziell sei er nicht dazu ernannt worden und habe auch keine Tätigkeit ausgeübt.

Ferner gibt der Betroffene an, dass er vor 2 1/2 Jahren von der Mil. Reg. überprüft worden sei, weil Fragebogenverfälschung vermutet wurde. Es handelte sich dabei um seine Zugehörigkeit und Tätigkeit in der Partei und seine Stellung als Referent beim Reichsführer SS — Reichskommissar für die Festigung deutschen Volkstums. Es sei im Dez. 1947 eine öffentliche Verhandlung angesetzt worden, zu der es aber nicht gekommen sei, weil das Verfahren wegen Nichtigkeit eingestellt wurde.

Auf Befragen erklärt der Betroffene, dass er die Tätigkeit als Referent beim Reichskommissar nur ca. 7 Monate als Student im Ferieneinsatz ausgeübt habe. Er habe sich auf eine Ausschreibung am schwarzen Brett der Universität dazu gemeldet, um Geld zu verdienen. Seine Tätigkeit in Kattowitz habe darin bestanden, Zeitungsartikel über den kulturellen Aufbau in Oberschlesien aus den Zeitungen herauszusuchen, auszuschneiden, aufzukleben und eine Kartei darüber zu führen. Er habe viel freie Zeit gehabt und sich während der Dienststunden noch schriftstellerisch betätigt. In den 7 Monaten seiner Tätigkeit sei er die halbe Zeit krank und nicht im Dienst gewesen. Über seine Einnahmen aus dieser Tätigkeit könne er nichts bestimmtes angeben.

Der Vorsitzende verliest die Angaben des Betroffenen im Fragebogen bezüglich einer Einnahmen, wonach er 1941 (Tätigkeit in Kattowitz) 1.500 RM verdient hat.

Der öffentliche Kläger stellt fest, dass der Betroffene das Amt in der Reichsführung SS freiwillig übernommen habe.

Es wird in die Beweisaufnahme eingetreten.

Der Vorsitzende verliest die Vernehmungsprotokolle des Entnaz.-Ausschusses in Göttingen vom 4. 3. und 16. 3. 1949 und die Eingabe des Betroffenen vom 27. 8. 1947.

Der Vorsitzende stellt fest, dass der Betroffene die bisherigen Angaben nicht wahrheitsgemäss gemacht hat und dass dadurch seine Glaubwürdigkeit in Frage gestellt wird. Die Mitarbeit bei der Reichsführung SS — Reichskommissar für die Festigung deutschen Volkstums — ist eine Belastung. Diese Betätigung muss genau erklärt werden. Er fragt den Betroffenen, ob er irgendwelche Handlungen gegen den Nat. Soz. nachweisen könne.

Der Vorsitzende fragt den Betroffenen, ob das Verfahren weiter durchgeführt werden soll oder ob er seinen Einspruch zurückziehen will.

Der Betroffene überreicht dem Ausschuss verschiedenes Material zur Einsicht. [not further named or listed]

Es tritt eine kurze Pause ein.

Nachdem wieder in die Verhandlung eingetreten wird, erklärt <u>der Betroffene, dass er seinen Einspruch zurückzieht.</u>

Die Verhandlung wird geschlossen.

Die Entscheidung im schriftlichen Verfahren: <u>Kategorie IV</u>

    <u>Massnahmen:</u>   Die Wählbarkeit wird auf 5 Jahre abgesprochen bleibt bestehen.

                       Hannover, den 2. Mai 1949

[name deleted]   Vorsitzender XVI

In this document from the hearing, Krolow presents his case as previously described and the public prosecutor adds comments for the record: he notes that Krolow concealed his work as block leader; the arbitrator or judge further notes that Krolow volunteered for work in the Reichskommissar für die Festigung deutschen Volkstums (RFdV); he notes that Krolow has on several occasions not told the truth about his activities, and that his work in that position still needs further examination and explanation. Finally, he asks Krolow if he ever undertook any action against National Socialism, and whether he wishes to continue the hearing or to retract his appeal. A pause ensues, and Krolow makes no response to indicate any actions taken by him against National Socialism. Instead, he withdraws his appeal, an action that in effect forestalls further review of his case and the exact nature of his activity in Kattowitz.

Subsequently, Krolow requested a reduction of the monetary penalty in light of his financial situation with two dependents, his wife and child. His request is granted and the fine reduced from 50 DM to 30 DM, twenty of which had already been paid, leaving only 10 DM still due. After having paid off that fine on September 7, 1950, nineteen months after the committee's decision went into effect,[5] Krolow writes again to request a change of status from Category IV to Category V, which is granted by the Office of the Public Prosecutor in Denazification Proceedings in the district of Hannover on September 27, 1950.

That pause in the proceedings, after Krolow was questioned about any actions that could demonstrate his attitude against National Socialism, remains as a significant silence throughout his later career in his poetics, his poetry, his poetic prose, and in his literary criticism. He never again comes close in any public form or forum, as far as I have been able to determine, to acknowledging or clarifying his activities as block leader or his work in the RFdV, or simply to describing his life during that period. In fact, his explanations of those activities, and of his exemption from military service during the period, remain in many respects implausible and subject to skepticism: was he allowed to serve casually as block leader? Could one assume such an office without official approval? If even possible, why would he agree to substitute? What were his circumstances in Breslau as a student? Or in Kattowitz? What did he notice there? Why would he take a job with the RFdV? Could one work there without good Party credentials? If he was working on cutting press releases "über den kulturellen Aufbau," did he not have to know exactly what else was going on in the Eastern territories, such as the euphemistic resettlement of Jewish populations, and particularly what was happening in nearby Auschwitz after 1940?[6] In all likelihood, without other documentation, these questions will go unanswered. What ultimately matters is Krolow's decision to stay silent about the topic: the final hearing above gives an exact administrative framework to that silence, which enters into the length and breadth of his later work, and of his long and busy career as a poet and critic. That silence remains at the core of Krolow's steady literary work for more than half a century and constitutes a secret center of willful amnesia beneath or behind the felicitous formulations of his prose, poetry, and poetics.

Notes

[1] This letter, dated January 18, 1948, can be found in the correspondence of Dolf Sternberger at the Deutsches Literaturarchiv in Marbach.

[2] See Opinion Sheet — Case No. GS/E/239; dated February 13, 1947, Göttingen.

[3] These materials can now be found in the Bundesarchiv.

[4] This is a specific reference to the letter of March 18, 1949 to the Public Prosecutor for Special Professions in the Denazification Commission of the City of Hannover.

[5] The result of this decision was a Category IV with monetary penalty and denial of the right to run for public office.

[6] The concentration camp at Auschwitz began in 1940, but underwent methodical and rapid expansion after the summer of 1941 (when the "Final Solution" went into effect). Krolow indicates that he responded to the job notice in the summer of 1941 and worked in Kattowitz until the summer of 1942. The gas chambers began operation in the summer of 1942, but the so-called cultural organization had begun years earlier. See Hilberg, esp. 562–66.

5: A New Start (The Late Forties)

Gedichte (1948)

K ROLOW'S SECOND VOLUME bears the unadorned and soberly generic title *Gedichte,* which is a far cry from the absurdly celebratory *Hochgelobtes, gutes Leben* (1943), an almost unbelievably silly,
gloatingly self-satisfied title; though not attributable to Krolow, that
first title must have compounded the anguish of self-misrepresentation
already present in his poems. After the complex hide-and-seek in that
shared collection, Krolow's first poem in the second volume appears as
a sort of liberation and is, in fact, a milestone that marks the real beginning of Krolow's public career as a poet and critic, once returned
from his particularly self-critical *inner emigration.* The poem is not yet
the type of poem he will later understand as a public poem, but it does
represent an opening, a coming out of hiding and the first step toward
going public.[1] The poetic voice declares itself present, without any
celebratory overtones or false transcendence and with due sobriety.
The poem stands in direct contradistinction to the last stanza of "So
nah am Tode": "Und weiß: ich bin mit Baum und Tier vertauscht,"
by beginning with the words "Ich weiß, dies Hemd und grobe Tuch
/ Sind mir nur ausgeliehen, / Und was ich je am Leibe trug — / Ich
nehm es dankbar hin" (17). The speaker acknowledges his appreciation for modest possessions that he owes to unnamed others. Like
Günter Eich's famous "Inventur," also published in 1948, this poem
confirms bare existence and affirms, through the simple denomination
of objects and the declaration of self, a new freedom of perception and
expression after the unreality of the last decade,[2] but Krolow goes beyond Eich's poem to foreshadow a profound existential disorientation:

> Im Spiegel ist zum anderen Mal
> Das Zimmer anzusehen,
> Die Vase, rund, der Leuchter schmal.
> Wie soll ich sie verstehn?

Des Nachts fahr ich mit fremder Hand
Mir zögernd durchs Gesicht.
Und hab ich mich im Licht erkannt,
Im Dunkel bin ichs nicht.

Ich finde Mond und Stern bei Stern
Und suche nach dem Sinn
Und spüre nur noch ganz von fern,
Daß ich im Leben bin. (17–18)

The question, which is not rhetorical but desperate, ratifies the private individual in the public sphere and at the same time destabilizes the reductive mimesis of Eich's poem. Here, that mimesis is given by the mirror which reflects the room, but against the solidity of objects, the subject seems to collapse into a state of anxiety and alienation ("mit fremder Hand"), in which body and consciousness drift apart to the point that identity even seems extinguished in the dark. A return to reality, to an undistorted and uninhibited relation between perceiver and perceived, is not as uncomplicated and self-evident as in Eich's poem. Though Krolow's poem performs the same function within his oeuvre as Eich's, a sort of *Kahlschlag*, it is more psychologically complex and tenuous in probing the implications of the moment for self-understanding. Krolow is not just reflecting the circumstances but reflecting upon the new terms of individual existence after the war. Now the subject looks at the expanses of nature that formerly offered some comfort in false transcendence and searches to make sense of what now seems so transparently meaningless.[3] After the long years of compounded self-estrangement for the inner emigrant, imposed from outside and assumed from within, identity has to be recovered and reconstituted, retrieved from a considerable distance: "Ünd spüre nur noch ganz von fern, / Daß ich im Leben bin."[4] In what will become a typical gesture of Krolow's poetry, the poem avoids any resounding slogan and locates the subject in an uncertain area of nuanced sensibility ("Und spüre"), both intellectual and intuitive. The subject retains the "hochempfindliche Dialektik" (Holthusen) from its incipient stages, but no longer employs it to hide, protect, and preserve itself in a cocoon of *Naturlyrik* in which one hears the chrysalis of selfhood rattling and squirming. The subject uses that dialectic to lay bare the historical vacuum of selfhood after the war and begins to recover a complex sense of self.

Krolow does not then reject the idiom of nature poetry. Instead, he proceeds to absorb it and exercise it fully on his own terms, using the vocabulary of natural detail now as so many anchors in physical reality, rather than as a bulwark against it. In the fourth poem, "Regnerischer Tag," the speaker now poses a question in wonder and bewilderment: "Haben je so wild gerochen / Fieberklee und Baldrian?" Against the sudden overwhelming fear of "das Nichts," the speaker invokes a sensuous embrace of the world: "Helft mir Sinne! Nehmt einander / In die Obhut des Gedichts."[5] The world in turn embraces the poet: "Klopft das Blut in den Gelenken, / Zieht's mich sanft zu Boden hin. / Will im Thymian bedenken, / Daß ich tief im Leben bin" (21).[6] The poetic voice is no longer "from afar," but rather "deep in life," whereby this poem adopts in its last line the title of the first poem with its alienated tentativeness. The word *selig* from two of the six poems in *Hochgelobtes, gutes Leben,* which characterizes in a word the tenor of false transcendence in that cycle, has now been supplanted by the word *sanft,* which will become an enduring mark of Krolow's idiom and his sensibility. It becomes a signal of the subtle range of nuanced feelings and perceptions that he so often seeks to bring into the poem.

The poem "Kurzes Unwetter" might seem in this first postwar volume a companion piece to the first poem "Der Wald" in his 1943 cycle, though the sleek column of five-syllable lines visibly pares down the stormy melodrama of the earlier poem from a heavily symbolic "Sturm" to an "Unwetter" that passes quickly. The scenario is still turbulent, but the short lines offer less allegorical pathos and turn toward a self-sufficiency of observed nature. In addition, the opening lines, "Die Wolkenpferde / Ins Licht sich stürzen," mark another pivotal moment in Krolow's development; he takes a similar metaphor from Oskar Loerke's poem "Landschaft im Strom": "Tief wittern die Nasen der Wolkenhunde" and makes it more vivid by changing to a more powerful, dynamic animal, enjambing it into the prepositional phrase, choosing a more dramatic verb, and transposing it to the end of the line so that the image plunges precipitously forward in ungrammatical, unbridled action.[7] These shifts to greater compression of line and concentration of image begin to show Krolow's abiding allegiance to the nature poem, though with a willingness to change its nature from within in such a way that signals in advance his proximity and susceptibility to the use of metaphor among surrealist poets outside of Germany. Interestingly, Krolow's second volume contains a series of four poems, "Waldgedichte" (25–27), that makes a direct connection to his first volume: he replaces the first poem, "Der Wald," which had announced the motif and the mood of danger and menace, with another, "Sommerwald" (25), that evokes foliage in synaesthetic density ("Oh, nichts als Grün! [. . .] Sonst Grün und Grün"[8]), and he includes the two others, "Waldmusik" and "Traum von einem Wald," that now read differently in the new context. In other words, Krolow inhabits the idiom of *Naturlyrik* and has not yet exhausted its energies, but has begun to transform it to his own purposes. He does not simply subscribe to a stable convention but creates within a common idiom a dialogue that will allow him to move beyond it.

The poem "Fische" (29–30) seems to acknowledge that distance to *Naturlyrik* while maintaining its contours. The first two strophes seem to offer, without becoming explicit, a subtle commentary on its practitioners, himself included:

> Die bei Molch und Alge schliefen,
> Sanft vom grünen Stein beschattet,
> Traumerstarrt in blinden Tiefen,
> Zeigen sich und drehn im schiefen
> Licht die Schwänze, früh ermattet.
>
> Ruhig leuchten ihre Flossen.
> Wind kämmt die gelöste Welle.
> Vogel kommt vorbeigeschossen.
> Und sie stehen, zart gegossen,
> In der jäh geweckten Helle.

The poem reprises the motif of "closed eyes" from the earlier poem "Traum von einem Wald," where it closed out the world and allowed the flight of false transcendence, which required a strained, anguished desire ("Ich wüchse selig," and so on). In an allusion to the poets of *Naturlyrik* or *Seinsdichtung* in the 1930s and 1940s, the fish resides in the depths in perfect calm, "Traumerstarrt in blinden Tiefen," in natural ignorance of the surface, where "Unkenruf aus Hollergräben / Tönt im Ohr wie ferne Trommel." Whether one understands these ditches allegorically as trenches and the drums as military, or not, the surface activity is only a distant echo, a place where the birds, like ballistics shooting by, do not disturb the calm. Krolow's new postwar vocabulary, with such key words as *sanft, zart,* and *ruhig* appears to create an image of poised passivity that is almost statuesque. The cascading commas in the first strophe lead into the sanctum of the depths; the poet, like the wind in the second strophe, a traditional image of inspiration, has smoothed every wave and harmonized the image in even meter and smooth, simple rhymes. But that calm is suddenly broken in the last strophe: "Räuber, der im Boote lauert: / Messer zuckt schon in den Händen! / Kühler Gott im Schlamme kauert, / Hilflos sieht er's an und trauert / Wie die Graugeschuppten enden." When the fish come to the surface, predators are waiting. The beauty of deep calm is no protection on the surface, and nature is not just a self-enclosed garden or lake. Here the figure of detached calm, both the fish itself and a separate representation of Nature now huddling helplessly in the mud, is unable to control the use of weapons against nature, against itself.[9] The abruptness of violence in the last strophe, "Messer zuckt schon in den Händen," puts that poise in a harsh new light, "In der jäh geweckten Helle," outside those depths; that poise and illumination below now seem like the false transcendence of the other poems, a false security in distance from the surface of life.

Another poem sets this relation more clearly into terms of human existence. The poem "Hinblick" (33–34) gives a perspective on the outside world from indoors, through a window: "Die bange Welt, vom Licht bemalt, / Schwebt hinterm Glas heran." The viewer is detached and can only imagine what goes on out there: "Ich ahn, . . ." Until making the link to the previous poem clear, he looks at "das stumme Fischgesicht" in the frying pan, "So schaut der Tod." That sight brings him to a sudden recognition of his own life in the depths of willful seclusion:

> Im Schweigen leb ich unverwandt
> Und spür die Angst in mir,
>
> Die quer durch meine Braue springt,
> Die Stimme mir belegt.
> Den Schatten seh ich, der durchdringt
> Die Mauer, die sich schrägt.
>
> Den Flugsand hör ich, der sich mischt,
> Das feine Zeitgesumm.

That distant drone of life outside, on the surface, suddenly comes close and reverberates in his consciousness. Krolow's poems in this volume are preoccupied with death as in the poem "Kommt die Nacht" (35–36), which is dedicated to Günter Eich: "Und ich halt die Augen / In das Finstre hin," whereby that awareness of death also creates an intense appreciation of life:

Mit der Kühlung saugen
Sie schon andren Sinn,

Sehen am Geäste,
Wie es mühsam rauscht,
Lautlos sich die feste
Frucht zur Kugel bauscht,
Die im grünen Sprunge
Sich im All verirrt,
Hinterm kühnen Schwunge
Stoff des Schweigens wird.

That dual consciousness of death and fullness or ripeness of life emerges as the attempt to create a metaphysical context or atmosphere for the tangible object, for the thing of nature as a palpable "Stoff des Schweigens," imbued with its own natural fatality, as in also the poem "Sonnenblumen" (37). Here Krolow is still close to a Heideggerean sort of "Being unto Death" that is saved from maudlin pseudophilosophical morbidity by the sculptural, and perhaps sepulchral, evocation of physical objects that hold the metaphysical context in balance: "Wie im Gras sich gattet / Geist mit zartem Hauch, / Sinke ich ermattet, / Schwind' zu feuchtem Rauch." Cercignani wrongly interprets this poem and strophe as the subject's discovery of illusion and the failure of nature to provide comfort against fear (207), whereas these lines, with the always positive cue in the word *zart,* demonstrate the impulse toward dematerialized anonymity and depersonalization in nature toward which Krolow strives in his poetry. The new postwar frankness of self-presentation also gives these poems a different coloration.

In "Oktoberlied" (39–40) the subject wonders whether his attempts at probing the mysteries of things have not been in vain:

Hab ich meine Zeit vertan
Als der Sommer Falter sandte,
Auf der Gartenmauer brannte,
Knisterte im trocknen Span?

Gab ich meine Tage hin
Als am Wehr der Fluß verrauschte,
Warmer Wind die Kleider bauschte?
Forscht' ich nicht geheimen Sinn

Im Geleucht der Hundstagsrose!
Roch nach Wermut nicht die Wiese!
Lattich wucherte im Kiese. —
Nun zerfällt die Herbstzeitlose.

An den Zäunen drehn die Winde.
Weinlaubbüschel tanzt im Staube.
Aus dem Nebel schwebt die Laube
Und der Baum verliert die Rinde.

Soll ich meine Augen schließen?
Soll ich harte Beeren sammeln
Oder Haus und Tür verrammeln
Und die frühe Lampe grüßen?

Nirgend ist für mich zu bleiben.
Soll ich Holz zum Feuer legen?
Unermüdlich geht der Regen,
Trommelt an die blinden Scheiben.

Laß den Garten ich verwildern,
Krähenvögel in ihm hausen?
Mögen sie die Hecken zausen!
Keiner kann die Schwermut mildern.

Keiner kann den Tod verlocken,
Wie ich mich vor ihm auch flüchte.
Greif ich fröstelnd falbe Früchte,
Fühle ich ihn im Nacken hocken.

The difference between Krolow's first and second volumes lies in the shift from the ecstatic exclamation to the rhetorical question. The former mode masked the existential uncertainties of the subject behind a specious impulse to merge with nature as the only available direction for expression, but which emerged as an elaborate artifice of dialectical subterfuge; the latter mode addresses directly the position of the subject, who no longer requires such subterfuge. In the above poem, the exclamation mark appears in the past in lines nine and ten. Now the subject no longer needs to seek studiously, in willfully blinding detail, a "geheimen Sinn" in nature, but can remain freely exposed to the uncertainties of life and certainty of death. But as in previous poems in this collection, awareness of death is a sign of life.

The queries reject the need to close one's eyes and lose one's self in dream: "Soll ich meine Augen schließen?" and to barricade one's self in a prison of domesticity. The question "Soll ich Holz zum Feuer legen?" has the same pathos as T. S. Eliot's Prufrock asking, "Shall I eat a peach?" or of Gottfried Benn's figure Rönne, who, in the story "Der Geburtstag" (1916), had also jubilated at the prospect of a fruit as a sign, however banal, of his efficacy in life, his sureness in mere existence. But here, this late German Prufrock finds precisely in a fruit a reminder of his frailty and mortality "Greif ich fröstelnd falbe Früchte, / Fühl ich ihn im Nacken hocken." That latter image recalls the many conventional late medieval and German Renaissance woodcuts of the figure of death — the skeleton — riding, bearing down on the person, but which here expresses the overwhelming consciousness of death in the postwar subject.

One might, however, see here a solipsism in those reflections because of the absence of sociohistorical content in the poems. But the solipsism is assertive and secures the individual in the world, recognizing, as in the first three stanzas of the poem "Der Zauberer," the limitations of the earlier *Naturlyrik:* "An den Westwind hab ich mich verschwendet, // An das Blühn der Wolfsmilch hab ich mich vergeben." In the second three stanzas, the subject reiterates four times the phrase "will ich" in the middle of four different lines to locate the centrality now of the subject in nature before adding in two further variations: "Nicht mit Leichtsinn noch mit Schwermut sparen, / Will der Tod und will das Leben sein." The subject seeks a broader embrace of the world that requires a new assertiveness: "Prangen muß die Quitte, wenn ichs will." Yet that assertiveness remains subordinate to the fatality of nature. Krolow has not departed from the ideology of nature poetry but has changed the terms within that idiom.

The productive, even liberating solipsism of the subject, has its limits in that fatality and in a rising horizon of historical reality in the poems, as in his poem "An meinen Sohn" (44–45). In this poem he implicitly sets the innocence of the newborn against the guilt, or at least non-innocence, of *Naturlyrik* faced with still unnamed historical adversities:

> Von der Welt getrieben wir
> Ihrem dunklen Geist:
> Denk, mit Blum' und scheuem Tier
> Lebst du unverwaist.

> Sammelst in der kurzen Faust
> Irdisches dir viel.
> Bist im sichren Tag behaust,
> Fügst ihn zart im Spiel.

The child cannot and should not be aware or concerned by historical events. He should realize naturally the self-imposed historical obliviousness of the nature poets that protected them against historical forces through a false innocence. The parents, however, without the solipsism of "Der Zauberer" (42–43) in the preceding poem, know the difference:

> Schreckt Vergängliches uns sehr,
> Bist von ihm verschont.
>
> Immer größer wächst die Zeit,
> Fällt wie Schatten dicht.
> Und wir schauen oft zu zweit
> Bang dir ins Gesicht.

Here the horizon of contemporary history emerges without specific details but as a force that determines the individual and conditions existential and parental anxiety.

When the sense of enclosure from the world appears, it is self-imposed, as in "Der Kranke," where the microscopic view of nature that closes off other perspectives is not at all self-evident:

> Mit offner Tube
> Die Tulpen wehn.
> Von meiner Stube
> Aus kann ichs sehn.
>
> Die Ammern singen
> Im Licht verzückt.
> Von nahen Dingen
> Werd ich beglückt.
>
> Vom Regen rauschen
> Die Ulmen noch.
> So will ich lauschen
> Nach innen doch.
>
> Stimmen beschwör ich
> In meinem Blut.
> Im Schweigen hör ich
> Sie lang und gut.

Die Tulpen röten
Sich tief wie Wein.
Die Ammern flöten
Für mich allein. (46)

The perceiving subject is ill, or at least thinks so, and is in retreat from the world, taking pleasure from the observation of "nahen Dingen," which recalls the practice of observation in Krolow's early prose sketches first published in the *Deutsche Allgemeine Zeitung* in 1944 and later as *Von nahen und fernen Dingen* (1953). That foreshortened perspective on the world is not imposed from without, but a conscious choice: "So will ich lauschen / Nach innen doch." The emphatic affirmation "doch," in response to a negation, reflects the lack of necessity, the velleity of the self-indulgent subject appearing in stanza four, the inclination to luxuriate in solipsistic hypochondria. That decision is valid, though not shared by others, and remains ("Für mich allein.") a sign of individual freedom to fashion one's existence without impositions from outside.

Krolow's poems here dwell overwhelmingly on the mood of despair and disorientation and combine closeness of observation with bleakness of outlook in a near reversal of earlier good spirits, however feigned. An elegy of sorts, or perhaps a poetic epitaph, "Der Tote" (52–53) offers in a morose reprise "vertanes Leben," in which decease is "Allerletztes Glück." That bleakness of mood is, however, not overweening and self-indulgent, but rather opens up, through the poetic underbrush of nature poetry, an area for the self in history as in the only dated poem in the collection, "Selbstbildnis 1945" (54–55):

Aus dem Schweigen bin ich kaum entlassen,
Das mir bitter aus der Kehle steigt.
Und ich spüre manchmal mit Erblassen,
Wie mein Atem sich im Nichts verzweigt,
Wie's augenlos endet,
Im Trübnis gewendet,
In lautlosem Drehen
Die Sinne vergehen,
Am Hexenzwirn hängend, vom Tollkraut berückt,
Zu Larven und kalten Gallerten gebückt.

The poet finds himself released from the domestic imprisonment of doctrine as an inner emigrant but choked with resentment at those years of self-distortion. He is alert to the fact that such an internalized straightjacket can not be thrown off overnight. The poet has to reconstruct an idiom but is first drawn to address that loss: "Und ich spüre manchmal mit Erblassen, / Wie mein Atem sich im Nichts verzweigt." Poetic breath has been restored ("mein Atem"), but that voice loses itself and branches out endlessly in an overwhelming sense of emptiness and nothingness. The shift to six-syllable lines from ten-syllable lines reinforces the feeling of historical vertigo at the sudden change. The poet remains hanging onto a deeply ingrained idiom, crouched down, deformed in microscopic inspection of eccentric details and oddities of nature. Those last two lines swell to eleven syllables. They indicate the poet's helpless return to an idiom of nature that is no longer imposed or serves as a retreat, but still serves as a crutch in the absence of other means and still has to be worked through critically and recovered or dispensed with on its own terms. Anything else would amount to a wholesale ideological discreditation of the idiom and would therefore be false and misleading. Krolow seeks instead to preserve the idiom in order to distance himself from it. While not rejecting it as a resource, he seeks to transform it by enriching it beyond the corruptions it underwent in the Third Reich, while recognizing its limitations as a subgenre.

In one of the last poems of the volume "Der Dichter spricht" (58), he addresses this constant focus on the marvels of nature: "Wunderliches Leben, das ich sage, / Unaufhörlich am Verstehn vorbei! / Wuchs es nicht wie Stille hinterm Schrei, / Dessen Schall ich noch im Ohre trage?" The poet finds a bond of continuity from prewar to postwar in the evocation of "Wunderliche[m] Leben," which by design during the Nazi period passed the censor "Unaufhörlich am Verstehn vorbei." That concentration on nature reflected inversely the poet's anguish at the horror of historical events, though that collapse of "Schrei," within history, into "Stille," outside or beyond history, can also seem silencing. The strategic duplicity of the poems in the first collection is not entirely absent here either, though that duplicity in the idiom is part of what the poet openly confronts. In lines that anticipate Celan's "Todesfuge," Krolow's poet exclaims: "Luft, die trauert! Und ich muß sie trinken, / Bis die Augen sich mit Schwärze sammeln." The poet here drinks the air that, even with the new atmosphere of freedom after the war, does not refresh since the imagined sanctum of nature outside of history that sustained him during the Nazi years is now inseparable from the facts of history that he had then avoided. Nature can only appear as mourning within the given historical context, and that mourning in nature contains here, to my mind, mourning over the poet's own half imposed, half adopted silence. The dialectical duplicity that had been useful and pragmatic during the Nazi period as a strategy of survival in poetry, now appears, to some degree, as complicity though under coercion. Even the poet recognizes this complicity in retrospect. In this poem those lines of recognition lead only to a disappointing sort of redemption: "Hell im Gras erlöst mich Grillenstammeln, / Und ich kann in sanfte Dämmrung sinken." Though the word *sanft* marks Krolow's new sensitivity, his search for nuances of feeling after the war is thwarted and sinks with the echo of Trakl into the obscure twilight of cliché.

Something closer to recognition of the historical situation of *Naturlyrik* emerges in the last poem of the volume "Lobgesang" (59–60), dedicated to his friend Friedrich Rasche. In the first three dense sestets of thirteen- to fourteen-syllable lines, he reiterates the command to praise nature, though with mounting irony ("Lobe die Mücke, . . . Lobe die Blase im Schlamm"). In the fourth stanza, his praise becomes open lament:

> Traumnetz der Nächte lob, das man uns übergeworfen,
> Das uns im Schlafe mit jeglichem Wesen verstrickt,
> Quälenden Alp, der uns aufsitzt, mit Schrammen und Schorfen,
> Algenumwunden, und dumpfe Verhängnisse schickt.

The poet now suddenly views the idiom of *Naturlyrik* during the Third Reich, including his own dialectical variant, as a dream net that contained and trapped him, politically subdued him, linking and binding him to the realm of nature in the poem as he intended, but also unintended, to the Reich that oppressed him. In retrospect the dialectic of inner escape is a net of contradiction in which the poet is entangled. It is both witting and unwitting complicity with or within the Reich. The garden sanctum of nature has become the object of ironic, self-indicting praise, the "Quälenden Alp, der uns aufsitzt, mit Schrammen und Schorfen, / Algenumwunden, und dumpfe Verhängnisse schickt." Yet the poem continues to list objects of ironic praise in such a way that the critical insight here is not elaborated but curtailed. The poem rejects, through bitter irony, the nature idiom during the Reich. It marks its limits, thereby freeing it from those prior uses and recovering it at the same time into the existential idiom of Krolow's first postwar volume. In other words, Krolow tightens the torque of a strained idiom once more, both binding himself more tightly to that idiom but also freeing himself more surely. Krolow finds his way back into and out of a tradition that frames his beginnings as a poet.

Heimsuchung (1948)

The title of Krolow's third volume contains complexities in that single word. The most direct meaning is, of course, the affliction of the war as it affected individuals; the first connotation suggests the search for a home, both the retreat into whatever domesticity was possible during the war or the search after the war for an old home in the rubble or a new one, though with the reminder also of the frightening invasion of privacy in the common *Durchsuchung* of one's home. On another level, the title suggests a search for the meaning of *Heim* or for even the ponderous possibility of *Heimat* in postwar Germany, an inquiry into the question of national identity. That single word triggers a number of associations that link the private and personal dimensions of the poetry to the public and historical context without ever making that latter dimension explicit. The volume is divided into three sections, *Die zweite Zeit*, *Widerfahrung*, and *Hoffnung*, that suggest a dialectical structure to the volume.

The title of the first section refers to the time after the war, after the Zero Hour or Stunde Null of May 8, 1945, and the end of Nazi domination, though Krolow, with his intense, almost exclusive focus on the genre of poetry, would not subscribe to the notion of a historical caesura implicit in the term Stunde Null.[10] His own career illustrates the variation in continuity of German poetic traditions of *Naturlyrik* through the 1930s to the present. Yet the variations that show the richness of a tradition emerge ever more strongly. The first poem, in stark contrast to the transhistorical impulses of nature poetry in the Nazi period, is titled "Gegenwart" and begins:

> Der Mauerputz blättert
> In rötlichen Schuppen,
> Weht unter die Füße
> Mir Schmetterlingspuppen.
> Im Aussatz des Steines, im kalkigen Grind,
> Blühn fleischlich die Tage, die jenseitig sind. (69)

The direct frontal perspective on a shabby wall suggests the immutable reality of concrete, external existence, like the opening frame of Roberto Rossellini's postwar film *Paisan* (1946), stripped of poetic illusions. Here however, against the grain of that veristic, documentary impulse, the tradition of *Naturlyrik* emerges in the word *blättert*, meaning to leaf, to peel, to scale or flake off. The plaster on the wall loses chips that have turned reddish and blow underfoot like autumn leaves. A traditional image of autumn has been inscribed into an un-traditional, unnatural object to make immediately palpable a sense of time, the conventional task of a poem about autumn. The reference to butterflies in line four contrasts to the leprosy of the stone, its sickly rash, which blossoms in the last line, conflating autumn and spring, and compressing into few words the passage of time from birth to sickness and death, and beyond: "Blühn fleischlich die Tage, die jenseitig sind." The intermingling of metaphors bring opposite seasons, animate and inanimate objects, animals and humans, life and sickness, death and afterlife, all into play. The sense of transhistorical, all-encompassing rhythms of life and death common to *Naturlyrik* in this period offers small comfort and abundant delusion in the postwar period. It is adumbrated but neutralized by the poetic means of metaphoric compression, which brings to life, against ingrained habits of mind, a more adequate sense of the reality of death. The dimension of magic is still present but overwhelmed by the immediacy of death: "Es atmet der Schimmel / Mit offenen Poren. / Ich bin ans Gewimmel/ Der Geister verloren." Across the idiom of *Naturmagie* (nature magic), Krolow conjures a landscape that leads back into, not out of, the historical reality of postwar Germany. In the last stanza, the use of mythological allusion is sharply ironic and highlights the inadequacy of such references: "Der Bremsenton hebt sich / Aus faulender Grube. / Sieh, Ceres belebt sich / Und schwebt durch die Stube!" What one sees is the putrefaction in the ditch encircled by flies, against which the classical allusion might offer abstract consolation since Ceres as the summer "duftet und dauert" in the last words of the poem, but which is also a transparent fiction that evaporates before the reality of what is in the ditch, and of the "spirits" that are lost.

The subsequent poems revolve around the topic of isolation and anguish, with a tendency toward darkly magical narration and a variety of rhyme schemes. Krolow seems to try from many angles to explore and confront the psychological and existential implications of the historical moment without entirely abandoning familiar idioms, and perhaps, by opening those idioms to more candid inquiries into the status of a newly recovered selfhood in poetry, to make that magic a means of questioning the links of the individual to the real world and thereby binding that individual to the world. In other words, Krolow's use of traditional idioms is now framed by new knowledge; in the tripartite poem "Das Nachtessen" (70–71), the narrator contemplates "Die Finsternis, die immer dichter fällt," which, with the play on the word for poet, *Dichter,* reverses the relation of sovereign poetic voice and world to suggest that now the dark historical moment, the circumambient atmosphere, creates and forms the poetry, not the simple transcendent or escapist impulse of the poet:

> Ich pfeife leise, hebe meine späte,
> Entfernte Stimme auf. Es wird kein Lied,
> Nur kleines Flüstern, das das Schweigen säte,
>
> Wie sichs durch meine Einsamkammer zieht.
> In meiner Brust ersticke ich die Schreie,
> Mit denen altes Leben mir entflieht.
>
> Ans Fenster tret ich, und ich horch ins Freie.

Instead of a song with its confident relation to the world, the poem has become just a "tiny whisper" that contemplates "the silence." That silence, in turn, represents the cries or screams from the period past ("altes Leben") that still define the present. In that last line, the narrator tries to step away and find release in the traditional Romantic motif for transcendence by looking through the window "ins Freie," but such a conventional and generalized dodge is no longer possible. The freedom lies precisely in individual confrontation and personal conscience, no longer in sublime sublimation; that line at the end of part two of the poem is just the sort of false transcendence that Krolow and many others had negotiated during the Nazi period, but here the narrative impulse of the poem carries over and culminates at the beginning of the next section, after the caesura, with the bluntly powerful lines: "Es saugt das Draußen an den toten Scheiben. / Ich fühl die Angst, die auf die Haut sich legt."

Though many of the themes are consistent with earlier poems such as drinking ("Der Schnapstrinker," "Selbstbildnis mit Rumflasche" [84]), nature ("Verfallene Laube" [78–79], "Neumond" [80], "Nachtstück" [85], "Seestück" [86]), or weakness and helplessness (*Ohnmacht* in "Augen im Schatten" [81], "Die Augen im Spätsommer" [82–83], "Der Gewaltlose" [88–89]), the focal point of these poems in the first section remains the "Abgrund im Innern" (77) of the individual. *Naturmagie* and historical awareness come to their most refined expression in the poem "Nächtliches Flötenspiel" (90–91) in the convergence of music and darkness:[11]

> Ihr flüchtigen Bilder,
> Gemalt in die Lüfte!
> Der Mondfisch streift milder
> Die Wasserminzdüfte.

Er springt aus dem Grase,
Er fliegt durch die Bäume
Beim süßen Geblase,
Schenkt Inbrunst der Träume.

Wie Öl zischt im Feuer,
Mit bebender Flanke,
Fährt Wind durchs Gemäuer: —
Ein dunkler Gedanke!

Die Töne, die Klagen
Fliehn perlend nach oben,
Vom Lufthauch getragen,
Zur Nacht aufgehoben.

Verstrickt in Verlangen,
In altes Gelüsten,
Ziehn — mondkrautbehangen
Sie Milch aus den Brüsten.

Die Klagen, die Töne,
Dem Holze entsprungen,
Sind tief schon ins schöne,
Ins Fleisch eingedrungen

Und tragen den Wandel
Ans Ohr, ein Erwecken,
Bis unter die Mandel
Als seligen Schrecken.

The first stanza makes audible music visible, nearly three-dimensional, and palpable as "Bilder, / Gemalt in die Lüfte!" where the air as a plural noun takes on an almost swirling, impasto quality, reminiscent of Van Gogh's *Starry Night*. It moves and takes form from the musical images, but the plasticity of image only highlights their ephemeral character. The surreal image of the *Mondfisch* lends startling liveliness to the darting and flitting of moonlight through the night airs and fragrances. The poem comes alive in these two remarkable images, and the active verbs, such as *springt, fliegt, schenkt, zischt, fährt,* and so on, maintain that magical sprightliness of image and sound. In the fourth stanza, that music appears as such, and as lament: the participle *perlend* gives again a swirling nacreous luster to the immaterial sound, but the verb *fliehn* at once reiterates their transience and adds an ominous ambiguity as the notes rise like smoke. Music is sensual and almost carnal in its eroticism ("Verstrickt in Verlangen") and, like some succubus, both lubricious and maternal, draws "Milch aus den Brüsten" and penetrates "tief schon ins schöne, / Ins Fleisch. . . ." Music gets under one's skin and effects change by appealing to levels of awareness beneath rational consciousness: "Und tragen den Wandel / Ans Ohr, ein Erwecken." The aestheticization here of lament, in terms of painting and music, carries deeply into the individual "Bis unter die Mandel," a recognition that strikes almost bodily "Als seligen Schrekken." The last word undercuts the seductively aesthetic terms of the whole poem and changes their value by galvanizing the distant, ominous connotations of the poem into a sudden awareness of historical horror, which is *selig* not only in the aesthetic trappings of devotion, but as the first step toward responsibility and contrition. Krolow joins his contemporaries, especially Nelly Sachs and Paul Celan, in addressing the aestheticization of horror in the Holocaust and recovering art as a valid means of response, both emotional and cognitive, to recent history. Unlike those two other poets, Krolow had, as far as we know, no direct experience with the Holocaust or with death in combat, but here he works, though thematically at a greater distance, to open the genre to an overwhelming historical necessity of coming-to-terms in poetry with the historical facts of atrocity.

After that confrontation with atrocity, Krolow arrives at one of the first poems that can be said to carry his signature, though the poem ("Pappellaub," 93; I, 16) bears strong resemblance to a poem with the same title by Wilhelm Lehmann and demonstrates his strong influence on Krolow:[12]

> Sommer hat mit leichter Hand
> Laub der Pappel angenäht.
> Unsichtbarer Schauder ist
> Windlos auf die Haut gesät.
>
> Zuckt wie Schatten Vogelbalg,
> Spötterbrust, als winzger Strich:
> Ach, schon wird es Überfall,
> Wie sie blätterhin entwich!
>
> Luft, die unterm weichen Flug
> Kurzer Schwinge sich gerührt,
> Schlägt wie blaue Geißel zu,
> Die die dumpfe Stille führt.

Grüne Welle flüstert auf.
Silbermund noch lange spricht,
Sagt mir leicht die Welt ins Ohr,
Hingerauscht als Ungewicht. (93)

The poem demonstrates close observation of nature, but also shows Krolow's own facility at capturing a moment "mit leichter Hand" through vivid metaphors, especially those of sewing and sowing in stanza one, that deftly anticipate his interest in surreal imagery, and place him on the cusp between *Naturmagie* and surrealism. The sylvan setting of foliage has become *Silbermund,* the voice of nature that whispers to the poet "sagt mir leicht die Welt ins Ohr, / Hingerauscht als Ungewicht." Whereas Lehmann's poems tend toward concretion of the image through naming of details, Krolow's poem balances concrete image with its metaphoric equivalent, and then extracts a sense of the ethereal with the words *leicht* and *Ungewicht* that anticipate so much of Krolow's later development in shedding descriptive ballast from the poem. The poem becomes more abstractly intellectual without losing any of its sensuality, as the world evanesces from image into color, sound, and idea. In those last lines, Krolow, with the help of Lehmann, has recovered a poise in intimacy with the world.

The fragility of that poise is visible in the subsequent section *Widerfahrung,* when Krolow turns to direct confrontation with the historical reality of the war in postwar Germany. The first poem "An Deutschland" (99–100) opens with the question "Wo bist du nun?" In these poems, Krolow moves abruptly away from that preceding lightness of touch in giving contours to personal experience and moments of perception; instead, he seeks, rightly but heavy-handedly, to register the horrors of the war and its aftermath. For the most part, the poems maintain a constant rhythm in iambic pentameter and a uniform rhyme scheme of *abab, cdcd,* and so on that together create a transparency of poetic means and shift attention to the graphic images, recalling the macabre images of Otto Dix and Ludwig Meidner. The poems are vehemently rhetorical, with stark visions composed of stacked phrases that are powerful, but ultimately remain phrases that lack the necessary nuance of observation or emotion to transmute them into profound encounters with historical experience. The effect is less descriptive than declamatory, less emotive than emblematic.

The poems chronicle the anguish of the poet and his attempt to open the poem and his own sensibility to the grand scale of historical reflection in general after a long period of interdiction and to the specific horrors of wartime devastation and loss. The stark change in direction for Krolow is marked by the distance between "Pappellaub," where the *Silbermund* of nature "Sagt mir leicht die Welt ins Ohr," and the poem "Stimme aus der Landschaft" (103), whose title evinces the same motif and rootedness in nature and in nature poetry, though now the speaker in the poem does not listen but bluntly and brutally calls up the dead "mit Schüssen durch die Stirn, / Mit schwarzen Bärten und verrenktem Kiefer, / . . . / Ich rufe sie, die starben wie Geziefer!" The poet-speaker in the poem tries to cover or bury them: "Ich werfe zartes Laub euch hinterdrein, / Ihr Leichtgewordenen sollt nicht ruhmlos liegen." The motifs of foliage and lightness or desubstantiation and the word *zart* all reappear in the changed context of honoring or consecrating the defiled dead, but what registers is the weakness of Krolow's idiom, elsewhere a more sensitive medium, in coming to terms with the war. The word *Ruhm,* used here to protest an indecorous burial that should not remain "ruhmlos," is contaminated Nazi discourse and remains, even with presumably different intent, distant from reality. In the last stanza the discrepancy between poetic means and the poem's meaning is itself remarkable: "Ihr werdet heiter sein in eurem Reich, / Ins Netz der letzten Dämmerung verstrickt. / Wie Träume seid ihr schon und seid euch gleich, / Wie ihr versöhnt aus tausend Augen blickt." The poem imposes nature magic on the dead, who then should be *heiter* in another *Reich,* another infelicitous and contaminated word, and forces upon the dead, grotesquely, a reconciliation with death.

Krolow's awkward wrestling with history in these poems culminates in the longest poem of the cycle, "Vaterland" (114–17), where he elongates the line over four numbered sections in order to try to attain elegiac somberness, but the poem instead remains mired in banal formulations such as "Große Ruine nun, Vaterland, sternwärts geschossen, / In die Plejaden geschossen vom Schmerzenskatapult" and so on. The strained effort to bring large areas of the world back into the German poem of *inner emigration* only brings Krolow full circle to late Expressionist oratory in the manner of Franz Werfel or Johannes R. Becher. The poems are interesting in their attempt to find images to express visceral anguish and to lament, and in their inability to disturb conventional patterns of poetic language despite the shift in theme from beauty to horror. Some poems do remain valid as enduring expressions of the historical moment by finding, instead of mere empty phrases, a more personal tone of anger and of remorse, as in the topical poem "Land im Gericht" (106–7):

Ich bin das Land, das ohne Hoffnung ist,
Mit Gräberkreuzen neben jedem Weg
Und schief im Kräuticht, das die Ernte frißt,
Gedünst von Blut im Boden, trüb und träg.

In meinen Städten hängt die Sonne still
Wie ein Geschwür, von Fliegen dicht umflort.
Ich bin der Kehricht, drin die Ratte schrill
Vor Hunger pfeift und nur der Käfer bohrt.

Ich bin das Land, das man durch Tränen sieht.
Im Aug bleib ich als bittres Salz zurück,
Lieg unterm Netze, das der Himmel zieht,
Und fall ins tiefe Schweigen, Stück um Stück.

In meinen Wäldern lösen sich im Schrei
Die alten Geister. Und die Hölzer schwelen,
Vom Monde krank und blinder Zauberei.
Die Vögel flattern mit verbrannten Kehlen;

Und heiser wie der Wetterfahnen Ton
Fliehn ihre Stimmen an des Tages Rand
Zu Wolken auf, in denen Gifte drohn.
Verdammt bin ich und der Vampire Land.

Ich bin das Land, das im Gerichte steht,
Und allen Ländern bin ich das Gericht.
In meinen Schwären, die ich hergedreht,
Werd ich gerufen in das letzte Licht,

Ins Licht von drüben, wie es unverwandt
Einst auf mir ruht und mich nach oben zieht:
Das unter Qualen umgeworfene Land,
Das Totenland, das man durch Tränen sieht.

Here the poetic voice has entered into the catastrophe, rather than standing outside as in the other poems, and identifies with the country whose ruin is shared by individual and collective, the person and the country. The reflection on self is a reflection on nationhood, on culture, and vice versa. The rhythm is the same, with, if anything, even less inflection; the images are less numerous, less grotesque, and less allegorical, and less embedded in pat phrases, with the exception of the genitive "der Vampire Land," and can now coincide with that rhythm to render a tone of sober, melancholic matter-of-factness: "Ich bin das Land, das ohne Hoffnung ist." Though the poem does not break into new formations of language in order to find necessary new means to express grief, this poem at least observes that limit ("Und fall ins tiefe Schweigen, Stück um Stück"), which gives the poem's reflections greater depth. Line four even takes precise aim at, and makes precise use of, the propagandistic Nazi slogan *Blut und Boden* in order to translate it into a concrete reality, not as the basis of racist ideology but as its murderous result. In alignment with that recognition of a general insufficiency in the language, stanza four also specifically recognizes the particular failing of the idiom of nature magic in poetry, like the forest, a refuge for "blinde[ ] Zauberei." The three repetitions of the refrain "Ich bin das Land," each time with a different subordinate clause, add emotional intensity to greater conceptual complexity, as the speaker moves from despair ("ohne Hoffnung") to expressed grief ("durch Tränen") to questions of culpability ("im Gerichte"). Here Krolow touches the political dimension directly and links German society precisely and economically to Western and world culture through the question of guilt: "Ich bin das Land, das im Gerichte steht, / Und allen Ländern bin ich das Gericht." That point anticipates, for example, the adroit reflections of Camus's Jean-Baptiste Clamence in *La Chute,* but here any elaboration would seem only an inappropriate, since exculpatory, digression. Likewise, the rather typical metaphysical or quasi-religious ending could seem merely an apotheosis of anguish into cliché, but is capped by the final distich that, by mentioning "Land" (country) and "Totenland" (land of the dead), secures the link between individual and country in grief.

At times the poems do contain surprising effects, as in "Elegie vom Harren in der Nacht" (118), about the futility of the hopes and perseverance of the inner emigrant. The poem alternates quatrains with indented tercets to create an effect of gradually increased force, an inert dead weight of oppression that closes in. Each quatrain begins with the refrain: "Dumpfer Ruf, der mich würgt wie mit Krallen," alluding to the pressure to join and to conform, and continues in stanza two, "Und mein Harren vergeblicher macht," or in stanza three, "Mich in ratlosem Harren verwaist." The position of the inner emigrant, tenuous to begin with, becomes more isolated and pointless. The poem then concludes, as the individual expires, with the lines: "Wenn erloschenen Blicks ich mich kehre / Den Stimmen zu, schmerzlich, der Welt / Der schönen Maschinengewehre." The speaker turns back to the world to discover not some form of release or salvation but only the aestheticization of violence that forced his retreat to begin with. The historical framework is uncertain and could include both the Nazi period and beyond since it subtly addresses an enduring mechanism, defined by Walter Benjamin as the aestheticization of politics in fascism. Likewise, another elegy, "Elegie für ein spielendes Kind" (120), evokes a future untouched by despair but concludes with a devastating sketch of the period:

> — Bei Bier und Zigarren
> Frieren die Mörder und treten verlegen im Kreis,
> Kauen Erbrochenes im Mund hinter Zähnen und harren
> des Gerichts, das sie ausläßt, und singen ganz leis . . .

The postwar period resembles a Georg Grosz cartoon of bestial murderers, confined and discomfited but confident of their release. A new historical cycle will begin, culminating again in terror that will define the existence of the child. The elegy mourns the child's lost future.

The final section, more of a coda, is, like its title "Hoffnung," no longer a poetic exploration of personal anguish or historical crisis. Instead, the poems, four of seven previously published, all strike a conciliatory, even optimistic note, as in the last lines of "Lied der Erbsenpflücker" (128–29): "Wolln wir uns freudger regen, / Sind schon zur Hoffnung reif." Even "Nußernte" from his first volume loses its critical edge in the new context, as does, to a lesser degree, the poem "Lobgesang." The new poem, "Zauberglas" (130–31), seems to announce a recovery of spirits and return to the idiom of nature magic in lines 13–28:

> Blick verlor sein Aschengrau,
> Wie er an den Traum geheftet.
> Spiegeltiefe, die ich schau,
> Hat Vernichtung bald entkräftet.
> Der ich einst war gewillt,
> Schwermut, ist nun gestillt,
> Heitre Welt, Bild um Bild,
> Kommt auf mich zu,
> Zieht zart die Wolkenspur,
> Rückt an der Sonnenuhr,
> Gleitet als bunte Flur
> Mir unterm Schuh.

Und so dring ich froh bewegt,
Deute mir den Zauberhimmel,
Tauch, vom schönen Wahn erregt,
Selig unter im Gewimmel.

The mood now is sanguine. The speaker has overcome the existential melancholy by turning again to dream as an antidote to the reality (*Aschengrau*) of the war and Holocaust and the annihilation they caused (*Vernichtung*). The passage recalls Goethe's Faust leaving his study for a "bunte Flur" outside once called back to nature. The overly familiar words *Traum, Spiegeltiefe, Zauberhimmel*, and so on from the Romantic lexicon appear without irony in a straightforwardness that is both almost disarming and almost disturbing, until that vocabulary and mood become self-conscious as "schöne[r] Wahn." After two reprints of poems from his volume *Gedichte* of the same year, Krolow concludes *Heimsuchung* with a poem, "Mahlzeit unter Bäumen" (134) of lucidly sensuous impressionism: in the first stanza, "Luft kommt lau wie Milch gestrichen," and in the second, "Grüne Glut drang aus der Wiese." Instead of a hideout from the "starken Hirtengott" in the dense thicket of his earlier "Waldmusik," light, sound, and air all resonate in synaesthetic harmony: "Stille summt im Käferflügel. / Ruhn, vom Ahorn schwarz umgittert. / Auge schmerzt vom Staub der Kräuter, / Der im lauten Lichte zittert." In the last two stanzas, the wine runs over and hands begin to wander, and "Weiche Glieder, braungeschaffen, / Im bewegten Laube fließen." The poem is an erotic idyll that calls to mind both Biedermeier kitsch and Rokoko fluff; the vivid sensations and sensuous images rescue the poem from becoming a mere exercise in banality but not from exquisiteness and preciosity.[13] Krolow has staked out an area here in developing a poetry of light and sensation, and of lightness of affect, with a narrow margin for error but, paradoxically, a wide range of nuance: that is, Krolow's poetry often demands a minute discrimination of poetic affect. His poems often tend in the very opposite direction of so-called *dunkle Lyrik*, as described later by Hugo Friedrich in his *Struktur der modernen Lyrik* (1956). Rather than semantic compression, Krolow's poetry in this vein aims at decompression, a sort of *helle Lyrik* of liberated sensation, which is as interesting for its exclusions as for its rich internal modulations.

Auf Erden (1949)

This volume continues from that turn back to life and to nature at the end of *Heimsuchung* and consolidates his achievements in working through different registers in the poems of his *inner emigration* and postwar return, though *Auf Erden* neither extends nor deepens his range. The first poem, appropriately called "Lebenslied" (137–38), even harkens back to "Traum von einem Wald" in his first volume with its last line: "Bin ich selig an die Welt vertauscht." One of the most interesting poems of this collection, and very important for this phase of his work, is "Hand vorm Gesicht" (139–40), which does not really belong here. Krolow dates it from 1945 in his *Gesammelte Gedichte,* and it recapitulates with its verbal gesture the existential mode in his work of that period:

> Hand vorm Gesicht! Sie hält
> Kurz nur das Sterben ab.
> Grube im Nacken fällt,
> Beere am Aronstab.
>
> . . .
>
> Ratloser Mund! Er schweigt,
> Ins Schwinden still gedehnt,
> Wenn sich mein Schatten zeigt,
> Süß an die Luft gelehnt.
>
> . . .
>
> Über mir weiß ich schon
> Stimmen aus schwarzem Schall,
> Laubhaft gehauchtem Ton,
> Und spür den Stirnverfall.
>
> Rückwärts mit leisem Schrei
> Stürz ich ins Leere hin,
> Hart hinterm Tod vorbei.
> Fühl, daß ichs nicht mehr bin.

The speaker fends off death like a physical attack. The exclamations are a parallel gesture in words to the physical pose and negate the exclamations of wonder in the first volume. The narrow margin discussed above is also here, though in an anguished existential context, in the word *Süß* that captures the moment in balance between silence, shadow, and air. The speaker feels the oppression of "Stimmen aus schwarzem Schall, / Laubhaft gehauchtem Ton," or in other words, the necessity of confronting the specific individual deaths of the war and Holocaust, an overwhelming thought that pitches the speaker into echoing Gottfried Benn, "Stirnverfall," and then "ins Leere hin / Hart hinterm Tod vorbei," which unlike death, does not dull consciousness of such atrocity. Instead of engaging that emptiness, the poem concludes with a pose of narcissistic self-estrangement.

Most of the other poems in the volume do not show traces of that earlier dis-ease of consciousness, and instead, pick up the note from "Mahlzeit unter Bäumen" that concluded the last volume. "Sommerlied" (142) seems almost like a manifesto, perhaps for much of the immediate postwar generation, anticipating the 1950s: "Ganz innen will ich Freude sein / Und mich zum Licht entschließen." The poem seems to cross Jugendstil motifs with dream factory Hollywood production values: "Die hohe Luft zu Traum zerrann / Im Spiel der heitren Schatten. / Mit stillen Augen sehn sich an, / Die sich umschlungen hatten." The final lines adapt the Expressionist motif of *Entgrenzung* to technicolor-trained audiences: "Wie ich ins zarte Leuchten schau, / Weiß ich mich ohne Grenzen." That subtle-soft coloration characterizes many of these poems, though most others also retain an earthy solidity in the naming or description of objects. The phrasing and images are delicate and refined, rarely brittle; yet underneath remains a darker realm of anxiety that those images wish to banish: "Halt ein, du schwarzer Ton im Ohr! / Verbranntes Singen in der Luft" ("Abends," 145). Eight poems are each devoted to separate animals, mostly from the farm, though without the experimental flair and sweeping, orotund verbality of Marianne Moore's animal poems in the 1920s and 1930s. Krolow's earthiness is closer to, and directly influenced by, Georg Britting's southern German variety of nature poetry, along with Rilke's *Dinggedichte*. Krolow's poems aim at evoking a fullness of being as in the "Bauerngott" (160), "Mit braunem Bauche, zeigt den starken Nabel," and so on, as images of unshakable groundedness in existence, even though one of them, "Katze im Sprung," also captures emblematically Krolow's later ideal of a poetry of hovering weightlessness, without gravity: "Vom Fluge gewichtlos gemacht. / . . . / Wie die Windsbraut ins Leere, mit / schwindenem Sinn, / Der den rasenden Absturz nicht kennt" (149). In the delicate poem "Die Schwangere" (166), the speaker contemplating death is at the same time most fully aware of herself: in the first two lines, "Ich fühle manchmal mich bis ins Gelenk / Der dünnen Finger, die ich langsam biege" and in the last two, "Ich hör mein Blut in seinem stillen Gange / Und bin für alles Außen plötzlich taub." The poem comes full circle in describing the centeredness of the woman's consciousness and body upon itself, on death and new life, and ever so subtly, suggests a symbolically positive image in the last line of a natural sort of *inner emigration*.

The same circular structure reappears in the last poem, "Traumfahrt" (170–71), which provides the overarching trajectory of Krolow's development from (1) his *inner emigration* into the magic of *Naturlyrik* during the Nazi period to (2) his freely adopted return to that idiom after the horror-of-war poems and existential phase in the immediate postwar period, and (3) anticipating his surreal variations of that tradition in subsequent years. The first stanza reads:

> Bin hingereist
> In andres Land,
> In Träume ausgeschlüpft.
> Dem heitren Geist
> Werd ich verwandt,
> Der Bild mit Bild verknüpft,
> Der von der Schwere ungebeugt,
> Den Sinn aus wachen Sinnen zeugt.

And the last of seven:

> So reife ich
> Geduldig aus
> Als Frucht im Fabelland,
> Durchschweife ich
> Das Träume-Haus,
> Hab mich am All erkannt,
> Und zieh als treuer Wandelstern
> Dem Geiste nach, dem Weltenherrn.

The opening of the first stanza directly addresses the matter of *inner emigration* and thereafter captures the defiance and inner resistance of someone who as a poet "Bild mit Bild verknüpft." The turn toward the senses signals an imaginative freedom "von der Schwere" of state oppression and adds another political sense to the poems drawn from the physical senses ("Sinn aus wachen Sinnen zeugt"). That residue of imaginative freedom in *inner emigration* in the dream of nature becomes a private mythology that renews the poet. The poet turns in upon himself: "So reife ich / Geduldig aus" in a private universe of dream. Yet that political sense is double edged: even though an inner sense of resistant integrity is preserved, outwardly the poet follows "als treuer Wandelstern / dem Geiste nach, dem Weltenherrn." The term *Wandelstern* possibly refers to Emil Barth's autobiographical novel *Der Wandelstern* (1936–38), whose first chapter also bears the title "Auf Erden Sein"; Franz Norbert Mennemeier characterizes Barth's work, relevantly, as "das Erwachen eines Ichs aus kindlicher Traumbefangenheit zum schmerzhaften Bewußtsein des Todes und Vergänglichkeit" (II, 747). The poem recapitulates the course of Krolow's early career and suggests that to remain in the service of a private vision ("dem Geiste nach"), to subscribe to the individual supremacy of imagination, can nonetheless put one in the service of much less sublime forces of the reigning ideology ("dem Weltenherrn").

Notes

[1] For Krolow, the German terms "offen" (open) and "Öffentlichkeit" (the public sphere) are central to his understanding of poetry, and he eventually applies them as generic classifications. The relation between the two is significant. The individual and the poem are open to reality; society is open to the poem. Thus, the personal poem of individual sensitivity and perception is, *prima facie,* also a social text, even if not explicitly political.

[2] Unless otherwise noted, all page numbers in this chapter refer to the reissue in 1989 of these four volumes from the 1940s, *Auf Erden: Frühe Gedichte,* Frankfurt am Main: Suhrkamp, 1989. In his afterword to that edition, Krolow writes of that time before and after the end of the war:

> Es schien keine andere Macht der Welt mehr zu geben als die Ohnmacht. Die sinnliche Aufmerksamkeit war noch einmal stark: Sie ist nie wieder *so* wahrgenommen worden wie in Augenblicken, in denen die Sinne zu schwinden scheinen, in denen jedenfalls unsere fünf Sinne nicht mehr gelten, denn aus Sinn wurde Abersinn, Unsinn und jene Bodenlosigkeit, die ein In-den-Boden-Versinken ist. (175)

Of course, he is describing the affects of Nazi doctrine, censorship, threats of punishment, and the general climate of menace. For a detailed description of the distortions of language and sensibility in that period, see the diaries of Victor Klemperer (1933–1945) as well as his *LTI: Lingua Tertii Imperii or The Language of the Third Reich,* published as *LTI: Notizbuch eines Philologen* (1947).

[3] Fausto Cercignani finds in this poem and these lines "die Enttäuschung und Verwirrung des Menschen gegenüber dem undurchdringlichen Geheimnis der Schöpfung" ("Zwischen," 202) and thus views the poem in a religious-existential

context, rather than a historical-existential context, as I do. The poem demonstrates rather the collapse of the abstract constructs that create and support identity, and thereby raises the question of the situation of that collapse.

[4] For a comparative discussion of this problem faced by writers after the war in Germany and Japan, see my article on the development of postwar literatures in those countries ("An East-West Comparison of Two War Novels: Alfred Andersch's *Die Kirschen der Freiheit* and Ōoka Shohei's *Fires on the Plain.*" *Comparative Literature Studies* 24, 1 [1987]: 58–82).

[5] Cercignani sees this exclamation, inexplicably, as "ein hoffnungsloser Anruf, keineswegs eine Rettungsankündigung" (204). Without adopting either such reductive extreme, hopelessness or salvation, the poem and poetic voice evince a powerful presence, alive to its insecurities.

[6] Cf. Wilhelm Lehmann's poem "Augustwolken": "Nichts ist mehr irdisch als ein Ruch von Thymian" (I, 75). See Hans Dieter Schäfer's *Wilhelm Lehmann* for a discussion of Lehmann's influence on Krolow in this period. Cercignani rightly defends Krolow against Schäfer's criticisms there, which he finds "ziemlich übertrieben" (204).

[7] Hans Dieter Schäfer comments very pertinently on the general use of metaphor in this period: "Grundsätzlich kann über die Bildlichkeit der dreißiger und vierziger Jahre gesagt werden: Die Metaphern wurden sparsam verwendet, stimmten zumeist mit der Erfahrung und der Natur überein oder wurden auf das Niveau des allgemeinen Sprachgebrauchs herabgesenkt. In der Lyrik hatte man kein Verständnis mehr für kurze Bildimpulse aus verschiedenen Bereichen" ("junge Generation," 490). Krolow's use of metaphor stands out against that background and constitutes a radical departure from that atrophied sense of metaphor.

[8] Cercignani makes a brief comparison to G. Britting's poem "Feuerwoge jeder Hügel" (206).

[9] The "Kühler Gott" is not only a representation of nature, but also, from a more socio-historical perspective, of the school of nature poetry in this period: the term alludes to Oskar Loerke's "Der grüne Gott" from his poem "Geleit" (dedicated to Wilhelm Lehmann) from his *Silberdistelwald* (1934). Lehmann then used that term as the title of his own volume in 1942.

[10] This caption, *Die zweite Zeit,* recurs in Krolow's work with different meanings: in his acceptance speech upon receiving the Büchner-Prize in 1956, he uses the phrase to suggest a parallel other time in which poetry exists, in which past poets speak to us in the present; and in 1995, at age eighty, he published a volume with that same title, indicating the state of advanced age.

[11] This motif is common to the immediate postwar period in poems by Nelly Sachs, Paul Celan, and Ingeborg Bachmann, among others, and illustrates what Hugo Friedrich later, in his epoch-making study, called *Dunkle Lyrik*. For a discussion of the motif, see my essay on "Adorno's Philosophy of Poetry after Auschwitz" (57–70) in Brockmann/Trommler, eds. Also in my *Voice and Void: The Poetry of Gerhard Falkner* (19–34).

[12] See Hans Dieter Schäfer, *Wilhelm Lehmann,* 259–60. In contrast, though noting Krolow's debt to Lehmann, Walter Hinderer singles out this poem, playing it off the poem "Die Zisterne" by Wolfgang Bächler, to indicate that traditions of

Naturlyrik still can retain some critical force and not sink into escapism, but he does not demonstrate in any detail how Krolow in this poem achieves what he calls "das seltene Kunststück" (130).

[13] Hans Dieter Schäfer classifies this poem as the "intimen Stil der neobiedermeierlichen Anakreontik" (*Das gespaltere Bewußtsein*, 45). See my reading of the poem in terms of erotic content in chapter 8.

6: Modernism in a New Key (The Fifties)

Die Zeichen der Welt (1952)

M<small>ORE THAN HIS POETRY</small> of the late 1940s, his first volume of the 1950s, *Die Zeichen der Welt* (1952), placed Krolow among the most interesting and highly regarded poets of the postwar years with Bächler, Bachmann, Celan, Eich, and Huchel. In a review of that volume, Alfred Andersch even remarked: "Sieht man von dem Schaffen der älteren Meister ab, so stellen Krolows Gedichte, neben denen Günter Eichs und Stefan Hermlins, die einzige konsequente Annäherung an die große lyrische Form seit dem Ende des Krieges in Deutschland dar" (42). The first poem of the volume, "Irdische Fülle" (6–7), recalls the crosscutting hypothetical jubilations of *Hochgelobtes, gutes Leben:* "Schöne Erde! Wer sie wüßte! / Wer die süße Weise fände!" The last lines indicate the continuing debt to *Naturlyrik,* the existential climate of the times, and Krolow's turn toward an analytical surrealism: "Erdenhaus, vom Nichts umlauert! / Und ich bin auf sel'ger Reise! / Daß es mir als Wesen dauert, / Wird es Traum und Geist zur Speise" (7). Krolow remains true to and extends the tradition in which he learned his craft ("Daß es mir als Wesen dauert") by changing and enriching it.

The poem "In der Fremde" (I, 7–8) was published for the first time in *Die Zeichen der Welt,* but Krolow later dated the poem from 1944 and put it at the beginning of his *Gesammelte Gedichte.* This highlighted its significance as a transitional poem but also raised the question of why he chose not to include it in the earlier volumes in the 1940s. The poem belongs to the mood of the late war years and early postwar period, as in his previous "Hand vorm Gesicht," but here the poem brings the idiom of *Naturlyrik* into direct, open collision with wartime reality and frames, between a flight from devastation among ruins ("die verbrannte Mauer") and toward symbolic plenitude in Nature ("die runde Nuß"). It reveals a situation of disorientation and fear in a hostile environment: "Ich fühl die rauhen Sterne im Genick. // Ich hör die fremden Schritte um mich her." Without specific historical detail, as given for example in Alfred Andersch's *Die Kirschen der Freiheit,* also published in 1952 and also about fleeing war, Krolow's poem is more suggestive than descriptive and merges physical with symbolic flight from reality and conjoins them in an existential, but also transhistorical anxiety ("Laut pocht das Herz im Hals"), a general condition of fear.[1] Nonetheless, in a two-step process, that anxiety exposes the speaker, all at once, to new and unsettling depths of experience and creates an openness to such exposures: the former causes fear and the latter knowledge, "Die Toten nehmen in der Dämmrung zu. // Und [ich] fühl sie nahe, die vergessen waren." The poems leads to a positive anamnesis, a first step to necessary mourning and recognition, emotional and intellectual coming-to-terms with the recent past, but also subtly indicts, in the passive voice, whoever forgot or ignored the dead or, to be exact, the then still living.

"In der Fremde" captures the position of Krolow wresting himself free from the cocoon of *Naturlyrik,* despite the internal dissonances he developed in that idiom, and committing himself to openness, while also fearing that exposure. This quandary goes back to his earliest publication, as a student, on Rilke's "Ausgesetzt auf den Bergen des Herzens" and anticipates his efforts in the 1950s to make the poem increasingly open to fresh language and experience, including influences from abroad and to use language to bring the greater world back into the closed, crowded, and cramped realm of German nature poetry. In *Die Zeichen der Welt,* Krolow still tries to confront the past with jarring images of battlefield carnage ("Gesichter wie zerquetschte Beeren, / Die man aus einer Schüssel fischt" [I, 33]) that deconstruct the comfortable, otherworldly earthiness of *Naturlyrik,* but these poems still depend on a vocabulary of exaltation. In the poem "Lied, um sich seiner Toten zu erinnern" (I, 33–35), thirteen of fourteen strophes evoke the dead as they are transformed from the world of violence into ghostly lightness as they blend back into nature: "Und lächelt aus den Augenwinkeln / Begrünung, vom Vergessen schwer." Paradoxically, their substance lies in their forgetting, in their detachment from the world, whereas the survivor, not yet expired into the airiness of death, is trapped by the gravity of living: "Indes ich als ein Haufen Kleider / Begraben bin vom Welt-Gewicht." Other poems like "Nachtstück mit fremden Soldaten" (I, 35–36) only underscore the dreary datedness of eternity in poems where death appears as beautiful and beatific, as "himmlische Wahrheit," even though that hymnic elevation is undercut by short strophes that suggest new menace: "Hör ich im Laube lachen / . . . / Soldaten, fremd, mit flachen / Maschinengewehraugen." That dialectic appears, likewise, in "Männer"

(I, 48–50): "Hinter der lyrischen Landschaft der Jäger und Hirten / Lauert der Waffen Gestrüpp." Krolow uses the fulsome language of exalted nature but sets it in relation to a violent reality that threatens always to burst forth.

Another means of separating himself from that ingrown idiom of *Naturlyrik* is to reach back to traditional metrical forms, though not in the manner of humanist-traditionalist poets like Rudolf Schneider, Werner Bergengruen, and Rudolf Hagelstange, who did not question inherited forms nor try to adapt to the present.[2] At times, Krolow adopts traditional forms but subverts them to his own purposes, like his use of terza rima, where the second line of a tercet should give the first line of the following tercet in a pattern of *aba, bcb,* and so on, which combines musical subtlety with a deterministic rigor of construction, as in Dante's *Divine Comedy.* In his "Terzinen drei Uhr nachts" (1948) Krolow alters slightly the repeated line in order to loosen that construction and interlace startling metaphors that emerge from the "Leuchtgas meiner Träume" in the first strophe: the poem has the form of a structured disorientation, an outwardly ordered derangement of the senses (Rimbaud) of lucid hallucination: "Der Dschungel Nacht der leeren Zeit, / Wenn aus den Uhren Leguane / Ins Zimmer kriechen, wenn es schneit // Den Schnee der Frühe, die ich ahne" (I, 23). The surreal images and slightly altered repetitions from stanza to stanza undermine any narrative momentum and lend the poem an oneiric and ornamental quality, exemplifying what Hans Dieter Schäfer has called a "Rokoko-Surrealismus" in postwar German poetry with Krolow in mind.

In "Terzinen vom früheren Einverständnis mit aller Welt" (1950; I, 21–22), an epigram by Apollinaire, "Erinnerungen sind Jagdhörner / Deren Ton im Wind vergeht," sets a new course, like a rudder in Krolow's work, marking his shift in orientation away from *Naturlyrik* and toward French modernism in the surrealist vein. It was a turn that he had already prepared for in his years as a student of Romance languages during the Nazi period and had continued first in a series of works in translation from French. Visits to Paris also began at this time. Klaus Jeziorkowski rightly sees in Apollinaire, and in this epigram, for Krolow an "Angelpunkt für die Erfahrung von Moderne generell" (223).[3] However, aside from citing Apollinaire, the poem looks only backward at Krolow's origins in the "magic" of nature: "Die schöne Stille der Gewächse / — Zerbrechlich wie die Fabel Welt — / Umschlang ich sanft im Arm der Echse." The epigram consigns that closed period, like a fleeting memory, to the past. Jeziorkowski links the poem, through its form of terza rima, to the eschatology of Dante's *Divine Comedy* and to Hofmannsthal's *Terzinen über Vergänglichkeit* (1894). To be sure, Krolow's poem alludes to *Terzinen* but it probably owes more to Hofmannsthal's Chandos letter (*Ein Brief,* 1902). The letter serves as a model for his definitive break in *Weltanschauung,* looking back, across a breach of sensibility, to a lost world of seemingly harmonious but also illusory empathy and identification with nature and myth: "Erheiterte der Geist sich still, / Mit allen Wesen einverständig, / Zypressenfeuern, Asphodill. // Mit allen Wesen einverständig, / Beharrlich, ohne Ungeduld, / Und wie das Flötenholz lebendig." Jeziorkowski's interpretation, though not incorrect, imposes onto the poem the overarching schemas of the expulsion from Eden, admittedly secularized "als Parabel vom verlorenen Paradies und der verlorenen Unschuld eines seligen, hingegebenen Zustands" (225), though it is impossible to imagine that Krolow's period of imagined aesthetic insularity or *inner emigration* between 1940 and 1945 would actually fit such a description as paradisal time of innocence. Here, by enlarging the historical context into myth and overstating the terms given by the poem, the interpreter falls into the trap set by his own interpretive framework.

Krolow's use of nature was never a so wholly unified fiction as Jeziorkowski might assume in his overly tidy interpretation, and Krolow's nature poetry had a political dimension, which gets lost in the parable. The poem is also, necessarily, "vom früheren Einverständnis" in his political stance, to whatever degree of participation, in the Third Reich. After the dissonances and dissimulations of his early work, and the attempts to confront the war in his existential poetry after the war, now this poem announces: "Kein Kartenspiel der Schwermut mehr: —," borrowing Gottfried Benn's existential full colon and dashes to separate a concluding utterance for the new period: "Wie Süßigkeit, die frei von Schuld // Verschwendet sich im Ungefähr." Almost pointedly, Jeziorkowski does not comment at all on these final lines, which — if the rest of the poem is so decidedly about a break from the past — must have resounded in the immediate postwar period with topical immediacy ("frei von Schuld") to announce or anticipate a poetry of exquisite and luxuriant sensuality in the present that circumscribes certain questions without trying to address them directly.[4] The ending that trails off here announces that the historical dimension has entered the poem as an ellipsis that does not become, as it does in Paul Celan's poems, a reduction of language into compacted, historically sedimented, and eloquent silence. Rather that ellipsis generates more and more language ("Verschwendet sich") as a dialectic of ornate approximation and avoidance ("im Ungefähr"), not far from the phenomenon Krolow dubs, in his vignette on the semiotics of Parisian streets, "vitale Girlanden. . . . eine Welt ohne Tiefe, wohl aber der spontanen Fläche" (*Minuten-Aufzeichnungen*, 38–40).[5]

Before Krolow settled into the form of the short poem of faceted surface, brilliant or bristling, that has become his signature, he tried his hand at long poems, probably under the influence of St. John Perse and Archibald MacLeish, mainly in the early 1950s.[6] That form allows a flowing verbality that is less decorative of that historical ellipsis than directly descriptive; the poem "Heute" (I, 41–45) seems, in this light, a programmatic statement in four sections of this new *inner emigration* into the immediate present of mysticized or magical sensuality, but at the same time, a reflection on that aesthetic:

> Unausdenkbar: ein Tag wie ein Leib, der aus Gras,
> Aus duftendem Grase gehöhlt ist im heißen August,
> Der mit leuchtender Anmut — ein Scherben aus
>   rötlichem Glas —
> Die Luft spannt und lockert, die sich zu rühren gewußt
>
> Über der Welt der Minute, den sanften und langsamen
>   Gesten
> Eines Manns, einer Frau, die ihre Herzen erpreßten. (I)

Immediate contact with nature defies conception or analysis ("unausdenkbar"). The day does not belong to history but to sensory impressions. The emptying of historical content creates a hollowness ("gehöhlt"), a space for the senses to dilate "mit leuchtender Anmut."[7] Yet since the poem articulates this position, the senses are not immediate but mediated by a fiction of autonomy: "Und ich leb in der Mitte der schönen Vernunft, bei Gefühlen, / Die in des Schweigens abstraktem Gestein die Stirne mir kühlen." The solipsistic universe of the perceiver is rational and feelings do not erupt directly into words; rather, feelings are set by consciousness into images that only appear concrete and immediate or unmediated, but as artifice, those images in fact cover over or take the place of an unsettling silence ("des Schweigens abstraktem Gestein").[8] Abstraction is no longer a stylistic means to communicate visceral anguish through forceful disjunctions that implicate the epoch but a means of simulation and dissimulation that conceal an epoch.[9] The poetological implications of the poem belie its opening word *unausdenkbar,* which seems more like a cue for later criticism.

That function also brings random objects, which again harkens back to Hofmannsthal's Chandos letter, into new phenomenological immanence as monuments of pure presentness:

> An die Wand gelehnt einen Augenblick lang, an das Jetzt, wie
> ein Fahrrad, die Leiter des Tünchers oder gebündeltes Stroh!
> Ganz einfach ein Gegenstand ohne Zeit, ohne Angst, und allein
> Mit der Lepra des Steins in der Mauer, ihrem Aussatz, und so
> Auf das Vergessen zu hoffen, auf das Ertrinken im Heute
> Der leblosen Fremde, den Fliegenschwärmen zur Beute!
>
> Heute und Jetzt. [. . .]   (I)

Krolow delineates landscapes that glisten in luminous presence but also throw a shadow:

> Ahn ich, was möglich ist, was mich erhellt und beschattet:
> Reine Stimmen und Augäpfel, rascher Genuß
> Eines zarten Gesichts, schöner Taube aus Hoffnung und
>   Bangen,
> Da schon der Himmel erdrosselt in Bäumen gehangen. (II)

The adjectives *rein, rasch, zart,* and *schön* give the coordinates of Krolow's aesthetics of immediate but refined, delicate sensation captured in breathtaking tableaus, behind or beside which looms, at the opposite pole of experience, equally breathtaking violence. Likewise, the inverse of that refinement of sensation, that epidermal excitement, is a fear that gets under the skin ("Hinter der Haut [. . .] beginnt das Entsetzen").[10] In this particular "Landschaft der Fremde," that exquisite sensibility in discriminating sensations ("die Waage der Zärtlichkeiten") is a response, as in his earlier poem "In der Fremde," to an anxiety that rests like a "Dolch im Genicke." Fear registers, like a psychic seismograph, the shock of historical experience that sits deep in the individual psychology and sensorium.

The poem even questions its own beginning and the implicit escapism of that aesthetics "Unschuld des Lichts: zählt das wirklich?" (III). In describing the landscape, the poem also adumbrates the concealed absence at its core "Dahinter das Loch in der Luft, die Leere" (III) of unpresented history that nonetheless indicts. At times, though, haunting images float into the poem out of the past with uncanny specificity:

Nun nur ein totes Gehöft noch, bespieener Garten
Ohne Feierlichkeit und gut für Verbannte und für
Erschießungskommandos, die ihre Opfer erwarten.
Schakale umstreichen die offene Abtrittstür,
Heulen und stoßen die Schnauzen ins flache Gewimmel
Horniger Vipern an einer Erde aus Schimmel.
Das alles ist gültig noch hinter geschlossenen Lidern
Und zählt wie die zarte Flora der Herzen, . . .
[. . .]
Wie ein Vorhang gepanzerter Luft umfließen mich Schatten,
Die mit zeitlicher Last mich gefoltert hatten. (III)

Knowledge of recent history (*Verbannte, Erschießungskommandos*) tortures the speaker; historical content, memory of the past, is a burden that weighs on the present and closes one off like an existential iron curtain from the free play of the senses.[11] The poem works through the difficulty of anamnesis in a dialectical struggle between sensuality and memory, present and past, but does so in order to disburden the present, to recover amnesia! In the final section, the pulse of life ("Schöner und knisternder Starkstrom der Herzen im heißen / Elektrischen Abend") grows slowly and galvanizes the senses, "und dringt / Langsam als Fieber ins Fleisch uns." That intensity is purchased with the coin of forgetting: "Vergessen / Ist nun die zerstoßene Stirn und die Unordnung, die uns besessen." Despite its formal features as an elegy, described by Weissenberger, "Heute" is an odd elegy that does not mourn human loss but celebrates the loss of memory for the sake of art.

That distance from the past releases new energies, new imagery, and opens a distance into the future: "oben phantastisch / Der Himmel ein eiliger Fisch ist aus Silber, der flach / Ins Unendliche schwimmt, in die Wonnen der Weite." Once rid of the past, the speaker exults in a frenzy of self-creation outside of history in a transcendental present: "Im Kohlenfeuer der Blicke, undeutlich und selig, erfinde / Das Jetzt ich: den Vogel, der eines ward mit dem Winde." The present is invention or artifice.[12] In the overcoming of historical trauma, without critical examination, the passage recalls the rhapsodies of Gottfried Benn in his Rönne stories, though Krolow carefully distances himself from Benn in a review of his influential lecture "Probleme der Lyrik" (1951).[13]

The proximity of beauty and violence in Krolow's work in the 1950s appears prominently in his poem "Der Täter" (I, 47), which describes some sort of execution. The poem sustains itself through the tension between clear metaphor and cryptic brutality:

> Der Morgen, die traurige Taube, schmilzt
> Mir langsam im Aug und verdirbt
> Mit blauem Gefieder. In Lüften aus Kork
> Steht schwach meine Stimme und stirbt.
>
> Die Worte zersprangen mir trocken im Hals,
> Wie raschelndes Laub, ohne Ton.
> Hinterm Schrei, der wie brüchige Münze klirrt,
> Schwillt die Traube der Stille schon
>
> Und wächst mir durch die erbitterte Hand,
> Die das Holz des Messergriffs faßt,
> Die unter die fremde Achsel greift,
> Wie in Wasser, voll zorniger Hast.
>
> Das Schweigen, das leicht nach dem Flintenschuß
> Durch die Dornengebüsche bricht:
> Die Auferstehung aus Rosen und Wind
> Reicht jäh ans verfärbte Gesicht.

This poem narrates a central action, but the atmosphere of the moment is not evoked through description that leads into the action as in a novel; the atmosphere is given indirectly in abstracting metaphors such as *Morgen, die traurige Taube,* and *Lüften aus Kork,* and similes that diverge or distract from that central action.[14] The protagonist loses his voice and outward presence, and also as a consciousness, recedes in estrangement from the action performed by his hand while simultaneously "die Traube der Stille" swells outside in nature, behind the action carried out in "zorniger Hast." That action takes place between the third and fourth strophes, involving a knife and a gunshot. Its victim, present as "die fremde Achsel," is entirely estranged and objectified by the metonym. Once over, raw silence breaks out, no longer poeticized as "die Traube der Stille." "Schweigen" reflects consciousness and language that is withheld. The one who remains silent, or performs that "Schweigen," also knows what happened. In the last lines, the resurrection seems, however, to belong to the perceiving protagonist, who sees beauty in nature ("Rosen und Wind") in sharp juxtaposition to the discolored face of the victim.[15] In short, Krolow's poem dramatizes Bertolt Brecht's famous comment on nature poetry in his poem "An die Nachgeborenen": "Was sind das für Zeiten, wo / Ein Gespräch über Bäume fast ein Verbrechen ist / Weil es ein Schweigen über so viele Untaten einschließt!" (723). Here the exact nature of the *Untat* remains uncertain, but the action is included in the poem as *Untat* and as *Schweigen,* against both of which the poetic figures of the poem create referential dissonance, establishing a distance between the language and the content, and a strong, strange tension. The poem "Männer" (I, 48–50) puts that matter more simply: "Hinter der lyrischen Landschaft der Jäger und Hirten / Lauert der Waffen Gestrüpp" (I, 48).

In Krolow's intricate dialogue with historical experience in "Heute," he overcomes deep fears through a sort of ecstasy that remains intellectual invention, the construction of an expanded temporal present, an artifice of anonymous self without past, that is reinforced by his practice of montage; that practice links his poetry to models outside of Germany, to what one could call an international, impersonal otherhood of poets, as a means of depersonalization, but which also skirts the boundaries of inspiration, influence, and plagiarism.[16] In effect, Krolow realizes in his poetry Rimbaud's dictum "Je suis un Autre," though, to be sure, in a different, very specific context that is both poetological and historical. In "Die Entdeckung der Güte" (I, 45–46), Krolow again cites Apollinaire in an epigram and tries to maintain the expansive euphoria of the senses that he arrived at in "Heute," here in the second stanza:

> Hör ich wie Rascheln von wachsendem Weizen die Stimme,
> Brennende Lunte des Glücks, lebendig und zart
> Zwischen unbezähmbaren Steinen, den Laut, drin ich
>   schwimme
> Wie in alten Gewässern, mit flüssigem Lichte gepaart,
> Den Mund, der mich lange schon meint, der aus melodischer
>   Kehle
> Umarmung und Hoffnungen singt, denen ich ganz mich
>   befehle.

But that register of uplifting sensual lyricism cannot be maintained through calculated artifice. The contradiction appears in the last line above, where the speaker commands himself "ganz" to sing of embraces and hopes, but that command removes the spontaneity and authenticity of the song. The last word of the poem, *Güte,* coincides with the title and the motto with the contrary intellectual effect of a scientific proof. As Rümmler notes: "Doch fehlen der Krolowschen Mischung letzten Endes die Apollinaireschen Ingredienzen Optimismus und Vitalität. Krolow ist weniger vital, sein Daseinsgefühl schwankender, sein Blick skeptischer, bei ihm herrscht latent immer die Resignation; seine 'Entdeckung der Güte' ist mehr nachvollzogen, mehr erlitten als in aktiver Weise mitvollzogen" (173). Rümmler has put his finger on a central aspect of Krolow's sensibility that renders his long poetic line, almost by nature, into an ultimately ill-suited medium since more rhythmic and less analytical, more musical and less starkly visual, though the long line does remain important for Krolow at this juncture as a means of assimilating French and American influences and in developing his concept of the open poem.

After his programmatic retreat into the immediate present, detached from the past, without memory, Krolow is able to return to history, in a particular sense as the limited present without the past, a position that largely coincides with West German culture in the fifties. For the first time, a date appears in a title, which marks for his work a new beginning or Zero Hour of sorts. In "Ode 1950" (I, 51–52), Krolow alternates the elegiac, dactylic long line with stanzas of short lines to emphasize the dialectic that was, in "Heute" for instance, already present:

Nicht mehr das traurige Stichwort: Bequeme Parabel
Ist die Rede vom Nichts wie von herbstlichem Laub, das
                        zersetzt
Sich zu brüchigem Rost. Die unbarmherzige Vokabel
Schreckt nicht mehr als der Fisch des Tobias zuletzt,
Wenn sie verbraucht ist im Munde, die als gespenstische Mode
Wie ein Feuer im Heu war und noch einmal Geist wird als Ode.

Aber was bleibt zu tun
Vor der trägen Gewalt
Des Daseins als auszuruhn,
listig und mannigfalt:
Flüchten mit leichten Schuhn
In die Fabelgestalt
Oder auf äschernen Flüssen
Langsam treiben, von Küssen
Umarmenden Windes benommen
Der aus der Höhe gekommen.

Formel der Früchte: wer nennt sie? Auf tönenden Tischen
Der Tage gebreitet, in silbernen Schalen der Nacht!
Sinnlich und nah und zu greifen. Ich suche mit Worten
                                    inzwischen
Die Flüchtigen aufzuhalten: mit einer Algebra, zart erdacht
Aus atmenden Silben, einem Bündel Gedanken, die baden
Im steigenden Halbmond wie das Geflecht der Plejaden.

> Aber mit diesen
> Namen aus Zauber
> Ist nichts erwiesen:
> Der gurrende Tauber,
> Die süßen Geräusche
> — Erhört wie bewußtlos —
> Vergehen. Ich täusche
> Sie vor als ein Sinn bloß
> In Worten, in Zeichen,
> Die keinen erreichen.

Also wieder ein Abgrund?—Kein Abgrund: Versuchung schon eher
Und ein zärtlicher Hinterhalt, dem man erliegt,
Poetische Falle, gestellt, wenn im Mittag der Mäher
Oder im Abend aus Schilf es melodisch sich biegt,
Das Bewußtsein, die Fähigkeit, zuversichtlich und heiter
Gewähren zu lassen, den Geist aus den Geistern zu ziehn
Und die Zeit zu erkennen, die vorbeijagt — phantastischer
                                    Reiter
Durchs Gewölk der Geschichte, in dem die Verhängnisse fliehn.
Ich lasse die summenden Drähte, das klingende Gitter
Der Worte zurück auf dem Grunde des Seins. Er ist leuchtend
und bitter.

Krolow distances himself at the outset from the existential philosophy that had also, along with *Naturlyrik,* played an important part in his formation as a poet, yet seems to him now "gespenstische Mode."[17] In renouncing that source, that depth of reflection, the second strophe ponders the options and foreshadows his later developments "listig und mannigfalt," suggesting again nature magic ("Fabelgestalt") or rhapsodic sensuality ("von Küssen . . . benommen"), both of which now belong to the repertoire and will still recur in his work. Krolow sees the danger, as Knörrich puts it, of falling into "eine Art modischer Konfektionismus" (49). The third strophe marks his shift, under the influence of Jorge Guillén, to a mathematics of the senses that structures perception of objects in the present and lends them a trans-temporal monumentality. That algebra constitutes a "New Objectivity" of sorts after the related obscurities of existential philosophy and nature magic but shares the same shortcoming as simply another kind of magic with a new formula.

Knörrich cites the fourth strophe, "Aber mit diesen / Namen aus Zauber / ist nichts erwiesen," in a long rumination on the nonreferential character of poetic language in modernism and ascribes to Krolow an incipient skepticism, but Knörrich cites the stanza out of the context of the poem, as is so often the case with Krolow criticism. Krolow is not skeptical about language, but consciously affirms the nonreferential character and the poetological assumptions of aesthetic modernism during the previous century, taking Baudelaire as a starting point, like Hugo Friedrich does, while he remains conscious of art's relation to history. The nonreferential character of art is not an exploration and intensification of the medium as it was earlier but has now become a self-conscious instrument of illusion ("Ich täusche / Sie vor als ein Sinn bloß / In Worten, in Zeichen, Die keinen errei-chen."), de-hermeticized, or voided of historical and philosophical content, without the semantic abyss of that tradition from Mallarmé to Celan.[18] The poem has become a "poetic trap," adopting the appearances of that or other traditions while maintaining a detached, conscious distance from the existential urgency of original poetry.

Krolow develops here an aesthetics of clinical, diagnostic detachment toward the genre in which he works, which allows him to observe, with utmost attention and sensitivity, its changes in mood and developments in form: "Das Bewußtsein, die Fähigkeit, zuversichtlich und heiter / Gewähren zu lassen, den Geist aus den Geistern zu ziehn / Und die Zeit zu erkennen, die vorbeijagt." His extensive criticism reinforces this aspect of his poetry, since his poetry is also partly commentary through conscious stylized imitation of dominant impulses in the genre at a particular historical moment. Krolow, despite or because of his ahistorical aesthetics, is acutely aware of historical context as his criticism demonstrates. The magic of nature poetry, with its historical and existential depths, has become a style of felicitous derivation, a means of riding the currents of historical development without entering into their substance: "phantastischer Reiter / Durchs Gewölk der Geschichte, in dem die Verhängnisse fliehn." In this way, Krolow remains contemporary with each generation of poetic development in the postwar period. Krolow's poetry no longer contains

"Verhängnisse," which would determine his development. Instead, Krolow can react and respond in his poetry to other poetry and to the times. The distinction here to Paul Celan is staggering, whose "Sprachgitter" is anticipated by this poem's final lines: "Ich lasse die summenden Drähte, das klingende Gitter / Der Worte zurück auf dem Grunde des Seins. Er ist leuchtend / und bitter." Knörrich cites these lines as "programmatisch" without further explanation. The program, however, is in the previous lines! The "phantastischer Reiter" leaves behind what Hugo Friedrich calls the *dunkle Lyrik* of modernist abstraction with its binding ontological implications. It makes a clean distinction between the "Ich" and the "Grunde des Seins. *Er* ist leuchtend und bitter" (author's emphasis); as opposed to that ground of being, that binding ontology, the speaker remains apart, "zuversichtlich und heiter."[19]

In "Huldigung an die Vernunft" (I, 58), the Apollonian reason of the poet mediates, outside of history, between metaphysical anguish and sensual ecstasy, translating those uncontrolled feelings into "die leuchtende Dauer. // Schmuckloses Bildnis, . . . / Ohne Erinnerung, doch mit genauem Gesicht, / Lächelnd und sachlich vor der beweglichen Öde, / dessen was war." The long cycle "Gedichte von der Liebe in unserer Zeit" (I, 53–56) maintains the framework of the dehistorical present ("Die Zeit hier / ist längst schon phantastisch"),[20] but continues the dialectical working through of that position in the elegiac terms of an intimate relationship that once filled the moment "porös und aus Küssen gemacht," and that foreshortened historical time into sensual immediacy: "Jedesmal ohne Gedächtnis! Berührung und Nähe," but that euphoria could also reverse into "die Wahrheit, die Wirklichkeit . . . des Nichts hinterm Rausche." The two poles allow an amplitude of melancholic feeling between the speaker and the other, but the intimacy of that dialectic now elides the question of historical content outside of the circle of that relationship: history or "die Zeit" is "nur Attrappe noch . . . ein anderes schönes Bild, schnell projizierbar / An die Wand des Bewußtseins." What remains is intimate memory: "der geistige Kuß . . . entrückt wie ein Traum" (56).

In the hymn "Erde" (I, 63–67), the earth is apostrophized and conjured in long, flowing lines as the realm "Ohne Gedächtnis," and in the last section, that flow is arrested by a jarring shift in perspective to the substance of history or the meaning of human activity in the past: "Bewältigt ward nie das Geheimnis, was eigentlich war unter Menschen . . ." where again the ellipsis marks the absence of historical reflection that the poem circumscribes. Without this remark, the evocation of earth would take on a mythic, chthonic hue as in St. John Perse, but Krolow keeps the poem set in relation to history at a safe distance. Unlike Benn's absolute poem, Krolow's poetry remains open to historical reflection on the past which it also deconstructs and reduces into ahistorical montage or to the limited historical present. The poem "Koreanische Elegie" is immediately topical and addresses the Korean War, even making a more or less direct reference to the thirty-eighth parallel that separates North and South Korea: "Eine gerade Linie ging einst durch alle Gesichter [. . .] diese riesige Lunte, die glimmt," which links that flash point in world politics in the early 1950s to the map of divided Germany. The poem evokes both countries, or all countries, as a "Hypothetische Heimat!" Against that notion of *Heimat,* which is already problematic, is set the vague menace of world politics that could disturb such metaphysical domesticity. Though monitory, the poem retains, on a broader geopolitical plane, a conventionally sentimental notion of *Heimat* and of war without any analysis. The poem is flat and rather mechanically invokes "die toten Soldaten" now as guarantor of correct earnestness. Though relatively well known in his oeuvre, the poem demonstrates the difficulty Krolow has, despite his versatility, in approaching historical material, even in the limited present, in any meaningful way.[21]

Despite the breach with the past in "Terzinen," but in accordance with the aesthetics of "Heute," nature is not at all just cast off, but rather simply appears under different auspices, in less density, no longer as a bulwark against the world beyond or as a mooring in physical reality outside of history, though that still persists as in "Weide" (I, 11). In the poem "Warmer Herbst" (I, 15), nature begins to dematerialize into ciphers as in the line "Im zarten Wind ist aufgehängt / Die Vogelschwinge," to become "Zeichen der Welt" ("Spätherbst" [I, 38]), and as such, as signs to enter into new concretions and constellations:

> Die Luftorange bebend
> Im Wasser steht,
> [. . .]
> Die süße Frucht aus Stille
> und grauem Wind,
> Die mir in der Pupille
> Zu Licht gerinnt.
> ("Notturno am Fluß" [I, 31–32])

The images become tactile and light floods into Krolow's poetry: "Die Frühe hat mit gelbem Rahm / Die Bettstatt mir gezinkt. / . . . / Indes die Nacht versinkt" ("Morgenlied" [I, 29–30]). His duly famous poem "Verlassene Küste" of 1951 (I, 26–27) demonstrates his new use of metaphoric shorthand to amalgamate a jaunty corporeality with a breezy lightness of metrical touch to create images of jolting novelty:

> *Wenn man es recht besieht,*
> *so ist überall Schiffbruch.*
> *Petronius*
>
> Segelschiffe und Gelächter,
> Das wie Gold im Barte steht,
> Sind vergangen wie ein schlechter
> Atem, der vom Munde weht,
>
> Wie ein Schatten auf der Mauer,
> Der den Kalk zu Staub zerfrißt.
> Unauflöslich bleibt die Trauer,
> Die aus schwarzem Honig ist,
>
> Duftend in das Licht gehangen,
> Feucht wie frischer Vogelkot
> Und den heißen Ziegelwangen
> Auferlegt als leichter Tod.
>
> Kartenschlagende Matrosen
> Sind in ihrem Fleisch allein.
> Tabak rieselt durch die losen
> Augenlider in sie ein.
>
> Ihre Messer, die sie warfen
> Nach dem blauen Vorhang Nacht,
> Wurden schartig in dem scharfen
> Wind der Ewigkeit, der wacht.

Here, an epigram calls to mind the sociohistorical context ("überall Schiffbruch") and also creates an intellectual detachment for analysis of the unlikely images. The opening line, a phrase of metonymic abbreviation, works memorably and has the abruptness of Melville's "Call me Ishmael," but instead of leading into a narrative, calls up instantly a whole field of associations to rugged but hardy life at sea.[22]

The steady assonance of the line gives it an implacable rightness that overrides the apparent lack of expository sense and forces a cognitive leap to metaphoric association. The dangling relative clause in line two adds "Gold im Barte" that calls to mind pirates, treasure, gambling on deck, reflected sunlight on doubloons and in drops of water in beards, and the palpable sound of ringing, clinking laughter, which takes on weight, color, brightness, and form. That heartiness is, however, "faded" and evaporates in a series of compelling similes, both visual and olfactory; the expired laughter, light, and movement recoils into a center of felt emptiness, of mourning that becomes concrete through equally compelling and sensory similes. Though the centerpiece of this poem, the notion of mourning has here, unlike the "black milk" of Celan's "Todesfuge," little historical resonance and is associated with "black honey," and excrement or guano ("frischer Vogelkot") as a subtle form of death ("leichter Tod"), set against the jaunty carmine of the sailors' cheeks ("heißen Ziegelwangen"). The sailors in their card game sit in monumental self-centeredness in the pure present, isolated unto themselves "in ihrem Fleisch allein." In a variation on Rilke's "Panther," where the "Vorhang der Pupille" lifts to allow in an image that penetrates into the core of that animal's being ("Und hört im Herzen auf zu sein"), the sailors drift along into sudden, arresting awareness, when the laughter subsides, of their insignificance and transitoriness, like the wafting tobacco smoke: caught on deck between the passing of time in card playing and the sense of an awesome timelessness, the sailors throw their knives in an irrational act of frustration and pointless vengeance, "nach dem blauen Vorhang Nacht," in piercing ("schartig . . . scharfen") recognition of their own mortality. The poem gains a depth of philosophical reflection without historical definition. His "Matrosen-Ballade" (I, 46) and "Männer" (I, 48) use the same images of manly immediacy in the present.

In *Zeichen der Welt,* Krolow dramatically opens up the space, already visible in earlier poems, between the existential and aesthetic poles of his sensibility and plays the one against the other: "Mit Süße verdrängen / Läßt sich das Nichts. / Die Kirschen hängen / Sanften Gewichts" ("Kirschenzeit" [I, 60]). Within that space, one might say he evasively explores the matter of history in the poem, forming it as a specific absence or refracting it through metaphors that are brilliant and blinding, or annulling it in the artifice of montage. In all these poetic maneuvers is displayed Krolow's characteristic "zarter Widersinn" ("Sommermorgen" [I, 61]) a calculated contrariness of means and substance that emerges in delicate dissonances and rebarbative refinements of language that are both exquisite and exasperating. Like the hanging cherries in the above poem, dangling from a philosophical concept ("das Nichts") and the incarnation of its repression into sensual fullness ("Süße"), the poem illuminates a situation, a scene, a landscape, or an object and obscures it at the same time; each motif appears, as Rudolf Hartung has written, "ebenso sehr in seinem Wesen erfaßt wie diesem entfremdet" (107). As Hugo Friedrich notes of Krolow's landscapes, but which applies as well to all his work, the artful duplicities or double-edged ironies "verweigern das Bequeme" (79).

Wind und Zeit (1954)

The first poem in the volume, "Worte" [I, 75], draws the consequence of Krolow's developments in *Die Zeichen der Welt* and constitutes a poetics for his next volumes in the 1950s:

> Einfalt erfundener Worte
> Die man hinter Türen spricht,
> Aus Fenstern und gegen die Mauern,
> Gekalkt mit geduldigem Licht.
>
> Wirklichkeit von Vokabeln,
> Von zwei Silben oder von drein:
> Aus den Rätseln des Himmels geschnitten,
> Aus einer Ader im Stein.
>
> Entzifferung fremder Gesichter
> Mit Blitzen unter der Haut,
> Mit Bärten, in denen der Wind steht,
> Durch einen geflüsterten Laut.
>
> Aber die Namen bleiben
> Im Ohre nur ein Gesumm
> Wie von Zikaden und Bienen,
> Kehren ins Schweigen um.
>
> Vokale — geringe Insekten,
> Unsichtbar über die Luft,
> Fallen als Asche nieder,
> Bleiben als Quittenduft. (I, 75)

Krolow had amply prepared this development by separating, yet invoking, the existential depths of mourning from the brilliant metaphoric fireworks of the poem as in the soulful "Niemand wird helfen" (57), where "Der nackte Text nur besteht, / Nachlesbar in der Stille." Now that naked text no longer registers emotional destitution or the agonies of repressed anguish but has arrived at a new and disarming, though artificial, innocence: "Einfalt erfundener Worte," composed almost anonymously and from an impersonal distance ("hinter Türen") is in sharp contradistinction to, or even negation of, the closeness of perspective in nature poetry as well as to the broodingly dark emotionalism of existentialist verse. Otto Knörrich finds in this poem "eine Wende, die in der modernen deutschen Lyrik nach 1945 von einschneidendster Bedeutung wurde. . . . Kurz gesagt, zunehmende Entzauberung, Ernüchterung, Abkühlung, ja Unterkühlung, 'Entpoetisierung' der Sageweise, damit verbundenen Verkürzung, Reduktion, Verzicht auf poetische Aufwendigkeiten, . . . den Lyrismus und seine Reizwirkungen" (52–53). In his history of German poetry in this period, Knörrich necessarily has to adopt a foreshortened perspective on the individual writer's work. As a result, his lavish description here of this point, in order to embellish the poem's significance for the epoch, overshoots the mark in terms of Krolow's own development. The poem should not be confused with Krolow's later work that Knörrich anticipates.

The poem appears to cut itself off from external reality as a separate "Wirklichkeit von Vokabeln." Yet, contrary to Knörrich's view, a strong link still remains to Krolow's earlier work in the tradition of *Naturlyrik*. Now the depths of mystery and magic have simply migrated from objects in nature into the enigmas of objects in nature, equally impenetrable to analysis, at least in principle, as a sort of free-floating, *plein air* hermeticism. The mystery is still there, but as enigma, it is now cerebral, starkly intellectual. Language has supplanted nature as a separate ontology of inscrutable depths. Krolow has evolved in his work from the *Silbermund* in the poem "Pappel-laub" to the *Silbenmund* of "Worte." His poetic universe is now different but not dissimilar.[23] His poetry has attained a secure distance between its content and its means, between the signifiers (*die Namen*) and the signified. In so doing, Krolow has brought German *Naturlyrik* fully into alignment with the main course of European modernism as defined by Hugo Friedrich in *Die Struktur der modernen Lyrik*. Instead of the fiction of direct representation, Krolow inserts the self-conscious fiction of indirect re-presentation. In other words, as poetological text, the poem reflects on its status as artifact. The signified is, however, still drawn from nature and refracted through consciousness by the mediation of language; nature is now denatured, a second nature of verbal autonomy and lexical construction, divorced from the world it abstractly represents as a montage ("geschnitten"). The world of denatured language, of textuality, as previously with the world of nature, remains a mystery that was once scenic but now cerebral, requiring deciphering. Against the obscure realm of nonlanguage (*Schweigen*), the words, the particles and sounds once invoked, or put into voice (*Vokale*), simulate events in nature: "ein Gesumm, / Wie von Zikaden und Bienen"; "*als* Asche"; "*als* Quittenduft" (author's emphasis). By a new poetological route, in sharp contradistinction to earlier practice, the poem concludes with a precise sensory impression of language as nature, the latter disembodied and invisible ("unsichtbar"), but as presence within the former at the same time sensuous, palpable, and enduring.

The poem "Wind" (I, 94) thus embodies that new sensuous lightness of material insubstantiality. The object of the poem is invisible and immaterial, without weight or shape, flowing and ephemeral, taking its contours from outside: "Wind, Wind, der auf der Wange / Und überm Herzen steht, / Im Laub als grüne Schlange / Aus fremder Luft vergeht!" Wind defines itself entirely in the linguistic distinction to "Luft," which brings to mind the sensuous difference between unfelt air when still standing and the bodily feel of air in movement. Krolow aims at a cerebral and epidermal refinement of the senses through intellect and vice versa, and tries to capture tactile moments in language as "Ein fliegendes Entzücken / Des Nichts." That latter term re-presents the somber existential nothingness of his earlier poems as an almost ornamental backdrop, against which sensory moments gain their contours: "Wind, Wind, der flüchtge Spuren / Auf Herz und Wange schreibt, / Vergängliche Figuren, / Dem Schweigen einverleibt." Fully in the later sense of deconstructionist thinking, language and nature are fleeting rhetorical figures of textuality, detached from the external reality they gesture toward and always on the verge of disappearance back into the abyss of nonlanguage, into nothingness, into silence. The poem, which has the rhythm of a children's rhyme or even a limerick, winds around its topic in neatly rhymed lines as an ekphrasis of an absence, an "Ungewicht," or in the following poem, "Strand" (I, 95), where the bodies in the sand, not the one nor the other, appear as "Zarte Figuren, sich spiegelnd in Lüften," as pure disembodied contour, or "Im Rückspiegel" (I, 98), where "Dein leichtes Profil / Wird zur Wolke."[24] Krolow describes a sensuous nimbus that momentarily flashes into consciousness around objects that flee, that cannot be grasped physically or intellectually, but only momentarily perceived.

That acute sense of transience automatically bears an elegiac note, which Krolow exploits in the second section of *Wind und Zeit* in long poems that harken back to his work in *Die Zeichen der Welt,* such as in his "Elegien auf den Tod eines jungen Dichters" (I, 84–88), where at the end, "schwarzer Wind spitzt seinen Mund zur Klage" (88), or in the cycle "Gedichte gegen den Tod" (I, 89–93), where, in a contrary movement, "alles schnell vergessen ist und leichte Wolke wird" (91) and the speaker senses "Freude in mir wie Wind, / Der vor dem Tod keine Furcht hat" (92). That elegiac timbre emerges with greater concentration in "Schatten in der Luft" (I, 109) and with great poignancy in "Gedicht für J. S." (I, 76), where the sadness behind the initials is private, not declamatory, and almost impersonal. Unlike what one might expect, this love poem does not set a monument to a lover but consigns a lover to the past. From inside a departing train, the speaker looks out at his lover; the window marks his aesthetic distance from the scene, and from her: "Auf dem Dezember-Bahnsteig in der ersten Stunde nach Mitternacht / Dein Bild in die Kälte geschnitten." The next two strophes begin each with "Ich erfinde dich noch einmal." The crowds and noise have been blocked out of the image. He is first aware only of her: visually in stanza one, and then emotionally in stanza two, yet an interior bond ("Zärtlichkeit," "Verlangen nach Glück," "Zuneigung") are only attributed to her, and do not seem to figure here as shared feelings; and then he considers his own distanced aesthetic conception of the scene, of her, perhaps of their relationship. As he waves from the lowered window, he also pictures himself in that action, separated from the feelings that his action should signal: "Ich erfinde dich noch einmal: geschaffen nun, / Um mit mir zu gehen, einem anderen: / Mann im hochgeschlagenen Mantelkragen, / Der das Fenster im Fernzug-Abteil herunterläßt und winkt." The poem turns on these lines as he reinvents her once again: either she is different in order to accompany him, or she accompanies him, who would have to be different. The scene becomes a self-consciously anonymous participation in familiar sentiment and empty convention as if on a stage. As the train pulls out of the station, the speaker also withdraws emotionally:

Du bleibst zurück, auf Fluten grauen Windes treibend,
Zurück mit Umarmung und Kuß und dem Geruch deiner Haut.
Das schwarze und weiße Schachbrett der Schneenacht
Liegt über deinem Gesicht; und ich weiß,
Daß nichts an dir für mich bestimmt ist.

The currents of wind that engulf them both, she standing on the platform, he in the window, as the train leaves, reflect the passing of time over them. In his feeling of isolation and analytical anonymity, he takes leave of his physical senses, his sensual memories of her, and instead, effaces ("Liegt über deinem Gesicht") his lingering intimacy with her with a stark metaphor of calculation and opposition ("Das schwarze und weiße Schachbrett") as the train disappears into the snowy night. The poem imposes a seemingly neutral geometry onto the fluid intimacy of their relationship that has now ended and concludes with a moment of analytical recognition that links the two of them by their incompatibility ("nichts an dir für mich"), presented as an objective fact, a configuration on the chess board that forces such conclusions. In the next poems, that geometry will no longer be imposed on a dramatic situation; it will reside within objects.

After the explorations of melancholy that culminate in the analytical resignation of "Gedicht für J. S.," the middle section of *Wind und Zeit* picks up the impulse from section one "mit wachsendem Entzükken / An die leichte Luft gelehnt! . . . Metamorphosen / Wurden Beute süßer Dauer" ("Aufschwung," I, 102–3).[25] The sense of time narrows to discrete momentary sensation in "Augapfelfarbe / Der Morgen-Minute" ("Zum Mittag hin"; I, 105) and the sense of mathematical exactitude, of geometrical calculation, emerges fully in "Drei Orangen, zwei Zitronen" (I, 107):

Drei Orangen, zwei Zitronen: —
Bald nicht mehr verborgne Gleichung,
Formeln, die die Luft bewohnen,
Algebra der reifen Früchte!

Licht umschwirrt im wespengelben
Mittag lautlos alle Wesen.
Trockne Blumen ruhn im selben
Augenblick auf trocknem Wind.

Drei Orangen, zwei Zitronen.
Und die Stille kommt mit Flügeln.
Grün schwebt sie durch Ulmenkronen,
Selges Schiff, matrosenheiter.

Und der Himmel ist ein blaues
Auge, das sich nicht mehr schließt
Über Herzen: ein genaues
Wunder, schwankend unter Blättern.

Drei Orangen, zwei Zitronen: —
Mathematisches Entzücken,
Mittagschrift aus leichten Zonen!
Zunge schweigt bei Zunge. Doch
Alter Sinn gurrt wie ein Tauber.

The title suggests a still life, as in a painting, but no description follows. The first stanza explains the title as, instead, an equation, a formula or calculus that resides in nature ("Algebra der reifen Früchte!"). As an equation, the poem does not develop a narrative of any kind but seeks immediate balance, a universal equality of luminescence, whose palpable radiance makes itself felt first in the oxymoron "umschwirrt / lautlos." In the first distich of stanza two, the noontime sunlight penetrates everything and makes all objects transparent to Krolow's algebraic pantheism; in the second distich, the lines achieve poise in a discrete moment, pivoting on the enjambment ("im selben / Augenblick") but balanced by the repetition of "trockne[m]" between rooted stasis "Blumen" and movement "Wind." The title repeats three times in the first lines of stanzas one, three, and five to extend the constant equation to new variables of imagery as "ein genaues Wunder" and a "Mathematisches Entzücken" or "Mittagschrift aus leichten Zonen!" Light is not a symbol of reason or enlightenment but a mystical sensation that blinds reason by appealing to it and instead glorifies the unquestioned senses. Such sensual communion requires no language and consists of abstract consciousness of the physical senses: "Zunge schweigt bei Zunge." That conscious eroticism heightens, but does not hide, an instinctive carnality: "Doch / Alter Sinn gurrt wie ein Tauber."

The third section of *Wind und Zeit* carries the same title as its first poem, "Aufschwung," and taken as a whole, constitutes the axis of this volume and of Krolow's development in these years. "Orte der Geometrie" (I, 110) is a companion piece to "Drei Orangen, Zwei

Zitronen" and compresses further, under the influence of Jorge Guillén, the aesthetic enunciated by that poem in order to gain an additional degree of logical clarity and visual simplicity:

Orte der Geometrie:
Einzelne Pappel, Platane.
Und dahinter die Luft,
Schiffbar mit heiterem Kahne

In einer Stille, die braust.
Einsames Sich-Genügen
In einem Himmel aus Schaum,
Hell und mit kindlichen Zügen.

Alles wird faßlich und Form:
Kurve des Flusses, Konturen
Flüchtender Vögel im Laub,
Diesige Hitze-Spuren,

Mundvoll Wind und Gefühl
Für blaue Blitze, die trafen
Körperschatten, die sanft
Schwankten wie Segel vorm Hafen.

Image and poetics go side by side, each determining the other: the image renders the concept concrete, the concept renders the image intellectual, as a metaphor of itself, perceived and apperceived, registered by the senses and reflected upon by consciousness. The poem becomes an intellectual landscape in which idea and image come together without merging the real and the cognitive, contraries conjoined by juxtaposition, which requires an act of visual intellection, as would an oxymoron ("Stille, die braust"), whereby neither element points beyond to a larger order of coherence to become allegory. Both terms simply reflect back and forth upon each other as an "Einsames Sich-Genügen" of metaphoricity. As such, as "Orte der Geometrie," the landscape becomes both sensuous and abstract, an object and its universal: "Alles wird faßlich und Form: Kurve des Flusses, Konturen." The poem achieves flashes of cognition and recognition ("blaue Blitze") in the metaphorical dimension of language between description and proposition, between the language of nature and denatured concept, or, for example, in the abstract interstices of the tautological compound "Körperschatten," where each part adumbrates the other just as a body throws a shadow and vice versa, a far less common thought. For Krolow, that interstice of intellection is not a gloomy abyss but the bright light around the shadow, its nimbus, the negative space around the object. In this manner of refined expression, the leitmotif of wind in this volume does not even require direct utterance since it is present, though unseen, in the image and fills the "Segel vorm Hafen" like thought within language.

These last two poems are often anthologized and demonstrate Krolow's sophisticated "Mittagsschrift aus leichten Zonen" (107), another kind of *Artistik* unlike Gottfried Benn's eruptive *Ligurian-Komplex,* which instead remains coolly intellectual and controlled, composed in measured cadence and in rhyme, not irregular, ecstatic and instinctual. These compositions do not at all seem to arise out of existential depths, and instead, they point outward, away from the subject: "Krümmung der Ferne, / Blicken entzogen, / Wie ich sie gerne / Fasse als Jenseits: / Landschaft mit Schiffen" (I, 112). The abstracted landscape is a self-conscious construct beyond the horizon, out of sight, outside of history: "Unschuld der Schwebe, / Aus Luft und Anmut ein / Loses Gewebe . . .," whose breezy innocence of composition calls into question its opposite pole, beyond the horizon in the other direction, beyond what the poem "Verdacht" (I, 113) calls also the "Unschuld der Bilder."

In six strophes, the poem "Wo endet das Auge?" (I, 114) orients Krolow's poetics, his "Unschuld der Schwebe," in relation to history and addresses that vanishing point. The repetition of the title question in strophes 1 and 5 divides the poem into two uneven sections, the latter of which responds to the former:

> Wo endet das Auge?
> Leicht hinter der Linie
> Des Horizonts, glücklich
> Im Lichte der Glyzinie,
>
> Im blauen Gewoge
> Des Himmels, im Garten,
> Korbweidenumstanden,
> Beim Mittags-Erwarten.
>
> Darüber die Tiefen
> Des Jenseits, erraten
> Vielleicht noch: gespenstisch
> Von toten Soldaten

Und Engeln bevölkert,
Die unsicher fliegen,
Mit Bildern, die hinter
Der Netzhaut schon liegen.

Wo endet das Auge?
Beim heiteren Raunen
Der Nähe, des Daseins. —
Im raschen Bestaunen

Der leuchtenden Fläche
Verlangt es nicht weiter.
Es weist ihm nach oben
Aus Luft eine Leiter.

The vanishing point is both optical and reflective: Both far- and near-sightedness are set off against memory. In its structure the poem locates the vanishing point between its two sections, the first four and the last two strophes, where the poem turns away from its perspective of depth and focuses on proximate surfaces. The first section describes an optics of distance, a far-sightedness that loses itself beyond the visible horizon in "Tiefen / des Jenseits" that remain inaccessible to the eye, but nonetheless might still be discovered ("erraten vielleicht noch"). That mystery lies however in the experience of war; that background still haunts the foreground, the past looms over the present: "gespenstisch / Von toten Soldaten." Even the angels, that might otherwise represent an "Unschuld der Schwebe," are weighed down by memories, by images from the past: "Mit Bildern, die hinter / Der Netzhaut schon liegen." The first section of four strophes invites inquiry into those images, into the history that has receded beyond sight but not beyond memory; the second section of two strophes collapses that space of historical inquiry into the "heiteren Raunen / Der Nähe, das Daseins. —" which then appears as an exclusion of historical depth in general and of the war, which still lies on the horizon. The immediacy of the senses and the closeness of focus on brilliant surfaces, otherwise in itself unobjectionable, appears here as a conscious denial of history, a retreat behind the façade of "der leuchtenden Fläche." Thus filled by immediate sensations, the eye "verlangt [. . .] nicht weiter" and does not lose itself beyond the horizon where optics and memory converge. Instead, that overdetermined sense of wonder directs the eye of the viewer/reader not into the depths of history but rather "nach oben" with a poetics of desubstantialized artifice ("aus Luft eine Leiter"), a transcendence out of history.

After this central articulation of a poetic position, the remainder of the volume turns back toward the world, first in a section devoted to poignant "Liebesgedichte[n]" (I, 77–82) and then in the last section, called "Moralische Gedichte" ("Vorgänge" [115–23]), which invokes history, with resignation as fatalistic backdrop:

> Ein Hut voller Singvögel, in rosa Luft geschwenkt:
> Versuch des Jahres,
> Durch Wohllaut zu erschüttern!
> Aber die arkadische Tonleiter
> Wird rasch unsicher
> Im Himmel, und die Käfige
> Der Vogelfänger stehen weit offen.
>
> Jemand ließ einen Entwurf machen
> Von einem Leben ohne Trauer.
> Die historischen Voraussetzungen indessen
> Waren nicht günstig,
> Und wie das Singvögel-Sterben
> Waren einige Umstände nicht
> Aus der Welt zu schaffen:
> Es blieb dabei, daß
> Zu viele etwas vom Waffenreinigen verstanden,
> Daß Herzen durch Wolken
> Sich dem begangenen Verrat entzogen
> Und obszöne Kreide in obszönen Fingern
> Auf Ziegelmauern die Beschreibung vom Menschen gab.
>
> Aber in jedem April
> Wiederholt der Versuch sich,
> Zierlicher Vorgang: —
>
> Ein Hut voller Singvögel, in rosa Luft geschwenkt!

This poem locates the poet in a generalized historical context and defines a tension between art and historical circumstance. The decorative opening image is a charming blend of sound, image, color, and gesture, which is qualified at once as routine failure ("Versuch des Jahres") that nonetheless has a certain heroism ("Durch Wohllaut zu erschüttern"). The "ladder of air" from the poem "Wo endet das Auge" reappears here, also disembodied, as a musical scale, the "arkadische Tonleiter," which suggests both the range and essence of art and nature, but which, again like the angels in "Wo endet das Auge," becomes "unsicher," presumably at the sight of the cages of the bird catchers. The opening strophe borrows some of the musical and operatic charm of Mozart's *Zauberflöte*, which the motif of the bird catcher calls to mind, but here such innocent charm of a Papageno is sobered by the symbolism of the cage that now — in a shift of allusion from Mozart to Max Weber's "golden cage" of capitalism — upsets the song of nature and threatens to capture the "Singvögel." Politics intrudes into the whimsical pantheism of artists who attempt to transcend into apolitical nature through art. A note of self-criticism rings through all the more so in the next strophe, even in the impersonal "Jemand." By noting the failure to live "ohne Trauer," the poem brings in a dimension of historical sorrow, linked to concrete but unspecified circumstances in the world, in history, which is explicitly referred to. The ominous death of the songbirds suggests either the annihilation of artists in the Nazi period or the suffocation of poetic exuberance in postwar materialist culture, or both. The poem confirms an enduring and repeating disappointment, a longing for poetic transcendence that remains frustrated by history ("Es blieb dabei") as defined not by art but by violence. Nonetheless, art regains a defiant charm in its perseverance: "Aber in jedem April / Wiederholt der Versuch sich." Now Krolow's poetry, already refined, is a "Zierlicher Vorgang" tempered by historical awareness so that the final line is both mournful in recognition and triumphant in defiance of the bird catchers' cages of society: "Ein Hut voller Singvögel, in rosa Luft geschwenkt!"

The last poem of the volume completes that turn to the world of politics, to history, in the poem "Politisch" (I, 134–35). The poem renounces rhyme and shows a new analytical sobriety of reflection on society, as if Krolow were now set to explore the real implications of his cage symbolism from the previous poem. Instead of the earlier transports of his nature poetry or the glistening and complex metaphors in the surrealist vein, this poem registers insights in slogan; part I defines the invalidity of imagination in a bureaucratic apparatus of control: "Ein Paß ist besser als / Ein Traum zu lesen." Part II deserves quotation in full:

> Falte die Decke.
> Lösche die Lampe.
> Die trügerische Anästhesie
> Des Dunkels ist verantwortungslos
> Wie der Schlaf.

Falte die Decke.
Lösche die Lampe.
Die Nacht birgt wie Bernstein
Eine Mücke: Dein Gedächtnis!
Dein Gewissen!

Falte die Decke.
Lösche die Lampe.
Der Staat, das ist
Der steinerne Gast.
Er erscheint: allen Abwehrgesten
Zum Trotz.

Falte die Decke.
Lösche die Lampe:
Die Zeit ohne Dokumente
Ist dennoch nicht im Anbruch.

Falte die Decke.
Lösche die Lampe.
Schon nähern sich Schritte
Deiner Tür. Wirst du dich
Ausweisen können?

Falte die Decke.
Lösche die Lampe.
Deine Stunde wird
In jedem Fall schlagen!

The six strophes all begin with the refrain in the lumbering rhythm of resigned fatigue as if in the weary routine of hiding out. The first strophe attacks the anodyne of obscurity, which characterized much of Krolow's own earlier work and which Hugo Friedrich at this time was about to canonize as the sign of the modern. The second strophe discovers in that darkness the functions of memory and conscience that earlier poems seemed to have pointedly excluded. The third stanza alludes, of course, to Don Juan's devil, who comes to collect him; the state here gathers up souls without pity or reprieve. The fourth strophe negates the utopian hope for the dawn of a "Zeit ohne Dokumente," but in doing so, also raises that thought as a criticism of dehumanized bureaucratic apparatus. The fifth strophe personalizes the anonymous threat of bureaucratic menace that comes to one's home where one's fate then depends on the correctness of one's papers. The last strophe puts the individual in the moment of historical decision when the anonymous state bears down upon him or her, though here without circumstantial detail that is all too familiar in this century. Krolow's poem gives a lean and forceful evocation of the exposed self in an anonymous state system; his alternation of refrain and varied caption creates an emotional and intellectual engagement with the predicament and subtly argues for historical, that is, critical consciousness of society in the present. In light of Krolow's work to date and his personal past, the poem almost surprises for its somber and sober analysis, with only a modicum of monitory pathos. This poem therefore anticipates Krolow's later turn to engagement with everyday life and eventually to topics of everyday concern in society.

Tage und Nächte (1956)

Tage und Nächte appeared in the same year that Karl Krolow received the Büchner Prize, the highest literary honor in the Federal Republic of Germany. His address on that occasion reflects his thoughts on his own poetry up to this time. He speaks about his development, as is appropriate to the occasion, in relation to Georg Büchner's *Leonce und Lena* (1836–37) and remarks, in particular, on those features ("Es sprang etwas über, Anonymes, Zauber, Geheimnis, Berückung" 196) that affected him at a particular historical moment:

> es wurde mir in *dem* Moment wichtig, in dem ich mich von den Bedrückungen zu befreien, von jenem Cauchemar zu lösen versuchte, der als schwerer Schatten über den poetischen Äußerungsversuchen der ersten Nachkriegsjahre lag, ein Schatten, in dem sich ein für allemal alle triste Erfahrung mit der deutschen Szene, alle an Leben und Existenz gehende Widerfahrung gesammelt, verdichtet zu haben schien. Ich wollte mich aus der Umklammerung der Erinnerung befreien, die ich an die Zeit zwischen meinem zwanzigsten und dreißigsten Lebensjahre hatte, damals kurz nach 1945. (196–97)

Among other sources as well, Krolow finds in Büchner's play just what he is looking for: a means of separating himself from the past, from the oppressions of that period. Krolow does not seek a means to come to terms with the past through critical examination of his own experiences and reflection on specific issues of the Nazi period and the war, but rather he openly seeks a means of freeing himself atmospherically, in terms of his mood, from the oppressiveness of the past. Yet he establishes a direct link between his work and its historical context. That relation is inverse: his poetry reflects through that specific absence what it does not represent. Krolow defines his work as an attempt not to remember, analyze, and understand, but to release or liberate himself from the "grip of memory," from his memories of the decade between 1935 and 1945, the period between his graduation from the Gymnasium and the end of the war. He alludes to memories, but in all his writing, he has never given an account of that time or of any specific instances or circumstances that weighed upon him, which the earlier chapters here have now documented for the first time. That historical period and the gap in what is known of his experience in that period nonetheless defined his style, invisibly as it were. His silence on the past has become over time also, one might say, increasingly explicit as a form of systematic misrepresentation and biographical stylization.

Krolow defines here, in stark contrast to Paul Celan's Büchner Prize address "Der Meridian" in 1960,[26] a poetics of forgetting after the historical experiences of the Nazi period in Germany and the destruction of war. From his own unnamed experiences, Krolow moves to the general situation of the genre in the mid-1950s:

> Inzwischen hat sich einiges im deutschen Gedicht der Jahrhundertmitte gewandelt. Es hat sich in der Tat vom Schock zu lösen vermocht. Die von der Realität überwältigte Vorstellungskraft hat sich bemüht, die Benommenheit abzustreifen. Das geschah mühsam genug, und es hat den Anschein, als wenn nach gewissen barbarischen Ereignissen auch die Lyrik die *Realien* mehr, als das lange Zeit erwünscht und praktiziert war, in ihre Sprache einbezöge. Sie hat sich dem Verhängnis gestellt und hat gesehen, daß der Schrecken, der den Sensiblen so oft in ihrer Einbildung geläufig gewesen war, greifbare Gestalt annehmen konnte, die alles vorgestellte Maß übertraf. Dennoch mußte das Gedicht wieder darangehen, *zaubern* zu lernen, mußte es alte, alterslose Fähigkeiten und Fertigkeiten entwickeln, die verlorengegangen schienen. Es mußte nach der Atemlosigkeit wieder zu Atem kommen. Die Imagination war wieder ins Spiel zu bringen. (198)

Instead of incorporating the past into the present, and the German individual and collective experiences into his poetry, Krolow engineers for the genre a break from the past, as if the genre had, once and for all, "sich in der Tat vom Schock zu lösen vermocht." He allows that the genre had confronted already "dem Verhängnis," but suggests that that phase is now (in 1956!) over, and that the genre has to start once again "*zaubern* zu lernen . . . alte, alterslose Fähigkeiten und Fertigkeiten zu entwickeln." Krolow's vocabulary, such as *Verhängnis* and *alterslose,* obfuscates by projecting the genre into timeless metaphysics; Krolow separates poetic practice from history instead of seeing them in relation to one another. In Krolow's speech, the ability to conjure or perform magic in poetry, to which he refers, is vague and without specific definition, but does take on the definite aspect of avoiding or projecting beyond historical issues. In the penultimate sentence above, Krolow seems to call for what Celan called an *Atemwende,* where poetry hovers between speech and speechlessness precisely for the purpose of bringing history to consciousness through transformed or deformed language in order to reflect in new ways on the shocks of history, "solcher Daten [20. Jänner] eingedenk zu bleiben" (Celan, 196). On the other hand, Krolow sets imagination as play, apart from, not together with, history: "eine Poesie der Schwebung, der Balance, des geistigen Vergnügens an einer Einsicht, der man alles Schmerzhafte nahm" (201). In the postwar period of the so-called "economic miracle" (*Wirtschaftswunder*) Krolow advocates an aesthetics of anaesthesia that numbs the pain of coming to terms with the past with an artistic acrobatics that gives pleasure without pain and appeals to the mind without troubling the conscience.

Krolow closes his speech with the contrast of the poetry he calls for with that of the postwar avant-garde of experimental poetry: "Der Mut zum Zauber, zum Spiel, zur intellektuellen Heiterkeit, zum Charme scheint mir größer zu sein als die nervöse Tätigkeit einsamer Manipulation" (202), but in fact both of these tendencies reflect an ahistorical aestheticism. Krolow's contrast elides the question of a poetry between the two poles that incorporates historical reflection. Krolow attaches his idea of poetry, however, to the same idea of progress that informs the scientism of experimental poetry, though with a different accent: "Der Fortschritt liegt weniger im Herausbasteln von Kleinigkeiten als in unmerklichen Verschiebungen des Gesamtklimas" (202). He thus sets his ahistorical understanding of poetry into the historical context of postwar Germany with the function of changing the "Gesamtklima." The scintillating surface of the poem evinces a magical refinement of sensibility that also forecloses historical inquiry and critical reflection.

The first poem, "Blätterlicht," of *Tage und Nächte* (I, 125) demonstrates that evacuation of depth, historical or otherwise, from the poem, which then appears purely as scintillating surface:

Blätterlicht, Amalgam
Silber in grüner Luft!
Zärtliche Ferne kam
Zu dir und blieb als Duft.

Modelliert zur Figur:
Schatten, der leicht sich dehnt
Und mit genauer Spur
Sich aus dem Laube sehnt

Hin in ein Land, drin heiß
— Heiteres Element —
Wange des Windes weiß
Über dem Staub verbrennt.

In the opening two lines, three appositions meld sensations of bright light and dark green in evoking the image or the sense of foliage in sunshine as intermingled color fields. The word *Amalgam,* though itself infelicitous, abstracts the image away from simple description and causes it to hover between description and concept without becoming either. Further, that intermediate state between thing and thought is both perceived and conceived as air. The negative space of the image or sensory impression becomes predominant. The affect of the first distich hovers between flashing light and dark, between air and solid, between green and silver, visual image and concept, and thereby titillates the retina and the cerebrum without extending further. Conceptual depth, like the visual perspective, as exquisite delicate distance ("Zärtliche Ferne") is drawn into the foreground and evaporated into *Duft.*

The negative space of the shadow takes on form "Modelliert zur Figur" as does the personified "Wange des Windes." Nature is dissolved into disembodied sensory impressions that are light, precise, white, and full of desire, projected toward another space, which Krolow defined at the end of his Büchner Prize speech as "die reizende Topographie eines Landes der Phantasie" (203), where the separate impressions in turn merge into an ensemble as "— Heiteres Element —." That combination of light and air, geometry and fantasy, in the poem and image of *Blätterlicht* characterizes this volume, as also in the pair of linked poems "Für Celine, vor Zeiten gestorben" (148–49) that follows, which transform the premature death of an unknown girl, whose name Krolow had noticed as a youth in the local Hannover cemetery, into an exquisite and fleeting verbal confection

("Ein Atemzug Süße").[27] The portrait disappears as it comes into being but scatters shimmering and ephemeral impressions: "Ein Bildnis, das zwischen / Den Fingern verrinnt / Und schwebenden Fischen / Im Blätterlicht gleicht." *Blätterlicht,* first as title and opening and then as the closing of a poem, conveys the synaesthetic liquefaction of his poetry here.

The poem "Zuflucht im Kühlen" (I, 124–25) contains many of the same features of the Celine poems, such as the meter, diction, and simple rhyme scheme of *abab,* without the aspect of memorial portraiture, and extends that liquefaction thematically into the language:

> Die leichten Gewächse
> Der Luft, dran ich lehne!
> Im Laub der Reflexe
> Auf Haut mir und Sehne!
>
> Bewegung im Schatten,
> Gewürzt wie Pistazie,
> Im Armen des matten
> Geleuchts der Akazie,
>
> So bin ich von der Hitze
> Versöhnt ich und gleite
> Durch grünliche Blitze
> Ins Kühle, ins Weite,
>
> In Wasser, das zwischen
> Den Fingern rinnt: — Silben
> Aus Licht, die verwischen
> Beim raschen Vergilben
>
> Der fiebrigen Blätter
> die lautlos sich drehen,
> Im feurigen Wetter
> Des Sommers vergehen.

In the foliage there takes place a constant play of light and shadow ("grünliche Blitze"), of solid substance and weightlessness ("Die leichten Gewächse / Der Luft, dran ich lehne!"), and of heat and coolness that provides a refuge from the world outside and restores the speaker for a return to that world. In that play, nature becomes a language ("Silben aus Licht") that is fleetingly inscribed onto the leaves of trees or books, a liquefied process of signification "das zwi-schen / Den Fingern rinnt." Textuality becomes an artificial nature rich in its own nuances, its own sensuous play of oppositions. "Zu-flucht im Kühlen" gestures toward the outside world only as the an-tipode to the enclosed realm of aestheticized nature in language.

Here, as in the "Celine" poems, that dissolution into refined nu-ances of imaginative natural aestheticism attempts to employ language as a means of casting off its own referential function. The figure of Celine is the displaced referent, the missing signified, who was never known as family or friend or local history but only as sepulchral script, who now exists as playful and sweetly nostalgic inflection in the lan-guage of poetry, a poetic figure of representative absence, who inhab-its the time and terrain of fantasy; Krolow also evokes, again with an allusion to music, in the first strophe of his poem "Fabelzeit" (I, 125): "Süße, die sich gefügt / Im Pergolesi-Ton, / Geisterhaft sich ver-gnügt / An anderem Leben schon," but here strangely conveys a dif-ferent sense of that exquisiteness that, for all its direct sensuous appeal, draws its substance, with vampiric parasitism, from "anderem Leben."[28] Language, however self-enclosed in its own rhetoric ("Mo-delliert zur Figur"), retains a referential substrate that it cannot long deny, like a corpse that will not stay hidden.

That dissonance between detached aestheticism and historical background, the nonreferential and referential uses of language, in-creases when the dead subject of the poem belongs, unlike Celine, not to the realm of private association and recollection, but to the definite context of public memory as in the case of war in the poem "Meta-morphose" (I, 127):

> Blonde Soldaten aus Wind
> Und Träumen der Stunde Null,
> Lang füsiliert schon: sie sind
> Leicht wie ein Vers des Catull
>
> Versetzt in die Scherbe Blau,
> In Himmel, und ruhen aus
> Bei einem Bad von Tau
> Im heiteren Niemandshaus.
>
> Die Karabiner im Arm,
> Wie Bilder auf altem Email
> Und Luft, die geduldig und warm
> Durchrieselt das grüne Detail:

> Zerbrochne Gebüsche, Geruch
> von Leder und Koppellack —
> Aus fließendem Schweigen ein Tuch . . .
> Entfernter Dudelsack
>
> Beklagt sie, die ohne Bart
> Und Orden wie Schatten tun,
> Wie Geisterseher, und zart
> Auf ihren Gewehren ruhn.

In this romantic elegy for fallen soldiers, the transformation out of history and into timeless artifice strips death on the battlefield of its political implications and its individual pain. The adjectival specification of "blonde soldiers" in general links the topic to the specific context of Nazi ideology. The notions of wind and dreams no longer seem so innocent, though the soldiers, themselves perhaps not ideologically committed to war, dream of its end and a new beginning ("Stunde Null"). Their violent death ("Lang füsiliert schon") seems to figure, in this poem, only as necessary precondition for their transformation into the exquisite lightness of "ein Vers des Catull." When the dead soldiers come to rest "Im heiteren Niemandshaus," the *Heiterkeit* of Krolow's poetics, as advocated in his Büchner Prize speech, seems a willful imposition of a fixed point of view onto material that resists such neat framing into images of folksy heroism "Wie Bilder auf altem Email." The bodies are covered metaphorically in the poem with a catafalque of silence ("Aus fließendem Schweigen ein Tuch"); that silence also enters then directly into the poem as an ellipsis, but the silence of the poem is not metaphoric. The poem does not engage any meaningful aspects of its putative topic of death, war, or mourning but remains distant like the "Entfernter Dudelsack." Krolow's now familiar term *zart* to signal aesthetic refinement leaves the dead soldiers in the final lines in a posture of tranquil repose with their weapons to complete their metamorphosis. The dead have been stripped of all links to the world that they have left behind and that expedited their departure ("lang füsiliert schon") and have been transformed into decorative props, ornaments "ohne Bart / Und Orden."

That aesthetic of *Heiterkeit* is more successful in such poems as "Sommerlich" (I, 159) where no residue of historical experience troubles the surreal elegance of the imagery: "Das Zündholzlicht / Des Monds verging / Im Tag, der dicht / In Ulmen hing." Though even here Krolow includes the dialectic of metaphysical abstraction

away from any grounding in historical experience: "Zerblitzt die Zeit /
Zu Immer, Nie, / Schmilzt hin das Leid." The dialectic also appears
in the relation between the title and body of a poem, as in "Schwer-
kraft der Zeiten" (I, 160), where *Zeiten,* the times, is used in the plural instead of time as a singular metaphysical category (which suggests
the tug of gravity in historical experience), but the poem gives a different answer:

> Die Schwerkraft der Zeiten
> Im Schnitt des Gesichtes!
> Das Blau legt auf Lippen
> Patiencen des Lichtes.
>
> Die heuschreckenleichte
> Unordnung des Laubes
> Auf Kleidern, die wehen
> Im Atem des Staubes.
>
> Es gehen und kommen
> Minuten, die schweben,
> Ein Rudel Delphine,
> Vergängliches Leben!
>
> Der Augenblick drängt sich
> In leichte Profile,
> In Augen, die kämpfen
> Um Schatten zum Spiele.

That gravity may have left its mark ("Schnitt") on the individual that
raises questions, but ephemeral changes of light defeat further inquiry
and dissolve such depths. Again, though unnamed, *Blätterlicht* is that
solvent, here as "heuschreckenleichte / Unordung des Laubes,"
which illuminates without enlightening; the play of light blocks scrutiny that wants to probe beneath the visible surfaces and thereby releases the object from its gravity into a pure temporality of the
moment, like dolphins that hover above the depths, glistening in the
air and sun, without ever plunging back below the surface. In a variation of cubist method, the moment cuts profiles that fill the eyes with
light and shadow. The limited temporality of the *Augenblick* puts
blinders on the *Augen.*

When the scope of the poem expands to include more of the
world than just metaphors of the moment, the poems take on a para-

tactic quality that recalls the poetry of Alfred Lichtenstein as in the poem "Handstreiche der Dämmerung" (I, 164):

> Handstreiche der Dämmerung: —
> Die Radler verirren sich
> Im blauen Staub des Himmels
> Und kommen zu Fall.
> Der Nachmittag erscheint noch einmal
> Als Film auf heißen Ziegelwänden.
> Passanten schütteln den Kopf
> Und bekennen seinen Abschied.
> Das Zwielicht macht aus einer
> Entblößten Brust im Hauseingang
> Ein schwarzes Idyll.
> Eine rasche Bewegung zerstört es,
> Während die Schatten der Abendkleider
> Vorüberhuschen.
>
> Nun kann die Nacht kommen
> Und die Bilderrätsel lösen!

The rapid suite of images becomes a puzzle, though the pieces of the puzzle do not fit together to form a whole. The random events of the world are related through the passing time of day, by the evening as night begins to fall. In that crepuscular half light, objects and events briefly loom large and then recede into night. The evening, like the poem itself, offers a magic, a legerdemain of fleeting, mysterious impressions, whose mystery, once suggested and adumbrated, is dissolved, not solved. The poem provides no penetration of a depth and no depth to penetrate, only a series of poetic gestures that opens and closes upon itself, without issue or consequence.[29]

For comparison, the poem "Die Zeit veränderte sich" (I, 167) presents a similar suite of impressions but manages to convey a sense of history and individual emotion:

> Es gibt niemanden mehr,
> Der die Denkmäler der Zärtlichkeit
> Mit blauer Farbe anstreicht.
> Die Liebkosungen blonder Frisuren
> Und Strohhüte sind vergessen.
> Die Kinder, die den ermüdeten Singvögeln
> Im Park ihre Schulter hinhielten,
> Wuchsen heran.

Die Zeit veränderte sich.

Sie wird nicht mehr von jungen Händen
Gestreichelt.
Die Lampen tragen nun andere Glühbirnen.
Die Tennisbälle kehrten aus dem Himmel
Nicht wieder zurück.
Die gelben Badeanzüge
Sind den Schmetterlingstod gestorben;
Und alle Briefumschläge
Zerfielen zu sanftem Staub.

Aber dafür sind die Straßen voller Fremder
Mit Fahrkarten in den Taschen!

Though the opening line announces the sense of anonymity and loss of individual subjectivity that characterizes Krolow's work in these years ("Es gibt niemanden mehr"), the impressions of this poem nonetheless evince a sense of melancholy as a reflection on the passing of time in the historical context of an individual life in society. Because of that implied context, the random and apparently insignificant minutiae of daily life become, in retrospect, "Denkmäler der Zärtlichkeit," a marvelous phrase that might describe most of the poems in this volume. The speaker recalls the erotic innocence of youth, and images from childhood "Im Park," and ponders his hands that show his age. A sense of public history enters in the detail of "nun andere Glühbirnen." The image of tennis balls that do not fall back to earth conveys, in playfully surrealist defiance of the laws of nature, a sudden feel for an individual's disorientation in his or her own history, as a life passes on and heads to its own "Schmetterlingstod," like just another fashion. The image of crowds ("Straßen voller Fremder") as statistics of mass transit, duly ticketed, concludes the poem with a sense of intimate individual anonymity observing the historical changes in society and in one's life.

In *Tage und Nächte,* anonymity or depersonalization as a theme moves from the realm of nature to the realm of society. The linked poems "Jemand" (I, 144–45) anticipate the changes in Krolow's work in the next volume *Fremde Körper* (1959):

> I *Jemand hat Licht brennen lassen*
> Jemand hat Licht brennen lassen
> In der Wohnung, die ich früher
> Besaß.

Jemand lacht in meiner Wohnung.
Oder ist es ein Weinen,
Das sich hinter kaltem Rauch
Von Zigaretten verkleidet?
Jemand hat hier geliebt
Bei Tabak und Resten
Vorjähriger Nelken.
Das Blumenwasser
Leuchtet noch blau.
Jemand hat hier einsame Mahlzeiten
Eingenommen bei Geraune
Aus der Luft.
Die Zeit hat hier jemanden erstickt,
Ehe er das Licht in den Zimmern
Löschen konnte.

II *Der Augenblick des Fensters*
Jemand schüttet Licht
Aus dem Fenster.
Die Rosen der Luft
Blühen auf,
Und in der Straße
Heben die Kinder beim Spiel
Die Augen.
Tauben naschen
Von seiner Süße.
Die Mädchen werden schön
Und die Männer sanft
Von diesem Licht.
Aber ehe es ihnen die anderen sagen,
Ist das Fenster von jemandem
Wieder geschlossen worden.

The four repetitions of *Jemand* as a refrain in the first of the two poems underscore the anonymity of that person but also create a certain intimacy with the unknown occupant "in my apartment." The speaker's identification with the space of his or her former existence lends a residue of individuation to the present occupant, whose life might follow the same pattern in that apartment, first ownership and self-possession, fully engaged in life with confident laughter, or even crying and loving, but finally left alone, haunted by "Geraune / aus

der Luft," and ultimately, a victim of violence and loneliness, "suffocating" by the circumstances of his or her life. The light in the apartment first represents the fullness and intensity of living in that space,
and then the anonymity of a public utility that continues without notice of the life that has expired there. The light is not extinguished,
but the individual is. The anonymous occupant has become a projected Doppelgänger for the speaker tracing his or her own path of
self-estrangement. The speaker is dispossessed of the apartment and of
a sense of selfhood and livelihood. The absence of rhyme creates an
openness in the poem to the world, even as that world appears closed
to the individual subject, just as the open window in the second poem
floods the street with light that illuminates the world outside, casting
its beneficent glow on objects and people and then is shut. The human agency has disappeared behind the discrete actions registered in
the poem, which leads to the *Fremde Körper* of Krolow's next volume.

Fremde Körper (1959)

Tage und Nächte marked a movement from an extraordinary delicacy
of impressions in nature that dissolved historical and metaphysical
depths, under the rubric of *Blätterlicht,* into a fluid and transitory sensuousness along the surfaces of objects — to a new sense of anonymity
within those impressions. Individual subjectivity had disappeared in
those poems or existed only residually as an ambient awareness of the
subject's absence in a social context. That absence of subjectivity registered as solitude, loneliness, self-estrangement, and increasingly as
violence. These two tendencies link *Tage und Nächte* to *Fremde Körper* and can be briefly illustrated in two of the fifteen poems that Krolow chose to carry over from one volume to the other.[30] In the poem
"Ziemlich viel Glück" (I, 137–38), the first tendency appears in an
image reminiscent of Marc Chagall's paintings:

> Ziemlich viel Glück
> Gehört dazu,
> Daß ein Körper auf der Luft
> Zu schweben beginne
> Mit Brust, Achsel und Knie,
> Und auf dieser Luft
> Einem anderen Körper begegne,
> Wie er
> Unterwegs.

Die Atmosphäre macht
Zwei innige Torsen aus ihnen.
Unbemerkt beschreibt ihr Entzücken
Zärtliche Linien in Baumkronen.
Eine ganze Zeit noch
Ist ihr Flüstern zu vernehmen,
Und wie sie einander
Das schenken,
Was leicht an ihnen ist.
Glücklichsein beginnt immer
Ein wenig über der Erde.
Aber niemand hat es beobachten können.

The image of levitation in defiance of gravity releases the subjects from any binding weight of groundedness. Krolow's key terms of *Luft* and *schweben* propel the bodies, metonymic collages of body parts in the manner of synthetic cubism, upwards, where they meet "unterwegs." The "lovers" have no passion, no psychological depth, but a certain charm; they are brought together and dissolved as subjects, truncated and inverted, turned inside out as "innige Torsen" and released into the atmosphere, where the flash of sensual intimacy between them becomes an ornate "Entzücken / Zärtliche Linien in Baumkronen," in effect again a *Blätterlicht* of softly shaded contours and shifting configurations, an abstract swirling, whispering, rustling in the treetops, a strobic aural-visual synaesthetic titillation of intermingling light and lightness. The earth, as the ground that binds, anchors, or supports a subject or a discourse, recedes; happiness begins with that detachment from groundedness and grows as the subjects float, like lost balloons, out of sight into a surreal space of an antimetaphysical transcendence beyond empirical inquiry ("Aber niemand hat es beobachten können").

The second poem here in question is "Einsamkeit" in four parts (I, 139–41), with the caption "'Je suis l'autre' *Gérard de Nerval.*" This long poem translates the situation of the poem "Jemand" into more precisely psychological terms by introducing a visible individual ("Jener träumerische Mann mittleren Alters:") into a similar scenario at the window: "Er läßt seine Hand aus dem Fenster fallen / Wie ein Staubtuch." The surreal images of hallucinated self-estrangement into body parts, like a mannequin, registers his insanity, which radiates like a lunar nimbus of lunacy ("Es ging ein stilles Leuchten / Von ihm aus") that is set in relation to his isolation in society ("Seine Hoffnung war, bemerkt zu werden, / Wie er in seinem Zimmer auf und ab ging, / Das Dunkel erhellte / Und die unbestimmte Sehnsucht nach Geselligkeit / Zwischen Gaumen und Zunge spürte"). The situation in "Jemand" centers upon an individual subject but enters into the dissociated consciousness of that subject, whose hallucinations nonetheless register his attempts to form personal bonds to the world outside: in his disturbed mind extending his hand to others, as it were, by dropping it out the window. Finally, in his isolation he conceives of "eine schwarze Braut" in order not to be alone any longer, but that bride is the night of insanity that will also kill him: "Natürlich weiß er, / Daß die Nacht das blaue Rasiermesser ist, / Mit dem sie ihm, / Ohne Umstände zu machen, / Das Haupt vom Rumpf trennt." The idea of suicide accompanies him and relieves his solitude by providing a ceremonial link between the two sides of his dissociated consciousness; ultimately, however, the "Nacht" [night] of his *Umnachtung* [madness], the bride of his schizophrenia, will consummate his isolation in the act of suicide performed by an imagined Other, separating consciousness from the body ("Das Haupt vom Rumpf trennt") and transforming the individual into an estranged and dismembered object.

In the poems of *Fremde Körper,* these traits of dissolution into nature and out of history and dissociated subjectivity in society come together in numerous variations with a plethora of brilliant metaphors. Rhyme has largely disappeared and given a new degree of prominence to metaphor. In the first section, titled "Andere Jahreszeit" (7–45), the thirty-eight poems stay closer to the first of these two poles of sensibility, in the conciseness of imagery and closeness to nature, though mostly without the particular lightness and charm of "Ziemlich viel Glück." Instead, the beauty of nature is conjoined with the violence of mankind, often with a morbid sense of fatality: "Die Stunden mit welkem Laub im Nacken / Vergehen nicht anders / Als die Blutspuren im Asphalt, die / Vom letzten Zweikampf herrühren" ("Notiz durchs Fenster" I, 186). Between these two poles of nature and violence, often with the same vocabulary, phrases, and motifs, Krolow's poems turn, kaleidoscope-like, in ever new constellations. Among these new poems, at one end of that spectrum of kaleidoscopic variations, the poem "Der Baum" (I, 195) provides the best parallel to "Ziemlich viel Glück" and a measure for the subsequent fluctuations in diction and tone:

Gestern habe ich einen Baum gepflanzt
Und ihm den Namen
Meiner Unruhe gegeben.
Heute umspringt seine Hüften
Die Forelle des Lichts.
Das Silber kleiner Gespräche
Dringt durch sein Laub.
Es ist Versteck für alle Mittage.
Später lehnt der Abend
Eine goldene Leiter
An seine Krone.
Die Nacht benutzt sie,
Um mit ihrer Hilfe den Himmel zu verlassen
Und in die Arme einer Gestalt zu sinken,
Die sich mit abgeblendeter Laterne
Bereit hielt.

The speaker plants a tree and names it after his "Unruhe," which is not further explained. In this manner of psychological allegory, the image of nature then eclipses a presentation of that subjectivity, which recedes behind the tree, which is in turn personalized ("seine Hüften"). The dissolution of the subject takes place with the familiar motif of *Blätterlicht,* though without the appearance of that term. Instead, two literally brilliant metaphors, found in lines five and six, capture the rapid play of light and dark, the sweeping arched lines of the branches as leaping trout, and the splashing liquidity in that pool of light and shadow, as well as the sight and sound, the flashing and rustling, of the leaves. The foliage absorbs the light, then increases in density of shade and shadows as the sun passes its zenith and the afternoon wanes: the foliage becomes a "Versteck" for the daylight, and by implication, for the observing subject immersed in observation of its surfaces and depths. The "goldene Leiter" marks the gradual motion of the sunlight up the tree as the sun sinks below the horizon. Observing these changes during the course of the day, as in Monet's paintings of poplars or the cathedral at Rouen, the individual subject loses itself and becomes anonymous, a positive process that transforms the suffering subject into part of nature and that culminates in an embrace with the night that falls "in die Arme einer Gestalt." The same positive anonymity in nature figures in the poem "Siegreiche Vegetation" (11; I, 180–81) where "das Leben verlor / Sein Selbstbewußtsein." No viewer perspective is directly present in this poem; the individual perceiving consciousness is defined only as the absent indirect object in the first line ("Damals fiel auf") and as a simply detached perspective, belonging to no one or everyone, in the last lines: "Der Anblick der Pflanzen / Machte Brust und Hüfte / Überflüssig." Nature has engulfed the individual; the metonymic dismemberment of the body represents the individual presence only in a form of fragmentation and negation.

In the poem "Der Blätter-Schütze" (I, 194), the same basic image of a tree, as in "Der Baum," takes on a different tone, which is characteristic of this volume:

> Der nach den treibenden Blättern zielte,
> Verletzte den Himmel
> In einem Augenblick, in dem er
> Sich unverwundbar wähnte.
> Es werden Wolken kommen
> Und nach dem Schützen suchen.
> Ihre Fäuste drohen schon
> Hinter einer Baumgruppe am Wasser.
> Er wird nicht davonlaufen können.
> In keinem Wind wird er sich
> Von Stund an mehr verstecken.
> Nicht umsonst hat er der Luft
> Die Geduld des Herbst-Mittags
> Gestohlen.

Here an individual subject is only present as a definite article, an agent of violence, who shoots at leaves and injures the sky. Nature is no longer pristine and "unverwundbar," but rather hurt by the anonymous violence of depersonalized humankind and intent on revenge. This evocation of a storm has become a scene of violence, revenge, of hunter and hunted, of flight and refuge, with weapons, an atmosphere of fear, menace, relentless persecution, and punishment ("Er wird nicht davonlaufen können"). The hiding place of nature has now become political and historical, though only through metaphoric extension, without grounding in details.[31] Nature is permeated with the atmosphere, figured here as clouds, of historical violence.

In the poem "Einöde" (16; I, 166–67) that atmosphere becomes more concrete with the presence of barracks, signaling a wartime scenario for that violence. As in "Siegreiche Vegetation," the forces of Nature compete with mankind, though here the violence of war seems to have struck a balance with the slow relentlessness of nature:

Die Wellblech-Baracken
Werden vom Geruch
Heißer Stauden umarmt.
Rauchen verboten!
Und der Aufenthalt in der feindlichen Luft
Greift an die Kehlen.
Draußen beginnt die Ferne
Nach ein paar Schritten
In der Sonne.
Das Handgemenge zweier Schatten
Endet in der Stille.
Nur der Traum vom Wasser bleibt
Und das Bild eines Mannes,
Der am Horizont von seinem Gewicht
Zu Boden gezogen wird.

Unlike the embrace of floating figures in "Ziemlich viel Glück" or the embrace of night in "Der Baum," the embrace here is not tender or transcendent. Nature surrounds a military outpost; nature and the artifice of civilization do not merge in this embrace. The two forces are anonymous agencies competing for space but indifferent to each other. The individual as a perceiving consciousness with memory and emotions has disappeared completely; unnamed figures in the military are also conscripted into the poem by implication, as unthinking reflexes of the second nature of civilization at war, inhabiting the space (*Baracken*) and time (*Aufenthalt*) of their tour of duty. The text of a sign, "Smoking forbidden!" suggests the presence of ordnance; the general atmosphere is also explosive, galvanized by the threat of attack, which further reduces all individuals to "shadows." The skirmish of hand-to-hand combat ends in violent death but only figures in the poem as the play of light and shadow, noise and stillness, a form of *Blätterlicht*, an ominous aesthetic moment. The poem creates a scenario of historical experience that is then voided: the historical space divides in the last four lines without issue between a dream and an image, a deep psychological moment of escape into nature and the aesthetic construct of a dying man. The dream is named, not given; the poem presents an image only, an image of a dying hanged man. In this way, the poem backs away from the scenario it had set up and retreats from poetic or historical insight, which remains over the horizon given in the poem. The two types of distantiated and abstracted perception supplant observation and serve to collapse the "distance" of historical inquiry or emotional empathy onto the surface of decorative imagery.

Contrary to reigning impressions of Krolow's work, an atmosphere of violence and mystery appears in numerous poems. In "Verrufener Ort" (22; I, 196–97), a deserted farm appears as a group of shepherds pass by; the second strophe presents an unspecified historical incident in some detail:

> Immer noch riecht es hier
> Nach kranken Tieren.
> Das Echo von Pistolensalven
> Schläft wie eine Erscheinung
> An den Stallwänden.
> Doch überschlägt sich keine Stimme mehr
> Im Tode.
> Der letzte Hahn
> Wurde längst geschlachtet.
> Sein kopfloser Schatten
> Taumelt noch manchmal
> Im Kreise.

Sick animals have been slaughtered in the stalls and the farm abandoned. The place smells of illness "immer noch" even though the last of the animals was "längst geschlachtet." The space of the stall also still carries the echo of pistol shots, an unusual method for killing livestock, and frenzied voices (*Stimme*), a term which personalizes the slaughter and extends its metaphoric range to humans, distinct from animals by their voice. Of course, the necessary slaughter of sick animals would not make a place notorious or infamous. Without explanatory detail, the denotative level of "Pistolensalven" and "Stimme" does not seem to fit easily with recognizable reality, but the connotative or figurative level of metaphor here, "Schläft wie eine Erscheinung," adds a haunting note to the scenario like the revenant rooster whose headless shadow runs in circles "noch manchmal." Brutal violence in the foreground of the poem creates and ultimately collapses an inscrutable background that nonetheless unsettles as aestheticized brutality.[32]

Elsewhere, in "Nach und Nach" (37; I, 204), that violence is explicit but not described. It is invisible but present as a concentration of atmosphere and implication leading to a horrific ellipsis:

Nach und nach fiel sie
In die Hände seiner Worte.
Die Bäume auf dem Wege zu ihm
Waren rasch verblüht,
Die Gebüsche zerbrochen, in denen
Ihre Zärtlichkeit die Wange
An seinem Gesicht rieb.

Sie war nun in seiner Gewalt
Wie zwischen großen Hunden,
die jedem Fremden
Nach dem Leben trachten.
Langsam verging sie, umstellt
Von Dolchen des Gesprächs,
Das er mit ihr führte.

Sie hatte keinen Willen mehr,
Wenn der Schatten seines Bartes
Unter dem Mond auftauchte
Und seine Stimme befahl,
Ihm zu folgen . . .

Here the primary, literal level of the poem suggests physical violence with terms such as *Hände, Gewalt, Hunden,* and *Dolchen,* but the secondary, figurative level indicates that the violence is verbal and psychological as evidenced by *seiner Worte* and *des Gesprächs.* Trees and bushes figure as embodiments of tenderness, intimacy, and eroticism that once bloomed or flourished between them, or at least in her, but that has now withered and been broken. The woman has become an object of hatred, an Other that has been forced into submission through terror "wie zwischen großen Hunden, / die jedem Fremden / nach dem Leben trachten." The feral intensity of that image negates any possible distinctions between physical and psychological and verbal violence: violence in this poem is all-encompassing and reduces the woman to abject subjugation ("keinen Willen mehr") at the sight or sound of the man, whom she then must blindly follow. The ellipsis at the end of the poem is itself also a metaphor, in which the primary denotative level of signification has fallen away, but the secondary connotative level of comprehension gains correspondingly in force of signification and alludes, inevitably in this context, to a fatal act of sexual violence.

Likewise in the poem "Nach der Arbeit" (43; I, 206), precise language and imagery mediates an uncertain but ubiquitous sense of violence:

> Die Soldatenmützen sind in den Nacken geschoben.
> Es ist so weit, daß man sich
> Die Augen reibt und nach der Sonne sucht,
> Die untergegangen ist.
> Aus den Häusern stürzen
> Wasserfälle des Lichts.
> Sie verlieren sich im Efeugebüsch,
> In dem ein Schatten gebeugt bleibt.
> Andere machen woanders ihr Glück.
> Schon ist die Nacht auf der Suche
> Nach denen, die unter ihrem Messer
> Fallen sollen.

Soldiers, anonymous and dehumanized by their reduction to the metonym *Soldatenmützen,* are on their free time at the end of the day. The brilliance of the metaphor of cascading light from the windows illuminates the poem at its center. Around that pool of light, however, the soldiers lose themselves surreptitiously into the bushes. One shadow does not come back out of the bushes but, on the contrary, remains "gebeugt," which seems to indicate some kind of vulnerability or victimization, either in sex or violence. The others move on to seek their separate or further pleasure. Again the exact details of what transpires here are lost in the metaphoric penumbra around the words, subject to speculation and without definite specification. But again, in the final lines, the secondary, figurative level of the metaphor has become primary: the concrete, denotative signification is simply that the sun has set and night has fallen, but the metaphor of predation, menace, and murder looms in the foreground. The metaphor does not coincide with its object as in "Wasserfälle des Lichts"; the "Nacht auf der Suche," with its knife, has meaning in excess of its initial signification of night falling. That excess of meaning lies in the suggestions of intent, of relentless stalking, or of searching broadly and of murder, which all transfer and attach to the only agents of action in the poem, the "Soldatenmützen." Outside the pool of light, the night is alive with menace, with violence that might be, beyond the campfire or light of civilization in the feral world of humankind, just another person's cruel pleasure.

Fremde Körper is populated with images of menace, flight, pursuit, choking, suffocation, ambush, knives, and weapons, usually emerging after several unrelated images. In "Entführung" (91; I, 128), as in the above reading of "Nach und Nach," the eroticism of nature only introduces sexual subjugation and violence:

> Der Wind, . . .
>
> Öffnet deine Bluse am Hals.
> . . .
> Die Taube in deinem Herzen
> Ist in seiner Gewalt.
> Ohne Widerstand
> Läßt sie sich töten.

Nature harbors menace and does not offer refuge; in "Die Bildsäule" (36; I, 174): "Seither sind aus den Bäumen / Gewehrmündungen auf sie gerichtet." In "Das Schweigen" (17; I, 178), travelers lose their way: "Ihre vom Sommer entblößten Körper / Hängen tot / Im Schatten eines Walnußbaums."[33] The poem "Blut der Nacht" (45; I, 212) concludes as follows: "Auf der Flucht vor dem Tod / Blickt sich niemand um. / Die letzten Schritte / Ersticken im aufgelösten Haar / Des Windes." The ornate genitive metaphor, recalling pre-Raphaelite imagery and Jugendstil design of sensual, abundantly swirling hair, jars as an image of a death struggle, in which the fleeing person is literally out of breath in frightened flight for his or her life; in "Manchmal" (42; I, 213), the atmosphere is explosive, literally and figuratively: "Ganz nah ist mit roter Pupille / Eine Flamme auf der Suche / Nach einer Lunte. // Jedes geflüsterte 'Wer da?' / Käme zu spät." The attempt to identify friend or enemy in the darkness is a fatal hesitation. In "Laß den Himmel" (44; I, 220), as the title suggests, the possibility of any floating transcendence out of the gravity of violence seems far: "Und nachts wird geschossen, / Wenn im Dunkeln / Zwei Augen leuchten." The gleaming light of *Blätterlicht* now means ancient predatory menace lurking in the darkness with modern weaponry.[34]

After the inclusion of fifteen poems from *Tage und Nächte,* under the caption of "Wahrnehmungen" (49–66), the section "Gesang vor der Tür" (67–94) reflects a gradual turn away from nature as a scene of violence and toward society. Accordingly, the subject returns to the poem, though in isolation. The first poem of the three poem cycle, "Robinson I" (69–71; I, 209–10), demonstrates this distant relation of the subject to society, as "ein Ausgesetzter" (199). Krolow himself describes the subject in his essay in Hilde Domin's collection of complementary essays by poets and critics, titled *Doppelinterpretationen: Das zeitgenössische Gedicht zwischen Autor und Leser*.[35]

> Immer wieder strecke ich meine Hand
> Nach einem Schiff aus.
> Mit der bloßen Faust versuche ich,
> Nach seinem Segel zu greifen.
> Anfangs find ich
> Verschiedene Fahrzeuge, die sich
> Am Horizont zeigten.
> Ich fange Forellen so.
> Doch der Monsun sah mir
> Auf die Finger
> Und ließ sie entweichen,
> Oder der Ruder und Kompaß
> Brachen. Man muß
> Mit Schiffen zart umgehen.
> Darum rief ich ihnen Namen nach.
> Sie lauteten immer
> Wie meiner.
>
> Jetzt lebe ich nur noch
> In Gesellschaft mit dem Ungehorsam
> Einiger Worte.

As in the poem "Einsamkeit," the individual subject as "das personifizierte Verlangen nach Kontakt und zugleich die Widerlegung einer derartigen Anstrengung" (200) extends a hand to the outside world, but remains, within the larger context of society, lost or shipwrecked in a sort of semantic isolation where words no longer can grasp anything. On the one hand, the theoretical loss of referential function in literature and in poetry, and on the other hand, the unquestioned and empty referential status of language in journalism, both maroon the individual subject, the linguistic consciousness, on a metaphoric island, though in real isolation. Reality cannot be captured in language any longer "mit der bloßen Faust." Instead, in order to form a link to what is "am Horizont," the subjective consciousness has to pay close attention to its language, the vehicle of expression with its content, its cargo of meaning ("Man muß / Mit Schiffen zart umgehen"). Though that scrupulousness and scrutiny with language carries the risk of further isolation in narcissistic monologue ("Darum rief ich ihnen Namen nach. / Sie lauteten immer / Wie meiner"). Yet within the context of society, language remains the ground, the terra firma, even if as an island, for survival as a subject, as a linguistic and historical consciousness. Krolow has subtly adapted the theme of Robinson Crusoe, the Enlightenment hero of rational self-sustaining intelligence, to the context of twentieth-century linguistic consciousness and late capitalist social abstraction. But that linguistic consciousness is also bound and bounded by history: in this poem and in Krolow's work overall, poetry is the ship that brought him to the island of his isolation, to his exile from reality in pure metaphoricity, in language cut off from its groundedness in history, that distant coast to which he waves from afar. As Benno von Wiese has noted, in an otherwise helpless and hapless essay on the poem: "es sind Schiffe der Phantasie, die trotzdem etwas Wirkliches intendieren" (*Doppelinterpretationen*, 205). Robinson is here the historical subject that is both separated from and linked to society and history by its language, and in that double consciousness, is "geisterhaft wirklich, dennoch leidend an den Nachstellungen einer Realität, an der er zu tragen hatte" (*Doppelinterpretationen*, 200); Robinson seeks to exist outside of society and history, and figures that ambiguity into this poem: "So verstanden, gleicht der Verlauf des Gedichtes einer vergeblichen Geste, der vergeblichen Anstrengung, von sich los zu kommen" (200) and thus to achieve a "Freiheit von Folgerungen und Folgen" (201). History does not disappear from Krolow's works but resides or hovers out of sight just over the horizon.

Subsequent poems translate that solitude back into society as an inhabited architectural space, often given metonymically as a window, a door, or an interior, as in "Das Haus" (I, 201):

> Bevor aus seinen Fenstern
> Schwarze Fahnen wuchsen,
> War alles in ihm ruhig gewesen.
> Die Katze saß über der Falltür.
> Die gestorbene Frau
> Winkte auf der Treppe.
> Man konnte mit den weißen Petunien reden,
> Die aus Nischen blühten.
> Immer war gerade vorher
> Einer fortgegangen und hatte
> Mit den Zehen zarte Namen
> In den Staub geschrieben.

> Die Stunden trugen die Haare
> Ins Gesicht gekämmt.
> Aber nun sind die Bettlaken
> Schwarz geworden vom Abdruck
> Fremder Körper, die im Hause
> Nächtigten.
> Die Zeit, die sie miteinander verbrachten,
> Wächst unaufhörlich in den Himmel.

The "schwarze Fahnen" seem to represent the darkness in the windows that looms outward, as if in mourning as a sign of death, like the light used to do as a sign of life when the house was inhabited. Now the woman has died and the animation in the house, the conversations and coming and going, has all disappeared. The house is now occupied by shadows of its former occupants, who have left their imprint ("Abdruck / Fremder Körper") as negative impressions, explicit absences, a sort of sediment of memories from former times that endure "unaufhörlich."

In "Der Wind im Zimmer" (74; I, 203), that space comes alive through the wind that enters the house like a prowler: "Unter Gelächter und Türenschlagen / Findet er ins Zimmer," which recalls the first line of Krolow's earlier poem "Verlassene Küste." The wind slips through the house and leaves its tracks in windblown hair: "Wer ihn im Dunkeln fängt, / Wird am anderen Morgen aufwachen / Mit einer fremden Windrose im Haar."[36] In the fourth section of *Fremde Körper*, the violence of mankind in a natural setting and the anonymity and estrangement of the individual in society converge in poems like "Die Gewalt" (96; I, 185):

> Sie kam aus ihrem Versteck
> Und erweckte totes Metall zum Leben.
> Die letzten Unterhändler
> Streiften die Handschuhe über ihre Finger
> Und gingen. Ihr Lächeln
> Zahlt sich in keiner Münze mehr aus.
>
> Sie kam aus ihrem Versteck.
> Der Erdstrich, auf den ihr Blick fällt,
> Ist verloren.
> Die Türen springen auf.
> Die Fenster zerbrechen.
> In die Augen streut man

Asche und Mörtel.
Lippen schließen sich
Unter Faustschlägen.
Die unreine Nacht hält
Überfälle und schwarze Minuten bereit.
Bald werden die Herzen
Aufhören zu schlagen
Hinter dem Vorhang von Ruß.
Sie kam aus ihrem Versteck.
Sie wird Hand an uns legen.
Noch dürfen wir die Häuser verlassen
Und in den Glühbirnen-Himmel sehen.
Aber in den Vorstädten
Sind schon Spruchbänder gespannt.
Bald werden die Straßenkämpfe
Uns erreichen.
Bald werden wir allein sein
Mit den Gewehrmündungen.
Wer unter uns ist der erste,
Der an seinem Tische
Vornüber sinkt? . . .

Violence is allegorized as a woman, who emerges from hiding to unleash destruction and chaos.[37] The refrain picks up the familiar motif of a place of hiding, but that violence now moves with implacable progress from nature through the outlying suburbs into the city where banners are hung and street fights imminent. The poem seems at first to address at least the scenery, if not the substance, of social unrest, but gives no specific historical details or insight into a general situation of protest and the legitimacy, or not, of violence or pacifism. The poem opens a context that it does not fulfill, and instead seeks to generate fear, without analysis, which then figures only as sensationalist pathos. In effect, each repetition, without rhythmic sonority or concrete detail in a developing situation, only empties the poem of specific emotional or intellectual content. The violence that was so prevalent in the other poems, in situations of ambush or sexual violence, now inspires, in a social context, melodramatic fear.[38]

The poem "Wollen wir es nicht versuchen?" (104; I, 191) goes furthest in this volume in trying to enter into the dynamics of contemporary history. In the rhetorical question of the title, Krolow addresses himself perhaps more than others:

Wollen wir es nicht
Mit den anständigen Leuten versuchen?
Die Republik hat genügend verirrte Hände,
Die sich auf jemandes Schultern legen lassen
Oder über unseren Scheiteln
Zu vereinigen sind.
Vorläufig verlieren sich die Tage noch
Mit den zuvielen Banknoten.
Vorläufig ist die Ratlosigkeit noch
Den Verwandlungen der Cellulose
Beigegeben.
Der Himmel voll kalter Linien,
Die die Luft aufteilen.

Wollen wir es nicht
Mit den anständigen Leuten halten?
In unserem Land vergißt man so schnell
Die hingerichteten Augen.
Die getäuschten Herzen
Warten noch auf ihre Zeit.
Die auf der Straße vorbeigehen,
Werden sie bald schon
Wahrnehmen . . .

The reference to the republic broadens the scope of the poem, though the speaker retreats from the political arena, presented in lines two through six as a sort of Big Brotherly chaos ("verirrte Hände") viewed from below. The word *Vorläufig*, followed by allusions to inflation and materialism or the "economic miracle," to the development of rayon and to air traffic, gives a sense, which is unusual in Krolow's work, of history in process, though at the center of that process is still "Ratlosigkeit." After the rhetorical refrain, the second stanza alludes, with a direct reference to the war and perhaps to the Holocaust, and to the willful amnesia of the fifties and the inevitability of anamnesia, the eventual recollection of the "getäuschten Herzen," who will gain their recognition among the people on the street in the everyday life of contemporary Germany.

The last poem of the volume seems to bring to culmination the tendency to address, at least superficially, the matter of history and bears as its title, "Historie" (105; I, 192):

Männer trugen über den Platz eine Fahne.
Da brachen Centauren aus dem Gestrüpp
Und zertrampelten ihr Tuch
Und Geschichte konnte beginnen.
Melancholische Staaten
Zerfielen an Straßenecken.
Redner hielten sich
Mit Bulldoggen bereit,
Und die jüngeren Frauen
Schminkten sich für die Stärkeren.
Unaufhörlich stritten Stimmen
In der Luft, obwohl sich
Die mythologischen Wesen längst
Zurückgezogen hatten.
Übrig bleibt schließlich die Hand,
Die sich um eine Kehle legt.

In the first lines, history begins as the triumph of brute force, of mythological man-beasts, over politics, figured here either as protest or partisanship and represented by the flag. Here again as in previous poems, though set in the public arena, violence surges out of the underbrush of nature and overwhelms a peaceful demonstration of political engagement. Orderly governments become "Melancholische Staaten" doomed to dissolution, to chaos in the streets ("an Straßenecken"). Speakers become fanatical and discourage discussion or debate with the threat of raw force ("Bulldoggen"). In this climate of bestiality, young women paint themselves for the powerful. The chaos becomes self-perpetuating ("Unaufhörlich stritten Stimmen"). The suite of scenes recalls the images of Georg Grosz, though without the satire and critical sense of the grotesque; instead, they lead here to a forceful conclusion in the separate distich that advances an ideology. Whatever the political constitution that governs the surface of daily life, once the bestial nature of mankind, which is transhistorical or mythological, has burst out of the depths, chaos reigns. In this poem, the concept of history, however it might be more closely defined, collapses, from the public to the private sphere, to the overwhelming reality of brute force and violence: "Übrig bleibt schließlich die Hand / Die sich um eine Kehle legt." This view of history precludes any further examination of society in its different, less grandiose or horrific dimensions. In fact, a contrary understanding of history, as the contestation of various political, economic, personal, and psychological factors, does not enter at all into this poem; a complex understanding of historical experience registers only as the sharp contours of its absence. The poem is powerful in its stark imagery, tightly tailored and precisely executed in its form, but primitive in its concept.

Notes

[1] Without naming Krolow, Hartmut Eggert discusses this motif in the fifties (drawing on Bachmann and Eich) and demonstrates the contemporary historical contexts of the seemingly vague dread that remained in the postwar period.

[2] Cf. Ziolkowski.

[3] Jeziorkowski considers the poem: "einer der zentralen Orte im lyrischen Werk Karl Krolows, fast möchte man sagen, in der deutschen Lyrik nach dem zweiten Weltkrieg" (216).

[4] Also, "Winterliche Ode" (I, 39–40) seems to present a seasonal poem, but the diction reveals an oblique portrait of the epoch and an individual psychology, whose vanishing point is historical and centers upon "schwarze Bündel Schuld" (39).

[5] Accordingly, that silence is not enacted, but named, in multiple varied phrases in this volume, as "Horizont der Stille" (I, 40), as "Dickicht der Stille" (I, 41), as "Traube der Stille" (I, 47), and as "Nullpunkt der Stille" (I, 49).

[6] Later, Krolow entered into a public debate with Walter Höllerer over this issue of the long versus the short poem. The long poem became a significant genre of *Alltagslyrik*.

[7] Rümmler points out that Krolow "borrowed" these several phrases, among the most arresting and interesting in the poem, and others from Stephan Hermlin's translations of Eluard. Rümmler uses the peculiar and contradictory phrase "passiv entlehnt" (164). See also his discussion (167) of other direct and verbatim appropriations.

[8] Rümmler cites these lines as figures that for "den Interpretanten nicht mehr nachvollziehbar sind, und nur noch unbestimmte Gefühlswerte liefern" (165).

[9] In explicating the first stanza of Krolow's "Die Überwindung der Schwermut," of the same period and volume, Otto Knörrich comments on this process that allows Krolow to resemble and reject the nature poetry he learned from: "Die Wörter sind ihres realen Benennungscharakters mehr oder weniger entkleidet. Indem sie in ein ungegenständliches, alogisches Beziehungsnetz eingesetzt werden, werden sie von den durch sie benannten Inhalten teilweise abgelöst. Es ist jener Vorgang der Abstraktion, dessen grundsätzliche Bedeutung für die moderne Lyrik immer wieder in Erscheinung tritt" (43). Knörrich rightly points out that *Naturlyrik* to some extent already had that dual character, as representation and presentation, as image and language, and played an important role in German poetic modernism, not outside of it. It therefore marks a shared point of departure for measuring the developments of most important German poets of mid-century.

While agreeing, I try here to articulate the precise use of that tradition with respect to historical content that distinguishes Krolow.

[10] Klaus Weissenberger mainly analyzes the metrical organization of the poem, but also notes its dialectical structure ("dialektisches Wechselspiel," 128) as it develops and disposes of different metaphysical positions.

[11] Curiously, in his rather long interpretation of the poem, Rümmler passes over this section with the note: "Im zweiten und dritten 'Heute'-Gedicht setzen sich die Erfahrung der Sinnlosigkeit des Lebens und die des Todes durch" (167), whereas the image itself is precise and seems to refer to a specific context since "Verbannte" and "Erschießungskommandos" are not general existential conditions as Rümmler seems to indicate with his gloss. Any connection Krolow might have had to the RKFDV, or even just his presence in Breslau and inevitable awareness of the invasion of Poland (see Walter Tausk's *Tagebuch*), would provide a context. In contrast, Weissenberger rightly notes: "Viel mehr Wirklichkeit als in der Metaphysik offenbart sich in den Bildern der Zeitgeschichte. [. . .] Es bleibt als Wirklichkeit die Folter der Vergänglichkeit" (129). Clearly Weissenberger means "Vergangenheit," but he himself sidesteps the issue by universalizing history into temporality, by shifting into the same metaphysics as Krolow, though Krolow is also clearly making the historical reference. Criticism of Krolow's work, by not noting the specific ahistorical tendency, has exaggerated that same tendency since those parts of the poems that are of actual historical interest are then simply dropped.

[12] In extrapolating from the earlier poem "Traumfahrt" where this process of voiding history begins, Horst Daemmrich had made a comment that is more pertinent here where Krolow is consciously working through that position: "Die Bildassoziationen sollen über die Jahrhunderte hinweg den geschichtlichen Raum zu einem Ideogramm verschmelzen. . . . zu einer zeitlosen Zusammenschau, welche das weit auseinanderliegende Geschehen zusammenfügt, ohne es kritisch zu bewältigen. . . . So erscheint die Geschichte als Fläche ohne scharfe Kontur" (43). He adds rightly, "In den Gedichten der fünfziger und sechziger Jahre setzt sich eine Auffächerung des geschichtlichen Raums durch" (44). Here it happens.

[13] See the final passage of his story "Gehirne" in his collection *Gehirne* (1916): "Wie ein Vogel aus der Schlucht." For an analysis of that passage in its relation to the story and the collection, see my *Forms of Disruption* (173–78). Yet Benn does establish a relation to the war and to Rönne's empirical experience as a doctor performing autopsies as a source of trauma. Hans Bender makes the connection of Krolow to Benn with the following distinction, which is also a contradiction: "Krolow ist anti-metaphysisch gestimmt (wie die Autoren des Nouveau Romans). . . . Er ist Benn, den er seltener zitiert als andere Lyriker, verwandt in der artistischen Haltung; in der Auffassung auch: das Gedicht sei anachoretisch, monologisch, 'an niemand gerichtet,' ein 'Kunstprodukt'" (113). Bender's equation is only partly correct, but at least underscores a certain affinity between the two despite Krolow's guardedness toward Benn. In "Not und Chancen des deutschen Gedichts" (April 1952), Krolow wrote of "Die Überschätzung *Gottfried Benns*" (6) and developed his critique in "Jugendstil und Gottfried Benn" (September 1952) to absurd lengths, describing his metaphors as "rein dekorativ" (3), a view which elicited sharp replies from Bode F. Ferber and Helmut Heissenbüttel (see

bibliography). In a letter to F. W. Oelze (March 4, 1953), Benn writes witheringly: "Die jungen deutschen Dichter: keiner primär, alle Halb- und Halbnaturen, wenig interessant. [. . .] Krolow ein 'Bewisperer,' Schule Wilhelm Lehmann, hat oft böse gegen mich geschrieben u. immer darauf hingewiesen, daß er selber viel bedeutungsvoller sei" (*Briefe an F. W. Oelze, 1950–54,* #629, 163–64).

[14] Alfred Andersch cites the first strophe of this poem as an example of Krolow's adoption of surrealist metaphor without the psychological depths from the unconscious, making the essential distinction that German postwar surrealism tends toward mannerism. About the conscious control of the technique that Krolow retains, Andersch remarks: "Das hat Vorteile: es fördert das Gelingen der Form, und Nachteile: es versperrt den Weg zu den Funden" (*Über Karl Krolow,* 43), yet Andersch himself then does not press forward to open a way "zu den Funden" and to examine its actual content beyond the brilliant metaphor Krolow writes and he in turn cites.

[15] Also, the commentator at times sees only the beauty, not the violence. Hans Egon Holthusen cites these last lines to make the point that "Die metaphorische Aktivität verzichtet mehr und mehr auf optische und logische Unterlagen und schöpft ihre Einfälle aus dem rein Vokabulären" (93–94; also in *Über Karl Krolow,* 15). Here, a critic of the same generation eliminates the relation to reality in the poem. See Helmut Böttiger on Holthusen's altercation with Peter Szondi over Paul Celan's poetry, which is relevant here.

[16] Rümmler documents in detail numerous verbatim borrowings and paraphrasings in the "Heute" cycle, mainly from Stephan Hermlin's translations of Paul Eluard (7), but also from Jules Supervielle. Some of the most striking phrases in the poem, such as "Waage der Zärtlichkeiten" and "Brücke der Blicke," among others, are lifted directly; as Rümmler notes: "Krolow montiert diese Metaphern unverändert in seinen Kontext" (167). Around the same time, of course, Thomas Mann was doing the same thing on a much larger scale (see my chapter 8 on "Erudite Montage" in *Forms of Disruption,* especially fn. 7) and referred to his practice in a quasi-confessional letter to Theodor Adorno dated December 30, 1946, concerning his use of Adorno's manuscript on *Die Philosophie moderner Musik* as "eine Art hoheres Abschreiben." Yet the smaller, tighter economy of the poem offers less context for integration.

[17] Paulus considers this poem Krolow's "erstes komplexes Poetik-Gedicht," though "Heute" precedes it, and he cites a conversation with Krolow on June 26, 1978, in Darmstadt, in which Krolow indicated "daß dieses Gedicht programmatisch zu verstehen sei und gegen die inflationäre Verwendung bestimmter fast schon modischer Ausprägungen des Existentialimus gerichtet war" (*Lyrik und Poetik Karl Krolows,* 35). The text seems clear enough on that point in the first stanza, though one would have to add that Krolow's work also added to that inflation.

[18] Cf. Neumann on "absolute metaphor."

[19] Indeed, Krolow develops this latter word as a centerpiece of his aesthetics in his Büchner Prize address.

[20] The distinction I wish to make with this term is that Krolow's poetry is not simply ahistorical, which would mean that it merely by definition and practice avoids

specific historical context, like Benn's absolute poem, and sublates it into myth, but rather that Krolow's poetry maintains a relationship to history, in as far as it consciously then rids the poem of history. Krolow's poetics, as theory and practice, includes the mechanism or the process of translating history into artifice, the past into the open continuum of the present.

[21] Almost alone among critics of the poem, Rudolf Hartung notes, with his usual acuity: "Hier zeigt sich, daß Krolow auf diesem Gebiet [the long poem with apparent political content] kaum Wesentliches, jedenfalls nichts Spezifisches zu sagen hatte — der Krieg in Korea beispielsweise bleibt in der 1951 geschriebenen *Koreanischen Elegie* ein gleichsam atmosphärisches Ereignis, die Dimension der Geschichte wird verfehlt. Das Gedicht ist in sich selber versponnen und langt nicht hinüber in die große schreckliche Wirklichkeit draußen" (*Über Karl Krolow*, 108). Heinz Piontek also indicates that, for Krolow in general, long poems are not "des Dichters Sache" (*Über Karl Krolow*, 92), but he dismisses the better ones with the lesser and does not note the importance of "Heute" and "Ode 1950," for example. This gesture, though distinct from that of Helmuth de Haas simply finding the long poems "voll schwingender Anmut" (*Über Karl Krolow*, 54), reinforces the de-historicizing tendency in Krolow and his reception by winnowing the work to separate out traces of historical content, and by gleaning metaphors out of context.

[22] This opening line in a much-anthologized poem is one of the most well-known in Krolow's oeuvre, and probably owes a debt to Georg Britting's poem "Der Morgen" (12), where "Kühl durch die Windgemächer / Rinnt grün das junge Licht / In den Tag, der mit Schlag und Gelächter / Anbricht." Krolow had cited the isolated phrase "Schlag und Gelächter" in his review essay "Betrachtungen zu Gedichtband-Titeln" (100).

[23] Here one can accept Knörrich's point that *Naturlyrik* in Germany cannot, in fact, be held apart from the modernist traditions outside of Germany, since nature only existed in its linguistic realization, a point which sounds more obvious than it is, and he emphasizes that magic realism in German *Naturlyrik* participates, ultimately though not at first glance, in the traditions of magic verbalism or linguistic experimentation of European modernism (52). See Doris Kirchner's treatment of the notion of *Magic Realism* in this period in Germany.

[24] Jong Ho Pee gives a full reading of this last poem in terms of its motifs, including a mirror and flamingos, and compares the poem to Rilke's "Die Flamingos," while remarking at the outset "Die bewegende Bildfolge verdeutlicht Schweben und Leichtigkeit" (63), which is an increasingly common feature of Krolow's work, as I demonstrate.

[25] Rümmler detects here in "Aufschwung" the first sign of Jorge Guillén's influence, which converges with the enduring influence of Wilhelm Lehmann (Rümmler, 185). He defines that combined influence as follows: "Das tragende Grundgefühl der heilen Natur- und Liebeswelt ist das zeit- und erinnerungslose Daseinserlebnis" (Rümmler, 188). Guillén's influence is marked by the sense of a precise mathematics in nature.

[26] See chapter 9 on Krolow and Celan.

[27] Krolow gives an account of the genesis of this poem in his essay "Celine 1/2" in *Ein Gedicht entsteht* (27–35). He remarks in summary: "Ich wollte die jugendlich Verstorbene in eine gleichsam durchhellte, leichte, schwebende Umgebung versetzen, in eine Welt, wie sie zu der Zeit ihres Erdenwandels gehört haben mochte, Welt des 18. Jahrhunderts, Zeitalter des Lichtes, der durchdringenden oder graziösen Vernunft, des hellen Geistes, der die Geisterseherei verabscheute" (30). In unintentional irony, however, this historical fantasy resembles more such "Geisterseherei" than an act "des hellen Geistes."

[28] Peter Härtling's brief and frivolous meditation (*In Zeilen Zuhaus*, 66–70) evokes, without any critical value whatsoever, what Härtling takes as the rococo spirit and scenario of the poem.

[29] Hans Dieter Schäfer (*Zusammenhänge der deutschen Gegenwartslyrik*, 168) notes that in this poem, as in so much of Krolow's work, the terms of metaphoric comparison between the various incidents given by the poem and the passing of day into night are linked by verbs of movement, usually discrete, which lend the poem as a whole, as an aggregrate of small metaphoric conceits, a kaleidoscopic quality.

[30] These poems are excerpted from the section "Wahrnehmungen" of twenty-one poems.

[31] As Martin Anderle alertly notes in his comparative discussion of Krolow's surrealistic metaphors: "das tertium comparationis ist kaum aufzuspüren, und der Vergleich wirkt nur noch als bizarre Chiffre" (175–76). In my readings, I attempt to push beyond prior criticism to discover the third term or locate, as exactly as possible through the metaphors, the contours of its absence.

[32] Rolf Paulus lists this poem among several whose "Spezifikum [ist] meist eine verschärfte Emotion, deren konkreter Anlaß nicht sichtbar wird" (*Text + Kritik*, 28). Here, the opposite is the case: the emotion recedes behind the concrete details that are ambivalent, but not unclear or invisible. That ambivalence between the literal and figurative usages, implicating animals or humans or humans killed like animals or animals killed like humans, unsettles and disturbs precisely because the concrete situation of a slaughter is clear.

[33] Rolf Paulus comments rightly that the poem "Das Schweigen" presents "eine beängstigende verbrecherische Szenerie" (*Text + Kritik*, 28–29), but again, he draws no conclusion. Instead, he paraphrases Dieter Schlenstedt to suggest that the visual details present an emotional structure that reflects the "Unbegreiflichkeit und Bedrohtheit der Wirklichkeit" (*Text + Kritik*, 29). That willingness to abstract each poem into a general existential situation obscures further whatever is already not obvious and defeats the purpose of criticism, which is to elucidate the text in question. See also, the following footnote.

[34] In his critical survey of Krolow's reception, Gerhard Kolter remarks rightly on the tendency to abstract away from specific, but unpleasant details of the text: "Konkrete Hinweise auf bedrohliche Elemente der Realität werden entweder konsequent vermieden oder in ein Bild umgesetzt (. . .), so daß die Bedrohung durch eine Abstrahierung wegstilisiert werden kann. Dadurch wird Realität verdunkelt, statt analytisch auf den Begriff gebracht zu werden. . . . Wenn Krolow z. B. konkret von Gewehrmündungen spricht, werden nur *Bedrohungen und Einsamkeiten* erkannt" (*Text + Kritik*, 42).

[35] Krolow links the poem to his other poems of anonymous subjects, such as "Jemand," "Er," and "Einsamkeit," and makes a reading of the poem dependent on that context. Of course, the notion of being "ausgesetzt" runs through Krolow's work and goes back to his first publication on Rilke's poem "Ausgesetzt auf den Bergen des Herzens."

[36] Reinhold Grimm comments on this metaphor in his discussion of this poem in *Strukturen* (190–91), building on H. Friedrich's comments in his preface of 1962 on Krolow's use of metaphor, but Grimm also notes how Krolow plays on the word as a technical term for the "face" of a compass. Further, one might note as a possible source a volume of poems by Peter Gan (a.k.a. Richard Moering) with that title in 1935.

[37] The poem "Die Freiheit" (102; I, 188–89) also allegorizes that concept as a woman, also creating chaos ("Die Leute sagen, sie habe den bösen Blick") as she flees (in the refrain: "Sie flieht vorüber, in sich gekehrt"). Her flight leads her into an ambush: "An der Ecke wartet auf sie / Der schwarze Wegelagerer:— / Gewalt, mit unbiegsamen Metall / In den Fäusten!"

[38] This poem was first printed in the *Frankfurter Allgemeine Zeitung* in November 1956. Rolf Paulus makes the relevant connection to the Hungarian Revolution (*Text + Kritik,* 29) that would have affected the reception of the poem; Paulus introduces the poem under the caption "Politische Dimension," but does not analyze the poem in that light or draw conclusions about it. That historical context would only make more urgent and necessary some specific analysis, detail, or at least, a point of view by Krolow and by Paulus. Given that context, the poem, despite first appearances, is all the more decidedly and perhaps egregiously apolitical. The melodramatization of violence would also seem to place unreflected blame on the insurgents and condone social stability, under whatever conditions, for its own sake. Of course, a poet need not take a stand on contemporary issues and events, but to write a topical poem for the occasion, in light of the event, and without entering into its substance, is simply a sensationalistic exploitation of contemporary history.

7: Professions of an Apolitical Man
(The Sixties)

Unsichtbare Hände (1962)

AFTER THE PONDEROUS INVOLVEMENT with history in *Fremde Körper* (1959), whose title itself suggests the culmination of Krolow's aesthetics of impersonality, Krolow's first volume in the 1960s, *Unsichtbare Hände*, likewise seems to constitute the culmination of his poetics of dematerialization with an array of images of tactile invisibility, as in his poem "The Fairy Queen: Nach der Musik von Henry Purcell" (I, 218): "Das Licht legt dir / seinen Mantel um / Nun bist du gekleidet / wie der geborstene Körper / des Mittags: durchsichtig." The physical material in this image is rendered transparent, though with palpable texture; the immaterial light and air are conversely rendered textile, as surface, as epidermis.

A poem like "Im Grünen" (I, 230) establishes the basic situation of a return to impressions of nature, though with an added degree of artistic mediation:

> Frauen- und Vogelköpfe
> im Laub, das aussieht wie Laub
> der Aquarellenmaler.
>
> Hier kann man sitzen
> und langsam mit der Luft sprechen.
> Grün: bis unter die Herzen,
> unter den Kinderhimmel,
> in dem jeder Verdacht
> zur Wolke wird.
>
> Es macht Kopfweh, weil es
> noch bei geschlossenen Augen
> grün bleibt.

> Aber man kann auch darüber lachen
> und sich ein blaues Fahrrad ausdenken,
> mit dem man den Horizont entlang
> fährt.

The familiar motif of *Blätterlicht* returns in the comparison to water colors, as opposed to oil paints, which provides a measure of lightness, dematerialization, and sweeping flourish. The simple sentence that begins the second stanza disperses the obscurity of the earlier motif of the hiding place that endured after Krolow's period of *inner emigration* with openness, air, and a casual dialogue with nature. The primary colors of green, blue ("Himmel") and white ("Wolke") in their simplicity dissolve suspicions of violence that used to lie in ambush in nature. Such suspicions that link the individual to a specific context, a particular reality, are evaporated "zur Wolke" by the light and air in the foliage. The individual becomes an anonymous but not estranged part of nature. The third stanza alludes back to Krolow's "Traum von einem Wald" (*Auf Erden*, 10) from his first volume ("Ich träume Grün. Wie ich die Augen schließe, / Ist noch das Dunkel meiner Lider grün."), but the motif no longer figures as defiant inwardness in retreat from outward, historical pressures in a National-Socialist state. Instead, that eidetic green registers merely as discomfort, the intensity of colors in nature, which as "Kopfweh" marks a counterpoint to joyous freedom of imagination; in the poem "Siebensachen" (I, 239), Krolow varies the motif without the "Kopfweh": "Jemand hat uns / Blätter auf die Augen gelegt. // Kühl ist das Grün." In these poems the dead appear as phantoms, as in "Stelldichein" (I, 240) or "Bei Tagesanbruch" (I, 230), without adding the specific weight of private or collective history; rather the dead radiate a surreal glow of nightly light. The sense of dematerialization links the dead as phantoms to angels. The poem "Himmel" (I, 237) portrays the upward movement out of historical gravity:

> Arena der Scherenschnitte!
> Sie kämpfen darum,
> Schneeflocken oder Lerchen
> zu werden.
>
> Der Sommer läßt in ihm
> sehnsüchtige, blaue Schiffe fahren.
>
> Auf ihrer Reise zum Zenit
> werden sie immer leichter.

> Die Engel des Horizonts
> warten schon mit Licht
> unter den Wimpern.

Silhouettes do battle like gladiators in the arena of paper that will define their existence, either as snowflakes or as larks. No individual is present in the poem, only as the "invisible hands" holding the scissors. That anonymous and metonymous individual is an empty vessel of imagination that the season inspires. The blue ships recall the blue bicycle in the poem "Im Grünen." The ships also represent, at another metonymic remove, the individual subject's transport "zum Zenit," its weightlessness and elevation upward toward the light on the horizon, toward the seraphic apparition whose eyelashes of light suggest the radiating rays of a rising or setting sun on the horizon.

In the above poem, as in the collection as a whole, Krolow seems to have realized the aesthetic principles he articulated in his self-interview of 1964:

> Ich glaube, daß die von mir im Gedicht bevorzugten Gegenstände ohne die Drastik ihrer Gegenständlichkeit, ohne das Gewicht der Materialität sind. Es sind in Veränderungen befindliche Stoffe, möchte ich sagen. Übergänge vom einen zum anderen. Und also bewegliche, sich entmaterialisierende Mitteilungen. Von ihrer Stofflichkeit erleichterte, über ihr schwebende, balancierende Themata. — Um es poetisch auszudrücken: ich möchte Rose oder Auge oder Mund oder Hand an ihre Umwelt, an Wind, Luft, Licht darstellen, an ein leichtes Ensemble, das den Einzelheiten hilft, so liquid wie möglich zu werden. Ich möchte gewissermaßen Leitern an die Gegenstände legen, mit Sprossen, die immer weiter nach oben, in ein unverdächtiges, offenes Blau führen. (10)

This passage contains the terms that recur in his descriptions of his own poetic practice, in his attempts to make the poem lithe, light, without substance, immaterial, liquid but floating, leaning like a ladder on its objects and leading into the opening sky, into a blue that is "unsuspicious" or "not placed under suspicion," where that unusual term (unverdächtiges, offenes Blau), unlike Mallarmé's transcendent azur, suggests a desired state of innocence beyond questions of worldly guilt.

In the poem "Der Zauberer" (I, 242) Krolow portrays indirectly the poet's role as a pantheistic force of nature:

In den Zikaden
ist ein Zauberer versteckt,
der singt.

Jung ist er
wie Laub und Zeisige,
die das Ohr verhexen.

Das Gemurmel der Krüge
ist das Echo seiner Stimme.

Mit unsichtbaren Händen
schüttet er Mittagsblau
vor die Haustüren.

Nachts ist er Spion
im Blut von Mann und Mädchen,
ehe sie in ihre Körper
zurückkehren.

Die Zikaden
finden keinen Schlaf.

In the sharply sibilant *Z,* the artist-magician is linked onomatopoeti-
cally to the buzz of the cicadas and casts his spell through the various
sounds in nature. In the line that gives the volume its title, the speaker
in the poem spills or splashes light and color before the doorways, like
buckets of water, in a moment of what Krolow calls "so liquid wie
möglich." In a world without God or gods, the artist-magician becomes the pantheistic omnipresence that calls life into being through
language. The conceit of the "Spion / Im Blut" suggests an aroused,
almost animal alertness between "Mann und Mädchen" on the look-
out for signs, hints of the other; the spy of desire in each extends toward the other in consciousness, if not also in touch, before returning,
recoiling upon its self in either nervous resignation or sated relaxation.
Behind the initially obscure metaphors lurks the certainty of desire and
uncertainty of fulfillment as part of the natural cycle of magical life:
"Die Zikaden / finden keinen Schlaf." The fullness of that cycle of desire and consummation or disappointment endures as a constant life-
affirming hum and buzz, a throbbing crepitation of cicadas.

That rhythm links the poem to what may be its companion piece:
"Winterliches Leben I" (I, 246) shows the tenacity of life against the
intensity of deathly cold in winter:

Die Zuverlässigkeit des Dunkels.

Es ist Tatsache, daß nun
eine Hand die andere leichter findet.

Feuer werden angezündet
vor den Augen der Kälte.
Die Erinnerung an gestern
ist die Geschichte von morgen:
die Worte frieren im Munde.
Die Sprache stirbt
vor den Lippen
als Rauch.

Die Krise des Lichtes hält an.
Der Frost ist eine singende Maschine.
Ihr Ton ist weit im Land
zu hören.

The certainty of early darkness is a small comfort. Hands are held more readily as a reflex against the cold, and fires are started as defense against the cold. The cold has eyes, like the "Spion / im Blut," that are alert to any opening where it can make itself felt, including the mouth: "die Worte frieren im Munde, / Die Sprache stirbt / von den Lippen / als Rauch." But the transition from physical cold around the hands to an existential chill around the words that silences speech turns on an axis in the middle lines of stanza two: "Die Erinnerung an gestern / ist die Geschichte von morgen: Die Worte frieren im Munde." Memory of the past in the present becomes, in the future, history. The thought of that inevitability of memory finding its way into history "freezes" speech, though the rhythmic cycle of nature defeats historical time. This hibernal poem reflects in its conclusion the vernal counterpiece in "Der Zauberer": just as cicadas resound in nature, so too the frost seems to supplant speech as an almost visible, crisp silence, which registers as a nearly unnatural intonation, "eine singende Maschine." Though seemingly less natural in its barrenness, the frost, as "singende Maschine," also affirms that cycle of nature.[1]

The last poem, "Schreiben" (I, 241), recapitulates the aesthetic that predominates throughout:

Papier, auf dem sich
leichter Wind niederläßt.

Unbedachte Linien: Wellen
eines Wassers, das die Hand
aus der Luft schöpft, Worte
auf meinem Tisch wie
Liebespaare, Körper
von Pflanzen.

Papier: wie schönes Wetter
drauf zu schreiben,
vergeßlich wie das Glück,
Girlande, welkend umgehängt
der Gegenwart des Todes.

The stanzas contain no main clause with a subject and an active verb. Instead, the first word or phrase attaches the thought in words to the page like a garland to a wall, and the dependent clauses then drop behind and hang across in undulating lines of rhythmically draping ornamentation. Writing has attained the lightness and slightness of wind, without central substance, only visible as the vibration of other objects, and since not binding, then ephemeral. In this neutral chain of signification, the "Unbedachte Linien" link words as metaphors for other words without priority of value: paper is wind is weather is lines of waves of water is lovers is bodies is plants are garlands that fade around the omnipresence of death, which is also voided of substance and reduced to a cipher, a linguistic reflex without physical or metaphysical urgency or presence. The meaning is inverted and annulled in an artful paraph in what Adorno calls the "Jargon der Eigentlichkeit." As in the image of garlands, the poems in this volume seem circumscriptions without center, without inner necessity of coherence or concept, as in mythographic or hermetic poetry, and without external imperatives of form, as in more traditional verse making. Rather the words hover without, or at least against gravity, like the "Vogelflug der Worte" in "Stele für Catull" (I, 232), as an antidote to or anodyne for historical reflection.

Gesammelte Gedichte I (1965)

Krolow's first volume of *Gesammelte Gedichte* (1965) also contains twenty-eight poems that appeared there for the first time in book form and constitutes for the years 1963 and 1964 a new volume of poems that adds a further degree of refinement to a tendency that emerged in *Unsichtbare Hände*. In comparison to a poem like "Himmel" (I, 237) or "Schreiben" (I, 241), the poem "Sommerblau" (I, 260) gives the measure of that further development:

> Aus Brunnen
> blutendes Blau:
> Wasser im Juni oder
> August.
>
> Licht: — eine
> hemdlose Brust wartet
> auf seinen Stilett-Stich.
>
> Konische Landschaft
> mit Pappeln und Staren,
> dem Rotwelsch der Luft —
> im Fensterrahmen
> aufgehängt als Kegelschnitt
> des Apollonios.
>
> Mit verbundenen Augen
> das mechanische Spielzeug
> der Minuten in Gang setzen.

The alliterative opening lines merge red and blue and the reflections of water and sky in sunlight, creating in the landscape an ambiguous space, both open and closed, flat like painted color fields and endlessly deep in appearance like the lost perspective in a mirror. The second stanza varies the garland-like stanza of the poem "Schreiben" by setting the first word and following utterance in equation, which increases relative to one another the force of the word *Licht* and disperses the force of the appended sentence; the passivity of the verb *wartet* captures, in a mix of eroticism (*hemdlose Brust*) and violence (*Stilett-Stich*), the appeal and threat of so much unshaded sunlight, the transition from sensuous warmth to burn of sunshine that is no longer dappled and refracted into *Blätterlicht*. The third stanza presents the perspective of an idyll, as viewed through a window, though here abstracted into geometric cones of ascending trees and starlings that gives form to their sounds, a sort of *Blätterlicht* of auditory impressions, a "Rotwelsch der Luft" that intermingles rustling leaves, flapping wings, wind and chirps. The last stanza negates the brilliant physical visuality of those images into a blind sense of time, as if before a firing squad. Taken together, the poem is voided, all at once, of human agency, of subjective consciousness, of *Ich*, through the elimination of active verbs. Only one remains in stanza two, but in an inversion of Rilke's "Archaïscher Torso Apollos," this torso does not exude light and energy; it awaits its blow like a helpless victim. In strophes one, three, and four, the verbs figure in turn as present participial adjective, as past participle, and as infinitive, all of which evacuate subjectivity and drama from the poem, which registers impressions that are decentered from a subject. In the poem "Kindertheater" (I, 278): "Jemand wird zu niemand." Nonetheless, the cryptic connotations of dramatic, violent action lurk in the sunlight as distant literal or denotative possibilities of the metaphors *Stilett-Stich, aufgehängt* and *verbundenen Augen*. Krolow's work continually inverts the normal priority of literal and figurative meanings in metaphor.

The poems in the final sequence in *Gesammelte Gedichte* I take on the porous quality that Krolow defines in his essays through their serial discontinuity of static images and utterances, though also without the staccato explosiveness of paratactic constructions in the Expressionist vein. Instead, what arises is a prismatic impression of adjacent sensations without aggregate force, which unfolds in new combinations across an endless surface from poem to poem to tease or titillate eye and mind without ever coming together into any density of formation, intensity of expression, or depth of reflection, though with an achieved lightness, a preciosity of felicitous affect. Krolow undertakes an origami-like folding and unfolding of an expanded temporal present into impressions paradoxically linked by their refraction from each other, by their angle of disjunction, of asymmetry. As he notes in the poem "Im Frühling" (I, 275): "Einer schneidet Vignetten / und verstreut sie als Vögel / zur Leibkosung der Luft." The poem "Blühen" (I, 276) marks Krolow's proximity, despite his various transformations, to the *Naturlyrik* whose features he describes and analyzes while carefully distancing himself from its excesses:

> Blühen
> kennt keine
> perspektivische Störung.
>
> Phantasien der Licht-Uhr:
> Grün, das von Baum zu Baum
> fliegt.

Die Natur ist älter
als Rousseau —
Unschuld der
sichtbaren Vergnügen.

Mit offenen Armen
stürzt die Zeit
in die Geschichten
duftender Vegetation.

Schlaflose Luft
trägt die Samen davon.

Instead of the dense, microscopic description that Krolow abjured in *Naturlyrik*, this poem offers cerebral captions to perceptions of nature without a presentation of the object in question, of nature. Again, metaphor precedes the object, connotation comes before denotation, as in the second stanza, which suggests the familiar affect, a retinal flitter of *Blätterlicht*, in yet another variation. The vanishing perspective of this poem, in the middle of the middle stanza, after the dash, is an "Unschuld der / sichtbaren Vergnügen" in nature, which absorbs, in the next stanza, historical time into its own cyclical "Geschichten / duftender Vegetation." Behind the different stylistic variations that distance Krolow from *Naturlyrik* there perdures the loss of history in the undergrowth of, if not nature, then of metaphor.

Landschaften für mich (1966)

Landschaften für mich (1966) begins with a poem of that same title with the noun in singular "Eine Landschaft für mich" (I, 264–66); nonetheless that poem consists of three parts, which highlight for this volume what might be called the deliberate arbitrariness of the images and utterances. This in turn seems a residue of Krolow's preoccupation with surrealism, though here no longer with explosive or provocative force, and even at times a certain flatness ("Baumschatten lassen / verschiedene Beschreibungen zu"). The addition in the title of the prepositional phrase and personal pronoun ("für mich") to Krolow's long favored motif of landscape suggests, in its limiting application, first, his consciousness of the motif's untimeliness, which might be partly its appeal for him, and second, a gradual turn away from the anonymity of previous volumes toward at least an ambience of affect between strophes and images that otherwise have no logical connection or cumulative force: "Ich lasse sie / vor meinen Augen / im trockenen Licht schweben." In this volume, that affect is often enough of jadedness, a world weariness of impressionism that alternates with new wonders of perception; in "Farben" (I, 259), the first line, "Schlafwandelnde Farben," suggests unconscious routine, but a later stanza, "Ein Lichtstrahl wird zur exotischen Zeichnung / des Augenblicks," awakens those unnamed colors into imagined movement and precision of contour that stretches from far to near: "Heimliche Liebe des Horizontblaus / zum Aderblau eines Mädchens."

In *Landschaften für mich,* Krolow achieves a new lucidity and limpidity of technique in a series of landscapes of light. These impressionistic poems are not merely images, but are more like engravings in their sharp optics, like cerebral "Werkzeuge für das Licht," as one poem is titled (II, 7). The impressions invoke, however, heightened consciousness without content. The perspective on history and violence in society or between individuals is now absent; in comparison to earlier poems of flight and disorientation, the vanishing point of history has itself vanished ("Der Grad der Freiheit / ohne Flucht / durch die Schatten"), leaving behind a glittering surface ("Der leuchtet / in der Helligkeit / geordneter Pomeranzen" or elsewhere in the poem "Frühjahr": "Die Helligkeit ist frei / von Schatten" [II, 9]). The poems collapse critical consciousness into an optics of sight and imagination with deadpan clarity but without visionary intensity as in "Augenschein" (II, 7–8):

> Alles ist Augenschein
>
> Die Bäume haben
> einen grünen Atem.
>
> Aus einem Schritt
> wird ein Luftsprung.
> Die Erde ist nicht mehr
> fest unter den Sohlen.
>
> Der kleine Himmel
> eines blauen Wassers.
>
> Die Fröhlichkeit ist
> ein junges Tier.
> Ohne Flügel nimmt sie
> ihren Weg nach oben.

The strophes are irregular, apodictic, and unlinked utterances without density of rhyme or rhythm but with a casual charm. The first line plays on the literal and figurative meanings of the word as "appearance to the eye" and "close inspection or visual examination and scrutiny." Here the critic looks closely for binding meanings and textual relations, but she or he is deceived by appearances that levitate, that take flight through unlikely metaphors, which erode the ground of representation and derange the points of orientation to create a space without gravity where physical laws no longer bind. The result is an uncanny openness and, in near contradiction, a strictly intellectual lightness of substance that avoids and approximates, all at once, both kitsch and content in a delicate balancing act. This poem and others neither slip into triviality nor plunge into depths of inquiry or intellection. Krolow maintains the tension of equilibrium, like a trapeze artist, through an invisible but strenuous exertion of exactitude, without looking into the depths. On his tightrope Krolow seems surefooted in routine execution of poetic caprioles, without new risks in the repertoire. The poems exude from the start a sense of disciplined exhaustion.

These landscapes draw upon Krolow's accomplishments in other volumes: the arrangement of the poems into seasons recalls Krolow's literary beginnings as inner emigrant in the Nazi period with seasonal poems about nature; the greenery recalls the botanical density of his earliest volumes; the geometry of perception as well as the metaphor of nature as script or text recall the poems in *Wind und Zeit* (1954), the *Heiterkeit* of images recalls the supple poems of *Tage und Nächte* (1956), and the anonymity recalls *Fremde Körper* (1959) and *Unsichtbare Hände* (1962).

Nonetheless, many of the poems here have attained a sort of classical self-sufficiency in their unabashed reflection of previous achievement; they do not break new ground, nor do they see the need to. Krolow displays his sure-handedness in the manipulation of what now appears as long established convention, as in "Laub" (II, 14–15):

> Romanische Tugend des Lichtes:
> Lotrecht fällt es auf den Scheitel
> einer Laubpyramide
> Segmente blauen Wassers
> zu ihren Füßen
> Über eine Baumleiter
> in den Himmel steigen!

Der wartet zerstreut,
unter sich den Sturzbach
der Blätter.

Each stanza recalls at least several others from poems in previous volumes, but those relations create no profundity or depth of reverberation; the surface beveling is brilliant, though not illuminating, since the poem has no direct function as inquiry, only as ornament of perception.

The poem "Im Frühling" (I, 275) seems almost programmatic in this respect:

Immer noch werden
idyllische Geschäfte besorgt.

Zeit ohne strenges Profil,
mit der Greisenerscheinung
des geflohenen Winters.

Einer schneidet Vignetten
und verstreut sie als Vögel
zur Liebkosung der Luft.

Häuser bekommen über Nacht
Gärten, in denen
das Licht scherzt.

Hölty's Freund mit
den schönen Gedanken,
die unsterbliche Locke
im Wind.

The poem announces with irony its untimely "idyllische Geschäfte." Krolow has commented on his desire to ignore the historical determinism of a genre and defy conventional and unconventional expectations (Kolter/Paulus "Gespräch mit Karl Krolow" [1983]: 47). Here Krolow scandalizes the expectations of an avant-garde by invoking eighteenth-century conventions that no longer seem to apply to serious poetry. The poet resembles the figure in the central stanza who scatters anecdotes like birds to caress the air while sunlight laughs in the gardens. Poetry becomes a form of social artifice, cultivated diversion with erotic or at least sensuous appeal. As in the conventional idyll, the images exist in a highly aestheticized nature and outside of historical time ("Zeit ohne strenges Profil").

In this sense, the poems are familiar in idiom but new in detail. They are not repetitive of earlier work, but openly derivative, at times as a form of ironic originality, as in "Erfahrung mit Blumen" (II, 12):

Erfahrung: Wiederfinden
eines Motivs.
Zum Beispiel
alternde Schnittblumen in
einer Hand.

Dahinter
der sichtbare Text
einer Landschaft ohne Tod,
mit zuviel Pflanzengeruch
durchlässiger Buchstaben.

Später das Blumenthema,
wiederholt von anderen
Fingern.

Das Bukett fällt schließlich
müde durch die einverstandene Zeit
von der man nichts
erfährt.

The poem is self-conscious about its representation of a prior representation, of a motif linked to other prior instances of that motif, and therefore thoroughly conventional. Consciousness of artifice defeats any mimetic function in the art; the "sichtbare Text einer Landschaft ohne Tod" supplants or conceals reflection of or on a landscape inhabited with life and death *hors du texte*. Each repetition of the motif evacuates mimetic meaning even further from out of the work and consolidates the motif as a "Blumenthema," an empty exercise in a given pattern in perpetuity, like the stripping of the aura in Walter Benjamin's thesis on mechanical reproduction. Krolow might have in mind Picasso's unavoidable image of a hand holding out flowers to another hand (*Paix,* 1958), whose endless reproduction and dissemination as a poster, postcard, and so on, exhausts it of its original charm, though it continues to sell: "Das Bukett fällt schließlich / müde durch die einverstandene Zeit / von der man nichts / erfährt." The historical perspective is not given in the reproductions, variations, and derivations of a theme but collapsed into an empty and endless presentness. But in this poem on the vacuity of artifice and of self-referential textuality, the aura has returned, not as the glow of time-lessness according to Benjamin's thesis, but as history. The absence of history is mimetic and points beyond the text to the missing historical context: "von der man nichts erfährt."

Yet the art of Krolow's metaphor is acute. The eight stanzas of the poem "Bei Tagesbeginn" (II, 15) stretch from "Dämmerung — Stichflamme / zwischen Bäumen" to "Azur — blaues Geräusch / des unerklärlichen / Horizonts" in a synaesthetic moment of expansive wonder. In "Junihimmel" (II, 17), the stanza "Euklidische Klarheit — / Spannung zwischen Licht / und Augapfelfarbe" captures neatly the interface of perception, consciousness, and external sensation; in "Hitzelandschaft" (II, 19), the "Umgangssprache leichter Kleider" gives an erotic twist to "Die an einem Gedanken / wie Quecksilber abgleitenden / Worte" where bodies do not even appear, but where casual thoughts disrobe with swift lubricity into a sensually charged silence; starlings appear wittily as "Luftiges Treibgut. [. . .] die in einem blattreichen Baum / Sprichwörter zurücklassen"; or the atmosphere resounds with "Esperanto / der von Vögeln besuchten Luft" in "Der Mai" (I, 261); in "Regen" (II, 26), recalling the French phrase "il pleut des cordes," the rain appears with indisputable force as "zu lange Sätze in einer toten Sprache, / Latein des Cicero"; in "Toter Herbst" (II, 33) the fading daylight figures as a "Zirrhose des Lichts"; in "Wenn es Tag wird" (I, 263) the cocks crow and "Ihr elliptisches Krähen / steht lange in der Luft," and in the poem "Im Frieden" (I, 270–71), the geometry of metaphor signifies a "Sieg der Ellipse / über den Tod. // Dahinleben." Krolow's fleetingly felicitous metaphors coruscate and combine without context in a weather-like variability; in the poem "Die Vorsicht" (I, 81), one reads "Ständig ändert sich / über meinem Haus die Wahrheit," like cloud formations.

The poems flash with striking images that expire quickly outside of any meaningful context. The poems inhabit the space between arch verbal wit or *Pointe* and discrete, stunning visual impressionism or pointillism ("Licht: leuchtender Punkt / auf der Netzhaut"). Image and wit do not merge; sight rarely leads to insight, though at times a certain formal integration, almost fortuitous, occurs as in "Insekten-zeit" (II, 23):

> Unauffindbare Grillen
> in der lodernden Luft
> wie die Rufe Schiffbrüchiger
> im blauen Sommerwasser.

Insektenzeit schwirrt
unter großen Bäumen.

Katzen verzehren Goldfische
im trockenen Teich.

Alle Pflanzen wachsen
gotisch in den regenlosen Himmel.

Die summenden Nerven
der Hochspannungsdrähte.

The initial conceit jars in the dissonance of its illogic — crickets are in
their element; drowning sailors are not — but that grating rasp swells
to endless frenzy in stanza two. Stanzas three and four intensify the
heat of summer that dried the ponds and withered the plants from
"baroque" lushness to "gothic" linearity. The last stanza reflects back
to stanza two, and recalls the last stanza of the earlier poems, "Der
Zauberer" (I, 242) and "Winterliches Leben I" (I, 246), to link the
insects' fierce buzz to crackling high tension wires and then metaphorically to the cracking nerves of an unseen auditor. On hot, dry
land, engulfed by the constant noise, one might still feel the sense of
madness and despair of a shipwrecked sailor lost at sea.

In "Worte im Winter" (II, 34) a seasonal poem becomes the state
of mind of someone trying to write or speak: "Schneeblind gebückt
über Papierweiß. // Langsam bewegen sich / Buchstaben über / ein
Schneefeld. // Das Alphabet friert." Winter is the near paralysis of a
writer alone before an empty page. The last strophes fight the cold
with the growing warmth of words as they begin to combine. The
poem ends auspiciously with the prospects of dialogue, though language remains exposed to hostile elements. In "Biographisches Gedicht" (II, 35–36) the question of personal history is raised but
remains too intimate to answer:

Biographisches Gedicht —
Liebschaft einiger Worte
mit der Lautlosigkeit.

Ein elegischer Körper
erwartet die erregten Hände
des Augenblicks,
an dem die Adjektive sterben.

Es bleibt Zeit
für die Geschichte
einer Mädchenhaut.

Sie endet im
unmerklichen Altern
bei Spaziergängen
durch empfindsames Gras.

That intimacy is the proximity of language to silence; momentary impressions can excite the body of language to a pitch of intensity, a climax in the poem, where qualifying words become irrelevant ("Adjektiven sterben"). History is reduced to superficial but sensuous epidermal sensations, a closeness of focus that intensifies consciousness of the physical body in the immediate present and excludes its abstract sociohistorical contexts. In contrast, in "Das Paar II" (II, 37–38), the same situation becomes erotic through a shift from the abstract anonymity of alienated confrontation in the first stanza ("Das andere Leben / mit zwei Augenpaaren") to first-person plural in the second:

Das andere Leben
mit zwei Augenpaaren.

Wir haben Fieber
wie die Steine
in der Sonne.

Stilleben abgelegter Kleider.

Unser Dunkel — leuchtendes Öl,
unsicher durchs Fenster geschüttet.

Im gemeinsamen Mund
fliegt unser Atem davon.

Desire builds in the two lovers like stones soaking up warmth from the sunlight. As invisible antipode to the "Stilleben abgelegter Kleider," the third stanza suggests an explosion of erotic movements; the fourth stanza lends a palpable, charged viscosity to the darkness that is illuminated and liquefied by the lovers' senses. Their fleeing breath suggests their merging flesh and their shared ecstasy.

Out of this art of continual poetic extrapolation away from a center, from the invisible center of history in the poem, Krolow begins to develop a less metaphoric, more casual language, as in "Solo für eine Singstimme" (I, 281): "Nimm das hin. / Laß es mich versuchen — / tonlos zunächst" or in the poem "Ohne Anstrengung" (I, 281): "Ohne Anstrengung, / nur so, gedankenlos / dieses und jenes — den Tag / als Wäscheblau auf der Leine." This new tone signals both a new prosaic quality in his poetry, a refreshing turn back to the individual subject in the world, but also a sign of exhaustion after so much dexterous legerdemain and defiant levitation against gravity and against history. Accordingly, "Ariel" (I, 282), the last poem of *Gesammelte Gedichte* I, picks up that theme:

> Auf irgendwas
> ein Gedicht, wie wenig,
> denkt man, und turnt
> den Handstand im Wind
> aus anderer Richtung.
> Die Zehen tragen den Himmel,
> die Wolke wie Frauenhaar
> weht durch die Luft, und so froh
> bleibt ein kleiner Engel.
> Sein Bilderbuch hält er
> mir vor. Meine Übung
> macht müde, am Ende
> kommt man doch wieder
> auf seinen Füßen zu stehen.
> Irgendwas
> ließ ich aus, vielleicht nur,
> wie zwischen den Beinen
> die akrobatische Landschaft
> ganz oben ist, dauernd
> zu hoch.

The poems seem, in their apparently casual, even arbitrary configurations, slight ("wie wenig, / denkt man"). The image of the magical sprite Ariel as an acrobat performing handstands becomes a figure of the poet, aspiring to the images in the angel's picture book, but tiring at the impossibility of remaining airborne and feeling the positive need to touch ground. Yet the "akrobatische Landschaft" becomes a metaphor for this use of metaphor, for his inversion of literal and figurative levels of meaning, and thus a means of inverting the inverted, in gymnastic athleticism, to arrive back "auf seinen Füßen zu stehn." That constant levitation seems, in retrospect, "dauernd zu hoch."

With an allusion to this particular poem, the influential poet and critic Hilde Domin reviewed *Landschaften für mich* in 1967 for the weekly newspaper *Die Zeit* with the title *Ariel im Handstand* and the subtitle *Karl Krolow schrieb seine bisher schönsten Gedichte*. Two weeks later she responded to the publication of her own essay with a letter to the editor, titled "Undifferenzierte Hymne" (*Die Zeit*, 13, March 31, 1967), where she indicted the newspaper for falsifying the intent of her original essay by stripping it of its carefully differentiated critical commentaries. The review later appeared for the first time in its entirety in *Neue deutsche Hefte*. Her essay alternates between praise and criticism, at times verging on nonsequitur, but begins with the confession that she had expected in the new volume "was man sich bei Krolow eben erwarten darf: intelligente Glossen, scharf oder überpointiert" (127), which immediately announced a critical candor apart from the usual respectful appreciation of Krolow's sensibility. After lamenting that the best poems get lost or obscured in the sheer mass of his poetic production, Domin attempts to define, with candor and concision, the difficulty that Krolow's poetry poses for critics:

> Es ist schwer zu definieren, was der Unterschied einiger dieser neuesten Gedichte ist im Gegensatz zu den vorigen. Vielleicht läßt sich dies feststellen: ein gewisser Leerlauf der Metaphern, eine sich auf hohem zünftigem Niveau bewegende Unverbindlichkeit, die gelegentlich wie Selbstimitation klingt [...] hat der Verbindlichkeit Platz gemacht, den Metaphern ist die Autonomie des hübschen Spracheinfalls beschnitten, ihre Beliebigkeit und ihr Exhibitionismus. (128)

Unlike most of Krolow's critics to date, Domin discriminates between the technical facility of the poems and the absence of a specific depth, which as absence cannot be exactly defined without becoming prescriptive. Domin employs the apt term *Leerlauf* to define that continual absence of binding semantic context of any kind, without which the words then, necessarily, seem arbitrary. Later she defines guardedly "nicht in allen, aber in einigen der Gedichte" the positive presence of "jenes Quäntchen 'Notwendigkeit' oder 'Gesetz' [...], das Spannung fühlbar macht und das das 'Sonderbare' (H. Friedrich über Krolow) ins Gültige wandelt" (129). She demonstrates the slackening of that tension into mannerism that continually empties itself of expressive force. The poems remain within the realm of the idyll and, as Domin notes pointedly: "Thematisch bringen diese Gedichte nichts Neues" (131). In light of her criticisms, she also concedes Krolow's historical importance after the war in opening German poetry to

European influences, but addresses the particularity, the unusual feature of Krolow's poetry: "Die 'Welt,' die Krolow uns gebracht hat, dies ist das Eigentümliche, bestand [. . .] fast nur im Technischen. Wiederum aber gibt es keine Sprachtechnik, die nicht die Sache selbst implicite mitbrächte" (132). What she calls "die Sache" should not necessarily be equated with the sense of political engagement that that term began to gain at this time on the Left, though that should not be excluded either; indirectly, she addresses here what Krolow advances in his various essays as his poetological aim: to jettison specific content from the poem as ballast. For Domin that cannot be done without reducing poetry to empty artifice; she suggests as much and indicates the dilemma of Krolow's improbable productivity: "Vieles bei Krolow bleibt in der Anwendung virtuoser Routine stecken [. . .] Das verdeckt den Rang dieses Werks. Die manierierten Gedichte drängen vor, rein zahlenmäßig" (133). She concludes her essay on a monitory note, turning Krolow's own words "Über meinem Hause / ändert sich täglich die Wahrheit" from the poem "Vorsicht" pointedly against him as criticism.

Domin's essay of 1967, in the middle of Krolow's career, confirms *in nuce* the impetus of this study, which tries to examine Krolow's poetry in its actual historical contours, that is, in its relation not only to literary traditions and to Krolow's contemporaries but also to his own historical experience. Domin, a distinguished poet and intellectual, stated in a prominent weekly newspaper, as a direct, almost blunt but always acute criticism, what had previously appeared in other commentaries only as discreetly stated reservations and which has never been addressed in the scholarship on Krolow. As perhaps a direct response to Domin's criticisms of the artful lack of content in his poetry, an essay by Krolow "Von der Zuständigkeit des Schriftstellers in der Politik," a very unlikely topic for Krolow, appeared in the very next issue.[2] In fact, echoing her criticisms, he remarks "Man bleibt ohnehin noch genügend der Gefangene der eigenen Begabung" (104). His posture throughout the essay remains defensive, "daß es für einen Schriftsteller nirgends einen Verhaltens-Kanon gibt" (103), although as he well knew as a writer in the Third Reich, there existed a strict "canon of behavior" as to who could write and what could be written; nonetheless, Krolow advocates the writer's candor, "wenn er redlich ist" (103). In general, the essay is convoluted in its argumentation and strained in its rhetoric, which departs from Krolow's normally clear and fluid style as an essayist on poetic topics. Initially, Krolow seems to advocate an openness to historical experience, even with a certain heroism:

Ich spüre die Gegenwart meiner Umgebung. Damit ist zunächst ganz einfach das Milieu gemeint, das es mir ermöglicht, so zu arbeiten, wie ich arbeite. Aber Umgebung ist schon sehr bald Umwelt, Zeitgenossenschaft. [. . .] Ich lebe in einem Dschungel von Stimmen und Gegenstimmen. Das kann verwirrend sein. Ich muß mich zurechtfinden. Ich muß Stellung nehmen. Ich muß reagieren. Ich muß [. . .] mich zu behaupten versuchen. Ich muß nicht sehend in einen Irrgarten geraten. Ich muß mich nicht unterkriegen lassen.[. . .] Ich muß mit den Menschen meiner Zeit, meines Landes in jenes einzig mögliche Verhältnis kommen, das es mir gestattet, meine Vorstellungen, Erfahrungen, Befürchtungen, Hoffnungen mit denen der anderen zu messen [. . .] Schreiben ist—so verstanden—zuallererst Auseinandersetzung, Stellungnahme, um sich selber, seine Position zu erkennen und sich im Erkennen zurechtzufinden. Das ist oft ein Auf-die-Suche-Gehen in einem unübersehbaren Gelände, in dem man rasch die Orientierung verlieren kann, weil der schmale Ausgangspunkt bald weit entfernt und undeutlich erscheint. [. . .] Bei einem solchen Auf-die-Suche-Gehen als Schriftsteller, wie ich es soeben beschrieben habe, bewege ich mich bereits auf einem im weiten Sinne *politischen* Boden. Ich gerate in ein Kräftefeld, in dem sich Stimmen und Gegenstimmen zu ordnen beginnen zu einer gesellschaftlich-politischen Ordnung, zu Macht und Gegen-Macht, zur Staats-Apparatur mit ihren Konventionen, Konflikten. (105–6)

With elaborate verbosity and a certain melodrama, Krolow describes the existential challenges of the writer. He draws upon familiar terms from his other literary-historical essays, such as *Kräftefeld,* that he had used exclusively with respect to the play of literary influences upon the writer, but now shifts that term to a sociopolitical context of ideological discourses and pressures. One might wonder how these principles developed from his experience during the Nazi period of *inner emigration* and outward careerism, when he seemed impossibly unaware of his surroundings and later described himself only in those terms, never accounted for his activities or wrote of his experiences, and never took a public position. He even defined writing as "ein Vorgang, der sich nur mit unverbundenen, mit offenen Augen bewerkstelligen läßt" (104). Given that discrepancy, the above notions of "Orientierung" and "zurechtfinden" seem to indicate that Krolow measures himself against others in order to find his way as a writer under different ideological circumstances. The above passage gives a generic description of how a writer survives or advances within a given system and is thus only political "im weitesten Sinne." The writer here is political in relation only to "sich selber" and the need to position himself among the voices and find his way through the jungle in order in effect to remain apolitical.

Krolow adumbrates the writer's awareness of the ideological field of discourses and, echoing existentialist beliefs in the moment of choice, states with authority: "Man muß diesen Augenblick verantworten und beantworten, beantworten mit seinen Mitteln: beantworten mit den Mitteln des Wortes, des Schreibens" (106). Krolow describes the writer's acute political awareness, then a sense of responsibility and then a response, a turn to action with various means, with the meaning of the word. He seems to advocate a certain activism, even if limited, but finally his logic comes full circle:

> Jeder muß das persönliche, das nur für ihn zutreffende Mittel wählen und anwenden. Nur so wird eine Äußerung, eine Stellungnahme verbindlich. Und allein so kann der Eindruck von Zuständigkeit aufkommen. Es ist eine Zuständigkeit, die an den Belastungen zu tragen hat, die in der schriftstellerischen Arbeit stecken, in der Labilität, der Schwäche des Metiers, in den vielen Fußangeln, die es bereithält, in seiner artistischen und in seiner stofflichen Problematik. [. . .] Gewissenhaftigkeit der Unsicherheit. (106)

The writer's activism, according to Krolow, consists of remaining preoccupied with the uncertainties of his or her existence. The specific conditions are not defined, whether the special difficulties are existential or material or both or other, and he offers no particular examples from his own experience. His understanding of the writer's position defies historical particularity:

> vielmehr die immer gleiche Lage — unter allen Umständen —, in der ich mich als jemand befinde, der mit Literatur 'zu tun' hat, der Gedichte schreibt, Gedichte, die ihre Stofflichkeit, ihre Thematik, ihre Materialität haben, und die gleichzeitig stoffflüchtig sind, die von Wörtern zusammengehalten werden, die sich durchaus entziehen. (107)

Here Krolow's exposition itself avoids any particularity. The description of the writer's trade is so general as to be meaningless and universally applicable to anyone using words. The breathtaking platitudes, however, serve the function of voiding the content of the words and essay, while also concealing that function. At this point, the essay, like the above passage, has itself become almost perfectly "stoffflüchtig." The redundancy in the phrase "immer gleiche Lage — unter allen Umständen" defeats historical analysis by denying and excluding context, but it also, in the consistency of the position, connects the experience of the writer in the Third Reich to later generations. His 1972 essay on the political responsibility of the writer enunciates the aesthetics and the politics of the inner emigrant whose position remains the same "unter allen Umständen."

Later in the essay Krolow confronts that reading with the remark: "Ich möchte nicht mißverstanden werden. Meine Gedankengänge und Zweifel haben nichts mit einem Ausweichen zu tun, einem literarischen Eskapismus."[3] His style in the essay, however, makes understanding difficult, and if one follows the logic of the argument, leads to the opposite conclusion that he does want to be misunderstood, that he wants a position of radical nonengagement and insularity to have the cachet of political engagement without the responsibilities. Set against the political activism of the day, concern for one's own writing and career should appear as "das empfindlichere, anfälligere, ungesichertere Engagement" (109). Once his position has developed to this point, the essay attains a certain clarity: "Ich bin deshalb der Meinung, daß er [der Schriftsteller] gar nicht erst den Versuch unternehmen sollte, mit ihm fremden Mitteln im öffentlichen Leben, in der öffentlichen Kritik in Konkurrenz mit derberen Kräften zu gehen" (109). Here Krolow has stated a clear position of apolitical reserve but has, in a wooly manner, separated it from literary escapism. Such a position of distance to society might at some level resemble Adorno's position on poetry in society, by which the poem attains its political agency dialectically through its concentration inward upon itself, upon its own language and semantic, rhythmic, and tonal density; Krolow does argue that "ein 'öffentlich' werdendes Poem sich seines komplizierten Wesens und Verhaltens in der Öffentlichkeit der politischen Gesellschaft bewußt ist" (110). Yet Krolow's conception of the poem remains porous, without the formal density central to Adorno's understanding of the poem's dialectical resistance to ideological pressures in society.[4]

Instead, Krolow's conception of the poem suggests an apolitical parallel to the poem of political engagement that Adorno repudiates, but which likewise remains, fleetingly, bound to the occasion:

Der literarische Einfall als literarische, geistige Verantwortung! Es geht natürlich hier nicht um artifizielle Handstreiche oder um ästhetische Scharmützel, vielmehr um die Fähigkeit zur Veränderbarkeit der literarischen Äußerung, so, wie sie dem jeweiligen Anlaß der Auseinandersetzung, dem Einspruch gemäß ist (111).

Thus, Krolow's poem would share the feature of spontaneous "engagement" with the political poem, but its own political substance would consist in its ability, not to concentrate its expression inwardly in dialectical resistance to society, but to evolve, in direct relation to society and in inverse relation to political poetry, in order to remain "open" but apolitical. For Krolow, "occasional" poetry is political in its lack of politics, which it most certainly is (dialectically), but not in the benign, positive manner he would like to project. Krolow's occasional poetry, especially what he wrote in the Third Reich, suffers from the shortcomings of both the politically "engaged" poem and of hermetic poetry as a negative synthesis of these two poles of poetic expression, lacking the content of the former while sharing its dependency on the moment, and lacking also the cryptic richness and density of the latter, while sharing its exquisiteness.

Alltägliche Gedichte (1968)

The title of the volume *Alltägliche Gedichte* can mislead if understood in the context of German *Alltagslyrik* in the 1970s, which it would seem at first glance to anticipate or join in common spirit.[5] That tendency introduced a New Subjectivity into the poem and into the historical scenario of common, everyday life, with the artless pretense of an unmediated registration of the particular in the everyday existence of an unexceptional individual, without the filter of transcendent conceptual categories, *Bildung,* or conventional poetic forms. In this volume Krolow continues to move toward a laconic sparseness of language and shares the deflationary rhetoric, stripped of pathos and pomp, of such poets as Nicolas Born (1937–79), Hans Magnus Enzensberger (1929–), Rolf Dieter Brinkmann (1940–75), Peter Handke (1942–), Karen Kiwus (1942–), and Jürgen Theobaldy (1944–), to name a few. Krolow's poetry anticipated their use of the *Momentaufnahme,* though without the sense of historical immediacy in the single moment of a poetic snapshot. The poets of *Alltagslyrik* tried, either through analytical pointedness, as in Enzensberger's poems, or more commonly, though a prosaic tendency to narrative exposition, to convey the texture of history through individual experience. In contrast, Krolow remains attached to the notion of literariness that runs counter to the demotic impulse of *Alltagslyrik*. Despite some similarities, Krolow's poetry is, in this particular point, fundamentally at odds with *Alltagslyrik*.

The first poem of the volume, "Zeit" (II, 43), announces in effect the distinction between Krolow and that contemporaneous tendency. The poem marks a transition from the last poem of the previous volume, "Vergänglich" (II, 39), and reinforces Krolow's understanding of time as a metaphysical, not a historical, category:

> Zeit: etwas
> das die Taschen
> feucht von Blut macht.
>
> Es regnet Leben
> aus offenen Körpern.
>
> Die Tage und
> ihr stilles Geschäft
> mit Menschen, die verloren
> gehen.
>
> Ein Monat malt
> dem nächsten sein Bild
> in den Sand,
> ohne Verwandtschaft
> mit dem, was kommt.
>
> Kein schönes Wetter
> verändert ein Karzinom.
>
> Die geordneten Papiere
> verbrennen Jahr um Jahr.

The full colon signals the disjunction between the conceptual category of time and the concrete incidents of daily life, characterized for Krolow by violence. In the first three strophes, time as abstract temporality squeezes the life out of "Menschen, die verloren / gehen." The third strophe names the topic of *Alltagslyrik* ("Die Tage und / ihr stilles Geschäft / mit Menschen") but does not describe, nor seek to create a texture of experience. This tangent comprises, despite the title, Krolow's actual relation to *Alltagslyrik* in this volume. From the named topic in common, Krolow moves in the opposite direction, away from descriptive detail, narrative exposition and coherence, and social analysis that characterized that tendency in German poetry. Krolow's poems retain the discontinuity of short stanzas that marked his surrealist phase, though now with less reliance on metaphor; that discontinuity figures for him as an openness to experience, but functions just as much to close off the poem to analysis and to limit the depth, if not necessarily the range, of experience that enters into the poem. In this example, the metaphysical category of time dissolves, here in the third stanza, the question of what happens to "Menschen, die verloren / gehen" and why. People, objects, and units of time do not impinge upon one another in a historical field of interrelations but remain "ohne Verwandtschaft" and thus inscrutable. The historical dimension of agency and its effects drops away and leaves an unbridgeable gap between the physical and the metaphysical, the micro- and the macrocosmic planes of experience, as in the lines "Kein schönes Wetter / verändert ein Karzinom," which seems surrealist in its conjunction of apparently unrelated and distant phenomena, and of beauty with ugliness, but the conjunction remains entirely logical despite its apparent illogic as a precise exclusion of the intermediate field between these phenomena as a means of obscuring or obliterating the dimension of historical experience.

The poem in two parts "Stundengedicht" (II, 44–47) reinforces that sense of time as the conceptual locus of impressions, whether lucid or banal, that remain inscrutable:

> Vieles fühlt sich
> wie immer an.
>
> [. . .]
>
> So geht das weiter.
> In den Taschen trocknet
> das eigne und das fremde Blut.
> Der Tag verstreicht.
> Die Augen: immer noch
> mit einem leichten Horizont beschäftigt.

Krolow presents the conceptual framework of time and the vanishing point of history on the horizon without the middle distance that might constitute historical experience. History has been absorbed into discrete impressions of time passing as in the intimacy of the aging body: "Das Alter stellt / die Lampe auf den Tisch. / Der Körper wird Geschichte, / lautlos von Haut gehalten, / weiter weißes Nachtfleisch." The poem describes concepts of perception, not objects ("Der Tag hat Stoff für Bilder. / . . . / Die Oberflächen sind / noch einmal gut zu sehen"). The landscape of the body or of nature serves to illustrate the metaphysical category of time.

The intimate images of aging represent concretely Krolow's consciousness of time outside of sociohistorical contexts in its affects upon the physical body as an object, as in the last three stanzas of the poem "Älter werden" (II, 47):

> In einem Zimmer
> mit sterbenden Buchstaben leben.
>
> Ein fremder Mund,
> der mir die Sprache raubt.
>
> Ihn geduldig
> den eigenen Namen nennen hören.

This poem anticipates Krolow's exploration of aging in his later poetry, especially in the volume *Die zweite Zeit* (1995), as I describe in my review of that volume (1996). Yet Krolow at this point does not examine aging in any other than existential contexts. Nonetheless, his understated poems on the topic attain both a genuine pathos in the individual who regards painfully the estrangement of the body over time and a sharp sense of irony in that same individual's sense of the detached superiority of consciousness over the body's increasing frailty. The measure of the individual's struggle to retain that superiority remains in language: "Die Wortfalle bleibt aufgestellt. // Aufmerksam / bewege ich mich / in ihrer Nähe." That consciousness turns tragic with the recognition of death's encroachment upon one's language: "Der Winter in den Worten / nimmt zu — [. . .] Eine Gleichung für das, / was später kommt. / . . . / Es bleibt kalt / unter der Zunge." Krolow's affective reflections on aging serve to focus his poetry upon that nexus of language and consciousness in literature. Krolow's *Alltägliche Gedichte* actually explore changing configurations of literariness rather than daily life.

In "Buchstabenkunde" (II, 44) Krolow creates a term, consciously antiquated, for the study of letters, of graphesis, as a natural science like *Erdkunde* for geography or *Menschenkunde* for anthropology. The word suggests a world of objects to explore and collect:

> Eine Landschaft,
> die sich mit Buchstaben
> füllt —
>
> unruhiges Spielzeug.

So wird Grammatik
sichtbar.

Vorsichtige Landvermessung
der Wörter.

Langsam taucht Jacob Grimm
auf im Schatten eines Satzes.

Die Freie Kunst
der Veränderung von Sprache.

Ihr leuchtender Körper
steht lange in der Luft.

Here, the letters of the alphabet fill the landscape as *Buchstaben,* a
word that returns to its literal meaning of beech staffs to populate the
landscape like so many trees. The natural becomes artificial and vice
versa. The letters as images are an "unruhiges Spielzeug," as in images
of Paul Klee, where ciphers become animate bodies, since their differences would become visibly palpable in this three-dimensional landscape once released from their standard linear order. The notion of
literariness takes on the dimensions of external reality as a field of vision and of verbal play, though that play is enunciated here, not enacted. The poem describes a type of poetry, such as concrete or
typographical poetry, that it does not itself embody. In the manner of
a simple poem of everyday life, this poem is, in fact, about a sort of
surrealistically playful experimental or concrete poetry.

In the conceit of this poem, grammar constitutes the visible relations between objects in that field of vision, a depth perspective, and
means of surveying the landscape, the wordscape, and taking its measure. In the imagined three-dimensional space of a written page, a
sentence can cast a shadow like a large tree. Here, in the manner of a
surrealist collage, the first writer of a dictionary of the German language, Jacob Grimm, sits in that shadow. Yet the twentieth century is,
of course, not the eighteenth. With the sum of words available as a
toy, the artist-poet can engage "Die Freie Kunst / der Veränderung
von Sprache." The process of putting words onto the page and setting
grammar into movement by combining words would explore those
relations in a visual field. Instead of fixing those words into the systematic order of a dictionary, linking them to their history as etymology, the activity of writing as such, the means as an end in itself,
releases the magic of words in combination: "Ihr leuchtender Kör-

per / steht lange in der Luft." Poetry has become for Krolow the means of releasing language from its contexts, from the forms of its boundedness to other realms of meaning, its etymology and its referentiality, to which it nonetheless must eventually return. Poetry is a self-contained acrobatics of language, a high-wire act of balancing on the poetic line; this poetological poem gives a series of different ways of thinking of the poem, as conceits without proceeding to create such poetry.[6]

Thus, the balancing act has its safety net. Elsewhere, Krolow's penchant for literary allusion and citation, and for careful derivations, provides the secure context for several poems and highlights the realm of literariness within which Krolow's "alltägliche Gedichte" appear. His "Meeresstille" (II, 52) and "Glückliche Fahrt" (II, 53) revise two poems by Goethe with the same titles and appear as ironic, whimsical commentaries on those poems. Goethe's "Meeresstille" reads:

> Tiefe Stille herrscht im Wasser,
> Ohne Regung ruht das Meer,
> Und bekümmert sieht der Schiffer
> Glatte Fläche ringsumher.
> Keine Luft von keiner Seite!
> Todesstille fürchterlich!
> In der ungeheueren Weite
> Reget keine Welle sich.

And Krolow's version:

> Eine schlafende Möwe — die Luft.
>
> Kein Salzkorn reibt
> im Auge.
> Die zu blaue Strömung
> wartet auf eine Flaschenpost —
> kein Wetter für Schiffbrüche.
>
> Ein Bündel Vegetation heißt
> Küste.
> Die Ferne ist ein Dampfer,
> leichter als seine Rauchfahne.

Goethe's poem centers upon the sailor as the central consciousness who perceives "anxiously" the calm all around him that, rather than suggesting repose, becomes increasingly ominous until "Tiefe Stille" from the first line escalates to panic in the exclamation "Todesstille fürchterlich!" in line six. Goethe's poem describes nature in its relation to a central perceiving consciousness; in Krolow's poem, that self is displaced and only metonymically present as "Auge." The only action in the poem does not actually take place ("Kein Salzkorn reibt"). The seascape is not described but given in metaphors for air, water, and distant coast. The ocean waits for a message in a bottle that, in the calm, would neither travel far nor convey its message, perhaps itself like the intertextual reference of Goethe's poem within Krolow's. Krolow decenters the concentrated rhythm and imagery of Goethe's poem and encapsulates it as *Flaschenpost* from another age within his poem as its content, which has been negated, though without which the poem, the bottle, would be empty; whoever receives the allusion recognizes the historical differences between Romantic and postmodernist poetry, which are then annulled, relative to one another, as a message in a bottle, as poetic text without origin or destination, afloat and adrift in an intertextual ebb and flow.

The poem "Nicht so schwer" (II, 56–57) seems programmatic in its articulation of whimsical lightness despite the unusual introduction of the first-person subject. In contrast, the poem "Sieg der Hitze" (II, 58–59) uses the same unrhymed, one or two word lines and two or three line stanzas to invoke an increasing sense of heaviness and lethargy in the heat:

> Von Graphomanen
> in den Sand geschrieben —
> Hitze.
>
> Bewegungslosigkeit
> einiger Stunden.
>
> Auf den Möbeln
> die Staubschicht
> nimmt zu.
>
> Die zu schwer gewordenen
> Schultern und Arme.
>
> Ein Steinhaufen
> sinkt lautlos zusammen.

> Lange Pausen
> zwischen den Sätzen.
>
> Das umgestürzte Glas
> bleibt liegen.
>
> Niemand hat die Kraft,
> den leer gewordenen Krug
> mit Wasser zu füllen.

Each stanza comes to a full, implacable stop. The poem reads down the page with the same slow deliberateness of a slowly rising thermometer and captures effectively the accumulation of heat and heaviness in objects, and the ensuing gradual loss of force, attention, and energy as an ode to inertia. The natural effect of heat still appears in terms of writing; the heat inscribes itself into objects as a frenetic script of "Graphomanen." The sixth stanza describes both the scenario of anonymous individuals who have fallen into silence in the heat and gives stage directions for the reading of the poem. In a contrary movement to the "leer gewordenen Krug" that remains empty in the heat, the conceit in the opening stanza creates a highly artificial vehicle or vessel that then fills with concentrated mood without the benefit of a literary citation as *Flaschenpost*.

The artificiality or literariness of nature reaches its most extensive realization in the cycle "Pomologische Gedichte" of seven poems, each devoted to a separate fruit, *Kirschen, Äpfel, Birnen, Pflaumen, Pfirsiche, Aprikosen,* and *Quitten*. The poems range from fifteen to twenty-three short, unrhymed lines of one to five words, divided into stanzas of varying length with no continual pattern to structure the poem as a whole. Each stanza, however, is a completed utterance, as in "Birnen" (II, 64–65):

> Wespen ertrinken
> im Saft der Bergamotten
>
> Mit gelben Birnen hänget —
> und der Birnbaum im Garten
> des havelländischen Herrn
> von Ribbeck:
> zur Familie der Rosengewächse
> gehörend.

Ihr nachgiebiges Fleisch
in der Tagesklarheit,
berühmt als Williams Christ.

Es duftet ohne
pomologische Namen
für Konserve und Obst.

Dreieckige Frucht
in einem russischen Gedicht,
sonst nichts als
die reife Geometrie

der Kegel- und Flaschenform.
Bildschnitzer befühlen
die Härte des Stammes.

(Und die Birnen leuchteten
weit und breit).

Krolow seems to return to the realm of nature, as in his very earliest poems, as the province of his poetry, though here that nature has become almost entirely literary, or at least textual. In each case, the idea of the particular fruit is surrounded by more or less random associations. Each poem is a montage of textual allusions as Adolf Fink remarks in the most detailed study of this cycle: "Natur enthüllt sich als eine erlesene. Das jeweilige Obst wird nicht als ein natürliches Erzeugnis zur primären Bedürfnisbefriedigung präsentiert, sondern als geschichtlich Gewordenes unserer sekundärer Hör- und Schaulust vermittelt" (467). However, by juxtaposing the allusions, both obvious and obtuse, to various texts and epochs, the poem does appear secondary, removed from primary impulses. But the poem does not, as Fink suggests, become historical or enter into the substance of historical mediation: rather, these "Pomologische Gedichte" put the idea of historical mediation on display as ahistorical and discontinuous textual references with breadth but without depth of reflection. Fink merely follows Krolow's own poetics to suggest that the poems "strahlen intellektuelle Heiterkeit aus" (471). The poems, to the contrary, collapse history into a random circuit of prosaic literariness that circumscribes the respective fruit as a textual cipher, as a literary moment, not as an observed object.

Unlike Krolow's later precise studies in prose, *In Kupfer gestochen: Observationen* (1987), in which an object appears as "ein Stück sinnlicher Phänomenologie" (*Etwas brennt,* 450), here each fruit appears in systematic refraction away, on the one hand, from its ontological core,[7] and, on the other hand, away also from any synthetic historical coherence, that is, no notion of historical embeddedness emerges from these montages. The fruit as historical or metaphysical object disappears into a constellation of names, of allusions that lead nowhere, and convey an atmosphere of museal exquisiteness only, of ahistorical literariness as erudite verbal ornament. Adolf Fink provides several pertinent but not necessary contexts along with the sources of the allusions, but he concludes: "Seien wir ehrlich: Der philologische Kraftaufwand steht mit dem Ertrag nicht im rechten Verhältnis. Das Zitat der Vergangenheit erweist sich als ein vergangenes Zitat. Es empfängt sein Leben allein im aktuellen Zusammenhang" (474). Yet Fink nonetheless draws the conclusion, contrary to his own evidence, that the suggestiveness of the poems resists the erosion, the dissolution of time ("Auflösung der Zeit"), whereas exactly the opposite occurs: Krolow's "Pomologische Gedichte" reduce history to tasteful literary pastiche.

The central section of the volume, after the opening poems on time as a category, on hours and on aging, roughly follows the progression of the seasons and calls to mind, for those few who know Krolow's work before 1945, his nature poems on the seasons; these later poems are equally remote from extrinsic contexts but now more self-consciously literary. What was implicit in the literature of *inner emigration* has become explicit and self-conscious here as a reaction to the increasing pressures of the force field of political poetry in the 1960s in Germany.[8] Despite his notions of the open poem, the actual range of experience that actually enters into these "alltägliche" poems remains closely circumscribed.

In his brief review of this volume, Klaus Jeziorkowski anticipates this criticism: "Aber das alles ist von einer kaum vorstellbaren Sicherheit und Nüchternheit des Tons, ist derart hellwach, ausgeschlafen und genau gesagt, daß dieser scheinbar enge Bezirk nirgendwo zum bloßen Würz- und Kräutergärtlein degeneriert, sondern in der Tat Welt repräsentiert" (*Über Karl Krolow,* 153), a claim which, aside from the puzzling critical terminology ("ausgeschlafen"), remains simple assertion. For contrast, Jeziorkowski sets Krolow's poems against "eine neue Pauschalvorstellung von modernster Lyrik: grimmig politisch hat sie zu sein, mit derben und auch etwas obszönen Griffen hat sie zuzupacken, mit Maschinengewehren und der Rassenfrage, mit Geschlechtsteilen und Guerillas hat sie zu fuchteln" (*Über Karl Krolow*, 152). Such a provocative rhetorical simplification overlooks the frequent presence of "Maschinengewehren" in Krolow's poetry, but does, at least as a defensive parry, recall to mind the historical moment.[9] Jeziorkowski finds in these poems "die historischen Beunruhigungen im Privaten, das Schwanken des Zimmerbodens, . . . das unterirdische Beben der Geschichte im Intimen," but he does not demonstrate or even indicate how that historical dialectic might work within the poems. Instead, his comments suggest indirectly or inadvertently a form of poetry that is self-consciously restored *Biedermeier*, self-consciously removing itself from a dialectical involvement with history, as in the poem "Winter auf einem bemalten Schild" (II, 74). Jeziorkowski seems to have simply accepted Krolow's argument from his essay "Von der Zuständigkeit des Schriftstellers in der Politik" (1967), as discussed in the previous chapter. Instead of the fiction of unmediated description or evocation of a scene or season, as in his poems in the Third Reich, these poems present the fact of artistic mediation in relation to nature as the main topic of the volume. Yet, again like the poems in the Third Reich, these poems only reflect a relation to society through their range of self-conscious exclusion.

With the introduction of the first-person pronoun, the poem "Ich gehe über die Straße" (II, 78) marks a move out of that enclosed space of nature as citation, which also distances Krolow from his longstanding precept of de-individualization. The four-part poem "Alltägliches Gedicht" (II, 78–80) confirms that new impulse to unmediated observation ("Eine Menge Stoff für Verse / liegt da herum" [79] . . . "Alles möglichst einfach" [80]) that finally allows a sociocritical perspective to emerge as in the poem "Familientisch" (II, 81):

> Der Familientisch verschafft
> die Illusion von Familie.
> Man sieht an ihm
> überall leere Plätze.
> Vater und Mutter sind
> hinzuzudenken
> bei rostiger Gabel, dreizinkig,
> einer zerstoßenen Tasse
> und behenden Rotweinflecken,
> die sich jeden Abend
> vergrößern.
> Eine Hintertür steht offen.
> Jemand schleicht sich hinaus.

A mundane object is the occasion for a meditation on the social ideal and social reality of the nuclear family that yields an insight into the (im)possibility of such unmediated observation of external reality. The poem gives few details, but the absences, the "empty places" at the table, illuminate the function of ideology in society to fill in the gaps and provide or impose an illusion. The table becomes a reflection on the social construction of what might otherwise appear self-evident. Simplicity is also artifice; in any attempt at unmediated perception, reality slips out the back door.

With that insight, Krolow returns to the notion of the poem as *Flaschenpost* that characterized the earlier poem "Meeresstille" as self-enclosed, self-referential text that is set adrift, disconnected from the author and possible recipient. In the poem "Briefwechsel" (II, 82–83), he seems to apply that concept to his own biography or to insert at least the question of his biography into the ambiguities of the poem's function:

> Mein Briefwechsel
> würde weit reichen, wenn es
> die Post gäbe.
> Ich erleichtere gern mein Gewissen.
>
> Ich habe ein Abkommen
> mit gestohlenen Tagen getroffen.
> Dann füllen Sterbenswörtchen
> das Papier.
>
> Ich beschreibe die Staatsraison
> oder mein früheres Leben
> in den Bäumen mit einer günstigen
> Himmelfahrt.
> In der richtigen Körperlage
> erzähle ich davon, daß ich
> Zuschauer blieb, während man
> um mich her immer ernsthafteren
> Beschäftigungen nachging.
>
> Außerdem fand ich niemanden,
> der bereit wäre,
> meine Post zu empfangen.

By negative hypothesis, that there is no mail service, the opening stanza rejects the possibility of direct communication: otherwise, the poetic persona would tell a great deal to a great many "correspondents" ("würde weit reichen") in order to ease "mein Gewissen." But poetry does not correspond to biographical reality and cannot document reality; the poem remains a message in a bottle that cannot be opened, cannot be linked to a specific content. On the one hand, without such a correspondence and its content of confession, the days seem stolen from that deferred reckoning of conscience; on the other hand, with such correspondence, the poetic persona can write with confidence at least about what he would write about. No one will receive that message. The third stanza describes the linked alternatives of either recognizing a political reality or of an apolitical escape into nature, into a poetics of ascension up through the trees into the heavens, as in Krolow's notion of floating *Leichtigkeit*. In hypothetically describing "mein früheres Leben," the fourth stanza goes further back to reveal that the poetic persona remained a passive spectator: the discrepancy between that passivity and knowledge of "ernsthafteren Beschäftigungen" relates back to and explains without specific detail the matter of "mein Gewissen." The poem elaborates the structure of a hypothetical confession without the content.

That paradox constitutes the basis for Krolow's ironic openness that marks a retreat, no longer directly into nature, but into an awareness of nature's literariness, which is both a critical commentary on tradition, on his own poetic roots, and a duplication of that predicament on another level. That doubleness is both Krolow's achievement and limitation: his ironic, critical rendition of literary tradition re-inscribes him into that same tradition in other terms. In "Neues Wesen" (II, 86–87), one of the best poems of the volume, Krolow manages to combine the volume's dominant tendency toward mere self-conscious literariness, as in "Pomologische Gedichte" and many others, with the more tentative impulse toward sociocritical registration of quotidian details:

> Blau kommt auf
> wie Mörikes leiser Harfenton.
> Immer wieder
> wird das so sein.
> Die Leute streichen
> ihre Häuser an.
> Auf die verschiedenen Wände
> scheint Sonne.
> Jeder erwartet das.
> Frühling, ja, du bist's!
> Man kann das nachlesen.

Die grüne Hecke ist ein Zitat
aus einem unbekannten Dichter.
Die Leute streichen auch
ihre Familien an, die Autos,
die Boote.
Ihr neues Wesen
gefällt allgemein.

The poem is a seasonal poem but an ironic derivation of Eduard Mö-rike's poem "Er ist's" published in 1832:

Frühling läßt sein blaues Band
Wieder flattern durch die Lüfte
Süße, wohlbekannte Düfte
Streifen ahnungsvoll das Land.
Veilchen träumen schon,
Wollen balde kommen.
— Horch, von fern ein leiser Harfenton!
Frühling, ja du bist's!
Dich hab ich vernommen!

Krolow's simile inscribes Mörike's poem into his own. Mörike's poem suggests the anticipation of spring in an intermingling of the senses, the color blue, the touch of wind, the smells, and the soft sound. The signs of spring are personified but still invisible, like the violet's dream of blooming. The extremely delicate intimations swell in significance and then come together, after the momentary pause of the hyphen, in a jubilatory recognition of spring's arrival marked by three exclamations. The poetic self, otherwise invisible, embraces spring like a lost loved one who has returned, as in the title "Er ist's," in full, joyous identification. Krolow's poem reverses the overflow of feeling from Mörike's poem: the plenitude of feeling in exultation is drained by the flat enunciation of endless repetition ("Immer wieder wird das so sein"). Each period point negates Mörike's exclamations; when Krolow cites the ecstatic line "Frühling, ja du bist's!" it has become static and reduced to a cliché ("Man kann das nachlesen") as with all impressions of nature that are derivative even if one cannot cite the source. Instead of concentrating inwardly upon flashes of sensory cognition, the poem registers the arrival of spring in the banal domestic activities around town. The spontaneous experience of nature has been supplanted by literary tradition and the ideological reflexes, fixed by the seasons, of a social community: the word for house-painting (*anstreichen*) shifts from the literal to the figurative usage between the third and the ninth sentences to suggest the whitewash of individuality in social habit. The notion of Hitler as the *Anstreicher,* the house painter, as he was often dubbed by Brecht, plays in the background as the risk of such proto-totalitarian conformity. The final lines invert all together the Romantic sense of spontaneous novelty in nature, the consumer's wish for new (looking) goods, and twentieth-century ideologies of ontological rebirth, whether in the Expressionist's *Neuer Mensch* or in fascist or communist plans of collective renewal: in withering irony, the multiple clichés of newness appear generally in the literal sense of the last word as *all-gemein,* a disreputable commonness that blossoms all around.[10]

In this poem Krolow goes beyond the ironic reflection on his pony or crib text to develop an insight into ideological formations in history, to create content beyond the technical negation of a model as a form of conscious literary derivation. Other poems in the latter part of the volume, however, fall back into the sort of repetition, in cynical negations, that they also seem to criticize as in "Gemeinsamer Frühling" (II, 87):

> Das haben wir nun
> wieder alles gemeinsam:
> einen singenden Baum
> mit Vögeln statt Blättern,
> die Brennesselkur, den Aufguß
> von Huflattich,
> das gemeinsame Motiv,
> die kollektive Luft.
>
> Uns gehören
> die Tauben auf dem Dach.
> Die Dose Bier
> schmeckt wieder im Freien.
> Nun muß sich alles, alles
> wenden.
>
> Die leeren Seiten
> füllen sich mit Bedeutung.
> Das Schreiben über den Frühling
> macht allen Spaß.

Here nature is experienced as commonplace, as textual platitude, as structural repetition, surrounding the "Utopian" moment of an open beer can out of doors: the increase of banality seems to arrive at a peak of despair, a moment of crisis ("Nun muß sich alles, alles / wenden"), in which the repetition of "alles, alles," the very inescapable ubiquity of banality should introduce a turn, a revolution, in history and in sensibility. But the last stanza curtails that suggestion of a redemptive possibility and annuls it by closing the circle of self-conscious text as denatured *Naturlyrik* that only reproduces the same fault as the object of its criticism: instead of naïve praise of nature, the poem produces a jaded tone of cynical negation that is equally self-contained and self-satisfied. Other poems such as "Frühling im großen und ganzen" (II, 88–89) all offer interesting nuances to the same basic model of ironic distantiation from a naïve view of redemptive nature.

The poem "Einen Satz lang" (II, 93–94) summarizes this model as a sort of *ars poetica* for Krolow in this volume:

> Einen Satz lang bleibt
> das ansehnlich,
> ohne Belastung durch Relativsätze,
> Kunststück mit Sonne, Welt —
> eine Kleinigkeit, freundlich
> bei günstigem Licht,
> soviel Gunst obenhin
> und bekömmliche Landschaft,
> eine wirkliche Szene,
> Schauspieler kommen und gehen,
> man holt gut Luft,
> das Leben hat man schon lange
> nicht so gut gefunden in einem Satz
> so wie Blumen auf dem Lande
> geradeaus wachsend hinter Bänken,
> auf denen niemand sitzt,
> den goldenen Rahmen
> vermißt niemand.

Krolow's denatured poems about nature strip the "goldenen Rahmen" and replace nature with text, with ironically self-conscious constructions of generic negation that depend still on the negated genre almost entirely for their substance. "Neues Wesen" comprises an exception. Hence the frequent praise of Krolow sounds more like an indictment for technical virtuosity with each repetition. The content of the poems, however consciously constructed, too often remains limited to ironic negation that strips an outdated, historical genre of its golden frame and does not pass beyond to open a new perspective. Only the framework has changed around a "Kunststück." Krolow risks falling into a mechanical cynicism toward nature that remains calendar poetry for a different year.

That automatic irony, whether sardonic or playful, can reverse upon itself into a surprising naïveté as in the poem "Staatsgewalt" (II, 95) that recalls the poem "Die Gewalt" for its surprising and even paradoxical presentation, both unanalytical and unpolitical, of its titular topic:

> Einen dieser sorgfältig verpackten Polizisten
> nehme ich aus der Schachtel,
> stelle ihn
> als blauen Schutzmann
> an die Straßenecke
> an einem Tag, der mit seinem blauen Wetter
> bis zum Lieben Gott reicht.
> Die Staatsgewalt lasse ich
> mit Stimme
> aus einem Buch mit schönen Gesetzen
> vorlesen.
> Die Passanten glauben ihr,
> die Haustiere, die Vögel.
> Sie halten an und staunen,
> daß alles so gut geht.

Irony seems to break down into a curious vision of order that extends from the "Lieben Gott" down to the "Staatsgewalt" and its representative on the street. This poem was written in 1967 at the beginning of student unrest in Germany[11] and during events such as the protests surrounding the Shah of Iran's visit to Germany in June of that year, the subsequent police reaction, and the death of Bernhard Ohnesorg.[12] The whimsical irony of the first line seems to trivialize the issues and then dwindles steadily into an image of a docile and gullible population, entranced by the voice of state power, no different from their pets and the birds. The omniscient poetic persona has created this scene as in a board game, perhaps to provoke criticism, but the irony boomerangs to present, however improbable, a desideratum of benign state control, or just the oddly unsure handling of such themes. Nonetheless, the final poems that broach social issues, "Differenz" (II, 96) and "Die Macht" (II, 97), suggest Krolow's uncertain emigration out of the realm of literary citation.

In his discussion of the poem "Neues Wesen," Otto Knörrich expands from that poem to the volume as a whole, and to this phase in Krolow's work in general, and makes an obscure link to Krolow's biography:

> Überhaupt wird durch die literarische Vermitteltheit des Frühlingserlebnisses jede Spontaneität des Erlebens ausgeschlossen. Sie ist eine Weise der Distanzierung. Das gilt für die Naturerfahrung ganz allgemein, für jenes Verfahren, den 'Landschaftstext' als literarische Zitatensammlung zu lesen. Letztlich entspringen diese Distanzierungsversuche dem Schutzbedürfnis des Dichters. (223)

The final poem of "Alltägliche Gedichte" seems to confirm Knörrich's surmise about that function of irony as a defensive mechanism: in "Sich vergewissern" (II, 98) Krolow drops that technique of ironic distantiation and returns to the anguished existential mode of the immediate postwar period:

> Ich versuche,
> mich zu vergewissern,
> daß ich vorkomme.
> Im selben Augenblick
> gibt es mich, bartlos,
> mit bleichem Zahnfleisch
> hinter der Lippe
> und halb geöffneten Augen,
> aus Furcht, zu viel
> zu sehen, was anders ist
> als Haut und Haar,
> die sich im Zusehen
> verlieren.
> Ich bin da. Meine
> rechte Hand fällt mir
> nicht durch die Tasche.
> Ich führe sie über Papier,
> um aufzuschreiben,
> daß ich lebe.

This poem, in its psychological drama, is the only one of its kind in *Alltägliche Gedichte*. In his essay "Selbstporträt 1971," Krolow draws the connection between this poem and his earlier self-portraits from 1945 and 1947 and suggests that the poems have in common a tentative, spontaneous, revocable quality, a certain fear or reluctance to make too much of one's self (202–3), and he rejects the notion of artifice in their appearance: "Es ist nichts von einem In-Szene-Setzen zu erkennen, glaube ich sagen zu können, nur diese flüchtige Da-Seins-Erscheinung" (203). Krolow makes a claim of artless authenticity for this poem, almost as a type of realistic, not surrealistic, automatic writing; the writing hand registers, seismographically, the shock and uncertainty of existence. The historical context that loomed behind the other two self-portraits in 1945 and 1947 is now absent; the frame of ironic literariness that characterized other poems in the volume has also fallen away and left only the persona's bare self-consciousness without the indirection and mediation of literary allusions. Yet as Krolow himself notes, despite his claim for the poem's lack of theatricality, the poem registers "literarisches Da-Sein" (203) and brings the self-conscious literariness of the preceding poems to the point of contact between writer's hand and paper in the immediate present. Instead of compositional technique of montage, the poem presents the process of automatic writing: "eine Sache ohne Aufwand, ein sachlicher Vorgang vor allem, hinter dem die Biographie desjenigen, der schreibt, verschwindet oder doch zurücktritt und uninteressant wird." Though unacknowledged and unexamined in a half century of criticism and scholarship on Krolow, this sense of poetry as a type of objective, automatic writing that effaces biography and enforces amnesia has always been central to Krolow's work.

Notes

[1] Jong Ho Pee compares "Winterliches Leben" to Hölderlin's "Hälfte des Lebens," but the comparison does not do justice to the nearly apocalyptic desolation of Hölderlin's powerful final image. Though both poems conclude with a lone sound resonating in the cold, Hölderlin's poem does not at all bear resemblance to the almost celebratory affirmation of ahistorical nature in Krolow's winter poem, arching from "Zuverlässigkeit des Dunkels" to the "singende Maschine." The isolation and desolation of Hölderlin's poem is historical (private and collective) in nature, whereas Krolow's poem sets nature over and above speech, memory, and history.

[2] Krolow also responds more indirectly to Walter Höllerer. In early 1965 in his journal *Akzente*, Walter Höllerer had published his "Thesen zum langen Gedicht," which marked an attempt to break or announce a break from the hermetic poem of the 1950s that he perceived as an impasse and to open the way for a

long, discursive form that would seek "Umgang mit der Realität" (128). The long poem constitutes a "Gegenbewegung gegen Einengung," which is "schon seiner Form nach politisch" (128). In the mid-1960s, Krolow became involved in public debates about the role of the poem in politics that coincided with an evolution in his own work.

[3] Marion Mallmann, in her thorough study of the journal *Das Innere Reich,* cites Krolow's essay and this particular passage in order to distinguish Krolow from the somewhat older group of poets such as Oda Schaefer and Horst Lange, who could never afterward directly confront or discuss their position as writers in the Third Reich. However, she notes "In diesem Aufsatz vermeidet er [Krolow] zwar die Anspielung auf das Dritte Reich und auf seine eigenen Gedichte dieser Zeit, aber er lehnt einen 'literarischen Eskapismus' ab, der nichts anderes als 'aesthetisch und regressiv' sei" (238). Uncharacteristically, she takes the statements of principle, the applause lines, out of context; as I have tried to show, the essay mouths certain principles, but reverses their meaning in order to adapt a familiar position to a contemporary sensibility. If a careful critic like Mallmann can be taken as an example, the strategy worked, though she does note, first, his silence about his own particular experience, and second, that the examples he cites of his political poetry are not representative of his work.

[4] In the third to last thesis, Höllerer admonishes: "Berufe dich nicht auf 'Schweigen' und 'Verstummen.' Das Schweigen als Theorie einer Kunstgattung, deren Medium Sprache ist, führt schließlich zu immer kürzeren, verschlüsselten Gedichten" (130). Höllerer is reacting to the ongoing discussion of Adorno's (misunderstood) remark on poetry after Auschwitz, to the tendency toward silence in Celan's poetry, and perhaps also to Ingeborg Bachmann's decision to stop writing poetry. See the discussion of Adorno's "Philosophy of Poetry" in my *Voice and Void.* Krolow finds himself forced into public discussion of his poetics in which he has to try to situate himself in relation to the poetics and politics of Adorno, Domin, and Höllerer.

[5] Michael Braun, for one, makes this obvious, but mistaken connection (*Der poetische Augenblick,* 111).

[6] Martin Anderle cites this poem as an example of "der zunehmenden Unverbindlichkeit der Krolowschen Metaphern" (187).

[7] Krolow reverses Gottfried Benn's metaphor of the novel, of literary form, as an orange, whereby each segment is self-contained and leads equally to the existential center of the phenotype. See chapter 7 ("Ecstatic Montage: Paratactic Visions in Gottfried Benn's Novella Cycle *Brains* [1916])" in my *Forms of Disruption,* especially 164–67.

[8] Krolow has often described *Kräftefeld* as a concept.

[9] The "Geschlechtsteile" appear in abundant detail and activity in 1970 in Krolow's volume *Bürgerliche Gedichte.*

[10] Krolow himself wrote a commentary on this poem, prefaced by a general statement of his understanding of poetry. His own reading of the poem as critic is surprisingly shallow and defuses the poem's intensity. Otto Knörrich had noted rightly of the ending: "Zugleich verstärkt sich hier gegen Ende des Gedichts der ironische Unterton. Der Schluß — und damit zugleich die Überschrift — ist bare

Ironie" (223). In contrast, Krolow emphasizes the ahistorical dimension of the poem's portrayal of an "alterslose[m] Frühlingsaugenblick" (*Ein Gedicht entsteht,* 42) and breaks the point off of any intellectual interpretation: "Der Text überläßt sich solcher — ich möchte sagen — frohgemuten, optimistischen, unkomplizierten Stimmung, diesem Gefühl, dabei zu sein [. . .] Und — bei beibehaltener leichter Ironie, die mit solchem Tun solidarisiert . . ." (42). Krolow's own banal interpretation turns the poem into a pretty little picture, without critique or particular content, of happy activity to welcome the spring ("neuer Mut, neue Initiative, neues Wesen nach dem Dunkel, der Mühsal winterlicher Wochen und Monate" 43).

[11] The exact date that Krolow wrote this poem is unknown.

[12] In October 1967, the Büchner-Prize recipient, Heinrich Böll, indicated Büchner's present topicality: "Es fällt nicht schwer, Büchners politische und ästhetische Gegenwärtigkeit zu sehen. Die Kerker-Torturen des Studenten und Büchnerfreunds Minnigerode mit jenen zwei, auf offener Straße durch amtliche Personen begangenen Morden in Beziehung zu bringen: der Erschießung des Berliner Studenten Ohnesorg und des Bundeswehrsoldaten Corsten, beides ungeheuerliche Fälle öffentlichen Mordes durch die Staatsgewalt" (Buck, 145).

8: The Vanishing Point of History (The Seventies)

Nichts weiter als Leben (1972)

THE FIRST POEM OF *Nichts weiter als Leben*, "Lesen" (II, 101), issues a challenge to critics. The poem narrows the circle of a literary domain drawn by Krolow in the last volume and defined by citation and allusion, which mediated existence and removed the individual, through the self-consciousness of the artifice, from questions and contexts outside of that realm of literariness. Here, however, no citations or allusions signal that realm and instead, the individual, the self of the first-person pronoun, is immediately present in the first word, describing a completed action that prepares for an ongoing action. The activity of reading becomes all exclusive:

> Ich habe alles
> liegen gelassen.
> Mein Schatten hinter mir
> wandert langsam
> von Norden nach Osten.
> Meine Erinnerung endet
> am Rande des Buches.
> Langsam neben mir
> im Glas trocknet
> das Wasser.
> Ohne Vorwurf vergeht
> die Zeit.
> Sie ist eine vollkommene
> Geschichte ohne
> Fluchtpunkt,
> auf den man zugehen könnte,
> um etwas zu finden.

The activity of reading does not appear directly in the poem but is only given in the title and has to be inferred from the separate, almost unrelated utterances. The first sentence separates everything else ("alles") from that central but invisible activity. The second sentence describes the passing of time by the movements of the reader's shadow. Both remarks suggest an intensity of concentration. That intensity, however, does not make time appear to go fast; rather, the word "langsam" repeats to suggest the languid passing of time, as if the reader were also conscious of time. Such an awareness of passing time distracts from "Lesen," perhaps a contradiction in the poem. But both the immediacy of reading as an activity and the awareness of time passing oddly preclude memory, since memory is a faculty of reading and would seem joined to an awareness of time passing as in Proust. The poem separates the self-contained activity of reading from any content in the book or any continuum with the past and links simply to an isolated sense of present time that passes then "Ohne Vorwurf." Without the engagement of memory and without engagement in the content, the disengaged, almost intransitive activity of reading becomes a sort of still life that collapses the notion of the past or of a narrative: "eine vollkommene / Geschichte ohne / Fluchtpunkt, auf den man zugehen könnte, / um etwas zu finden." The perfect story (*Geschichte*) is one without history (*Geschichte*), or in the poem's mixed metaphor, the perfect story is a picture without a vanishing point. The poem narrates in fact its poetics of reducing the poem, and by implication, the painting and the story, and history, to a standstill, a closed circle that describes only its own omission of content or *Geschichte* in either sense, that would lead beyond its isolation in the immediate present. The last lines suggest that such an immediacy would block inquiry into a content, would arrest the eye from pursuing a vanishing point. Or, my thesis argues to the contrary that precisely such an aesthetics of more or less open negation of content in general and of the past in particular creates a vanishing point in postwar German poetry that needs to be discovered and isolated for examination and inquiry. Thus, Krolow's poetics and his poetry have a content beyond their apparent, explicit, and insistent lack of content. All perspectives on Krolow's career in all its phases lead back to the vantage point of that invisible vanishing point.

This poem was chosen by Krolow for his own demonstrative interpretation, which first appeared in newspapers and in his collection of essays *Ein Gedicht entsteht,* and also at the end of the volume itself. In his interpretation he negates the historical nature of reading as an activity ("momentanes wie nicht Datierbares" 45) and then addresses the question of content directly: "Inhalt? Ich weiß mit den Jahren immer weniger, was es mit ihm in einem Gedicht für eine Bewandtnis

hat, oder gar, was für eine Funktion er in ihm übernehmen könnte"
(45). He concedes that some poems might have a certain content but
insists that "Lesen" is not such a poem: "Von dieser Art ist das Gedicht Lesen nicht. Ich weiß nicht, ob es überhaupt Absichten hat und
verfolgt. Ein argloses Gedicht, sozusagen, das einen Zustand repro-
duziert" (46). Krolow defines the poem as "arglos," even though
the poem does not simply reproduce a circumstance or condition
and is far from unselfconscious; rather, the poem states in its last
lines, almost defensively, a poetic principle that precludes critical inquiry.

The narrow restriction of content becomes the theme of the second poem "Sinn der Dinge" (II, 101–2), which reproduces the scope
of Krolow's early nature poems in poetological terms:

> Höhere Zustände,
> Luftschöpfen, diskrete
> Ontologie: — ich erhalte
> mir so, was ich brauche,
> Stimmung der schwankenden Form,
> beliebige Ausdehnung einer Jahreszeit
> als wiederholbaren Vorgang,
> mit Blättern, Hitze, langsam ablaufendem Wasser
> aus einem Bild im Raum,
> den ich mir geschaffen habe,
> zwecklos, minimaler Reiz
> der Wahrnehmung, Liebesbrief
> vegetativer Augenblicke,
> körperliches Leben mit
> einem geometrischen Garten.
> Ich nehme mir,
> was ich brauche,
> als Indiz für den
> Sinn der Dinge.

The poem appears at first paradoxically as a sort of manifesto for "dis-
krete Ontologie," though the body of the poem is structured by the
assertive, almost aggressive repetitions of proprietary actions: "ich er-
halte mir so, was ich brauche" and "Ich nehme mir, / was ich brauche." That egotistical Self is at the center of the poem, figuratively and
literally, in line ten of nineteen "den ich mir geschaffen habe." The
content of the poem remains in the realm of conventional nature po-

etry, evoked with some of Krolow's preferred vocabulary, *Jahreszeit, Blättern,* and *Hitze,* but negates itself as arbitrary, mechanical, and pointless, with terms such as *beliebig, wiederholbaren Vorgang,* and *zwecklos.* Yet that restriction of content to a minimal impression ("minimaler Reiz der Wahrnehmung") is not without purpose since it satisfies a need, "was ich brauche," and becomes to the contrary an affirmation of selfhood, a "Liebesbrief / vegetativer Augenblicke."

Without the range of literary allusion to structure the exclusion of other content, Krolow's poetry concentrates upon the articulation of Self, a confirmation of existence — in inverse proportion to the minimalism of content ("körperliches Leben mit / einem geometrischen Garten") — as a body in a defined space. Jong Ho Pee notes rightly: "Beide Wahrnehmungsweisen bleiben an der Oberfläche der Dinge, dringen aber nicht in die Dinge ein," but adds wrongly: "Wenn der Dichter die Sinnbeziehungen zwischen den Dingen erkennt, schwächt sich seine Bewußtseins- und Daseinskrise ab. Durch die Suche nach dem 'Sinn der Dinge' kann man die Erkenntnis der Wirklichkeit erlangen" (131). The poem, however, demonstrates no relations between objects that would begin to adumbrate the complex reality of a historical space, nor does the poem describe the profound reality of a phenomenological object. Instead of "Erkenntnis der Wirklichkeit," the poem presents only, from different angles, guarded distance toward reality, rather than a point of ingress or of intensification. The poem states a self-reflexive poetics for a no longer naïve *Naturlyrik* that precisely prohibits exploration into knowledge of reality. Self and nature or a social setting reflect each other in a tight radius of self-reflexivity that precludes a complex engagement with the world or with the past; without that relation to an object, the poem forecloses the possibilities of its own irony and the notion of irony collapses, leaving only its trace, a residue, a more or less steady posture toward the world that no longer delivers insights.[1]

That radius of self-reflexivity, given in the volume by his interpretation at the end of the opening poem, is first projected onto the landscape in a cycle of poems on the mechanics of perception, particularly of landscape. Krolow's poetry here concentrates upon the minimalist construction of images of nature that are self-conscious in their artifice as in "Außenwelt" (II, 103):

> Ich verschaffe mir Außenwelt
> mit ein paar Sätzen —
> Rundung des Blickfelds,

gleichmäßig verteilte Wärme
über der stilisierten Form
vegetativer Gebilde,
Baumschlägen wie künstlichen Objekten,
einfacher Linienführung
der Zivilisation
zwischen Hausfassaden
und statischem Himmel,
unter ihm verstreuten Figuren,
Menschen, die am Ganzen mitwirken,
einem Mitteilungsraum,
in dem ich mich bewege,
sprachlos.

The poem describes a compositional technique of landscape design but does not present an immediate image of a landscape. As elsewhere, Krolow's poetry here applies consciousness to objects, or the external world in general, without emotion but also without insight or irony. In this respect, the peculiarly deadening quality that at times afflicts Krolow's verse lies in its oppressive lightness as a formal exercise of consciousness in withholding substance.

Some poems put that thematics of perception and composition into an art historical perspective, which casts a certain irony upon itself, but also reduces the semantic scope of the poem to questions of its own technique as in the first stanza of "Perspektive" (II, 105):

Zuverlässiges Sehen weiß,
wozu Perspektive
taugt seit Brunelleschi
für Farbe und Luft.
Die Körper der Griechen,
verkürzt schon früher
vor dem unendlich fernen
Fluchtpunkt der Geraden,
die im Raum verschwindet.
Zuverlässig
ist Geometrie, wenn sie
sich verliert am Horizont.
Der Gesichtskreis zuverlässig
als Rahmen für ein
Schlachtengemälde,

einer Landschaft mit Leben,
das Leben nimmt oder
schenkt, wenn zwei
einige Körper sich
ein wenig verschieben
in der gemeinsamen Bewegung,
die uns alle ins Dasein
bringt.

The repetitions of the word *Zuverlässig* divide the poem into three parts: the first section describes the historical development of visual perspective in Western culture centered upon the linear vanishing point in the picture space; the second section reiterates that history of perspective as general principle, which raises the literal and figurative senses of horizon. That figurative level emerges in the term *Gesichtskreis*, which literally means the scope of sight or field of vision, and figuratively, the range of perception and comprehension, the ken, of the viewer. The literal sense of sight is "zuverlässig" in its limitations as a frame for battle scenes, landscape, or a scene of struggle, such as taking life, and coupling, such as making love and life. But in order to grasp the last meaning, one has to see figuratively. The third section develops one long sentence that departs from direct description in order to relate, in comic circumlocution, the act of love-making, which, though classical in its time-honored rhythm ("der gemeinsamen Bewegung, / die uns alle ins Dasein / bringt"), still disturbs the antique poise invoked by the first section. In this skillful poem, Krolow himself frames the semantics of the poem between compositional technique and existence, the "Fluchtpunkt der Geraden" and the vanishing point of "der gemeinsamen Bewegung." Krolow manipulates the play of nearness and farness, of depth and proximity, in order to exclude the middle ground of historical space.

Accordingly, Krolow approaches the same problem from another angle in the poem "Nähe" (II, 105) with the repetitions of the word *Blind* that derives from too close proximity: "Blind für das Büschel / der Geraden in der Ebene, / ein Stilleben, das / Perspektive tötet." The poem inverts the terms of the previous poem: instead of perspectival sight, blindness; instead of the life-giving rhythms of copulation, a still life that actively kills. Yet both perspectives reduce experience and remain within the purview of matters of technical composition.

The cycle on composition culminates in the poem "Der Horizont" (II, 106–7), which makes explicit an implication of the former poems on the relation between these questions of landscape and perspective, and memory:

> Der Horizont
> mit seinem Zubehör,
> Hauptpunkt, Distanzpunkte —
> ich sehe eine Allee
> Hainbuchen auf ihn
> zustreben und verschwinden
> wie Gedächtnis, das
> nach und nach Einzelheiten
> aufgibt als Verlust
> von erinnertem Reiz.
> Horizont, Streifen
> in Augenhöhe, zurückweichend
> vor der Sehnsucht, die sich
> auf ihn bezieht,
> wenn sie ihm eine Menge
> von dem entgegenschickt,
> was sie auf dem Herzen hat.

The visual horizon and landscape have been a metaphor in this group of poems for the picture space of a painting or drawing, which has been a metaphor, in turn, for art in general and the poem: now that visual horizon becomes a metaphor for the play of memory and feeling in the poem, of consciousness and conscience in relation to the past. Impressions are lost as they recede into memory, just as foreground recedes into background and loses itself in the vanishing point of the picture; the horizon recedes as one tries to approach with desires or regrets ("was sie auf dem Herzen hat") that lead like lines of perspective toward that vanishing point. Thus, the poem represents in the analytical vocabulary of spatial composition the pictorial impossibility of bringing together near and far, present and past, foreground and background, memory and desire, remembrance and regret. "Horizont" presents a structure that applies to the other poems in the volume and elsewhere in Krolow's work: his impressionistic poems still have a vanishing point, beyond the visible foreground of descriptive or sensuous immediacy and beyond the poetological background of analytical, self-reflexive commentary, on the horizon of his poetics. In some poems, one has to locate that vanishing point in the poem and the poetics, perhaps as here, in the dialectic between "Gedächtnis" und "dem Herzen."

In other words, all the poems have a semantic vanishing point. Whereas the hermetic poem enlarges that vanishing point and forces the critic to encounter the dense background all at once in the foreground and to speculate on the semantic depths just in order to locate the vanishing point where meanings might converge, these seemingly simple and accessible poems, such as Krolow's porous poems, appear in contrast as all foreground, with little to hide or reveal, without depths, as a kind of anti-hermeticism that defeats interpretation just by seeming not to require any. The critic has to take a longer perspective on that self-evident sort of poem in order to locate its vanishing point. The poem "Miniatur" (II, 109) provides a model for these critical assumptions:

> Auf einem kleinen Bild
> ist auch der blaue Himmel
> klein
> mit seiner winzigen Luft
> über allem,
> kleinen Verhältnissen und
> einem Stück Land,
> zurecht geschnitten für
> Bäume, Menschen und Haustiere,
> von einer unbekannten
> Intelligenz geordnet,
> die außerhalb des Bildes
> blieb und sich
> den Rahmen überlegte,
> in den sie Kleinigkeiten
> brachte.

However much reduced to minimalist proportions in terms of size or content, the poem bears the mark of its author's conscious construction. Krolow invokes this Flaubertian notion of the artwork for his poetic tableaux, his unassuming miniatures, from which the author, the unseen ordering intelligence, seems to have disappeared — or at least the poem states as much. For all its apparent simplicity, the poem offers a self-reflexive, poetological justification of minutiae. If that is the case, one has to question the aesthetic position and significance of such *Kleinigkeiten.*

The motif of *Kleinigkeiten,* already anticipated in the deflationary title, holds the volume together, which is divided into six untitled sections, within which some poems aggregate into poetic cycles. "Miniatur" completes the first section, which mainly revolves around the questions of artistic composition or perspective in art. It also contains a cycle on habitual actions, minutiae of routine, as in the poem "Trinken" (II, 107), which harkens back to "Selbstbildnis mit Rumflasche" from 1947 as a portrait of false transcendence but suggests a background: "Phantasie, immer noch / mächtiger als Gewissen — / ich will nichts / als dasitzen." The poem "Schlafen" (II, 108) invokes dreams "von wirklich schönen / Bildern, die nichts bedeuten, / Farboberflächen ohne Hintergrund [. . .] nur Abstufungen einiger Farben, die wechseln und die bloß / da waren . . .," which indicates a poetics that applies in general to Krolow's miniatures in *Nichts weiter als Leben*: the poetic persona *ich* gives a reading of the dreams as pure imagistic surfaces of changing color and nuance without meaning and without depth perspectives. The poems that describe a rational technique of composition also seek to eliminate depth and create foreshortened perspectives that seem "zwecklos" ("Sinn der Dinge"). The next section describes the changing seasons ("Abstufungen einiger Farben") and thereby returns again to Krolow's favorite theme since his earliest publications.[2] These tableaux do not present nature directly but describe, with an abundance of metaphors ("Der Himmel ist ein Schatz fernen Lichtes [116]), impressions of nature that are, as in section one, less physical observation than geometric composition as in "Schneevorhang" (II, 121):

> Manches gibt es nur jetzt:
> mangelnde Orientierung
> im Schneevorhang Luft,
> erfroren über der Fläche.
> Überall ist Norden im Winter,
> wenn man geradeaus geht,
> ohne anzukommen.
> Die Horizontale erstickt
> Schritte und Umkehr.
> Gedächtnis verliert sich
> wie eine Blickachse.
> Seine altertümliche Spur
> erlischt in der Längsrichtung,
> die immer weiter führt.

Here the method of geometric composition combines with the theme of seasons to the point that no image is present, only a presentation of concepts of perception before the metaphoric image of the "Schneevor-hang." As in the other poems of geometric composition, the first half of the poem delivers the conceit, the dominant metaphor or play of ideas, and the second half its significance: memory is lost in the pictorial van-ishing point of the conceived space, which is not otherwise described. This landscape poem has no primary image. The "Schneevorhang" blocks out the landscape and turns the poem indoors.

The next section focuses on more or less domestic scenes, interior spaces defined by objects, which fill the foreground: in "Auf dem Land" (II, 122), it is the "Einsamkeit / der Gegenstände. Ein Stuhl ist nichts / als ein Stuhl, eine Schere Schere, offen / oder geschlossen." The sense of seasonal recurrence or routine combines now with the nearness to objects to give access to the social realm as in the poem "Besuch kommt" (II, 122–23), where the first-person persona surveys "diese beliebten / Kleinigkeiten der Gastfreund-schaft" in the first half, and then in the second proclaims: "Ich sitze / unter meinen Habseligkeiten, / glücklich, sie dienstbar / machen zu können." The note of satirical irony is held in balance by a note of self-satisfied complacency. The poems maintain a steady clarity, with occasional nuance but little urgency, as technical exercises in subtly ironic composition. The self-reflexive poetological dimension of the earlier poems has fallen away. Many of the poems seem only flatly whimsical despite a touch of irony. The psychological portrait of a man in the poem "Allzeit mutig" (II, 128) marks a turning point in the volume; it is the description of a personal transformation, an awak-ening of conscience, that concludes: "Die empfindungsvolle Sicherheit / war ihm abhanden gekommen." Here, the cutting irony is balanced by a note of sympathy that gives the poem some depth of characteri-zation. The irony increases and begins to give the poems a discernible critical edge as the social realm of the poems expands; in "Bürgerlich" (II, 134) a social class is parodied:

> Seit längerer Zeit
> Klasse ohne Zukunft,
> gutgekleidet und angenehm
> beim Essen anzusehen,
> bürgerlich,
> mit aufgeheiterten Gesichtszügen,
> Verständnis für
> moralische Leistung und
> Kriegskunst.

Klasse ohne Ästhetik,
doch voll Menschennatur
im Gartenhaus:
Figuren, gut im Zeug,
soziologisch weiter
interessant.
Behagen schwebt
auf und ab.
Wir wollen tun,
was wir können,
fleißig und im Walde
feierlich,
als zeitvertreibenden Genuß
Gefühl für Höheres,
ohne Übereilung.

Unlike the prior portrait of an individual in that bourgeois class, this portrait of a whole social class is static, but that is the point. The features of the class are briefly stated in exaggerated generalization as in a satirical cartoon. A psychological inflection of interiority appears in the shift to first-person plural point-of-view, a sort of "stream-of-unconsciousness" of the whole class, in the recitation of a virtuous but modest cliché ("Wir wollen tun, / was wir können") that portrays the comfortable inner and outer paralysis of self-limitation in the middle class. Krolow extends this first-person portrait of self-confident complacency in the middle class in the four-part poem "Bürgerliches Gedicht" (II, 135–38), where the earlier artistic self-consciousness and self-reflection of the poetological poems appears in the *Bürger* as self-centered tautology: "Ich bekomme, was bekömmlich ist, / bequem in die Hand" (II, 136). The poems "Der Schrecken" (II, 138) and "Sterbliches" (II, 139) also address a social theme, one of violence. These poems indicate a tendency in the volume toward social engagement, though, as earlier, the poems reflect on violence only as a recurring, ahistorical phenomenon ("Die Szene wiederholt sich oft. / Blut ist billig / im Vergleich zum Goldwert, / für den Banken einstehn").

That notion of eternal repetition figures in the poem "Weltmaschine" (II, 139) in which Krolow seems to question the concept of history that informs his poems:

> Sanduhren, Attribute
> der unsichtbaren Weltmaschine,
> langsam laufend und poetisch
> als Erscheinung —
> man erfährt Ablauf
> von Geschichte als etwas,
> das durch Finger fällt,
> während fröhlich auf Leute
> geschossen wird, die
> nicht mehr verwendbar sind.
> Mit Genuß wird Vergangenheit
> verarbeitet als Zukunft.
> Die Botanik der Träume
> will gelernt sein,
> um aus ihr Nutzen
> zu ziehn für Utopie,
> die mit Grausamkeit
> nicht geizen soll.
> Die letzte Karte ist nie
> verspielt. Schon morgen
> werden wir mehr wissen.

Krolow sets the notion of history between the poetic image of the hourglass, as a perfectly functioning apparatus, and the notion of a utopia, both of which schemes annul historical specificity by subordinating it entirely to an aesthetic image, whose transfer from art to politics often entails "Grausamkeit." History slips through the fingers like sand as it does when viewed solely as temporality. Behind the perfect image, the reality of historical experience appears different; as usual in Krolow's work, history appears as one with violence, equated in this poem with an image, or the suggestion, of an execution of exploited human labor. After the long opening sentence, the poem turns on the pivotal sentence: "Mit Genuß wird Vergangenheit / verarbeitet als Zukunft," which captures a law of utopian thinking, and later of state propaganda, that tailors the past to fit its projection of the future and turns dreams into an instrument of practical manipulation, whose essence is its "Grausamkeit." Pee finds a hopeful note for a progressive utopianism in the penultimate sentence (68), but that line could also suggest, more logically, that the last card will be well played by the same party that knows to use the "Botanik der Träume" and will not spare cruelty. The conclusion remains ambiguous as in the phrase

"Schon morgen" that both anticipates and defers disillusionment. The future of utopian thinking always arrives too soon as a bitter reality.

Krolow seems to develop toward a more complex engagement with historical reality. The phrase *Botanik der Träume* in this context conflates his own earlier, unworldly phases of *Naturlyrik* and surrealism, distances him from them, and opens the way to the world. But the negated concept of utopia becomes a barrier for entry into the complexity of historical reality. It instead serves to extend and intensify that disillusionment, which registers reality only as timeless routine, as repetitions that undermine memory. In part five of the eight-part poem "Licht" (II, 140–44), sensory impressions no longer liberate experience, but have become their self-contained and intellectual universe, framed by literary experience, by the allusion to Paul Valéry's Monsieur Teste, about whom Krolow published an essay in 1966:

> Die Jahreszeit —
> ein grünes, nach Minze riechendes
> Haus, wie das Zimmer
> von Monsieur Teste.
> In der Fabelwelt der Erscheinung
> habe ich Gedächtnis
> für miteinander identische
> Vorgänge, während
> die Aufenthalte wechselten
> und vergessene Gedanken
> zurückblieben, hinterlassen
> als Wortparadies, Gesumm
> von Namen draußen im Land.
> Die Helligkeit wucherte
> grün als Landschaftsmodell
> mit Einzelheiten, unter denen sich
> der Geruch von Herrn Testes
> Minze erhielt.

In that unreal world of pure imagery ("Fabelwelt der Erscheinung"), memory retains only replications that defeat historical time and create a selective continuity in perception, which at the same time creates a selective discontinuity. With a change of place, specific thoughts ("vergessene Gedanken") and unwanted memories are left behind as mere words without relation to the present or to reality: "Gesumm / von Namen draußen im Land." Memory collapses into a lucid but artificial scene or scenario, whose artifice as landscape ("Landschaftsmo-dell") appears natural.

In another long poem, "Körper" (II, 144–49), individual exis-tence is likewise reduced to physical bodies in mechanical movement ("langsame Automatik der Verrichtungen als / Zusammenhalt" 144) like the *Weltmaschine* of history on a smaller scale. In five sections of short, prosaic lines, without inflection or affect, the individual only exists as a sort of grammatical shadow, the personal pronoun *er* for the body that goes through its motions. Pee wrongly interprets this poem as the realization of a sensualistic utopia (69) in section IV, which be-gins: "Utopie, eingelöst, Freiheit / als aufgehobene Spannung — / Li-bido, die vom Objekt / auf den Körper zurückfällt" (147) and ends: "Natürliche Zukunft / hat begonnen" (148), but does not change the flat tone of clinical detachment. The very lack of consciousness, emo-tion, love, or eroticism in the equation of utopia with ejaculation ("wenn ihm Sperma / verläßt im Stehen oder / Liegen, nach üblicher Art," 148) undermines that projection. This mechanical sensualism is rather a symptom of self-estrangement in a dull animality. The next section begins: "Das Abgestorbene, / das er in sich hat, / Empfin-dung, abgenutzt, / trotz ruheloser Augen." Like the tautological self-image of the *Bürger*, the individual becomes a robotic solipsist: "Der Zufall, abgeschafft, wie / das Gefühl. / Durchdachter Egoismus / als die Kunst, / wenig zu lieben." Krolow describes a type of trauma that ech-oes Gottfried Benn's descriptions in his Rönne stories (*Gehirne*, 1916), where Rönne's trauma appears in greater psychological detail in a concrete setting, in relation to clinical experience and, more dis-tantly, to the First World War. This trauma also gives rise to sudden visionary transports. Here, the "Körper" remains a statistic, a set of reflexes, a figure on a chart ("Leben als Tabelle / unnützer Phrasen") without relation to conscious experience as an individual. As Horst Daemmrich says of the figure in "Körper," and possibly of Krolow himself: "Jedes Verständnis historischer Prozesse ist abhandengekom-men" (55). The body here negates historical experience and represents reality in time but outside of history.

The sections of *Nichts weiter als Leben* create a trajectory from the self in the activity of reading to the technique of landscape composi-tion to portraits of the seasons to the Self in a private, social setting, and then in society at large and back to the body as the empty shell of self. As already indicated, the volume concludes with an interpretation of its first poem to create an overall self-reflexive structure; likewise, the last poem parallels the first poem and reflects a poetics, though perhaps not at first glance. The last poem gives the volume its title, "Nichts weiter als Leben" (II, 154), and thus necessarily takes on a programmatic character:

> Nichts mehr. Nichts weiter
> als eine Kleinigkeit wie
> unterbrochene Handschrift
> im Schulheft vor mehr als
> vierzig Jahren.
> Kein Geheimnis: Vergangenheit.
> So war das mit diesem und jenem,
> ein umgeworfener Stuhl,
> kalte Betten ohne Geruch,
> Augen, die in Bäume sehn
> und auf Gewalttat, Händeringen,
> Kopfschütteln und sparsames
> Gefühl — du edles Wild,
> nichts weiter als Leben,
> das einen verläßt, geduldig,
> bald oder jetzt, jetzt schon,
> zu früh, sagen welche, zu spät,
> meinen sie.
> Zurück bleiben diese
> dichten Bäume von damals,
> am grünen Abhang gemalt,
> wo ich umher mich leite,
> die andern Körper, die bekannten,
> auf mich gerichteten Augen.
> Es ist Zeit, sich fertig zu machen.

The title suggests a reduction of experience to the simple facts of physical existence as a confirmation of presence. What follows however presents a complex and cryptic narrative; the opening lines, without a verb, capture that reduction of experience to a *Kleinigkeit* in the immediate present, but that reduction is given a historical framework as a return to the time "vor mehr als vierzig Jahren" of school years, a time of simplicity and innocence. The repetition of "Nichts" in the first line and the return to an antecedent past create an emphatic ellipsis: "Kein Geheimnis: Vergangenheit." That historical ellipsis is framed as a trivial matter, not a secret, nothing more than a break, an interruption in the historiographic script, like a writing exercise in a school-book. The phrase "So war das" introduces that past as several inscrutable events, a partly revealed or partly unrevealed secret, but those uncertain events center upon an act of witnessing: "Augen, die in Bäume sehn / und auf Gewalttat, Händeringen, / Kopfschütteln und sparsames / Gefühl." Instead of feeling, the poem offers a literary citation, "Du Edles Wild" from Hölderlin's poem "Im Walde," which Krolow used as the title of an essay on Hölderlin in the same year.[3] Another citation follows from Hölderlin's poem "Der Spaziergang": "Am grünen Abhang gemalt, / Wo ich umher mich leite," which is followed in Hölderlin's poem, but not in Krolow's, by three lines on the redemptive function of nature: "Durch süße Ruhe bezahlt / Für jeden Stachel im Herzen, / Wenn dunkel mir ist der Sinn." As in previous poems, the citations consign fulsome, centered emotion to the past and emphasize disillusionment, if not trauma, and the erosion of Romantic feeling, but that is not what the poem is about.[4] At the center of the poem is an undefined act of violence, along with gestures of anxiety, confusion or denial, and halting emotional involvement refracted through literary allusion. The final image of Krolow's poem seems to define the uncited "Stachel im Herzen" from Hölderlin's poem that nature cannot assuage. The citations both circumscribe and circumvent a scene: "wo ich umher mich leite / die andern Körper, die bekannten, / auf mich gerichteten Augen." The act of witnessing at the center of the poem finds a counterpart in the act of being witnessed at the end of the poem: the bodies, the eyes are familiar, haunting, and seem to indict or force the poetic persona to a crisis of conscience with echoes of Rilke's "Archaïscher Torso Apollos" and of Paul Celan's "Corona": "Es ist Zeit, sich fertig zu machen." Here the vanishing point of history in Krolow's poems provides the locus, again also the vantage point, from which history as memory looks back.

Sex and the Inner Emigrant:
Bürgerliche Gedichte (1970)

As has been demonstrated, Karl Krolow's career shows very distinct phases with sharp changes in idiom. At each turn, some recapitulation allows a continuous perspective: Krolow emerged in the early postwar period as one of the leading figures in German poetry. Though also linked to an earlier generation of poets primarily associated with *Naturlyrik,* from Oskar Loerke and Wilhelm Lehmann to Peter Huchel and Günter Eich, Krolow represented, by dint of his numerous translations from French and Spanish poetry and the eclectic cosmopolitanism of his own poetry, a new wave of German poetry. Krolow's poetry was no longer rooted in suspect and provincial idioms and was now open to European and American influences. He stepped into the limelight for the first time in 1952 at the Gruppe 47 meeting in Niendorf along with Paul Celan and Ingeborg Bachmann. In 1956 he was awarded the Büchner Prize and entered the pantheon as one of only several German poets included in Hugo Friedrich's *Die Struktur der modernen Lyrik*. Though his career has been marked by many distinct phases, with critics repeatedly extolling his many-sided virtuosity and ability to transform himself, Krolow's poetic signature has always been the delicately sensitive poem of nature refracted through striking metaphors and surprising turns of phrase and form.

One of the earliest collected poems, "Mahlzeit unter Bäumen" (1944), represents the typical convergence in his *Naturlyrik* of bucolic idyll and a sort of rural Rococo eroticism:

> Sitzen im gefleckten Schatten
> Luft kommt lau wie Milch gestrichen.
> Kreis hat zaubrisch sich gezogen,
> Und die Hitze ist gewichen.

> Sicheln, die wie Nattern zischten,
> Klirrten am erschrocknen Steine.
> Grüne Glut drang aus der Wiese.
> Distel biß am bloßen Beine.

> Durch die Feuer der Kamille
> Flohen wir auf blanker Sohle,
> Heuumwirbelt, in die Kühle
> Von Lavendel und Viole.

> Stille summt im Käferflügel.
> Ruhn, vom Ahorn schwarz umgittert.
> Auge schmerzt vom Staub der Kräuter,
> der im lauten Lichte zittert.

> Und wir schneiden Brot und Käse.
> Weißer Wein läuft uns am Kinne.
> Des gelösten Geists der Pflaume
> Werden wir im Fleische inne.

> Hände wandern überm Korbe.
> Fester Mund, er ward verhießen.
> Weiche Glieder, braun geschaffen,
> Im bewegten Laube fließen.
> *(Gesammelte Gedichte* I, 10)

In the magic circle of a given setting, here in the dappled shade under a tree, the senses come alive to nature, in discrete impressions, which merge into an almost palpably synaesthetic experience of nature's surging sensual energies: "Grüne Glut drang aus der Wiese." In the last two stanzas, the couple appears in the first person as the flash point of this circumambient sensuousness of nature: overflowing like the wine, the released spirit of the bitten fruit ("Des gelösten Geists der Pflaume") signals the loosened spirits of the lovers. The eating of plums becomes an oral-erotic act suggestively rendered by genitive possession: the act of "innewerden," the delectation of the pulpy fruit, itself a sexual symbol, is both a heightening of consciousness and of concupiscence, that is, carnal desire, "im Fleische." Hands wander, mouths are firm, limbs bronzed from work in the fields now frolic and disport amorously, and then merge, flow together in titillating lique-faction. Krolow opens up in the magic circle of shade a richly sensual scenario of nature naturing all around and between two lovers, while the world beyond that magic circle, its historical horizon, magically disappears.

Likewise, one of Krolow's most famous early poems reflects that refined sensitivity, though not as eroticism but as an exquisite intimacy between perceived nature and the perceiver; in the first and last of four stanzas of "Pappellaub" (1946):

> Sommer hat mit leichter Hand
> Laub der Pappel angenäht
> Unsichtbarer Schauder ist
> Windlos auf die Haut gesät.
> [. . .]
> Grüne Welle flüstert auf.
> Silbermund noch lange spricht,
> Sagt mir leicht die Welt ins Ohr,
> Hingerauscht als Ungewicht. (I, 16)

The personified description of nature in the first stanza, "mit leichter Hand," suggests Krolow's own light touch in trying to capture an in-visible *frisson* on the skin. In fact, the repetition of the word *leicht* anticipates the aesthetics of *Leichtigkeit* that he developed and enunciated in the 1950s; his best poems, like this one, combine, through sharply etched metaphors, a rarefying of the physical senses with an expansion of consciousness in order to comprehend new degrees of physical discernment and perceived sensation. All the more surprising is the brutality and heavy-handedness of Krolow's volume of pornographic poems in 1970.

Even in his eclectic repertoire of verse forms, Krolow's *Bürgerliche Gedichte,* published under the pseudonym of Karol Kröpcke, constitutes a surprising, even puzzling, anomaly. When Krolow identified himself as the author and even gave a public reading, the volume caused some mystification and a little uproar, and still manages to shock, or at least to put off further examination: the volume has never received any serious critical attention that would situate it in the trajectory of Krolow's long and prolific career. Yet despite the graphic and deliberate indecency of the volume, that is, the coarseness and lack of subtlety that seem so at odds with Krolow's sensibility elsewhere, the volume nevertheless shares certain features characteristic of his work in other phases. In fact, his pornography in 1970 seems a curious inversion of the poetry he wrote in the very earliest phase of his career, not under a pseudonym at the time but also not otherwise acknowledged. Both the poems from *Bürgerliche Gedichte* and the poems he wrote and published before 1945 are excluded from the four volumes of his *Gesammelte Gedichte.* There, he included only five poems for the year 1944 as his earliest work, among them "Mahlzeit unter Bäumen" (1944). Prior to that date he had published over 100 poems in newspapers and journals that ranged from *Das Innere Reich* to *Das Reich.* Both his unknown and uncollected corpus of poetry from the days of the Third Reich and his post-1968 pornography exhibit a claustrophobic narrowness of focus and closeness of perspective, a hard core microscopic zoom onto nature's nooks and crannies. Both phases, a quarter of a century apart, enforce that restricted focus with an arcane nomenclature in the manner of either exotic floral taxonomy, on the one hand, or inventive bathroom graffiti, on the other. In short, both of these little known phases of his long career reflect the same type of *inner emigration,* albeit under changed historical circumstances.

Of course, the title of the volume suggests a dimension of social critique and seems to bring Krolow into alignment with post-1968 attitudes of defiance and sexual revolution, but that framework, that assumption, allows him to maintain in his poetry precisely the apoliti-

cal dimension that figures as a constant throughout the stylistic diva-
gations of his career. The first poem of the collection demonstrates
the initial presence of critique, and then its disappearance:

> Sein bürgerlicher Schwanz
> der für Geld mir
> von hinten hoch kam
> in die offene Dose,
> hinderte mich nicht,
> Gefühl für den Gegenstand zu haben,
> der für Geld in mir
> tätig war,
> ruhig und mit Gefühl
> für Zeit, die Geld ist,
> während mir das Loch
> langsam naß wurde und ich
> mich hüftaufwärts immer stärker
> nach vorn krümmen mußte,
> stehend, während er stehend
> seinen Stengel an die Gebärmutter drückte,
> heiß und langsam, und seine Eier
> irgendwo hinter mir schaukelten,
> ich nach hinten griff und
> zwischen Daumen und Mittelfinger
> die Hoden preßte, bis er für Geld
> entlud und mir sein Inneres
> langsam aus meinem Paradies lief,
> langsam die Innenfläche
> des linken Oberschenkels herunter,
> und ich mich wieder aufrichtete. (3)

Despite the archly desublimated crudity of the content, the poem does
at least enact a criticism, from a prostitute's point-of-view, of society
in the form of her steady stream of bourgeois customers. As a synecdoche, "sein bürgerlicher Schwanz" symbolically represents the lower
instincts of these monied male animals as a sociozoological group.
The almost clinical, procedural exactitude of her physical description
of this anonymous sex act demonstrates her detached control of the
situation; the repetition of the phrase *für Geld* keeps in view the unsentimental nature of this transaction, while the phonetic link of that
phrase to *Gefühl*, with the reversal of *fü* and the hard *Ge* sound, pro-

vides a measure of irony. The prostitute thinks feelingly of the money, which allows her to derive, in turn, a measure of physical pleasure, thus consolidating her control over the situation. The male author Krolow projects a female in the flesh trade, whose command of the transaction almost belies any lack of control or any difficulty in her situation beyond that momentary act. Krolow's characteristically close-cropped perspective on "nature naturing," which is here simple genital friction, renders invisible both the subjectivity of the male and the broader circumstances of the female. Her narration does not tell anything; her-story eclipses both his-story and history in which both subjects would otherwise participate. In the galvanized political atmosphere of the late 1960s and early 1970s, when Germany began to question both its present and its past, Krolow seems to seize upon sex as a means to appear contemporary and to displace the politics of the present and his past. What he calls in flippant vulgarity "the hole," as synecdoche of the woman in the poem, represents in fact the vanishing perspective of his historical consciousness, the hole or gap of memory. Explicit sexual excess forces a focus on the immediate present and thereby represents the same degree of denial of the past and of memory. In other words, the phallus that looms large here is also the fallacy of forgetfulness. In this respect, Krolow's *mise en obscene* in his *Bürgerliche Gedichte* shocks briefly for what it includes, but disturbs more profoundly for what it excludes. Behind the coldly abstract genital geometry of the poems lies an urgent denial of politics that avoids emotion and voids the past.

The language of the poems reflects their systematic emptiness of affect as mechanical variations of wording; to give one example, the penis as protagonist in this series of poems appears variously as: *dein hartes Stück, Pinkelmaschine, dein aufrechter Begleiter, Vögel-Pistole, deine Stoßstange, Bleistift, ein Steifer, Pimmel, Fick-Spitze, den Apparat, Wichs-Stange, Brecheisen, Beton-Ding, Wichs-Apparat, Sein Schlauch, Onanier-Gestell, Fleisch-Katapult, Werkzeug, Latte, den Langen, Bengel, Spritzmaschine, Tube,* and *Tiefbohrer.* What the volume does include amounts to a compendium of sex acts such as: urination, fisting, coprophagy (Krolow refers with labored and puerile wit to *Stoffwechsel-Schokolade*), rape, gang rape, S&M, group sex, anal sex and oral sex, masturbation, bestiality ("mit einem deutschen Schäferhund," no less), defecation, and in the last poem, the rape and murder of an elderly woman.

The last poem, which I will not quote, expresses directly the violence that pervades the other poems as well to lesser degrees, a violence directed against women, against aging, and, by extension, against the political currents in Germany at the time toward gender equality, the youth cult, the sexual revolution, and the growing pressures to reflect on Germany's past in the Nazi period. Krolow's volume might at first appear to constitute part of that post-1968 breaking of taboos, but instead it reflects a naked reaction to those tendencies. In line with the Mitscherlichs' thesis in *Die Unfähigkeit zu trauern* (1967), the anonymous brutality of Krolow's pornographic poems evinces the "Abzug der Affekte" (34), "auffallende Gefühlsstarre" (40), "mangelnde Einfühlung" (43), and "Unfähigkeit zum Mitgefühl überhaupt" (53) that the Mitscherlichs considered symptomatic of German society in this period because of its inability to come to terms with its past. Sexual violence is here above all a defense mechanism and exercise of control and dominance over the calls to conscience concerning the past. In one poem the political dimension of sexual violence in this context comes to the fore in a scene of sadomasochistic domination (S&M):

> Anmut, sagte er, ich will Anmut,
> mit seinem mehlweichen Ding, nackt,
> in Stiefelschaften, als er ihr
> die Lederjacke über den Kopf schob.
> Im Dunkel, wenn niemand sie sieht,
> fühlt sie sich anders an, und stopfte
> ihr den Mund mit Leder, damit er
> ohne Widerstand in sie hinein kam,
> mit seinem Schlagstock besser
> unter die Beine und besser
> den harten Gummi springen lassen konnte,
> ehe er ihr rasch
> den Kitzler kaute, und sie
> mundtot danach seine Erektion
> spürte, die ihr Rückgrat
> wie ein Messer traf und
> den schellen Erguß in Höhe
> der Lendenwirbel.
> Faschist,
> hörte er sie manchmal nach ihm
> stöhnen, später, wenn es ihm
> wieder zu rasch passiert war.
> Anmut, sagte er, ich will Anmut. (17)

The poem begins and ends with the man's express wish for charm or decorum, a sign of cultivated manners and savoir faire in civilized society. Between those two utterances, the man acts out, dressed as a Nazi, a scene of sadistic domination and political allegory, in which the female is rendered "ohne Widerstand" and "mundtot" until, at the peak of his domination, he ejaculates too quickly and she calls him *Faschist,* both confirming and questioning his staying power. This poem plays out as a sex game the very topic that the rest of the volume forecloses; the scenario is also a look behind the scenes and a cathartic enactment of what is otherwise repressed or violently displaced in the volume from politics onto sex. The magnified sex of Krolow's *Bürgerliche Gedichte* effaces in its overwhelming presentness the realm of historical reflection. The man's premature ejaculation in a sex game reflects inversely the poet's failure to come, in conscience and in public, to terms with his past. In these poems, sex is willful amnesia. Krolow's pornography is an act of *inner emigration* that runs parallel to, but in its violence seeks to repress or deny, his earlier *inner emigration* in the Nazi period.

Notes

[1] Pee notes elsewhere: "Auf dem Weg zur literaturästhetischen Wahrheit gebraucht Krolow ständig Ironie, weil sie innerhalb ihres Spielraums keine Täuschung über die Wahrheit zuläßt. Trotzdem wirft die Ironie aber auch kaum die Frage nach der verhüllten Wahrheit auf." Thus, irony cancels itself as a systematic approach to Krolow's poetry. When Pee extends his argument, the contradiction becomes clear: "Dieser Vorbehaltscharakter der Ironie ermöglicht die Darstellung der Welt und gewinnt ihr zudem etwas Positives ab. Die Ironie als Vorbehalt [. . .] ist die bedeutendste Triebkraft der Krolowschen Schwebungspoesie" (128). Yet Pee does not define what understanding or even "Darstellung" of the world is included or derived from such a narrow poetic basis. Gerhard Piniel's characterization of the volume is more apt: "Der bestimmende Eindruck insgesamt bleibt der eines behutsamen Abstandhaltens zu den Gegenständen. Der hier dichtet, schaut mit den Augen eines scheinbar Unbeteiligten, den keine Erinnerung belastet, . . . Bei solcher Zurückhaltung des Dichters können Pathos und Ironie nicht vorkommen" (*Über Karl Krolow,* 156–57).

[2] His continual return to seasonal poems during his career calls into question or at least qualifies the speculation by Kolter and Paulus that Krolow began with such seasonal poems in the early 1940s as a reaction to constraints in order to have a better chance of getting his poems published (Kolter/Paulus, 17). That theme certainly would not offend and probably pleased Nazi censors, but given Krolow's later affinity to seasonal poems, it is difficult to conclude that outward pressures were a decisive factor in the choice of topics.

[3] Krolow begins the essay with a description of his longstanding inability to comprehend Hölderlin, his puzzling "Unschuld" (W. H. Fritz, ed. *Karl Krolow: Ein Lesebuch*, 199) that he then came to understand as "Modell für absolute Sprache" (W. H. Fritz, ed. *Karl Krolow: Ein Lesebuch*, 201) that becomes also a model for the process of "Entpersönlichung" and then "Verstummen" in the language of twentieth-century poetry. Krolow works from Adorno's essay on Hölderlin but only restates familiar positions.

[4] In *Der Lyriker Karl Krolow*, Gerhard Kolter und Rolf Paulus give the two citations as examples of Krolow's technique of citation, but offer no further interpretation.

9: Comparative Contexts

Oskar Loerke as Karl Krolow's Model

WHEN KARL KROLOW continued his literary career after the war, his name was linked time and again with that of Oskar Loerke in order to situate him in literary history in the field of German *Naturlyrik,* though without exploring that link between the two poets any further. Through the connection to Krolow, Loerke's work certainly gained in stature and in familiarity to a broader audience, but by the same token, through Krolow's essays, Loerke's work lost out in the complexity of its reception because Krolow, in his estimation of Loerke, viewed the originality and particularity of his work in very narrow terms.[1] As a case study of the "anxiety of influence," the relation of Krolow to Loerke helps define the essential differences between the poets beyond the superficial, circumstantial, and atmospheric resemblances that seem to link them in literary history.

Born in 1915, Krolow read Loerke's poems for the first time in 1935 when he left the Gymnasium for the university. Krolow's own career began when Loerke's ended with his death in 1941. At this time Krolow was first trying to make his mark as a writer with numerous, widely scattered publications of poems and lyrical prose vignettes and with critical essays on poetry. In several lengthy review essays for the journal *Das Innere Reich,* Krolow does not even mention Loerke's work among the fifty volumes he discusses, perhaps because his last volume was already seven years old, but these essays nonetheless demonstrate in general how familiar Krolow was with contemporary German poetry in 1943.[2] Also in 1951, in an essay on "Das zeitgenössische deutsche Naturgedicht," Krolow speaks of Friedrich Rasche, Wilhelm Lehmann, Elisabeth Langgässer, Oda Schaefer, Horst Lange, Günter Eich, Georg von der Vring, and Peter Huchel, but again does not mention Loerke even once as representative of the direction in poetry for which he plays, in Krolow's later thinking, a so central role. Loerke would have fit in particularly well into this context, where Krolow tries to defend the genre of *Naturlyrik* against polemics that arose at the time, namely that it was "eine ahumane,

wenn nicht gar anti-humane Dichtung, lichtscheu und troglodytisch
[. . .] schließlich romantisierend, ja, reaktionär." In these founding
years of German democracy, Krolow argues that *Naturlyrik* is marked
by "ihr humanitäres Anliegen, ja, ihr ganz bestimmtes humanitäres
Pathos und eine sich in ihm ausbreitende Spiritualität." At this point
Loerke might well have found a place in the discussion.

In a shorter presentation of the same topic in 1953, Loerke's name
again does not appear next to that of the others named above. The
strong impression that Loerke's work made or is supposed to have
made on Krolow must have gestated beneath the surface and attained
awareness and expression much later. Krolow's critical encounter with
Loerke began in 1961, probably triggered by the two volume edition
of his work in 1958, twenty years after his death and after Krolow's
own beginnings as a poet; nine years after the volume *Die Zeichen der
Welt* (1952) had established Krolow as an important postwar poet;
five years after he received the Büchner Prize in 1956, and finally,
between the two volumes, *Fremde Körper* of 1959 and *Unsichtbare
Hände* of 1962, that together constitute the culmination of a tendency in his work that he now traces back to Loerke. Krolow's critical
encounter with Loerke finds its first expression in a series of texts over
the next twelve years. In these essays Krolow succeeds for the first time
as a critic to situate himself as a poet with respect to Loerke's work.

At the beginning of the second of his Frankfurter Lectures on Poetics (*Aspekte zeitgenössischer deutscher Lyrik*, 1961), "Möglichkeiten und
Grenzen der neuen deutschen Naturlyrik" (29–54), Krolow positions
Loerke as the key figure in his own development and for that of German poetry in general in the twentieth century. With the support of
commentaries by Heinrich Eduard Jacob before the war and by Wilhelm Lehmann and Hermann Kasack after the war, he links Loerke to
a concept of nature that is empirical as well as cosmic, visual as well as
expressive, static and ecstatic. Loerke represents a "Naturlyrik neuen
Typs" (29), whose appearance speaks for the continuity of the genre
and represents as much a particularly German feature as a general
European characteristic in poetry. For Krolow, Loerke set in his poems a completely different foundation for nature poetry as well as for
all poetry of the period because "er sich in ihnen [his poems] auf eine
seinerzeit, so noch nicht erlebte Weise aus seinen Versen 'heraus-
nahm,' als Person, als Individualität" (30–31). In Loerke's nature poems is "das Dasein weitgehend dem Zugriff der dichterischen
Individualität entzogen" (31). Krolow adds further: "Das war ein
Vorgang, an dem der Mensch als einzelner beinahe nicht mehr betei-

ligt wurde" (31). For Krolow, Loerke seems to constitute a sort of sluice through which a main current of modern European poetry streams into German poetry. Krolow ascertains: "Seit Loerke nun wird man gegenüber diesem Menschen zurückhaltender, vorsichtiger, ja indifferenter. Es ist ein Prozeß, bei dem das, was man 'Erleben' nennt, neutralisiert wurde" (31). Krolow names the core of this general development, which finds expression so poignantly in Loerke, the "Eliminierung des persönlichen Temperaments, [der] Teilnahme und Anteilnahme oder doch: ihre Reduzierung" (31). Loerke's work energetically dismantles the bridge to transcendence that the Expressionists had tried to construct through elevated pathos and high-pitched rhetoric between mankind and a utopian beyond. The individual as well as the concept of a beyond disappear with Loerke into the concept of an all-inclusive nature that animates mankind, not the other way around. The individual observes nature, to which he or she also belongs, but the individual occupies no privileged position in nature. According to Krolow's representation, Loerke promotes a sort of objectifying pantheism in which nature appears as the paradigm of the universe, though of course without mankind at the center. Loerke's poetic universe, though cosmic in conception, is held together by the analytical optics of proximity and distance, of micro- and macroscopics. The magic [*Magie*] of his poetry derives not from mystical conjuration that is full of feeling, but from subdued, analytical observation and densely compressed imagistic representation, whereby the typical use of rhyme with disrupted, broken rhythms plays a central role for Loerke. This optical objectification of the emotionally laden space of nature in poetry from Romanticism to Expressionism also becomes an objection to whatever might get called experiential poetry [*Erlebnislyrik*]; it becomes a form of de-individualization.[3] In this respect and with this term, Krolow perceives the path of modern poetry, and in Loerke, he recognizes the pathfinder for this development in Germany, although he also has to concede that there are "relativ wenig Stücke [. . .] an denen man den Vorgang abnehmen kann. Aber es sind wohl in jedem Falle Gedichte, die zu seinen besten gehören" (34). The circularity of this logic provides vivid testimony for the willfulness, or even arbitrariness, of Krolow's reception of Loerke and his work.

As proof of his understanding Krolow first cites four strophes from the poem "Gebirge wächst" (331–33), of which I cite only one: "Wie sich hier Zeiten, Schicht in Schicht, / Bewohnt von Laub und Tier, in Tier und Laub verschanzen! / Sich selber weiß — ich frage nicht — / Das Reich der Tiere in mir und der Pflanzen." Nature appears here no longer as a viewing screen for empathic projections, but shows itself now as "eine manchmal fast unmenschlich anmutende Ruhe, [. . .] mit der der einzelne nichts mehr zu tun hat, in der er sich selber aufgeben, sich verlieren muß" (35–36). The psychological situation and perspective of the observer of nature has been replaced by "das Reich der Tiere in mir und der Pflanzen" and later in the same poem: "Ich frage nicht, doch Antwort gibt / In mir das Reich der Minerale." External nature (lower case, that is, not ideational), which unfolds as a cosmos, overtakes and overwhelms the individual, who, in relation to it, begins to disintegrate and appears to disappear, as in the second poem cited by Krolow "Nächtliche Körpermelancholie" (36–37): "Mein Leib ist Nacht, verfließt mit Nacht im Kalten [. . .] Was ist nun Ich? — / Die Füße sind wie Berge in der Ferne, / Zu fremd und schwer, ich kann sie nicht bewegen." With this poem Krolow explicates the loss of subjectivity as the main characteristic of Loerke's poetry:

> Die Phantomisierung der Persönlichkeit, des Ichs, wird dadurch erreicht, daß das Ich zwar nicht gelöscht wird, aber im Zustand einer Überlagerung durch Kräfte der Außenwelt zu struktureller Veränderung gezwungen wird. . . . Es wird nicht nur in andere Gegenwart übergeführt, sondern fällt zugleich durch die Zeiten, durch die "Geschichte" von Wald, Fels, Fluß, durch die "Geschichte" der Elemente, "Geschichte" der Kreatur, der Pflanze, des Minerals.

Krolow explains this loss of self and subjectivity, however, in an unusual fashion. From his perspective, the process of depersonalization or de-individualization has little to do with the pathos of ecstatic transcendence, the process of social alienation, or the elevation of the individual through myth or religion. Rather, Krolow seems to perceive in Loerke a stage of development in the genre, in which a new understanding of the subject emerges. This "structural change" seems to consist for Krolow not in a complete disappearance of the subject, as one might at first assume, but in the disappearance or sublation of history, whereby the subject now is at the same time "brought to language." Opposite the "extra-human scenery" in a Loerke poem there appears for Krolow an extrahistorical individual or subject that manifests itself in language simply as language. This verbal manifestation of the subject is not binding and appears as a fleeting process "in dem Entstehen und Vergehen gleichzeitig sich ereignet" (38). As a verbal gesture in the poem without reference or relation to history, the subject is both affirmed and dissolved as an "Ansprechen auf Widerruf."[4] Krolow does not here surrender the subject in the poem, but insists on its presence, though under new conditions. In Krolow's interpretation, "dies Wiederauftauchen des einzelnen mitten im 'Überlagerungsvorgang'" is the point of departure for articulating his own poetics and creating his own poetic genealogy. By highlighting this trait of de-individualization in Loerke, Krolow also links himself and his poetics to the tradition of German *Naturlyrik* on the one hand, and to international modernism on the other, but puts himself at a distance, in one and the same maneuver, from the later *Naturlyrik* of Wilhelm Lehmann and Elisabeth Langgässer. Those two poets, in his view, succumbed, each in a different way, to a "Zwang zum Detail" (46), to an "Akribie der Darstellung" (50), by which the poet functions merely as a "Stenograf" (51). Krolow sets himself against this "doctrinaire" tendency in German *Naturlyrik*. This recourse to Loerke allows Krolow to separate and distance himself more fully from Lehmann und Langgässer, who actually had exercised a far greater influence on his own poetry. Apparently, Krolow speaks of himself when he emphasizes at the end of his discussion: "Auch in den letzten Jahren ist versucht worden, die Ausdrucksmöglichkeiten des Naturgedichts zu nuancieren, zu variieren, sei es, daß [. . .] surrealistische Tendenzen in es eindrangen, sei es, daß sich eine Neigung zur größeren Leichtigkeit der Mitteilung, zur spielerischen Anlage des Ganzen einstellte" (53). Both of these qualities allude entirely to Krolow's own work, which is supposed to have adopted from Loerke the de-individualization of the subject in nature without having succumbed to the excesses of Loerke's successors, their elaborations to the point of "vegetative[r] Überwältigung." Krolow's intention here is also to set himself beyond Loerke, whose lack of any inclination to playfulness Krolow had ascertained at the beginning of his essay, by virtue of his own playfully surrealistic "Leichtigkeit," which is also the central dimension in Krolow's poetics and signifies nothing less than the freeing of the poem from the weighty burden of metaphysics and history.[5]

A year later in 1962, Krolow brought these same thoughts in less detail but with verbatim formulations into his essay "Lyrik und Landschaft."[6] Only in 1965 does he then again go more deeply into the topic of Loerke in order to pinpoint more accurately his position in relation to him in the aptly titled essay "Oskar Loerke — mein Modell?"[7] Now his approach is autobiographical and correspondingly more personal in tone. Quotations from his own earlier essays comprise the core of his deliberations here; Krolow adds, in elaborate paraphrases, characterizations of Loerke's development and his work, and emphasizes what Loerke meant to him: "Mich faszinierte der starke Objektivierungszwang, der besonders in frühen Arbeiten Oskar Loerkes vorangetrieben wurde, eine Objektivation, die allerdings von einer magisch-pantheistischen 'Erweiterung' des Dargestellten begleitet war" (129). This combination of arguments about de-individualization and aperspectivism appears here in various formulations and elucidations as the conceptual scaffolding of Loerke's oeuvre, as the center of its significance.

Krolow clearly credits Loerke's work as the defining experience of his own development: "etwas höchst Ungewöhnliches und jedenfalls Aufregendes. Hier — spürte ich — war das zeitgenössische Gedicht, allen Vorschriften der politischen Machthaber zum Trotz, ein wirklich modernes Gedicht geworden" (131).[8] But in describing this dramatic scene of discovery, this primal scene for his own poetics, in which Loerke's work strikes him like a "revolutionary message," a revelation, Krolow also instrumentalizes this scene with the same sort of vivid description, though almost polemical, in order to bind Loerke even more tightly than before to the German tradition of *Naturlyrik* and thereby to limit his significance for the history of poetry: Loerke's work, because of its "isolated position" has "an extremely narrow foundation" and demonstrates generally the "Unfähigkeit des deutschen Gedichts, außerdeutsche Kontakte aufzunehmen und in eine [. . .] Korrespondenz mit einer international wirksamen Poesie zu treten" (132) because it is "too exclusive" in its content, and therefore suffers from a sort of poetic self-involvement or even "inbreeding." Despite the achievements that Krolow credits or concedes to Loerke, the kind of *Naturlyrik* of Loerke, Lehmann, and Langgässer constitutes a jungle or thicket of suffocating details, in which the modern or modernist features of their poetry get lost, for which reason it should be avoided by more contemporary poets: "Ich versuchte in dem, was ich an Gedichten schrieb [. . .] die notwendige Entfernung zu gewinnen und mit der Entfernung die Befreiung aus der stofflichen Überwältigung durch das vegetative Detail" (133). Krolow appears here as a poetic emigrant out of the "Stoff-Zwang" of *inner emigration,* who found his aesthetic exile in French and Spanish surrealism and who knew how to make use of that new range of metaphor. Krolow employs terms of political control to define his poetological position. Even here, in this aesthetic position, dangers loom: "An die Stelle der Knechtschaft des Stoffes konnte die Knechtschaft durch das Bild treten" (134). Krolow finds his own poetic style through the appropriation and overcoming of these two aesthetic currents of German *Naturlyrik* and of French and Spanish surrealism, by aiming for "eine

Balance [. . .] zwischen Stoff und Bild. . . . eine Art Schwebe-Vorgang" (134).

Thus, Krolow does not try to establish his own poetry as his own original achievement that springs from his inner self, but as a strategic maneuvering of avoidance in two directions; he thereby gives the point of origin in his development a negative framework. Within that framework he describes the progress of his development with, again, a negative accent as "die Zurückdrängung der Gegenständlichkeit" (134) that proceeded "Schritt um Schritt," — as the attempt to jettison "Gegenständliches . . . als Ballast, als Belastung." With this process of reduction and abstraction and without forgetting all he might have owed Loerke in productive impulses, Krolow seems here to distance himself from Loerke definitively for the simple reason that Loerke's work centers upon the vivid description of an object or a starkly visual representation of a concrete experience, as "Gesang der Dinge."[9] Whereas Loerke seeks to approach external reality through or by means of poetic language,[10] Krolow wants to dissolve and absorb reality into language, though without losing the subject entirely from the poem.

As a symptomatic feature of this development in his work, Krolow points to his gradual relinquishment of rhyme, a circumstance that allows a "trockene, lakonische Tonlage" and a tighter form, which more and more has the effect of grotesque-ironic play. With that, Krolow opens a perspective onto his own development into the mid-1960s and beyond, yet the connection to Loerke remains important for him, regardless of how strenuously he distanced himself, by his own accounts, from Loerke. But in another way as well, Loerke's work remained for Krolow a source of poetic security, a safeguard against the "Herrschaft des Einzelwortes," as it appears in Gottfried Benn's notion of *Artistik* or in the language games or verbal experiments of Heißenbüttel, Franz Mon, or Ernst Jandl; in Krolow's own words: "Loerkes 'Gesang der Dinge,' so sehr er für mich historisch geworden ist, so weit entfernt von ihm ich mich mit dem, was ich schreibe, auch aufhalte, ist vielleicht doch insofern noch wirksam als er bei mir verhindert, was inzwischen im Gedicht realisiert worden ist: eine Skelettierung von Stoff und Sinn und der aus ihr resultierende Verbalismus, einschließlich der Autonomisierung des Wortmaterials, die Autorschaft lediglich zu einem Pilotenamt macht" (135). Basically, it was Loerke's work that gave the young Karl Krolow, who had just begun to write poetry, a direction and path for his own development; it was the same Loerke, whose work helped the mature Krolow avoid excesses in this same tendency, in his development toward de-individualization. Krolow does not explicate this later turn of poetic events any more closely. Indeed, he claims to have remained under the spell of Loerke's influence, despite the numerous and varied impulses from abroad. Krolow often castigated Loerke and German *Naturlyrik* for its narrowness of perspective and material, of its forms and content, but he cannot bring himself to abjure once and for all the mimetic referentiality, the object concreteness that he finds so starkly, so specially and specifically, represented in Loerke's work. The two characteristics of *Entindividualisierung* [de-individualization] and *Entgegenständlichung* [de-objectification] capture for Krolow a desired process for his writing, but not an ultimate goal, which explains his later distance to experimental or concrete poetry.

Krolow criticizes in Loerke and in German *Naturlyrik* of this period its "weightiness of signification" and opposes it with his own attempts "den Worten größere Leichtigkeit und mit ihr größere Beweglichkeit zu verschaffen und der Zeichenhaftigkeit, der Chiffrenkunst eine Kunst der singbaren Formel einzuverleiben" (136). If he understands his own poetry opposite Loerke, Lehmann, and others as a lightening, in both senses of weight and light, and Loerke's work is a "Gesang der Dinge," the question remains: what are the things of which Krolow sings? What is the content, the positive substance of his poetry, which he has thus far defined only negatively, in aesthetic opposition? In his presentation of Loerke's influence on his work, Krolow offers circular logic, in that his poetics depart from Loerke and ultimately return to Loerke: "Die 'Aufhellung' von Bedeutung im Gedicht hat mich möglicherweise von meiner Ausgangsposition nicht so weit entfernt, wie das, artistisch gesehen, scheinen könnte" (136). But if one were to ignore aesthetic differences as he suggests, what would constitute the proximity or affinity that Krolow claims between himself and Loerke? Is it to be found between Loerke's "Bedeutungsschwere" und Krolow's "Leichtigkeit"? In the common front he wishes to build with Loerke against the later "Verbalismus" of experimental language poetry, Krolow insists, indirectly and implicitly, on an objectivity, a concreteness, in his poetry, without naming any such object. This much vaunted objectivity or referentiality of Krolow's, I would like to suggest, might best be understood as the reverse, the mirror image, of Loerke's "Bedeutungsschwere," precisely as the suspension of this substantive and binding weightiness of objective reference. Loerke's work consists of the attempt to bring together objectivity and specific objects, a worldview and a viewed world, concepts and image, logical sense and physical sensuousness, subject and object, the mind and the eye, the "I" and the "you," in a configuration that highlights their broadly arching connectedness, but also their widely diverging distinctness. His poetry wrestles with the relations of subject and object, *ich* and *du*, in various figurations of the object in the world and in language,[11] and ultimately in history. In contrast, Krolow in his poems aims for a finely faceted objectivity without deeper, more serious object, an immediate sensuousness without sense, in a world and a language that flee, are fleeting, without subject or object, without *ich* and *du,* without history. Krolow's poetry develops, opposite Loerke or even in opposition to Loerke, a sort of fascinating and frustrating lightness of touch [*Leichtigkeit*] and slightness of content, which, as a structural model, was inspired by his contact with Loerke's poems, but which distances itself from them at every turn. The poems of Oskar Loerke and Karl Krolow are distinct in their very essence. Through the representation of an external reality, Loerke wants to present an image of a suprapersonal, spiritual-intellectual inner life of mankind; the experience of suprapersonal nature in the world appears as unbounded individual interiority. Loerke's poems aim at concentrated expression: "Räumliche und zeitliche Nähen und Fernen streben alle einer Mitte zu, und zwar einer sinnlich faßbaren und gesicherten Mitte" (*Tagebücher,* 656); in contrast, Krolow's poems aim at a decorative "Heiterkeit." In the middle of the cosmos for Loerke is sorrow and suffering [*das Leid*], the experience of being in the world; for Krolow it is the lightness, the brightness of being [*die Leichtigkeit, die Heiterkeit*] in language, in metaphor.[12]

After the essay "Oskar Loerke — Mein Modell?" (1965), which is the highpoint of his engagement with Loerke, Krolow's preoccupation with Loerke trails off, although his positioning of himself in relation to Loerke repeats itself and consolidates itself in further publications, even though these do not deepen or complicate his thinking on the topic. Two essays on the same topic appear in rapid succession without attempting any broader or more detailed treatment of Loerke's work. Both texts repeat the same thoughts from "Oskar Loerke — Mein Modell?" more or less verbatim, but extend nonetheless, through some additions, his distance from both Loerke and Lehmann. In the essay "Warum ich nicht wie Oskar Loerke schreibe" (1967), two additional paragraphs of criticism of German *Naturlyrik* (110–11)[13] are added; in the essay "Literarische Vorbilder" (1968; also in *Ein Gedicht entsteht,* 1973) the influence of surrealism is treated at greater length. In this way Krolow sets himself at a greater distance from Loerke, and what Loerke represents for him in German

Naturlyrik, again and again always under a new title. In 1973 in his compendious contribution "Die Lyrik in der Bundesrepublik seit 1945" in *Kindlers Literaturgeschichte der Gegenwart* (347–533), Krolow treats Loerke in his discussion of "Eine Folgerichtige Entwicklung: Das Neue Deutsche Naturgedicht" (381–433) and sets him at the beginning of this development. In great brevity (382–83) Krolow outlines Loerke's "langsame und lange unauffällige Entfaltung" (382) in the now familiar framework, but the tone has changed in the meantime; Krolow no longer limits Loerke's work to the main features that were, in retrospect, important to him and his development. Instead, he indicates the greater stature of Loerke's poetry, and thereby also, though indirectly, the limits of his own prior readings and reception of Loerke's work by remarking that "Loerkes Verse jedoch wollen zögernd verstanden werden" (382), and then: "Im Vergleich zu Lehmanns visueller Kühle und Knappheit ist Loerke weicher, aber komplexer" (383), and he quotes the opening of Loerke's poem "Laubwolke" as an example "seiner zugleich zarten und tiefsinnig-prägnanten Gedichte" (383). This short explanation of Loerke's work actually seems fairer and more accurate than his much more detailed discussions because here he opens up the work for new readers, rather than foreclosing inquiry; despite the brevity of his analysis, one can hardly escape the impression that Krolow has found his way, with some difficulty, to a new understanding and appreciation of Loerke.

In the same year, Krolow published another general essay on the German nature poem as in 1951 and 1961: "'Wie sind meine Finger so grün': Natur und Mensch im deutschen Gedicht" (1973).[14] Here Krolow drops Loerke again from the picture, though not entirely, and in so doing, he has spanned and closed a trajectory in his reception of Loerke from 1951, when he did not even mention him in an essay on the German nature poem, to 1973, when he no longer ascribes to him, in the period from the seventeenth to the twentieth century, such a central role in the historical development of the genre. Framed between these two dates lies the period of Krolow's critical engagement with his erstwhile model Oskar Loerke. In this latter presentation of Loerke nonetheless, aside from the now routine descriptions of the autonomy of nature, that is, of de-individualization, and of the "gefährlich[en]" (237) one-sidedness, Krolow points out for the first time, if only indirectly, another new dimension of his work that had not been mentioned in any of the other essays: "die gelegentliche Behandlung der Stadt (Berlins) als besonderer *Natur*körper (etwa bei

Oskar Loerke)" (236). Krolow isolates a singularly modern or European dimension of urban or metropolitan poetry in Loerke's work (!), which had not made an impression on him in the previous twenty to thirty years of his reading of and writing on Loerke, when his essays had themselves perhaps succumbed to a certain one-sidedness.[15]

Just the year before he wrote this essay, the first monograph study of Krolow's poetry pointed out precisely this aspect of Loerke's work, his critical confrontation with the urban environment; it is possible that Krolow was alerted by this study, which he knew, to this dimension of Loerke's poetry. Artur Rümmler finds, in his detailed discussions of Krolow's use of metaphor, in which he systematically and thoroughly traces and tracks down Krolow's various borrowings and adaptations, only a single link to Loerke in the technique of mirroring. This actually does not even appear in Krolow's own thoughts on his relations to Loerke, although he does highlight the matter of aperspectivism as an important trait from Loerke:

> Die Spiegelung als Mittel zur poetisierenden Verfremdung der städtischen Umwelt, im Prinzip bereits der Einblendungstechnik des "Seestücks" (1946, *Heimsuchung*) zugrundeliegend, hatte Krolow bei Loerke vorgefunden, der "Die leichtre Welt im Spiegel aus Asphalt" im Gedicht 'Die gespiegelte Stadt' (*Pansmusik*) als zweites Gesicht der Wirklichkeit der Alltagswirklichkeit entgegenstellt. Dabei verschachtelt er beide Bereiche derart, daß eine Doppelwelt entsteht: die Gleichzeitigkeit von Oben und Unten, von Nähe und Ferne, ein Mit- und Ineinander von Traum und Wirklichkeit. Diese Simultaneität ist in ihrem Ergebnis von der des Kubismus und des Surrealismus nicht weit entfernt; deshalb kann Krolow, der inzwischen seit sechs Jahren surrealistische Mittel verwendet, auf sie zurückgreifen. Auch er läßt seine Imagination durch das dialektische Verhältnis von Bild und Spiegelbild, aus dem die metaphorischen Resultate hervorgehen, in Bewegung bringen, doch ist sein Medium künstlicher: nicht regennasser Asphalt, sondern ein technischer Gegenstand. (183–84)[16]

Rümmler's thorough study of 1972 was written in the period just after Krolow's most intensive preoccupation with Loerke in his essays prior to 1972. One can assume then that Rümmler would have been especially attentive to questions of such an influence. Rümmler demonstrates and documents borrowings and specific influences from, or adaptations of, Rainer Maria Rilke, Georg Heym, Georg Britting, Wilhelm Lehmann, and Hans Arp among the Germans; as well as Arthur Rimbaud, Paul Eluard, Guillaume Apollinaire, Pierre Reverdy, Jule Supervielle, Eugene Guillevic, and Jean Follain among the French;

and also Jorge Guillén, Rafael Alberti, and Federico García Lorca among the Spaniards. In Krolow's work, Rümmler is able to confirm numerous references, resemblances, verbal allusions, or discreet borrowings from all these poets, especially from García Lorca (the other Loerke!) and Wilhelm Lehmann.[17] Thus it seems at first quite surprising, but in this context also quite convincing that Rümmler can hardly ascertain in Krolow's work any borrowing or even similarities and resemblances to Loerke. In addition, his influence on Krolow is reduced for Rümmler to a poetic technique[18] and not, as one usually assumes, to the material, the content, of his poetic view of nature. Also surprising is his simple assumption that Loerke's slight influence on Krolow took place after Krolow's discovery and intensive engagement with the surrealists, as a reprise, which is very plausible in light of his later reception of and critical confrontation with Loerke after 1960, despite Krolow's own testimony to the contrary.

This retrospective review of Loerke gave a distorted view of Loerke's work in that Krolow viewed it only in relation to the tradition of German *Naturlyrik*. Other dimensions of Loerke's work that constitute his complexity as a poet were simply dismissed under the rubric of "Bedeutungsschwere" and not explored or examined further. Krolow's discussions of Loerke excluded his groundedness in empirical observation of the world, his sense of history and, by extension, his confrontation with modernity, as well as his humanitarian pathos and its corresponding sense of suffering or anguish, along with his development to social or even political criticism.[19] In response ultimately to his question "Oskar Loerke — Mein Modell?" one would have to say that Loerke served Krolow as a negative and simplified model, a sort of transitional object, for his own development and its critical representation. Against this negative model, Krolow was able to portray his own poetry and poetics as a decisive positive development in postwar German poetry, as progress out of provincial narrowness. Nonetheless, Krolow did, much to his credit, bring Loerke back into discussion and created a tightly circumscribed place for him in the literary history of the period and the genre. But just as Loerke served him as a negative model, Krolow's own reductive presentation of Loerke will serve, in turn, as a negative but provocative model for a more complex understanding of Loerke's multifaceted poetry.

Gedicht and *Gedächtnis:*
Karl Krolow and Paul Celan

Karl Krolow and Paul Celan figure in literary history as two of too few German language poets whose work signaled a new direction for the genre in the early postwar period. The work of both poets reflected and refracted German traditions such as *Naturlyrik* through the prism of European modernism, through French surrealism in particular, and accordingly, both represented a sharp departure from familiar poetic practice and a cosmopolitan openness to new impulses. Both published celebrated volumes of poetry in 1952 with the Deutsche Verlagsanstalt in Stuttgart, Celan's *Mohn und Gedächtnis* and Krolow's *Die Zeichen der Welt,* and both poets were also introduced in person to the German reading public in 1952, along with Ingeborg Bachmann, at the Gruppe 47 meeting in Niendorf. Then and there that trio constituted the new wave of German poetry in the 1950s.

Celan and Bachmann have long been acknowledged as the dominant figures of that period and since their deaths, their work has continued to receive scholarly examination and to gain in critical stature;[20] Krolow (b. 1915), who died in June 1999, continued his prolific career of over half a century through many phases — though with diminishing influence overall and relatively little serious and sustained critical analysis. But in the 1950s, Krolow's work was regarded with at least equal interest and attention. He was awarded the Büchner Prize in 1956 as the youngest recipient to date, and in that same year, he was also installed in the pantheon of late modernism as one of few German poets included in Hugo Friedrich's *Die Struktur der modernen Lyrik.*[21] Oddly, his relation to Celan has received virtually no attention in the vast and detailed literature on Celan, but their relationship is instructive about the tensions in the genre during the postwar period.

With an eye on the narrowness of German *Naturlyrik* that predominated in Germany during the 1930s and 1940s, both poets sought to open that field by drawing new impulses from outside of Germany.[22] Both Krolow and Celan were prolific translators. Krolow had studied Romance philology at the university and then published anthologies of translations from French poetry in 1948 and 1957, and of Spanish poetry in 1962. Like Celan, Krolow was a main conduit into the German language for the postwar influence of French modernism and surrealism: both poets had a particular appreciation of Apollinaire and Eluard.[23] Their affinity in literary appreciation indeed

led to more frequent personal contact, correspondence, and then
friendship, though an understanding of the exact contours and details
of their relations requires further research and reconstruction. However, in a memoir after his suicide in 1970, Krolow recalled Celan's
intense privacy, "so etwas wie eine unsichtbare Trennwand zwischen
ihm und seinem Partner, etwas schwer zu Überwindendes" (338).[24]
This essay addresses the nature of that invisible wall that seems to have
separated them all the more, the closer they were drawn together by
circumstance.[25] One year after their Group 47 meeting, the two poets
met again in 1953 in Paris at the first postwar French-German writers'
conference.[26] Later, in 1959, when Krolow received a UNESCO grant
to live and work in Paris for six months, the two poets met frequently,
"almost daily."[27] Celan even allowed a photograph to be taken then of
the two of them together, which was for Celan a significant and not a
casual act of trust and friendship.[28] However, their friendship seems to
have suffered soon thereafter to an uncertain degree from the fallout
of the infamous accusations of plagiarism by Claire Goll.[29] In point of
fact, Krolow was Celan's principal advocate in the literary press, and as
a member of the Darmstadter Akademie der Sprache und Dichtung
since 1953, he was probably also on the selection committee for the
Büchner Prize, which Celan received in 1960. The two poets may
have also met at the award ceremony on October 22, 1960. Krolow
signed a public declaration of support for Celan issued by former re-
cipients of the Büchner Prize against Claire Goll's charges of plagiarism. Krolow's sensitive appreciation of Celan's poetry remained
steadfast over the years,[30] yet at the core, their understanding of the
poem was sharply at odds.

Their speeches for the Büchner Prize, four years apart, reveal the
distance between them. Krolow isolates in Büchner's *Leonce und Lena*
(1836), a "Tendenz" (196) that appealed to him very personally: "Es
sprang etwas über, Anonymes, Zauber, Geheimnis, Berückung"
(196).[31] In effect, each of these qualities, depersonalization, magic or
mystery, sacralization or secrecy, decentering or displacement, represents an abstraction from prewar and postwar historical reality that
Krolow, in a rare moment, addresses directly:

> es wurde mir in *dem* Moment wichtig, in dem ich mich von den Be-
> drückungen zu befreien, von jenem Cauchemar zu lösen versuchte,
> der als schwerer Schatten über den poetischen Äußerungsversuchen
> der ersten Nachkriegsjahre lag, ein Schatten, in dem sich ein für al-
> lemal alle triste Erfahrung mit der deutschen Szene, alle an Leben
> und Existenz gehende Widerfahrung gesammelt, verdichtet zu ha-

ben schien. Ich wollte mich aus der Umklammerung der Erinnerung befreien, die ich an die Zeit zwischen meinem zwanzigsten und dreißigsten Lebensjahre hatte, damals kurz nach 1945. (196–97)

Krolow stayed in Germany during the Nazi period and the war, but in over fifty years of prolific literary, critical, and journalistic activity, he never described his life during that period which he delicately refers to in French as "Cauchemar" and "triste Erfahrung," whose "schwerer Schatten" still later loomed large. His here enunciated poetics, however, include that historical experience at its core only as a definite absence, which he deems a sign of liberation from the "Umklammerung der Erinnerung."

Krolow advocates in effect an aesthetics of amnesia for the postwar period; immediately after the war, the German poem had tried to register and recover from the shock of recent historical experience, and Krolow already declares this recovery successful:

Es hat sich [das Gedicht] in der Tat vom Schock zu lösen vermocht. Die von der Realität überwältigte Vorstellungskraft hat sich bemüht, die Benommenheit abzustreifen. Das geschah mühsam genug, und es hat den Anschein, als wenn nach gewissen barbarischen Ereignissen auch die Lyrik die *Realien* mehr, als das lange Zeit erwünscht und praktiziert war, in ihre Sprache einbezöge. Sie hat sich dem Verhängnis gestellt und hat gesehen, daß der Schrecken, der den Sensiblen so oft in ihrer Einbildung geläufig gewesen war, greifbare Gestalt annehmen konnte, die alles vorgestellte Maß übertraf. Dennoch mußte das Gedicht wieder darangehen, *zaubern* zu lernen, mußte es alte, alterslose Fähigkeiten und Fertigkeiten entwickeln, die verlorengegangen schienen. (198)

After a therapeutic interlude of documentary description and introspection, alluding to *Trümmerlyrik,* the poem need no longer preoccupy itself with the past, but rather now only exercise its freedom to be ahistorical in its ageless facility with words, to perform its own verbal magic [*zaubern*], a term that links Krolow's poetics in the 1950s back to the magic realism of literary *inner emigration* in the *Naturlyrik* of the 1930s.[32]

He describes the free flights of fantasy in the poem as *Spiel, Zauber, intellektuelle Heiterkeit, Charme, Grazie des Intellekts, Schwebung, Balance,* and so on, all of which amounts to both a coherent poetics and a rhetorical sleight-of-hand to make the past disappear from the postwar poem. Krolow had begun and diligently pursued a literary career under the Nazis with over 100 individual publications of poems, prose vignettes, and essays in literary criticism in newspapers and journals ranging from *Das Innere Reich* to *Das Reich*. In his Büchner Prize address, Krolow adapted to the postwar period the same aesthetics of *inner emigration* that defined his earlier writings — without essential changes; historical reflection is "Ballast" that must be jettisoned, since it weighs too heavily upon the poem: "Übrigens gehört ja auch zu den Freiheiten des künstlerischen Spieltriebs, sich von der 'Belastung' durch den Gegenstand zu lösen" (201). That "Gegenstand," that "Belastung," is, however, for Krolow, always the past, from which his poetics and poetry of *Leichtigkeit* seeks release.[33]

Celan's more familiar "Meridian" speech represents the opposite position; he asks: "Die Kunst erweitern? / Nein. Sondern geh mit der Kunst in deine allereigenste Enge. Und setze dich frei" (200). Both poets speak of the poem as a vehicle of liberation, but for Krolow that means freedom from the past, for Celan freedom through the past. For Celan the poem is intrinsically historical: he suggests "daß jedem Gedicht sein '20. Jänner' eingeschrieben bleibt," citing the date of Büchner's *Lenz* and of the Wannsee conference that planned the "Final Solution" and organized the Holocaust. For Celan the poem always contains and implicates the past to give a multilayered, complexly striated sense of history.

That fundamental distinction in their relation to history dictates the terms of Krolow's reception of Celan. His continual positive attention to Celan's work frames the conceptual breach between them: in effect, Krolow promotes, with utmost sensitivity, but also distorts Celan's work by stripping it systematically of its relation to history. As a literary critic and journalist, Krolow began reviewing Celan's poetry in 1953 and followed his career with close to forty publications on the poet, his works, and on Celan scholarship as it began to appear. As a literary journalist, who lived by his pen, Krolow commonly recycled his texts on Celan, which lends an additional consistency in variation to his commentaries. The frequency of Celan as his topic represents both the demands of the literary marketplace and Krolow's own guarded fascination with Celan, whose poems for him were "von jeher ganz in sich verschlossene Verse, Verse der Einsamkeit," unto themselves, a "Wortwelt,"[34] — but a world of words whose gravity of historical reflection Krolow never ceases to resist.

Krolow first commented in print on Celan's work in 1953 in a short review of *Mohn und Gedächtnis* as "ein Stück Bekenntnislyrik . . ., voller Verse von zarter Schönheit und Tiefe." He makes no mention there of the poem "Todesfuge."[35] In a review of *Von Schwelle zu Schwelle* in 1955 titled "Ein Rutengänger der Sprache," Krolow correctly distinguishes Celan from poets like himself "die sich in Wandlungen zu bewähren haben," perhaps suggesting indirectly a central theme to Celan's unfolding work — but Celan then appears as a refined postwar version of the Romantic poet, "der Typ des hochpoetischen Märchenerzählers von geisterhafter Sensibilität," in line with the tendencies of 1930s magical realism that Krolow himself had adhered to.[36] In locating the landscape of Celan's imagination in the artistic fairy tale, Krolow reduces the scope of his work to an "ebenso zärtliche wie ernste, schwermütige Traumwelt." The word *zart* from his first review appears twice here and increasingly signifies for Krolow a distance from historical content. A second review of that same volume, published in the *Frankfurter Allgemeine Zeitung* on October 1, 1955, also emphasizes the autonomy of Celan's "Phantasiewelt," reiterates that word *zart* twice, and locates the poems "jenseits von ästhetischen Schocks. . . . im gleichen märchenhaften Land der Celanschen Vorstellungskraft." His poems constitute "das Raunen des Märchenerzählers." In concluding this short review Krolow adds the phrase "die Geisterhaftigkeit der Sprache Paul Celans, die Schattenhaftigkeit ihres Wesens" and introduces two terms that define over many years the ethereal ahistoricism, the disembodied and purely aesthetic sensations that Krolow finds in Celan's work. This latter review builds upon but goes beyond his prior formulations and, in its approach and language, anticipates Krolow's understanding of Celan for years to come. His appreciative but willful misreading finds delicate beauty in the elision of historical content.

In 1973 Krolow cited Celan's death to mark the end of an era in the genre of poetry, an era that valued aesthetic qualities over political commitment: "Mit der zunehmenden Politisierung auch des Literarischen nahm dieses 'reine,' vordringlich ästhetische Interesse rasch ab" (1322).[37] Celan's posthumous poems figure as "eine Art Echo-Wirkung. . . . wie das Echo auf das, was gerade eben noch da war, nun aber nicht mehr zulässig erschien" (1322). He focuses on the "Schattenbeziehung" in Celan's work, its movement toward silence and toward "unmittelbarem Daseins-Ausdruck" (1323). Krolow defines in retrospect a sort of categorical imperative in Celan's sensibility that bound him and isolated him as a poet: "Er arbeitete beharrlich und einsam weiter. Er konnte gar nicht anders," but in an oblique reference that begs clarification, Krolow adds: "Er konnte aus dieser Situation nicht 'auswandern'" (1324).[38] That allusion telescopes into Krolow's presentation of Celan the context of emigration, exile, and

Holocaust that he otherwise never addresses, and it thus defines the gap in his appreciation and understanding of Celan's work.

By the end of that same essay, Krolow indirectly equates Celan with an impasse in the genre that can now be superseded by the inclusion of more realia from everyday life in the form of objects and emotions: "Die suizitäre Lage, in die das Gedicht bei uns schon vor einem Jahrzehnt zu geraten begann, könnte überwunden sein, wenn diese genannte Auffüllung mit Stoffen, mit Gegenständen, mit dem Arsenal von Gegenständlichkeit, wie sie der Alltag aufbietet, durchgesetzt werden und sich halten würden [*sic*], ohne Rückfälle in die balancierte Lyrik mit all ihrem Stoffschwund" (1327). Krolow fails to recognize the central content of Celan's poetry, its historical substance, and finds in Celan an admirable and exquisite aesthetic refinement of the poem away from the world. For Krolow, it seems that only the immediate and quotidian present counts as historical reality, not the past. Despite close and frequent attention to his work, and personal sympathies, Krolow cannot sound the depths of Celan's poetry and consigns it to the past: his manifesto for *Alltagslyrik* announced the transition in his own work. In his survey of German poetry after 1945 for *Kindlers Literaturgeschichte der Gegenwart* and also in 1973, Krolow distills his views on Celan's work and subsumes it under the captions of "Undurchlässigkeit," "reiner Sprachkörper," and "Existenz-Verdünnung" (439–51).[39]

Krolow's recollection in 1975 of Celan's *Mohn und Gedächtnis*,[40] which he had reviewed in 1953, brings his reception of Celan full circle, though he continued to comment occasionally on Celan. He emphasized the trait of "Gegenstandsflüchtigkeit" (15) that his own Büchner Prize speech had called for, but which Krolow by 1975 in his own evolution to *Alltagslyriker* otherwise condemns. For Krolow, Celan's first volume had changed the way poetry was read and written in the 1950s and signaled the arrival of an elevated sensibility equal to Rilke's in the 1920s, which gave the poem new contours and a certain "Schattenhaftigkeit," a feature Krolow had already highlighted in a sensitive appreciation of the poet shortly after his death in 1970.[41] Indeed, Krolow returns continually to forms of the word *Schatten*, but only outlines the shadow ("das Gedicht als Schattenriss") and does not address what in Celan's poetry throws the shadow.[42] In fact, the single mention of "Todesfuge" in this long review cites it only as an example of literary-musical technique, of "Fugen-Führung." Though highlighting Celan's importance, Krolow's appreciation of Celan in 1975, like his many other commentaries over the years, supplants specific historical realities with a vague existentialism, which remains consistent with his pointed comment from 1959 that Celan's poetry "nichts als Dasein aussagt."[43]

Notes

[1] Cf. Reinhard Tgahrt's trenchant observation about Krolow's "zwar produktive, aber partielle Aneignung [. . .], die Loerkes Gedichte zu eigensinnig einer Tradition zuordnet und damit auch verschließt" (in *Marbacher Kolloquium 1984*, fn. 3, 15).

[2] Karl Krolow, "Betrachtungen zu Gedichtband-Titeln," *Das Innere Reich* 1 (1943): 97–105; "Zur Gegenwartslyrik," *Das Innere Reich* 2 (1943): 165–97. Also in *Das Innere Reich*, he published reviews of Kurt Loup's *Die Wildnis* (1941); of Wolf von Niebelschützen's *Die Musik macht Gott allein* (1942); and Emil Lorenz's *Die Einweihung des Orpheus*.

[3] In his poetry Loerke writes against "das dumme Gefühl," as he puts it in his essay "Das alte Wagnis des Gedichts," where such feelings figure as "die ansteckende und vernichtende Seuche der Lyrik" (699). Instead of sentiments, one should feel in Loerke's poetry "das Pathos seiner Bedeutung" (706), which is not to be confused with conventional feelings.

[4] In the first essay on poetics, "Möglichkeiten zeitgenössischer deutscher Lyrik," he speaks generally about the poem as "empfindliche Ensemble [. . .] ein Gewebe, das sich von Moment zu Moment bildet und wieder auflöst, ein Gebilde auf Widerruf bestenfalls" (*Aspekte zeitgenössischer deutscher Lyrik*, 8). Krolow commented often on this dimension of his work and poetics, and emphasized it in his interpretations of his own poems (see Karl Krolow *Ein Gedicht entsteht: Selbstdeutungen, Interpretationen, Aufsätze* [Frankfurt am Main: Suhrkamp, 1973], especially his self-interview, 7–11 or 35). In this respect the difference to Loerke is particularly apparent, as when Loerke says: "das vollendete Gebilde kehrt nicht zurück, er ist nicht widerruflich, so wie einmal gelebtes Leben nicht widerruflich ist, selbst wenn niemand davon Kunde hätte" ("Das alte Wagnis," 708).

[5] In his address on "Intellektuelle Heiterkeit" for the Büchner Prize, Krolow succinctly describes his development after the war: "Ich wollte mich aus der Umklammerung der Erinnerung befreien, die ich an die Zeit zwischen meinem zwanzigsten und dreißigsten Lebensjahre hatte . . ." (*Ein Gedicht entsteht*, 197).

[6] "Lyrik und Landschaft" (7–38) in *Schattengefecht*. (1964). See especially 25–29.

[7] "Oskar Loerke — Mein Modell?" (1966), in *Ein Gedicht entsteht* (1973): 126–37.

[8] One hears an echo here from the beginning of Hermann Kasack's essay "Sinn und Gestalt: Zum 50. Geburtstag von Oskar Loerke" (*Die Neue Rundschau* 45, 3 [1934]).

[9] For example, Theo Elm speaks of the "Konkretheit der lyrischen Bildwelt" (*Marbacher Kolloquium 1984*, 93) in Loerke. Reinhard Tgahrt notes, "daß es bei [Loerke] eine Treue zum Gegenständlichen, eine Art semantischer Verantwor-

tung gibt" (*Marbacher Kolloquium 1984,* 44). Marguerite Samuelson-Könneker cites "kosmische Solidarität" as Loerke's fundamental attitude and defines that term as "das dichterisch-menschliche Verantwortungsbewußtsein für das, was er 'Welt' nennt" (*Marbacher Kolloquium, 1984,* 110).

[10] Here one recalls Loerke's observation from the afterword to "Silberdistelwald": "Ich hatte mein Erleben heimzuleiten in die Form seiner Existenz durch Sprache" (683).

[11] Cf. Gerhard Neumann's trenchant and detailed analysis of this dimension of Loerke's work in his essay "'Einer ward Keiner': Zur Ichfunktion in Loerkes Gedichten" (*Marbacher Kolloquium 1984:* 211–70; 229).

[12] The fundamental difference in the characteristic attitudes of both poets becomes apparent in their respective essays on Goethe's *West-östlicher Divan.* Both essays appear in the edition edited by Hans-J. Weitz (Frankfurt am Main: Insel, 1988). Loerke describes Goethe's "überpersönliche Natur," which emerges there and emphasizes that: "Seine Einbildungskraft verläßt niemals die Grenzen der Erfahrung, sie schleppt in der Tat immer die Weltkugel mit sich" (373). . . . "seine Phantasie [reicht] viel breiter und tiefer in die Wirklichkeit" (378). For Krolow, it is "die Leichtigkeit, die ständig Erfahrung einbezieht" (379), and further: "Die Leichtigkeit, die über dem 'Divan' liegt, widerspricht jeder Bemühung, jedem poetischen Fleiß und jeder Vorstellung von Bewältigung" (382).

[13] In the collection *Fünfzehn Autoren suchen sich selbst: Modell und Provokation,* ed. Uwe Schultz (Munich: Paul List, 1967), 103–16. All of the essays bear the same formulaic title "Warum ich nicht wie ———— schreibe," whereby each author cites a literary model.

[14] *Karl Krolow: Ein Lesebuch,* ed. Walter Helmut Fritz, 1973.

[15] In "Loerke's 'Das gelbe Pferd': Poesis und Zeit in der imaginierten Stadt," Anthony Stephens concludes: "In jeglicher Hinsicht erweist sich Loerke als ein Vertreter der zentralen Tradition der Großstadtlyrik der ersten Jahre dieses Jahrhunderts" (160).

[16] Although he does not cite him in this context, Rümmler probably derives this insight from Gerhard Neumann's first essay on Loerke ("Oskar Loerke," in *Expressionismus als Literatur: Gesammelte Studien* [1969]: 295–308), in which Neumann analyzes the poem "Die gespiegelte Stadt" and the technique of "Verfremdung durch Spiegelverdoppelung" (298–99). Rümmler cites this well-known collections of essays in his bibliography, but not Neumann's specific essay on Loerke. In his essay, however, Rümmler departs from Neumann's elucidation of the "absolute-metaphor" ("Die 'absolute' Metapher. Ein Abgrenzungsversuch am Beispiel Stéphane Mallarmés und Paul Celans." *Poetica* 3 [1970]: 188–225), and would therefore also have paid particular attention to that earlier essay as well.

[17] Rümmler rightly notes: "Was Krolows Thema, poetische Haltung, Motive und Metaphern vor 1946 angeht, so ist Lehmann . . . mit Abstand der wichtigste Lehrmeister gewesen" (126); Hans Dieter Schäfer cites particular examples of Krolow's debts to Lehmann in his *Wilhelm Lehmann: Studien zu seinem Leben und Werk* (Bonn: Bouvier, 1969): 252–63.

[18] Rümmler analyzes Krolow's poem "Im Rückspiegel" (1952).

[19] Eberhard Schulz, "Oskar Loerke und die Geschichte" (1968); Gerhard Schulz, "Zeitgedicht und innere Emigration: Zu Oskar Loerkes Gedichtbuch 'Der Silberdistelwald' (1934)" (1984). Eberhard Schulz appears to have in mind Krolow's essays at the time, when he emphasizes: "Es genügt nicht, in Loerke eine Art Erzvater der zeitgenössischen Naturlyrik zu sehen. Der Naturlyrik fehlt die Dimension der Geschichte und damit eine Spannung, der das Loerkesche Gedicht viel von seiner geistigen Elastizität verdankt" (189).

[20] The dissertation of James K. Lyon ("Nature: Its Idea and Use in the Poetic Imagery of Ingeborg Bachmann, Paul Celan and Karl Krolow," Diss. Harvard University, 1962) testifies to the circumstantial validity of this grouping at the time, though Lyon's conclusion separates Krolow fundamentally from the other two in his use and derivation of nature imagery. Cf. also Marlies Janz, "Haltlosigkeiten. Paul Celan und Ingeborg Bachmann" (1985). Janz explains the disinterest for Celan and Bachmann in the 1970s due to their high poetic tone, but acknowledges that those skeptics, however wrongheaded, had recognized something essential about the two poets: "daß sich diese beiden Autoren nicht vereinnahmen lassen: daß ihre Werke auf Distanz gehen" (31). Though she does not include Krolow, her remark helps situate him: in his adaptations to contemporary tendencies, his work sets no barriers to the reader, yet in its accessibility, it nonetheless creates impersonal distance, a central feature of his poetics. Krolow's impersonal adaptation to reigning tastes is tinged with irony that creates distance; thus, critics of his work tend to isolate his technical virtuosity, whether as a positive or negative feature, or both.

[21] Friedrich also then wrote an afterword to a selection of Krolow's poetry: "Nachwort," *Ausgewählte Gedichte* (Frankfurt: Suhrkamp, 1962), 49–59, in Fritz, *Über Karl Krolow*, 74–84.

[22] James K. Lyon notes acutely: "While Bachmann and Celan write from the outset in a larger European tradition for which nature has lost much of its intrinsic meaning (though it still has symbolic value when the poet chooses to work with its images), Krolow begins writing in a uniquely German tradition which affirms nature and uses nature imagery almost exclusively. By 1962, however, Krolow has completely abjured nature as a source of poetry and turned to the larger European tradition, whereas Bachmann and Celan, who have remained much closer to their origins, give nature imagery such a fundamental role in their poetry that one can decipher their central concerns through understanding it. This is not the case with Krolow" (301).

[23] Hans Egon Holthusen wrote the first serious and comprehensive review of Krolow's early work with the title "Naturlyrik und Surrealismus: Die lyrischen Errungenschaften Karl Krolows," in *Ja und Nein: Neue kritische Versuche* (Piper: Munich, 1954). As "Naturlyrik und Surrealismus" in Fritz, W. H. *Über Karl Krolow* (1972). Holthusen has entered Celan scholarship for his apolitical appreciation of Celan (Felstiner, 78–79) and later for ignoring an allusion to the Holocaust, which elicited a sharp rebuke from Peter Szondi (Felstiner, 222–23, and fn. 18, 320).

[24] Karl Krolow, "Paul Celan," *Jahresring* 70/71 (1970): 338–46.

[25] For comparison, a real wall, the Berlin Wall, came between Paul Celan and Erich Arendt at a time when their friendship began to intensify, as chronicled in W. Emmerich's: "Erich Arendt — Paul Celan; Korrespondenzen und Differenzen" ([1995]: 181–206, see 188).

[26] Karl Krolow, "Deutsche Dichter an der Seine: Zum Ersten Deutsch-Französischen Literaturgespräch in Paris," *Neue Literarische Welt,* no. 11 (June 10, 1953): 9.

[27] Karl Krolow, "Zum Tode Paul Celans," *Der Tagesspiegel* (May 7, 1970): 4.

[28] That photograph appears on page 127 in Rolf Paulus's *Der Lyriker Karl Krolow* (1983). Compare Celan's reaction to the possibility of being photographed with Heidegger on his famous visit to the philosopher's home in the Schwarzwald, as recounted in Gerhart Baumann's recollection *Erinnerungen an Paul Celan* (Frankfurt am Main: Suhrkamp, 1985), 62–63.

[29] Though I make no specific reference here to materials contained in the Krolow-Celan correspondence in Paul Celan's estate at the Deutsches Literaturarchiv in Marbach, Germany, I would like to thank Eric Celan for his permission to consult those materials, which reinforced my general sense of their friendship and collegiality.

[30] The general consistency of Krolow's support, despite some qualifications and reservations, is clear upon review of his scattered opinions. Bianca Rosenthal, in *Pathways to Paul Celan: A History of Critical Responses as a Chorus of Discordant Voices* (New York: Peter Lang, 1995), supports this impression and places it in the reception history of Paul Celan's poetry, where Krolow figures as a particularly sensitive commentator (9). With all appreciation of his merit I nonetheless essay to show some of the shortcomings and implications of Krolow's views.

[31] Krolow's essay "Intellektuelle Heiterkeit: Rede zur Verleihung des Georg-Büchner-Preises" is included in Karl Krolow, *Ein Gedicht entsteht* (1973), 195–203.

[32] See Kirchner's study of magic realism in the German context of this period: *Doppelbödige Wirklichkeit: Magischer Realismus und nicht-faschistische Literatur* (1993).

[33] Krolow introduces the term "Leichtigkeit" in his 1955 essay on "Intellektuelle Heiterkeit" in *Mein Gedicht ist mein Messer: Lyriker zu ihren Gedichten,* ed. Hans Bender (Heidelberg: Wolfgang Rothe, 1955): 58–65, which is essentially a draft of his Büchner Prize address. Cognate terms from the same essay that he will develop later on are "porös" and "offen," though these will reflect his later developments toward *Alltagslyrik.* Krolow returns to that central idea, however, in an essay ten years later: "Literarische Leichtigkeit" in his *Poetisches Tagebuch, 1964–65* (Frankfurt: Suhrkamp, 1966): 125–29.

[34] Karl Krolow, "Am äußersten Blickrand — Erlittene Dichtung: Paul Celans *Atemwende,*" *Der Literat* 10, 1 (1968): 4.

[35] In his 1959 commentary on Celan and Heinz Piontek, Krolow does speak briefly and inevitably about "Todesfuge" (11), now acknowledged as his most famous poem, but praises it as an artistic "Produkt solchen Kompositionswillens" that demonstrates how the theme of terror and "die Verhängnisse der Epoche ge-

rafft und in der Poesie auf atemberaubende Weise 'erleichtert' werden." What Adorno had feared in the aesthetic treatment of barbarity, Krolow welcomes and extols! See my discussion of "Adorno's Philosophy of Poetry" in *Voice and Void: The Poetry of Gerhard Falkner* (1998), 19–34.

[36] James K. Lyon makes the following observation: "Though no one could maintain that he [Celan] is a nature poet, the maze of Daseinsentwürfe through which Celan leads a patient reader abounds in nature imagery. Four main groups — images of a darkened landscape, a watery landscape, plant imagery, and stone imagery — unlock a large number of his poems and reveal his central concern. . . . No stretch of the imagination could bring him close to the *natur-magische Schule*" (208–9). Though Lyon also writes in his dissertation about Krolow, he is not aware of these early reviews of Celan by Krolow, in which Krolow does seem to make Celan's work resemble that school of inner emigrants such as Loerke, Kaschnitz, Eich, and many others.

[37] This passage first appeared in a review of "Schneepart" titled "Weit ausschreitende Stille" (68–69) in *Die Horen* 16, 83 (1971): 69, and then later, in his "Die neue Situation der Lyrik," *Universitas: Zeitschrift für Wissenschaft, Kunst und Literatur* 28, 7 (1973): 1321–28.

[38] In his earlier (1971) review of Celan's *Schneepart: Letzte Gedichte*, from which Krolow culled this passage, he had another sentence after "auswandern": namely, "Er konnte nicht emigrieren aus der Dichtung, die er bis zum Schluß machte" (*Die Horen*, 69).

[39] Karl Krolow, "Teil III: Lyrik" in *Kindlers Literaturgeschichte der Gegenwart: Autoren, Werke, Themen, Tendenzen seit 1945 / Die Literatur der Bundesrepublik Deutschland*, ed. Dieter Lattmann (Munich and Zürich: Kindler, 1973), 347–533. In his review of Klaus Voswinckel's study of Celan (*Paul Celan: Verweigerte Poetisierung der Welt*, 1975), Krolow repeats, paraphrasing his earlier view: "Das Gedicht wurde bei ihm zum reinen, absoluten Sprachkörper, zur einzigen Instanz" (*Frankfurter Allgemeine Zeitung*, Nr. 52 [July 5, 1975]). Krolow's remark aligns Celan with Gottfried Benn (!) and emphasizes, contrary to Voswinckel, the apolitical and isolated quality of Celan's person and poem. Krolow's view of Celan seems dictated by a distinction between the literary qualities of a text and whatever else might extend beyond the text into other realms: though he, on the one hand, faults Celan for too little external reference (or for "Stoffschwund"), he speaks of the "Gefahr des Umschlags ins nicht mehr Literarische" in Celan's work. Krolow seems to work his way carefully around the autobiographical and historical content of Celan's poems. Even when he cites a phrase from Adorno's essay on Hölderlin in order to isolate the "Fremde als Gehalt, von der Sprachform ausgedrückt," Krolow removes that strangeness or foreignness, contrary to Adorno, from any relation to a particular historical reality.

[40] Karl Krolow, "Erinnerung an einen grossen Gedichtband: Paul Celans "Mohn und Gedächtnis," *Die Tat* 3 (January 4, 1975): 15.

[41] Karl Krolow, "Paul Celan," *Jahresring* 70/71 (1970): 339.

[42] In a general portrait of Celan in 1961, Krolow did note, in a paragraph on his biography: "Die nationalsozialistische Ära wurde für ihn und für seine Familie in besonderem Maße zum Schicksal" ("Deutsch mit französischem Schliff"). In his

many reviews, Krolow only indirectly cites the extra-literary content of Celan's poetry, for example, its relations to the Holocaust, to his past, or to Judaic culture, when such perspectives are raised by other critics, as in Krolow's summary of Marie Luise Kaschnitz' laudatio at the Büchner-Prize ceremony (in Krolow's "Gedichte brauchen Hörer: Paul Celan anläßlich der Verleihung des Büchner-Preises") and in his summary of Beda Allemann's "Afterword" to Celan's *Ausgewählten Gedichten* ("Zwischen abgewrackten Tabus"). In the latter he notes Allemann's references [Hinweise] "auf die *im weitesten Sinn autobiographischen Aspekte* und besonders auf die *Vertrautheit mit der mystischen Tradition der Chassidim*. Auf diesen Punkt ist man meines Wissens bei Celan gar nicht oder genügend eingegangen." That latter comment indicates a welcome openness to such perspectives that had otherwise seemed foreclosed in his readings of Celan.

[43] Karl Krolow, "Das Wort als konkrete Materie: *Sprachgitter:* Gedichte von Paul Celan," *Deutsche Zeitung* (April 8, 1959): 17.

Works Cited

Works by Karl Krolow

Poetry

Hochgelobtes, gutes Leben. Das Gedicht. Blätter für die Dichtung. Vol. 9, no. 4. Hamburg: Hermann Ellermann Verlag, 1943.

Gedichte. Constance: Süd-Verlag, 1948.

Heimsuchung. With a foreword by Stephan Hermlin. Berlin: Volk & Welt, 1948.

Auf Erden. Hamburg: Ellerman, 1949.

Die Zeichen der Welt. Stuttgart: Deutsche Verlagsanstalt, 1952.

Wind und Zeit: Gedichte 1950–1954. Stuttgart: Deutsche Verlagsanstalt, 1954.

Tage und Nächte. Gedichte. Düsseldorf & Cologne: Eugen Diederichs, 1956.

Fremde Körper. Frankfurt am Main: Suhrkamp, 1959.

Unsichtbare Hände. Gedichte 1959–1962. Frankfurt am Main: Suhrkamp, 1962.

Gesammelte Gedichte. Vol. 1. [1944–1964]. Frankfurt am Main: Suhrkamp, 1965.

Landschaften für mich. Neue Gedichte. Frankfurt am Main: Suhrkamp, 1966. edition suhrkamp 146.

Alltägliche Gedichte. Frankfurt am Main: Suhrkamp, 1968. Bibliothek Suhrkamp 219.

Nichts weiter als Leben. Neue Gedichte mit einem Anhang "Über ein eigenes Gedicht." Frankfurt am Main: Suhrkamp, 1970. Bibliothek Suhrkamp 262.

[Karol Kröpcke, pseud.], *Bürgerliche Gedichte.* With 36 drawings by Arno Waldschmidt. Hamburg: Merlin, 1970.

Gesammelte Gedichte. Vol. 2. [1965–1974]. Frankfurt am Main: Suhrkamp, 1975.

Auf Erden: Frühe Gedichte. Frankfurt am Main: Suhrkamp, 1989.

Prose

Von nahen und fernen Dingen: Betrachtungen. With illustrations by Fritz Fischer. Stuttgart: Deutsche Verlags-Anstalt, 1953.

Poetisches Tagebuch. Frankfurt am Main: Suhrkamp, 1966.

Unter uns Lesern. Darmstadt: Gesellschaft Hessischer Literaturfreunde, 1967.

Minuten-Aufzeichnungen. Frankfurt am Main: Suhrkamp, 1968.

Deutschland, deine Niedersachsen: Ein Land, das es nicht gibt. Hamburg: Hoffmann & Campe, 1972.

Schatten eines Manns. With illustrations by R. Schoofs. Wülfrath: R. Schoofs and Horst Heiderhoff, 1959.

Von literarischer Unschuld: Matthias Claudius (Ein Portrait). Darmstadt: Gesellschaft Hessischer Literaturfreunde, 1977.

Etwas brennt. Gesammelte Prosa. Frankfurt am Main: Suhrkamp, 1995.

Criticism

Aspekte zeitgenössischer deutscher Lyrik. Gütersloh: Gerd Mohn, 1961.

Schattengefecht. Frankfurt am Main: Suhrkamp, 1964.

Unter uns Lesern. Darmstadt: Gesellschaft Hessischer Literaturfreunde, 1967.

Ein Gedicht entsteht: Selbstdeutungen, Interpretationen, Aufsätze. Frankfurt am Main: Suhrkamp, 1973.

"Teil III: Lyrik." In *Kindlers Literaturgeschichte der Gegenwart: Autoren, Werke, Themen, Tendenzen seit 1945.* Edited by Dieter Lattmann. Munich and Zürich: Kindler, 1973. 347–533.

Translations

Die Barke Phantasie. Zeitgenössische französische Lyrik übertragen von Karl Krolow. Düsseldorf and Cologne: Diederichs, 1957.

Bestiarium. Sieben Gedichte nach Guillaume Apollinaire's 'Bestiaire ou Cortège d'Orphée.' With lino-cuts by Flora Klee-Palyi. Wuppertal: Klee-Palyi, 1957.

Guillaume Apollinaire: 'Bestiarium.' Fünfundzwanzig Gedichte nach Guillaume Apollinaire's 'Le Bestiaire ou Cortège d'Orphée.' Gießen: Walltor Verlag, 1959.

Spanische Gedichte des XX. Jahrhunderts. Selected and translated by Karl Krolow. Frankfurt am Main: Insel, 1962. Insel Bücherei 722.

Guillaume Apollinaire: "Bestiarium oder das Gefolge des Orpheus." With woodcuts by Raoul Dufy. Frankfurt am Main: Suhrkamp, 1978. Bibliothek Suhrkamp 607.

Critical Essays and Commentaries

"Bemerkungen zu einem späten Gedicht Rilkes: 'Ausgesetzt auf den Bergen des Herzens.'" In *Junge Geisteswissenschaft/Göttinger Semesterhefte* 2, no. 2 (1938/39): 122–26. Göttingen: Gerstung & Lehmann, 1939.

"Betrachtungen zu Gedichtband-Titeln." *Das Innere Reich*, no. 1 (1943): 97–105.

"Zur Gegenwartslyrik." *Das Innere Reich* 10, no. 2 (1943): 165–197.

"Der Erzähler Curt Hohoff: Zum Bande *Der Hopfentreter. Erzählungen aus dem Krieg*, 1941." *Das Innere Reich* 10, no. 2 (1943): 219–24.

"Der Glanz des Ewigen im Gedicht." *Deutsche Allgemeine Zeitung* 82, no. 183 (April 17, 1943): 3.

"Die Musik macht Gott allein: Die Gedichte Wolf von Niebelschützens." *Das Innere Reich*, no. 3 (1943/44): 311–18.

"Das Wirkliche." Review of *Die Wildnis* (1941) by Kurt Loup. *Das Innere Reich*, no. 3 (1943/44): 333–36.

"Emil Lorenz: Die Einweihung des Orpheus." *Das Innere Reich*, no. 4 (1943/44): 431–37.

"Hinweis auf einen Vergessenen." [J. G. von Salis-Seewis] *Die neue Rundschau* 55, no. 2 (1944): 90–92.

"Das Gedicht in unserer Zeit." *Das Gedicht in unserer Zeit*. Edited by Friedrich Rasche. Hannover: Adolf Sponholtz, 1946. 3–9.

"Deutsche Lyrik: Versdichtung in diesen Jahren." *Die Zeit* 3, no. 20 (May 13, 1948): 4.

"Die Lyrik Stephan Hermlins." *Thema*, no. 8 (1950): 28–29.

"Das 'Absolute Gedicht' und das 'lyrische Ich': Zu Gottfried Benns Lyrik-Theorie." *Die Neue Zeitung*, no. 253 (October 27/28, 1951): 11.

"Das zeitgenössische deutsche Naturgedicht." *Aussprache* 3, no. 6 (1951): 478–81.

"Traum vom Sinn der Erde." Review of Wilhelm Lehmann. *Gegenwart des Lyrischen: Essays zum Werk Wilhelm Lehmanns*. Gütersloh: Sigbert Mohn, 1966.

"Vom Gedichteschreiben — Heute." Edited by Hans Bender. *Konturen: Blätter für junge Dichtung* 1, no. 2 (1952): 19–21.

"Not und Chancen des deutschen Gedichts." *Die Literatur* (April 15, 1952): 6.

"Wege, die man ging." *Stuttgarter Nachrichten*, no. 165 (July 20, 1952).

"Jugendstil und Gottfried Benn." *Die Literatur*, no. 12 (1952): 3.

"Überall schläft Zauber." *Almanach der Hannoverschen Presse für das Jahr 1954.* Hannover: Hannoversche Druck- und Verlagsgesellschaft, 1953. 23–24.

"Zwei neue Lyriker: Zu Gedichtbänden von Paul Celan und Walter Höllerer." *Die Neue Zeitung,* no. 68 (March 21/22, 1953): 23.

"Dichter des unbehausten Seins." *Freude an Büchern* 4, no. 3 (1953): 53–54.

"Deutsche Dichter an der Seine: Zum ersten Deutsch-Französischen Literaturgespräch in Paris." Edited by Frank Thiess. *Neue Literarische Welt,* no. 11 (June 10, 1953): 9.

"Wesenszüge deutscher Lyrik in diesen Jahren." *Deutsche Rundschau* 80, no. 5 (1954): 475–79.

"Ein Rutengänger der Sprache: Neue Gedichte von Paul Celan." *Stuttgarter Zeitung,* no. 232 (October 8, 1955): 34.

"Paul Celan." Review of *Von Schwelle zu Schwelle. Frankfurter Allgemeine Zeitung,* no. 228 (October 1, 1955).

"Intellektuelle Heiterkeit." Edited by Hans Bender. In *Mein Gedicht ist mein Messer.* Heidelberg: Wolfgang Rothe, 1955. 58–62.

"Intellektuelle Heiterkeit: Rede zur Verleihung des Georg-Büchner Preises." In *Ein Gedicht entsteht.* Frankfurt am Main: Suhrkamp, 1973. 195–203.

"Junge Lyrik und westdeutsche Öffentlichkeit." *Texte und Zeichen,* no. 2 (1956): 641–44.

"'Wo bist du, wenn du neben mir gehst?': Zur Liebeslyrik in diesen Jahren." *Zeitwende,* no. 28 (1957).

"Revolte gegen die Vernunft." *Frankfurter Allgemeine Zeitung,* no. 162 (July 17, 1958): 10.

"Das Wort als konkrete Materie." *Deutsche Zeitung,* no. 28 (April 8, 1959): 17.

"Paul Celan und Heinz Piontek." *Anstöße* vol. 6, no. 1/2 (1959): 5–18.

"Büchnerpreis für Paul Celan." *SPD-Pressedienst,* F/XV/179 (October 17, 1960): 3–4.

"Gedichte brauchen Hörer: Paul Celan anläßlich der Verleihung des Büchner-Preises." *Neue Rhein-Zeitung* (October, 25, 1960).

"Theodor Storm." *Triffst du nur das Zauberwort: Stimmen von heute zur deutschen Lyrik.* Edited by Jürgen Petersen. Frankfurt am Main and Berlin: Propyläen, 1961. 146–58.

"Jeder hat seine kleine persönliche Sahara: Lyriker und das erste gedruckte Gedicht." *Frankfurter Allgemeine Zeitung,* no. 217 (September 19, 1961): 20.

"Deutsch mit französischem Schliff: Die lyrische Sprache des Dichters und Übersetzers Paul Celan." *Das Schönste.* 1961. 42–43.

"Die Anwesenheit des Gedichtes in unserer Zeit." *Reclam Blätter* (May 2, 1962): 15–19.

"Die Gegenwärtigkeit des Gedichts in unserer Zeit." *Zeitwende. Die Neue Furche* 33, no. 6 (1962): 392–400.

"Erinnerte Trauer, erinnertes Glück." Edited by Karl Ude. *Besondere Kennzeichen: Selbstporträts zeitgenössischer Autoren.* Munich: List, 1963. 85–88.

"Unbegrenzte Schwermut." *Deutsche Zeitung,* no. 94 (April 22, 1961): 18.

"Vom Verlust des Reims." *Frankfurter Allgemeine Zeitung* (June 13/14, 1963).

"Landschaften des Gedichts: Zu neuen Lyrikbänden." *Hannoversche Allgemeine Zeitung* (February 8/9, 1964): 11.

"Der Lyriker als Kritiker." *Stuttgarter Zeitung,* no. 163 (July 18, 1964).

"Das Gedicht als Spiegel gesellschaftlicher Situation: Kritischer Blick auf unsere Lyrik." *Rheinische Post,* no. 218 (Sept. 19, 1964).

"Literarische Leichtigkeit." *Poetisches Tagebuch,* 1964–65. 125–29.

"Robinson I." In *Doppelinterpretationen* by Hilde Domin. Bonn: Athenäum, 1966. 198–202.

"Blaue Blume und Apfel der Hesperiden." *Der weiße Turm: Eine Zeitschrift für den Arzt,* no. 1 (1967): 31–32.

"Der Schriftsteller und die moderne Gesellschaft." *Duitse Kroniek* 19, no. 4 (1967): 130–36.

"'In den Mittag gesprochen' von Elisabeth Langgässer." In *Begegnung mit Gedichten* by Walter Urbanek. Bamberg: C. C. Buchners, 1967. 281–86.

"Der aufgerollte Redefluß: Musikalische und literarische Kuriosa." *Der weiße Turm: Eine Zeitschrift für den Arzt,* no. 2 (1967): 31–32.

"Vom Türmer Lynkeus zum Eiffelturm." *Der weiße Turm: Eine Zeitschrift für den Arzt,* no. 3 (1967): 31–32.

"Magische Poesie." *Der weiße Turm: Zeitschrift für den Arzt,* no. 5 (1967): 29–30.

"Mann am Fenster." *Der Literat: Zeitschrift für Literatur und Kunst* 9, no. 12 (1967): 188.

"Von der Zuständigkeit des Schriftstellers in der Politik." *Neue Deutsche Hefte* 115/14, no. 3 (1967): 103–14.

"Zwischen Ebene und Limes-Landschaft." *Zeitwende. Die Neue Furche* 38, no. 7 (1967): 471–76.

"Warum ich nicht wie Oskar Loerke schreibe." In *Fünfzehn Autoren suchen sich selbst: Modell und Provokation.* Edited by Uwe Schultz. Munich: Paul List, 1967. 103–16.

"Am äußersten Blickrand. Erlittene Dichtung: Paul Celans *Atemwende.*" *Der Literat* 10, no. 1 (1968): 4.

"Leuchtende Rätsel: Ungaretti in Celans Nachdichtung." *Der Tagesspiegel* 24, no. 51 (December 22, 1968): 39.

"Zur deutschen Lyrik heute." *ensemble: Lyrik, Prosa, Essay.* Edited by Clemens Graf Podewils and Heinz Piontek. Munich: R. Oldenbourg, 1969. 173–80.

"Zum Tode Paul Celans." *Der Tagesspiegel,* no. 7493 (May 7, 1970): 4.

"Höflichkeit und Diskretion der Dichter." *Stuttgarter Zeitung* 25, no. 107 (May 10, 1969): 50.

"Das 'absolute Gedicht' und das 'lyrische Ich': Zu Gottfried Benns Lyrik-Theorie." *Die Neue Zeitung.* n.d. n.p.

"Nachruf zu Lebzeiten." *Vorletzte Worte: Schriftsteller schreiben ihren eigenen Nachruf.* Edited by K. H. Kramberg. Frankfurt: Bärmeier & Nikel, 1970. 140–42.

"Paul Celan." *Jahresring 70/71: Beiträge zur deutschen Literatur und Kunst der Gegenwart.* Stuttgart: Deutsche Verlagsanstalt, 1970. 338–46.

"Selbstdarstellung einsamer Existenz. Lichtzwang: Paul Celans letzter Gedichtband." *Stuttgarter Zeitung* 26, no. 156 (July 11, 1970): 52.

"Über ein selbstverfaßtes Poem." *Stuttgarter Zeitung* 26, no. 234 (October 10, 1970): 50.

"Unendlich geerdete Schwermut: Paul Celans letzter Gedichtband." *Hannoversche Allgemeine Zeitung* (July 25, 1970). Also, in *Die Tat,* no. 274 (November 21, 1970): 34–35.

"Erscheinung eines Dichters: Erinnerungen an Paul Celan — Aus Anlass seines 50. Geburtstages." *Hannoversche Allgemeine Zeitung* (November 17, 1970): 25.

"Sprechzwang: 'Ausgewählte Gedichte' Paul Celans." *Badische Zeitung* (December 16, 1970): 21.

"Trauerdomäne: Die Lichtzwang-Gedichte Paul Celans." *Deutsches Allgemeines Sonntagsblatt,* no. 35 (August 30, 1970).

"Celan und H. Domin: Dokumentationen der Lyrik." *Deutsches Allgemeines Sonntagsblatt* 24, no. 6 (February 7, 1971): 23.

"Herr Teste." In *Romanfiguren.* Edited by Akademie der Wissenschaften und der Literatur. Mainz: Hase and Koehler, 1971. Also published in *Karl Krolow: Ein Lesebuch.* Edited by W. H. Fritz. Frankfurt am Main: Suhrkamp. 1975. 218–28.

"Morgenstunde." *Die Tat* (November 27, 1971).

"Selbstporträt 1971." *Motive. Deutsche Autoren zu Frage: Warum schreiben Sie?* Edited by Richard Salis. Tübingen and Basel: Horst Erdmann, 1971. 200–205.

"Unendlich geerdete Schwermut." *Die Horen* 16, no. 83 (1971): 67–68.

"Weit ausschreitende Stille: *Schneepart* — Letzte Gedichte von Paul Celan." *Der Tagesspiegel* 27, no. 7831 (June 20, 1971): 45.

"Weit ausschreitende Stille." *Die Horen* 16, no. 83 (1971): 68–69.

"Der Ernst der heiteren Verse." *Die Tat* (March 31, 1972).

"Nichts weiter als Gedichte: Überlegungen zu einer Beschäftigung." Edited by Rudolf de le Roi. *Jemand der schreibt: 57 Aussagen.* Munich: Carl Hanser, 1972. 43–48.

"'Wie sind meine Finger so grün': Natur und Mensch im deutschen Gedicht." *Die Tat* (December 29, 1973). Also included in *Karl Krolow: Ein Lesebuch.* Edited by W. H. Fritz. Frankfurt am Main: Suhrkamp, 1975. 229–41.

"Die neue Situation der Lyrik." *Universitas* 28, no. 7 (1973): 1321–28.

"Meditation über den Lauf der Zeit." *Die Welt,* no. 293 (December 15, 1973).

"Plötzlich bist du voll Gesicht und Namen: Briefe von Günter Eich." *Frankfurter Allgemeine Zeitung,* no. 261 (November 9, 1974).

"Erinnerung an einen grossen Gedichtband: Paul Celans *Mohn und Gedächtnis.*" *Die literarische Tat,* no. 3 (January 4, 1975): 15–16.

"Das Dunkel zu erhellen: Eine Untersuchung über Paul Celan." *Frankfurter Allgemeine Zeitung,* no. 152 (July 5, 1975).

"'Diese kleine verletzliche Handschrift. Das 'private' Gedicht — eine Tendenzwende der Lyrik." *Die literarische Tat,* no. 307 (December 31, 1975): 15–16.

"Günter Eich und Paul Celan: Zwei Interpretationsversuche." *Frankfurter Allgemeine Zeitung,* no. 155 (July 17, 1976).

"Nach der Engführung." *Ensemble 9: Internationales Jahrbuch für Literatur.* Munich: Deutscher Taschenbuch Verlag, 1978. 158–69.

"Eine Verweigerung: Paul Celan 'In Memoriam Paul Eluard.'" *Frankfurter Allgemeine Zeitung,* no. 169 (July 25, 1981).

"Von Jahr zu Jahr — Von Tag zu Tag." *Der Literat* 26, no. 1 (January 15, 1984): 2.

"Werkstattgespräch mit Karl Krolow: Weder Missionär noch allein." Interview by Christian Schmitt. *Börsenblatt,* no. 41 (1985): 624–25.

"Autoren lesen im Funkhaus Hannover: Karl Krolow." Introduction by Gisela Lindemann. Norddeutscher Rundfunk. Volume HW 207, 394/1–2. Taped on March 13, 1985; broadcast March 19, 1985.

"Die Neue Übersichtlichkeit." *Der Literat* 20, no. 1 (1987): 1–2.

"Die Leichtigkeit des 'Divan.'" *Goethes West-östlicher Divan.* 8th ed. Frankfurt am Main: Insel, 1988. Insel Taschenbuch #275. 379–86.

"Melancholie." *Melancholie in Literatur und Kunst.* Hürtgenwald: Guido Pressler, 1990. 9–13.

Works Consulted

Adorno, Theodor. *Jargon der Eigentlichkeit: Zur deutschen Ideologie.* Frankfurt am Main: Suhrkamp, 1964.

Anderle, Martin. "Die Entwicklung der Lyrik Karl Krolows unter französischem und spanischem Einfluß." *Seminar,* no. 13 (1977): 172–88.

Andersch, Alfred. "Gedichte in strömenden Wasser." *Frankfurter Hefte,* no. 7 (1952): 553–54. In *Über Karl Krolow.* Edited by Walter Helmut Fritz. Frankfurt am Main: Suhrkamp, 1972. 42–45.

Arnold, Heinz Ludwig, ed. "Karl Krolow." *Text + Kritik: Zeitschrift für Literatur,* no. 77 (1983).

Arntzen, Helmut. *Ursprung der Gegenwart: Zur Bewußtseinsgeschichte der Dreißiger Jahre in Deutschland.* Weinheim: Beltz, 1995.

Barbian, Jan-Pieter. "Literary Policy in the Third Reich." In Cuomo, *National Socialist Cultural Policy.* London: Macmillan, 1995. 155–96.

———. *Literaturpolitik im Dritten Reich: Institutionen, Kompetenzen, Betätigungsfelder.* Frankfurt am Main: Buchhändler-Vereinigung, 1993; Munich: Deutscher Taschenbuch Verlag, 1995.

Barner, Wilfried, ed. *Geschichte der deutschen Literatur von 1945 bis zur Gegenwart.* Munich: Beck, 1994.

Barth, Emil. *Gesammelte Werke in zwei Bänden.* Edited by Franz Norbert Mennemeier. Wiesbaden: Limes, 1960.

Basker, David. "'Für einen werdenden Schriftsteller keine schlechte Lehre': Wolfgang Koeppen's Literary Career, Pre-1945." *Modern Language Notes.* 88, no. 3 (1993): 666–86.

———. "Love in a Nazi Climate: The First Novels of Wolfgang Koeppen and Marie Luise Kaschnitz." *German Life and Letters* 48, no. 2 (1995): 184–98.

Baumann, Gerhart. *Erinnerungen an Paul Celan.* Frankfurt am Main: Suhrkamp, 1986.

Bender, Hans. "Individuelle Einheit in der Vielfalt der Versuche." In *Über Karl Krolow*. Edited by Walter Helmut Fritz. Frankfurt am Main: Suhrkamp, 1972. 111–13.

Benn, Gottfried. *Briefe an F. W. Oelze, 1950–54.* Wiesbaden: Limes-Verlag, 1977.

Beyer, Renate. "Untersuchungen zum Zitatgebrauch in der deutschen Lyrik nach 1945." Ph.D. diss., Universität Göttingen, 1976.

Bode, Dietrich. *Georg Britting: Geschichte seines Werkes.* Stuttgart: Metzler, 1962.

Bormann, Alexander von. Sections on West German poetry in *Geschichte der deutschen Literatur von 1945 bis zur Gegenwart*. Edited by Wilfried Barner. Munich: Beck, 1994.

Böttiger, Helmut. *Orte Paul Celans.* Vienna: Zsolnay, 1996.

Braun, Michael. *Der poetische Augenblick. Essays zur Gegenwartsliteratur.* Berlin: Verlag Vis-à-Vis, 1986.

Breuer, Dieter, ed. *Deutsche Lyrik nach 1945.* Frankfurt am Main: Suhrkamp, 1988.

Britting, Georg. *Gedichte, 1930–1940.* Edited by Walter Schmitz. Munich and Leipzig: List, 1993.

Brockmann, Stephen, and Frank Trommler, ed. *Revisiting Zero Hour 1945: The Emergence of Postwar German Culture.* Washington, DC: The American Institute of Contemporary German Studies, 1996. vol. 1.

Buck, Theo. "Angstlandschaft Deutschland: Zu einem Nachkriegssyndrom und seiner Vorgeschichte in einem Gedicht Paul Celans." In *Deutsche Lyrik nach 1945* by D. Breuer. Frankfurt am Main: Suhrkamp, 1988. 138–65.

Büttner, Ludwig. *Von Benn zu Enzensberger: Eine Einführung in die zeitgenössische deutsche Lyrik, 1945–1970.* Nuremberg: Hans Carl, 1972.

Cercignani, Fausto. "Dunkel, Grün und Paradies: Karl Krolows lyrische Anfänge in *Hochgelobtes gutes Leben*." *Germanisch-Romanische Monatsschrift* 36, no. 1 (1986): 59–78.

———. "Zwischen irdischem Nichts und machtlosem Himmel: Karl Krolows *Gedichte* 1948." *Literaturwissenschaftliches Jahrbuch*, no. 27 (1986): 197–217.

Cuomo, Glenn. *Career at the Cost of Compromise: Günter Eich's Life and Work in the Years 1933–1945.* Atlanta: Rodopi, 1989.

———, ed. *National Socialist Cultural Policy.* London: Macmillan, 1995.

Czernin, Franz Josef. "Wahngeschichten eines Zahns: Wohin bloß geht die deutsche Lyrik? Drei neue Gedichtbände von Krechel, Krolow, Pfeiffer." *Literaricum* (August 8, 1992): 10.

Daemmrich, Horst S. *Messer und Himmelsleiter: Eine Einführung in das Werk Karl Krolows.* Heidelberg: Groos, 1980.

De Haas, Helmuth. "Der grüne und der weiße Gott." In *Über Karl Krolow.* Edited by Walter Helmut Fritz. Frankfurt am Main: Suhrkamp, 1972. 52–59.

Del Caro, Adrian. *The Early Poetry of Paul Celan: In the Beginning was the Word.* Baton Rouge and London: Louisiana State UP, 1997.

Demetz, Peter. *After the Fires: Recent Writing in the Germanies, Austria and Switzerland.* San Diego, New York, and London: Harcourt, Brace, Jovanovich, 1986.

Denkler, Horst. "Janusköpfig: Zur ideologischen Physiognomie der Zeitschrift 'Das Innere Reich' (1934–1944)." In *Die deutsche Literatur im Dritten Reich.* Edited by H. Denkler and K. Prümm. Stuttgart: Reclam, 1976. 382–405.

Denkler, Horst, and Karl Prümm, ed. *Die deutsche Literatur im Dritten Reich: Themen, Traditionen, Wirkungen.* Stuttgart: Reclam, 1976.

Domin, Hilde, ed. *Doppelinterpretationen: Das zeitgenössische Gedicht zwischen Autor und Leser.* Frankfurt am Main; Bonn: Athenäum, 1966.

———. "Das Glück der offenen Augen: Karl Krolow zum 60. Geburtstag." *Frankfurter Allgemeine Zeitung,* no. 59 (March 11, 1975): 19.

———. *Neue Gedichte.* Review of Karl Krolow. *Neue Deutsche Hefte* 114/14, no. 2 (1967): 127–33.

———. "Undifferenzierte Hymne." Letter to the editor. *Die Zeit,* no. 13 (March 31, 1967).

———. *Wozu Lyrik heute: Dichtung und Leser in der gesteuerten Gesellschaft.* Munich: Piper, 1971; Frankfurt am Main: Fischer, 1993.

———. "Zum Leonce-und-Lena-Preis 1979: Rede auf Karl Krolow und Anmerkungen eines Jurymitglieds zu den Prinzipien der Preisvergabe." In *Gesammelte Essays: Heimat in der Sprache.* Munich: Piper, 1992.

Donahue, Neil H. "Adorno's Philosophy of Poetry after Auschwitz." In *Revisiting Zero Hour 1945.* Edited by Brockmann and Trommler, 57–70. Washington, DC: The American Institute of Contemporary German Studies, 1996. Vol. 1.

———. "An East-West Comparison of Two War Novels: Alfred Andersch's *Die Kirschen der Freiheit* and Ōoka Shohei's *Fires on the Plain.*" *Comparative Literature Studies.* 24, no. 1 (1987): 58–82.

———. *Etwas brennt. Gesammelte Prosa.* Review of Karl Krolow. Frankfurt am Main: Suhrkamp, 1994; *World Literature Today* (1995): 357.

———. *Forms of Disruption: Abstraction in Modern German Prose.* Ann Arbor: U of Michigan P, 1993.

————. *Ich höre mich sagen.* Review of Karl Krolow. Frankfurt am Main: Suhrkamp, 1992; *World Literature Today* (1993): 605.

————. *Voice and Void: The Poetry of Gerhard Falkner.* Carl Winter: Heidelberg, 1998.

————. *Die zweite Zeit.* Review of Karl Krolow. Frankfurt am Main: Suhrkamp, 1995; *World Literature Today* (1996): 395.

Donahue, Neil H., and Doris Kirchner, eds. *Flight of Fantasy: New Perspectives on Inner Emigration in German Literature, 1933–1945.* New York and London: Berghahn, 2003.

Drawert, Kurt. "Nachwort." In *Karl Krolow: Wenn die Schwermut Fortschritte macht. Gedichte, Prosa, Essays.* Edited by Kurt Drawert. Leipzig: Reclam, 1993. 349–62.

Drews, Jörg. "Das Tabu über Aggressivität und Kritik: Zu einer verborgenen Kontinuität der deutschen Literatur vor und nach 1945." In *"Gift, das du unbewußt eintrinkst. . ." Der Nationalsozialismus und die deutsche Sprache.* Edited by Bohleber and Drews. Bielefeld: Aisthesis, 1994. 114–31.

Eggert, Hartmut. "Metaphern der Angst: Zur Lyrik der fünfziger Jahre (Eich/Bachmann)." In *Die Gruppe 47* by Justus Fetscher. Würzburg: Königshausen and Neumann, 1991. 177-87.

Elm, Theo. "Aufklärung als Widerstand: Oskar Loerke's Gedicht 'Das Auge des Todes.'" In *Oskar Loerke: Marbacher Kolloquium, 1984,* by Reinhard Tgahrt. Mainz: Hase & Koehler, 1986. 89–106.

Emmerich, Wolfgang. "Erich Arendt and Paul Celan: Korrespondenzen und Differenzen." *Celan-Jahrbuch,* no. 6 (1995): 181–206.

————. "Kein Gespräch über Bäume: Naturlyrik unterm Faschismus und im Exil." In *Natur und Natürlichkeit: Stationen des Grünen in der deutschen Literatur.* Edited by Reinhold Grimm and Jost Hermand. Königstein: Athenäum, 1981. 77–117.

Engelmann, Bernt. *Im Gleichschritt marsch: Wie wir die Nazizeit erlebten, 1933–1939.* 2d ed. Munich: Goldmann Verlag, 1986.

Felstiner, Joel. *Paul Celan: Poet, Survivor, Jew.* New Haven and London: Yale UP, 1995.

Fetscher, Justus, ed. *Die Gruppe 47 in der Geschichte der Bundesrepublik.* Würzburg: Königshausen & Neumann, 1991.

————. "Spuren eines Spurlosen: Trauerarbeit im Schreiben Günter Eichs." In *Die Gruppe 47.* Edited by Justus Fetscher, Würzburg: Königshausen and Neumann, 1991. 218–38.

Fink, Adolf. "Natur als Lese-Früchte: Zu Karl Krolows Pomologische Gedichten." *Germanisch-Romanische Monatsschrift* 33, no. 4 (1983): 458–80.

Forster, Leonard. *German Poetry, 1944–1948*. Cambridge, UK: Bowes & Bowes, 1949.

Frei, Norbert. *Vergangenheitspolitik: Die Anfänge der Bundesrepublik und die NS-Vergangenheit*. Munich: Beck, 1996.

Freilinger, Hubert. "Karl Krolow 'Bürgerlich.'" In *Umgang mit Texten*. Edited by Jakob Lehmann. Bamberg: C. C. Buchners, 1973. 206–13.

Friedrich, Hugo. "Nachwort zu *Ausgewählte Gedichte*" (1962). In *Über Karl Krolow*. Edited by Walter Helmut Fritz. Frankfurt am Main: Suhrkamp, 1972. 74–84.

———. *Die Struktur der modernen Lyrik: Von der Mitte des neunzehnten bis zur Mitte des zwanzigsten Jahrhunderts*. Hamburg: Rowohlt, 1956.

Fritz, Walter Helmut. "Karl Krolows Prosa: Tagebuch, Aufzeichnung, Erzählung, Essay." *Text + Kritik*, no. 77 (1983): 61–71.

———, ed. *Karl Krolow: Ein Lesebuch*. Frankfurt am Main: Suhrkamp, 1975.

———, ed. *Über Karl Krolow*. edition Suhrkamp, 527. Frankfurt am Main: Suhrkamp, 1972.

Fröhlich, Hans. "Der Reiz der Überreizung: Ein bekannter Lyriker gibt sich pornographisch." *Stuttgarter Nachrichten*, no. 259 (November 2, 1970): 8.

Geißler, Rolf. "Form und Methoden der national-sozialistischen Literaturkritik." *Neuphilologus*, no. 51 (1967): 262–77.

Glatzel, Johann. "Das Bild der Melancholie in Karl Krolows 'Im Gehen.'" In *Melancholie in Literatur und Kunst*. Hürtgenwald: Guido Pressler, 1990.

Grimm, Reinhold. "Flamboyant Creativity: Some Notes on the German Poet Karl Krolow." *Pembroke Magazine* Pembroke, NC, no. 30 (1998): 2–9.

———. "Im Dickicht der inneren Emigration." In *Die deutsche Literatur im Dritten Reich*. Edited by Horst Denkler and Karl Prümm. Stuttgart: Reclam, 1976.

———. "Die Rohheit dieser Handlung: Versuch, Karl Krolows Gedichte in ihrer englischen Übersetzung zu lesen." *Neue Rundschau* 106, no. 3 (1995): 79–87.

———. "Versuch über Lyrik und Sprachbau." In *Strukturen: Essays zur deutschen Literatur*. Göttingen: Sachse and Pohl, 1963. 190–92.

Grimm, Reinhold, ed., with Heinz Otto Bürger. *Evokation und Montage: drei Beiträge zum Verständnis moderner deutscher Lyrik*. Göttingen: Sachse and Pohl, 1961.

Grimm, Reinhold, ed., with Jost Hermand. *Exil und Innere Emigration: Third Wisconsin Workshop*. Frankfurt am Main: Athenäum, 1972.

Härtling, Peter. *In Zeilen Zuhaus*. Pfüllingen: Günther Neske, 1957.

Hartung, Harald. *Deutsche Lyrik seit 1965: Tendenzen, Beispiele, Porträts*. Munich and Zürich: Piper, 1985.

Hartung, Rudolf. "Ein leiser Revolutionär." *Die Zeit* (March 12, 1965). In *Über Karl Krolow*. Edited by Walter Helmut Fritz. Frankfurt am Main: Suhrkamp, 1972. 105–13.

Haupt, Jürgen. *Natur und Lyrik: Naturbeziehungen im 20. Jahrhundert*. Stuttgart: Metzler, 1983.

Heissenbüttel, Helmut. "Karl Krolow. Gottfried Benn." [Letter to the editor]. *Die Literatur* 1, no. 15 (1952): 8.

Herf, Jeffrey. *Divided Memory: The Nazi Past in the Two Germanys*. Cambridge, MA: Harvard UP, 1997.

Heselhaus, Clemens. *Deutsche Lyrik der Moderne von Nietzsche bis Yvan Goll: Die Rückkehr zur Bildlichkeit der Sprache*. Düsseldorf: August Bagel, 1961.

Hilberg, Raul. *The Destruction of the European Jews*. New York: Quadrangle Books, 1961; New York: Harper & Row, 1961.

Hillebrand, Bruno. *Vernunft ist etwas Sicheres: Karl Krolow, Poesie und Person*. Mainz: Akademie der Wissenschaften und der Literatur, 1985. 15.

Hinck, Walter. "Überleben im Gedicht: Karl Krolows frühe Lyrik kann wieder besichtigt werden." *Frankfurter Allgemeine Zeitung*, no. 293 (December 18, 1989): 32.

Hinderer, Walter. "Verlust der Wirklichkeit: Eine Ortsbestimmung der Westdeutschen Lyrik nach 1945." *Studi Tedeschi* 20, no. 2 (1977): 117–67.

Hinze, Diana Orendi. "The Case of Luise Rinser: A Past That Will Not Die." In *Gender, Patriarchy and Fascism in the Third Reich: The Response of Women Writers*. Edited by Elaine Martin. Detroit: Wayne State UP, 1993. 143–68.

Hirsch, David. "Deconstruction and the SS Connection." Ch. 7 in *The Deconstruction of Literature: Criticism after Auschwitz*. Hanover, NH and London: UP of New England and Brown University Press, 1991. 143–65.

Hirschenauer, Rupert, and Albrecht Weber. *Wege zum Gedicht*. Munich: Schnell & Steiner, 1968.

Höllerer, Walter. "Deutsche Lyrik 1900 bis 1950: Versuch einer Überschau und Forschungsbericht." *Der Deutschunterricht*, no. 4 (1953): 72–104.

Hoff, Kay. "Zur lyrischen Not Karl Krolows." Letter to the editor in response to Krolow's essay "Not und Chancen des deutschen Gedichts." *Die Literatur* 1, no. 6 (1952): 8.

Hoffmann, Charles W. *Opposition Poetry in Nazi Germany*. UC-Publications in Modern Philology, 67. Berkeley and Los Angeles: U of California P, 1962.

Holthusen, Hans Egon. "Naturlyrik und Surrealismus: Die lyrischen Errungenschaften Karl Krolows." In *Ja und Nein: Neue kritische Versuche*. Munich: Piper, 1954. 86–123; In *Über Karl Krolow*. Edited by Walter Helmut Fritz. Frankfurt am Main: Suhrkamp, 1972. 9–41.

———. "Stationen eines Talents: Karl Krolow." In *Plädoyer für den Einzelnen: Kritische Beiträge zur literarischen Diskussion*. Munich: Piper, 1967. 163–67.

Ihde, Wilhelm, ed. *Handbuch der Reichsschrifttumskammer*. Leipzig: Verlag des Börsenvereins und deutscher Buchhändler, 1942.

Jacob, Heinrich Eduard. *Verse der Lebenden: Deutsche Lyrik seit 1910*. Berlin: Propyläen, 1924.

Janz, Marlies. "Haltlosigkeiten: Paul Celan und Ingeborg Bachmann." In *Das schnelle Altern der neuesten Literatur: Essays zu deutschesprachigen Texten zwischen 1968–1984*. Edited by Jochen Hörisch and Hubert Winkels. Düsseldorf: Claassen, 1985. 31–39.

Jaspers, Karl. *Die geistige Situation der Zeit*. 1932. Reprint, Berlin and New York: de Gruyter, 1979.

Jenny-Ebeling, Charitas. ". . . wie sich's in Trauer mischt: Frühe Gedichte von Karl Krolow." *Neue Zürcher Zeitung*, no. 285 (December 8, 1989): 47.

Jeziorkowski, Klaus. "Karl Krolow." In *Deutsche Dichter der Gegenwart: Ihr Leben und Werk*. Edited by Benno von Wiese. Berlin: Erich Schmidt, 1973. 395–412.

———. "Zu Karl Krolows 'Terzinen vom früheren Einverständnis mit aller Welt.'" In *Gedichte und Interpretationen: Gegenwart*. Edited by Walter Hinck. Stuttgart: Reclam, 1982. 216–27.

Jung, Werner. "Vom Alltag, der Neuen Subjektivität und der Politisierung des Privaten: Anmerkungen zur Lyrik der 70er Jahre." Edited by Dieter Breuer. *Deutsche Lyrik nach 1945*. Frankfurt am Main: Suhrkamp, 1988. 261–83.

Karst, Karl, ed. *Günter Eich: Rebellion in der Goldstadt: Texttranskript und Materialien*. Frankfurt am Main: Suhrkamp, 1997.

Kasack, Hermann. "Oskar Loerke." *Mosaiksteine: Beiträge zu Literatur und Kunst*. Frankfurt am Main: Suhrkamp, 1956. 134–61.

———. "Sinn und Gestalt: Zum 50. Geburtstag von Oskar Loerke." *Die Neue Rundschau* 45, no. 3 (1934).

Ketelsen, Uwe-K. *Literatur und Drittes Reich*. Schernfeld: SH-Verlag, 1992.

Kirchner, Doris. *Doppelbödige Wirklichkeit: Magischer Realismus und nicht-faschistische Literatur*. Tübingen: Stauffenburg, 1993.

Klemperer, Victor. *Ich will Zeugnis ablegen bis zum letzten. Tagebücher, 1933–1945.* 2 vols. Edited by Walter Nowojski with Hadwig Klemperer. Berlin: Aufbau, 1995.

———. *LTI. Notizen eines Philologen.* 1947. Reprint, Leipzig: Aufbau, 1996.

Knörrich, Otto. "Im Schnittpunkt der Richtungen." In *Die deutsche Lyrik der Gegenwart, 1945–1970.* Stuttgart: Alfred Kröner, 1971. 215–24.

Koebner, Thomas. "Die Schuldfrage: Vergangenheitsverweigerung und Lebenslügen in der Diskussion 1945–1949." In *Zur deutschen Literatur in der Weimarer Republik, im Exil und in der Nachkriegszeit.* Munich: *Text + Kritik,* 1992.

Koehl, Robert Lewis. *The Black Corps: The Structure and Power Struggles of the Nazi SS.* Madison, WI: U of Wisconsin P, 1983.

König, Helmut, Wolfgang Kuhlmann, and Klaus Schwabe. *Vertuschte Vergangenheit: Der Fall Schwerte und die NS-Vergangenheit der deutschen Hochschulen.* Munich: Beck, 1997.

Kolter, Gerhard. "Liebe, Eros, Sexualität. Stichworte zu Karl Krolows Bürgerlichen Gedichten: Ein Essay." *Text + Kritik,* no. 77 (1983): 81–85.

———. *Die Rezeption westdeutscher Nachkriegslyrik am Beispiel Karl Krolows: zu Theorie und Praxis literarischer Kommunikation.* Bonn: Bouvier, 1977.

———. "Typen der Lyrikrezeption am Werk Karl Krolows." *Text + Kritik,* no. 77 (1983): 37–45.

Kolter, Gerhard, and Rolf Paulus. "Gespräch mit Karl Krolow." *Text + Kritik,* no. 77 (1983): 46–54.

Korte, Helmut. *Geschichte der deutschen Lyrik seit 1945.* Sammlung Metzler, 250. Stuttgart: Metzler, 1989.

Kreuder, Ernst. "Dichtung als existentielles Experiment." In *Jahrbuch 1956 der Deutschen Akademie für Sprache und Dichtung.* Heidelberg & Darmstadt: Lambert Schneider, 1957. 93–100; In *Über Karl Krolow.* Edited by Walter Helmut Fritz. Frankfurt am Main: Suhrkamp, 1972. 60–69.

Landwehr, Jürgen. "Anläßlich 'Krolow': Formen der Mimesis im Gedicht." *Text + Kritik,* no. 77 (1983): 7–18.

Lehmann, Jakob, ed. *Umgang mit Texten: Beiträge zum Literaturunterricht.* Bamberg: C. C. Buchners, 1973.

Lehmann, Wilhelm. "Freundschaft mit Oskar Loerke." *Gegenwart des Lyrischen: Essays zum Werk Wilhelm Lehmanns.* Edited by Werner Siebert. Gütersloh: Sigbert Mohn, 1967.

Lehnert, Herbert. *Struktur und Sprachmagie: Zur Methode der Lyrik-Interpretation.* Stuttgart: Kohlhammer, 1966.

Lettau, Reinhard. "1952 Niendorf." In *Die Gruppe 47: Bericht, Kritik, Polemik.* Neuwied and Berlin: Luchterhand, 1967. 72–79.

Ley, Robert, ed. [Herausgeber: Der Reichsorganisationsleiter der NSDAP, Dr. Robert Ley.] *Organisationsbuch der NSDAP.* Munich: Zentralverlag der NSDAP, 1943. [7. Auflage: 301.–400. Tausend.]

Loerke, Oskar. "Das alte Wagnis des Gedichts." In *Oskar Loerke: Gedichte und Prosa.* Vol. 1. Edited by Peter Suhrkamp. Frankfurt am Main: Suhrkamp, 1958. 692–712.

———. *Gedichte und Prosa.* Edited by Peter Suhrkamp. Frankfurt am Main: Suhrkamp, 1958. Vol. 1. Edited by Reinhard Tgahrt. st. 1049. Frankfurt am Main: Suhrkamp, 1983.

———. "Der Goethe des 'West-östlichen Divans.'" (1925). In *Goethe's West-östlicher Divan.* Frankfurt am Main: Insel, 1974. Insel Taschenbuch 275. 8th ed. 1988. 364–78.

———. *Tagebücher, 1903–1939.* Edited by Hermann Kasack. Deutsche Akademie für Sprache und Dichtung, Darmstadt. Heidelberg and Darmstadt: Lambert Schneider, 1955.

Loewy, Ernst. *Literatur unter dem Hakenkreuz. Das dritte Reich und seine Dichtung.* Frankfurt am Main: Europäische Verlagsanstalt, 1966.

Lumans, Vladis O. *Himmler's Auxiliaries: The Volksdeutsche Mittelstelle and the German National Minorities of Europe, 1933–1945.* Chapel Hill, NC: The U of North Carolina P, 1993.

Lyon, James K. "Nature: Its Idea and Use in the Poetic Imagery of Ingeborg Bachmann, Paul Celan and Karl Krolow." Ph.D. diss., Harvard University, 1962.

Maier, Rudolf Nikolaus. *Das moderne Gedicht.* Düsseldorf: Schwann, 1959.

Mallmann, Marion. *Das Innere Reich: Analyse einer konservativen Kulturzeitschrift im Dritten Reich.* Bonn: Bouvier, 1978.

Martens, Erika. *Zum Beispiel "Das Reich."* Cologne: Verlag Wissenschaft und Politik, 1972.

Mason, Timothy. *Sozialpolitik im Dritten Reich: Arbeiterklasse u. Volksgemeinschaft.* Opladen: Westdeutscher Verlag, 1977.

Massoud, Fatma. *Epochengeschichtliche Aspekte in der Lyrik Karl Krolows.* Europäische Hochschulschriften. Vol. 405. Frankfurt am Main: Peter Lang, 1981.

Meckel, Christoph. *Suchbild: Über meinen Vater.* Hildesheim: Claassen, 1980; Frankfurt: Fischer, 1983.

Mitscherlich, Alexander and Margarete. *Die Unfähigkeit zu trauern.* Munich: Piper, 1967; Munich: Piper, 1991.

Mondstrahl, Felix. "Felix Mondstrahl beleuchtet Karl Krolow, einen neuen, wenn auch 'arrivierten' Benn-Epigonen." *Baubudenpoet,* no. 1 (1959/60): 65–67.

Monhardt, Stefan. "Das Kartell der Ignoranz: Keine Chance für neue Lyrik." *Rheinischer Merkur / Christ und Welt*, no. 24 (June 14, 1991): 13.

Müller, Hartmut. *Formen moderner deutscher Lyrik*. Paderborn: Schöningh, 1970.

Neumann, Gerhard. "Die 'Absolute' Metapher: Ein Abgrenzungsversuch am Beispiel Stéphane Mallarmés und Paul Celans." *Poetica*, no. 3 (1970): 188–225.

———. "Oskar Loerke." In *Expressionismus als Literatur: Gesammelte Studien*. Edited by Wolfgang Rothe. Bern and Munich: Francke, 1969. 295–308.

———. "'Einer ward Keiner': Zur Ichfunktion in Loerkes Gedichten." In *Marbacher Kolloquium 1984* by Reinhard Tgahrt. Mainz: Hase & Koehler, 1986. 211–70.

Orlowski, Hubert. "Krakauer Zeitung 1939–1945: Auch ein Kapitel deutscher Literaturgeschichte im Dritten Reich." *Text + Kontext* 8, no. 1 (1980): 411–18.

Paetel, Karl O., ed. *Deutsche Innere Emigration: Anti-nationalistische Zeugnisse aus Deutschland*. With commentaries by Karl O. Paetel. New York: Friedrich Krause, 1946.

Paulus, Rolf. "Karl Krolow." *Kritisches Lexikon der deutschsprachigen Gegenwartsliteratur*. Munich: Text + Kritik, 1990.

———. *Karl-Krolow-Bibliographie*. Frankfurt am Main: Athenäum Verlag, 1972.

———. "Die Lyrik Karl Krolows." *Text + Kritik*, no. 77 (1983): 19–36.

———. *Lyrik und Poetik Karl Krolows: Produktionsaesthetische, poetologische und interpretatorische Hauptaspekte seines "offenen Gedichts."* Bonn: Bouvier, 1980.

———. *Der Lyriker Karl Krolow: Biographie-Werkentwicklung-Gedichtinterpretationen-Bibliographie*. Bonn: Bouvier, 1983.

Paulus, Rolf, and Gerhard Kolter. "Gespräch mit Karl Krolow." *Text + Kritik*, no. 77 (1983): 46–54.

Pee, Jong Ho. *Karl Krolow und die lyrische Tradition: Ironie und Selbstreflexion*. Cologne: Müller Botermann, 1991.

Perels, Christoph, ed. *Lyrik verlegen in dunkler Zeit: Aus Heinrich Ellermanns Reihe Das Gedicht: Blätter für die Dichtung, 1934–1944*. Munich: Ellermann Verlag, 1984.

Picard, Max. *Hitler in uns selbst*. Erlenbach-Zürich: Eugen Rentsch, 1946.

Piniel, Gerhard. "Nichts weiter als Leben" (1970). In *Über Karl Krolow*. Edited by Walter Helmut Fritz. Frankfurt am Main: Suhrkamp, 1972. 155–58.

Piontek, Heinz. "Musterung eines Oeuvres." In *Über Karl Krolow*. Edited by Walter Helmut Fritz. Frankfurt am Main: Suhrkamp, 1972. 89–104.

Profit, Vera B. *Ein Porträt meiner Selbst: Karl Krolows Autobiographical Poems (1945–1958) and Their French Sources*. New York: Peter Lang, 1991.

———. *Menschlich: Gespräche mit Karl Krolow*. Studies in Modern German Literature. New York: Peter Lang, 1996. vol. 78.

Reichsorganisationsleiter der NSDAP, ed. *Organisationsbuch der NSDAP*. 7th ed. Zentralverlag der NSDAP. Munich: Eher, 1943.

Rolleston, James. *Narratives of Ecstasy: Romantic Temporality in Modern German Poetry*. Detroit: Wayne State UP, 1987.

Rosenthal, Bianca. *Pathways to Paul Celan: A History of Critical Responses as a Chorus of Discordant Voices*. New York: Peter Lang, 1995.

Rucktäscherl, Annamaria. *Zur Sprachstruktur moderner Lyrik: Ein Versuch über Karl Krolow*. Ph.D. diss., Ludwig-Maximilians-Universität, Munich, 1968.

Rühmkorf, Peter. *Dreizehn deutsche Dichter*. Reinbek bei Hamburg: Rowohlt, 1989.

———. *Die Jahre die Ihr kennt: Anfälle und Erinnerungen*. Reinbek bei Hamburg: Rowohlt, 1972, 1986.

———. "Die Körpersprache der Poesie: Rede auf Karl Krolow." In *Dreizehn deutsche Dichter*. Reinbek bei Hamburg: Rowohlt, 1989. 141–53.

———. [Leslie Meier, pseud.] "Meiers Lyrik-Schlachthof." Column on Karl Krolow on the occasion of Büchner Prize. *Studentenkurier* vol. 2, no. 8 (December 1956): 5.

Rümmler, Artur. *Die Entwicklung der Metaphorik in der Lyrik Karl Krolows (1942–1962)*. Bern: Lang, 1972.

Sabais, Heinz Winfried. "Karl Krolow." In *Schriftsteller der Gegenwart: Deutsche Literatur, Dreiundfünfzig Porträts* by Klaus Nonnemann. Olten und Freiburg i. B.: Walter, 1963. 200–204.

Samuelson-Könnecker, Marguerite. "'Das Schaufenster': Das visionäre Gedicht als Spiegel inneren Zwiespaltes." In *Marbacher Kolloquium, 1984* by Reinhard Tgahrt. Mainz: Hase & Koehler, 1986. 107–26.

Schäfer, Hans Dieter. *Die Entwicklung der Metaphorik in der Lyrik Karl Krolows (1942–1962). Die Beziehungen zu deutschen, französischen und spanischen Lyrikern*. Review of Artur Rümmler. Bern & Frankfurt: Lang, 1972; In *Germanistik* 15, no. 3 (1974): 713–14.

———. *Das gespaltene Bewußtsein: Über deutsche Kultur und Lebenswirklichkeit, 1933–45*. Munich: Hanser, 1981.

———. "Kultur als Simulation: Das Dritte Reich und die Postmoderne." In *Literatur in der Diktatur: Schreiben im Nationalsozialismus und DDR-Sozialismus.* Edited by Günther Rüther. Paderborn: Ferdinand Schöningh, 1997. 215–45.

———. "Naturdichtung und Neue Sachlichkeit." In *Die deutsche Literatur in der Weimarer Republik.* Edited by Wolfgang Rothe. Stuttgart: Reclam, 1974.

———. "Die nichtfaschistische Literatur der 'jungen Generation' im nationalsozialistischen Deutschland." In *Die deutsche Literatur im Dritten Reich: Themen, Traditionen, Wirkungen.* Edited by Horst Denkler and Karl Prümm. Stuttgart: Reclam, 1976.

———. "Die Wandlung Karl Krolows." *Neue Rundschau* 86, no. 2 (1975): 330–34.

———. *Wilhelm Lehmann: Studien zu seinem Leben und Werk.* Bonn: Bouvier, 1969.

———. "Zur Periodisierung der deutschen Literatur seit 1930." *Literaturmagazin,* no. 7 (1977): 95–115.

———. "Zusammenhänge der deutschen Gegenwartslyrik." In *Deutsche Gegenwartslyrik: Ausgangspositionen und aktuelle Entwicklungen.* Edited by Manfred Durzak. Stuttgart: Reclam, 1981.

Schaefer, Oda. *Auch wenn Du träumst, gehen die Uhren: Erinnerungen bis 1945.* Munich: Piper, 1970; Reprint, Munich: Piper, 1980.

———. *Die leuchtenden Feste über die Trauer: Erinnerungen aus der Nachkriegszeit.* Munich: Piper, 1977.

Schama, Simon. *Landscape and Memory.* New York: Knopf, 1995.

Schlenstedt, Dieter. "Lyrisches Ich in der Zugluft: Bemerkungen zur Poetik Karl Krolows." *Neue Deutsche Literatur* 11, no. 2 (1963): 97–104.

Schoeps, Karl-Heinz Joachim. *Deutsche Literatur zwischen den Weltkriegen: Literatur im Dritten Reich.* Frankfurt am Main and New York: Peter Lang, 1992.

Schmid, Gerhard. "'Gedicht für J.S.' von Karl Krolow." In *Begegnung mit Gedichten: 66 Interpretationen vom Mittelalter bis zur Gegenwart.* Edited by Walter Urbanek. Bamberg: C. C. Buchners, 1967. 324–31.

Schmidt, Adalbert. *Literaturgeschichte unserer Zeit.* In *Wege und Wandlungen moderner Dichtung.* Rev. and enl. ed. Salzburg and Stuttgart: Verlag Das Bergland-Buch, 1957, 1968.

Schnell, Ralf. *Geschichte der deutschsprachigen Literatur seit 1945.* Stuttgart: Metzler, 1993.

———. *Literarische Innere Emigration, 1933–1945.* Stuttgart: Metzler, 1976.

Schonauer, Franz. *Deutsche Literatur im Dritten Reich: Versuch einer Darstellung in polemisch-didaktischer Absicht.* Olten & Freiburg im Breisgau: Walter, 1961.

Schulz, Eberhard Wilhelm. "Deutsche Lyrik nach 1945: Zur Phase II der Moderne." In *Wort und Zeit: Aufsätze und Vorträge zur Literaturgeschichte.* Neumünster: Karl Wachholtz, 1968.

———. "Oskar Loerke und die Geschichte." In *Wort und Zeit: Aufsätze und Vorträge zur Literaturgeschichte.* Neumünster: Karl Wachholtz, 1968.

Schulz, Gerhard. "Zeitgedicht und innere Emigration: Zu Oskar Loerkes Gedichtbuch *Der Silberdistelwald* (1934)." In *Zeit der Moderne: Zur deutschen Literatur von der Jahrhundertwende bis zur Gegenwart.* Edited by Hans Henrik Krummacher, Fritz Martini, and Walter Müller-Seidel. Stuttgart: Kröner, 1984.

Schwerte, Hans. "Karl Krolow: Verlassene Küste." In *Wege zum Gedicht.* Edited by Hirschenauer, Rupert, and Weber. Munich and Zürich: Schnell and Steiner, 1956. 384–91.

Seidler, Manfred. *Moderne Lyrik im Deutschunterricht.* Frankfurt am Main: Hirschgraben, 1975. 104–8.

Siemes, Christof. *Das Testament gestürzter Tannen: Das lyrische Werk Peter Huchels.* Freiburg im Breisgau: Rombach Verlag, 1996.

Stephens, Anthony. "Loerkes 'Das gelbe Pferd': Poesis und Zeit in der imaginierten Stadt." In *Oskar Loerke: Marbacher Kolloquium, 1984,* by Reinhard Tgahrt. Mainz: Hase & Koehler, 1986. 127–60.

Steuler, Ursula. "*Renes-Zügel* oder *Königinnen*? Ein Beitrag zu Krolow als Übersetzter: Apollinaires 'Le Bestiaire ou Cortege d'Orphée' in Übersetzungen von Karl Krolow." In *Karl Krolow.* Edited by Ludwig Arnold. *Text + Kritik,* no. 77 (1983): 72–80.

Strothmann, Dietrich. *Nationalsozialistische Literaturpolitik: Ein Beitrag zur Publizistik im Dritten Reich.* Bonn: Bouvier, 1960.

Suhrkamp, Peter, ed. *Oskar Loerke. Gedichte und Prosa.* Frankfurt am Main: Suhrkamp, 1958. vol. 1.

Tausk, Walter. *Breslauer Tagebuch, 1933–1940.* Leipzig: Reclam, 1995.

Tgahrt, Reinhard. "Dichterische Existenz." In *Gegenwart des Lyrischen: Essays zum Werk Wilhelm Lehmanns.* Edited by Werner Siebert. Gütersloh: Sigbert Mohn, 1967.

———. *Oskar Loerke: Marbacher Kolloquium, 1984.* Mainz: Hase & Koehler, 1986.

———. *Zeitgenosse vieler Zeiten: Zweites Marbacher Loerke-Kolloquium, 1987.* Mainz: Hase & Koehler, 1989.

Trommler, Frank. "Emigration und Nachkriegsliteratur: Zum Problem der geschichtlichen Kontinuität." In *Exil und Innere Emigration.* Edited by Reinhold Grimm with Jost Hermand. Frankfurt am Main: Athenäum, 1972. 173–97.

———. "Die nachgeholte Résistance: Politik und Gruppenethos im historischen Zusammenhang." In *Die Gruppe 47.* Edited by Justus Fetscher. Würzburg: Königshausen & Neumann, 1991. 9–22.

Urbanek, Walter, ed. *Begegnung mit Gedichten.* Bamberg: C. C. Buchners, 1967.

Weissenberg, Klaus. *Formen der Elegie von Goethe bis Celan.* Bern & Munich: Francke, 1969.

———, ed. *Die Deutsche Lyrik 1945–1970: Zwischen Botschaft und Spiel.* Düsseldorf: Bagel, 1981.

Wiese, Benno von. *Deutsche Literatur in unserer Zeit.* Göttingen: Vandenhoeck & Ruprecht, 1959.

———. "Robinson I." In *Doppelinterpretationen.* Edited by H. Domin. Frankfurt am Main and Bonn: Athenäum, 1966. 203–6.

Witte, Bernd. "Von der Trümmerlyrik zur Neuen Subjektivität: Tendenzen der deutschen Nachkriegsliteratur am Beispiel der Lyrik." In *Deutsche Lyrik nach 1945.* Edited by D. Breuer. Frankfurt am Main: Suhrkamp, 1988. 10–42.

Wittstock, Uwe. "Krieg, Traum, Sprache: Wolfgang Bächler wird siebzig." *Neue Rundschau* 106, no. 2 (1995): 175–77.

Wulf, Joseph. *Presse und Funk im Dritten Reich: Eine Dokumentation.* Frankfurt am Main and Berlin: Ullstein, 1966; abridged 1983.

Ziolkowski, Theodore. "Form als Protest: Das Sonett in der Literatur des Exils und der Inneren Emigration." In *Exil und Innere Emigration* by Reinhold Grimm and Jost Hermand. Frankfurt am Main: Athenäum-Verlag, 1972. 153–72.

Zürcher, Gustav. *"Trümmerlyrik": Politische Lyrik 1945–1950.* Kronberg: Scriptor, 1977.

Index

Weissenberger, Klaus, 107,
   157nn.10, 11
Werfel, Franz, 90
Winkler, Eugen Gottlob, 34
Wohmann, Gabriele, 2
Wulf, Josef, 37n.5

zart (as poetic term), 16, 31, 45–
   47, 75, 77, 80, 90, 93, 96,
   106–7, 109, 114, 116, 119,
   135, 150–51, 238, 244–45
zero hour (or Stunde Null), 3, 9,
   84, 110, 135
Ziolkowski, Theodore, 156n.1